Gertrude Moeller

Project
Portfolio
Management

Project Portfolio Management

Selecting and Prioritizing Projects for Competitive Advantage

Lowell D. Dye and
James S. Pennypacker,
editors

Center for Business Practices

Center for Business Practices
A Division of PM Solutions, Inc.
316 W. Barnard St.
West Chester, PA 19382

Publisher's Cataloging-in-Publication Data

Project portfolio management : selecting and
    prioritizing projects for competitive advantage /
    Lowell D. Dye, James S. Pennypacker, editors. —
    1st ed.
      p. cm.
    Includes bibliographical references and index.
    ISBN: 1-929576-00-5

    1. Industrial project management. 2. Portfolio
management. 3. Strategic planning. I. Dye,
Lowell D. II. Pennypacker, James S.

HD69.P75P76 1999   658.4'04
                         QBI99-1343

For information on all business publications available, visit the Center for Business Practices on the World Wide Web at www.pmsolutions.com/cbp

10 9 8 7 6 5 4 3 2 1

Printed in the United States of America

This book is dedicated to our families without whose support, assistance, and understanding this work would never have been completed.

Gertrude Moeller

Table of Contents

An Introduction to Project Portfolio Management

Lowell D. Dye and James S. Pennypacker

Projects are essential to the survival and growth of organizations....The pathway to change will be through development and process projects. Future strategies will entail a portfolio of projects, some of which will survive and lead to new products and/or services and the manufacturing and marketing processes that will beat out the competition. With projects playing such a pivotal role in future strategies, senior managers must approve and maintain surveillance over these projects to determine which ones can make a contribution to the strategic survival of the company.

—*David I. Cleland*

Project portfolio management has become a significant factor in the long-term strategic success of project-oriented organizations. Its growth and acceptance as a management practice can be attributed to its link to business policy and organizational strategy. Project portfolio management is concerned with more than the advanced mathematical modeling of business, more than the mechanics of formal project planning systems. At its best, it is concerned with the role of top management and key decision makers in creating purposeful project investments and in formulating and implementing goals and objectives.

It is this view of project portfolio management that has guided the selection of articles for this collective work. The purpose of this work is not to tell the reader how to select a project, nor is it to evaluate and recommend a specific approach or tool. Its purpose is to provide the reader with a variety of ideas, present proven methods, and share some lessons learned from a cross section of industries. The major sections—Overview; Selection and Prioritization; Tools, Techniques, and Methods; and Best Practices and Applications—reflect the breadth of the subject. The articles themselves reflect the depth with which these topics are explored and their practical significance. It is this combination of the broad scope of the field, the important concepts and findings the writers have added, and the orientation toward the practical problems of top managers, project managers, and other decision makers, that explains the impact and acceptance of project portfolio management.

Project Portfolio Management

A *project* is a temporary, unique endeavor undertaken to create a product or service within defined parameters [1]. The parameters are typically scope, time, and cost. Examples of projects include designing a new automobile, implementing a new customer service process, changing an organization's structure from functional to matrix, modifying an enterprise information system, starting a new business. Projects must compete for an organization's scarce resources because there are usually more projects to choose from than there are resources to support them all. But projects are essential to an organization—they are the prime investment in the organization's future.

A *portfolio* is a range of investments. Synonyms include "collection," "aggregation," "variety," "accumulation," "multitude," "assortment," "ensemble." Therefore, a *project portfolio* is a collection of projects that, in the aggregate, make up an organization's investment strategy.

Project management is the art and science of applying a set of knowledge, skills, tools, and techniques to project activities in order to meet or exceed stakeholder needs and expectations from a project [1]. The science of project management is knowing how to use the various project management tools such as the work breakdown structure, network diagrams, Gantt charts, resource histograms, etc. The art of project management is knowing when to use the various tools and under what circumstances.

Project portfolio management is, therefore, the art and science of applying a set of knowledge, skills, tools, and techniques to a collection of projects in order to meet or exceed the needs and expectations of an organization's investment strategy. It seeks to answer the questions What should we take on? and What should we drop? It requires achieving a delicate balancing of strategic and tactical requirements. Project portfolio management often requires determining what is possible (Do we have the capability, the resources?) and what is needed (Does it make good business sense?). Balancing capability and need generally results in defining the best that can be achieved with the limited resources available, rather than attempting to find the perfect solution (which in a perfect world would include infinite resources).

Management Models and the Business Environment

Decision makers have found that the business environment in which they must operate continues to become increasingly more complex. Gone are the days when management appeared to fully understand the consequences of their decisions and could accurately forecast the impact of projects on their organizations and the community in general. In fact, the gap is widening between the business environment historically presented by most management science models and the environment in which most projects are actually undertaken.

Today's business environment reveals that many decision makers and many decision influencers operate in a dynamic organizational environment rather than a single decision maker operating in a stable environment. Information about projects and their characteristics—outputs, values, risks—are difficult to specify. Uncertainty accompanies all estimates. Management models often describe well-known, invariant project goals. In reality, goals are ever-changing and fuzzy. Today, decision making information is no longer concentrated in the hands of the decision maker. Instead, that information is highly splintered and scattered piecemeal throughout the organization, with no one

---

Table 1. Project Selection and Resource Allocation Methods

Benefit Measurement Methods	**Strategic Planning Methods**
• Comparative Approaches	• Portfolio Maps (Bubble Diagrams)
• Q-Sort	• Cluster Analysis
• Ordinal Ranking	• Cognitive Modeling
• Normative Models	• Regression Models
• Pair-wise Comparisons	• Decision Tree Diagramming
• Interactive Group	• Decision Process Models
• Scoring Models	• Expert Systems
• Multiple Criteria	**Ad Hoc Methods**
• Multiple Attribute Utility	• Profiles
• Analytical Hierarchy Process	• Interactive Selection
• Benefit Contribution Models	• Top-Down Methodologies
• Cost-Benefit	• Genius Award
• Risk Analysis	• System Approaches
• Economic Return (NPV, IRR, ROI, EV)	**Optimization Methods**
• Marketing Research	• Integer Programming
• Consumer Panels	• Linear Programming
• Focus Groups	• Non-Linear Programming
• Perceptual Maps	• Goal Programming
• Preference Mapping	• Dynamic Programming

part of the organization having all the information needed for making the best decisions. In most management science models, projects are viewed as independent entities, to be individually evaluated on their own merits. They have a single objective, usually expected value maximization or profit maximization, and constraints are primarily budgetary. In reality, projects are often, if not usually, technically and economically interdependent. They have multiple objectives (sometimes conflicting) and multiple constraints, often non-economic in nature. And finally, management science models often determine the best portfolio of projects solely on economic grounds. Budgets are "optimized" in a single decision, and one, economically "best" overall decision is sought. In today's project environment, good project portfolios possess many non-economic characteristics, an iterative budget process is used, and what seems to be the "best" decision for the organization may not be seen as the best by each stakeholder, giving rise to conflicts. Today's project environment is far more complex than described in most management science models, and this complexity needs to be taken into account in any process used to determine the "best" portfolio of projects to undertake [2].

The current popularity of project portfolio management makes it seem as though it's a relatively recent phenomenon. In fact, since 1959 there have been hundreds of articles, books, and other publications published on the subject. Table 1 presents some of the types of project selection and resource allocation methods that have been generated over the years. (This list is not all-inclusive—there are more than 100 documented methods—but is a good sampling of methods available[3].)

Much effort has been applied to developing ways to improve our ability to discriminate among a variety of project alternatives. The primary focus has been to clearly define the value of project-related investments to the organization. Mathematical formulas that predict a single rate of return or "best estimate" are not enough. Other values, particularly strategic fit and project balance, are clearly critical as well. And, although much of the literature has been on research and development (R&D) projects, portfolio management is not limited to R&D alone. It applies to any project environment that is competitive (both internally and externally), constrained by limited resources, concerned with making intelligent, sound project selection and prioritization decisions that are in strategic alignment with corporate goals and objectives.

The articles that comprise this work can be applied to all types of organizations, all types of projects, all types of industries. They capture the essence of 40 years of business modeling and management science applications and present project portfolio management in a clear and informative manner for the reader to use in their own practice. It will become obvious to the reader that a simple answer to the question, how to best select and prioritize a portfolio of projects is not to be found in this book. But the path to the answer is here. It's up to the reader to take the knowledge expressed in this work and add it to their own knowledge of their organization and its project management processes, and to select the methods and techniques most appropriate to their organization in order to develop their own best practice approaches to selecting and prioritizing projects.

Methodology for Selecting Articles

The objective of compiling this work was to select articles that contribute to the project management profession and help project stakeholders develop a process to determine which projects can best make a contribution to the growth of their organization. Toward that end, several criteria were established that guided the selection of articles published in refereed and non-refereed journals, as well as unpublished working papers. The selection criteria, in no specific order, included:

1. The article must focus on project portfolio management. Several articles reviewed were oriented toward financial portfolio management or managing multiple projects. Although these are important concepts and are often critical factors in project success, they were outside the scope and objectives of this work.

2. The article must be recent. Understanding that recent is a relative term, and that the disciplined study of portfolio management and model development dates back to 1959, most of the articles contained in this work were published after 1994.

3. The collection of articles must present a broad view of the art and science of project portfolio management, but not be so broad that value is lost. Many articles reviewed presented the same or similar concepts as those selected for this work. Therefore, only those articles that best captured the main themes or challenge the reader were selected.

4. The selected articles had to come from a variety of sources. Great lengths were taken to do an exhaustive literature search to ensure that a variety of industry, business, and technical journals were represented. To weight the work toward one or two specific sources would provide the project management profession and the reader with little or no benefit. At best, it would provide a lopsided view of project portfolio management.

5. The articles selected must present practical application of project portfolio management concepts and principles. The desire was to provide a useful reference document, not a theoretical one.

To meet these criteria, the right combination of articles had to be found. A publication search generated more than four hundred abstracts of potential candidates for inclusion. The abstracts were reviewed, and those that seemed to have the strongest fit per the above criteria were selected for full-text review.

Once in hand, each article was briefly scanned for key words, phrases, concepts, and themes, then ranked from one to ten, again using the above criteria. Candidate articles ranked one through four were read through completely and categorized by topic area—Overview; Selection and Prioritization; Tools, Techniques, and Methods; and Best Practices and Applications. Within topic area, articles were sub-categorized "A", "B", or "C" based on their relative strength and how well each met the selection criteria.

Articles initially ranked five through ten were then reviewed. Those articles that, upon detailed review, provided something new or made a significant contribution to the overall work were sub-categorized within their topic area.

Although this work contains only a sampling of the excellent articles available, the Appendix contains a detailed bibliography of articles, books, and publications available on project portfolio management.

Contents of This Work

The four sections of this book not only provide a way of organizing the articles but also define the broad scope of project portfolio management. Within each section, some of the articles develop general concepts and frameworks, whereas others present specific study results and applications.

Overview

Despite the numerous articles and books written on the subject of project portfolio management, it is important to look at the topic from a general perspective before addressing the specific elements of selection, tools, and applications. The purpose of this section is not to define project portfolio management nor is it to provide a tutorial on the concepts of project portfolio management. It is assumed that the reader has some familiarity with the concepts of portfolio management, as well as a general understanding of project management. The intent of this section is to provide a look at the strategic context of project portfolio management and the importance of integrating business and technical objectives. Throughout this section, many ideas and practices are presented, some of which will seem familiar, while others will allow the reader to look at project portfolio management from a different perspective.

Selection and Prioritization

When investing and allocating organizational resources, the techniques used to justify those investments make a big difference. Most organizations have more opportunities for investment than their limited resources will allow. Management needs a dynamic, robust set of selection criteria to identify and select projects that accurately reflect the corporate strategy. The emphasis in this section is not on tools and techniques, although some are addressed here, but on the various approaches to setting selection criteria, ensuring projects are in strategic alignment with organizational goals, and the general process for ranking and evaluating projects to ensure corporate resources are used in the most efficient and effective manner possible.

Tools, Techniques, and Methods

In the business of project portfolio management, there is no magic wand, no silver bullet, no crystal ball that will answer the question of which project to select. What is needed is a good, comprehensive set of tools that can be used by management to help evaluate the challenges and risks, bring insight from a variety of perspectives, guide the selection of projects that are complementary and that can be logically ranked as a "portfolio" rather than just an independent collection of resource-consuming activities. Over the years, there have been many project selection and evaluation tools, techniques, and methods each with their own advantages and disadvantages. This section provides the reader with several known and proven tools and introduces some lesser known approaches, with a single focus in mind—providing practical approaches to selecting and prioritizing projects.

Best Practices and Applications

Experience is the best teacher. Experience can also be the toughest teacher. Through a variety of actual cases and best practices, this section presents the experiences of several organizations from different industries and how they have applied various tools and techniques to help them select and prioritize projects. It is important for the reader to realize that whenever discussing best practices, there is the likelihood of discussing various tools, techniques, methods, selection criteria, etc. These various approaches to project portfolio management, however, cross industrial, functional, and project boundaries and can be applied successfully in most cases with appropriate adaptation.

Many executives and project managers contend that their environment and situation is unique and not amenable to models, tools, or techniques that have been proven in other environments or situations. However, hundreds of articles discussing project selection and prioritization have been published supporting and reinforcing the benefits of a variety of techniques for effectively managing project portfolios. Many of these articles show precisely how project portfolio management is working at specific organizations. The knowledge and best practices exist. The purpose of this work, then, is to provide management, project managers, and decision makers with a sampling of that current knowledge to help them address project portfolio decisions, especially in selecting the proper project mix that aligns with organizational goals and objectives, maximizes limited resources, and strengthens their organization's competitive advantage.

References

1. Adapted from Project Management Institute Standards Committee. 1996. *A Guide to the Project Management Body of Knowledge.* Newtown Square, PA: Project Management Institute.

2. Adapted from Souder, William E. 1978. A system for using R&D project evaluation methods. *Research Management* 21(5): 33.

3. Adapted from Hall, David L. and Alexander Nauda, 1990. An interactive approach for selecting IR&D projects. *IEEE Transactions on Engineering Management* 37(2) and Archer, N.P. and F. Ghasemzadeh. 1996. Project portfolio selection techniques: a review and a suggested integrated approach. *Innovation Research Working Group Working Paper No. 46.* McMaster University.

Part 1:

Overview

The Strategic Context of Projects

David I. Cleland

The most dangerous time for an organization is when the old strategies are discarded and new ones are developed to respond to competitive opportunities. The changes that are appearing in the global marketplace have no precedence; survival in today's unforgiving global marketplace requires extraordinary changes in organizational products, services, and the organizational processes needed to identify, conceptualize, develop, produce, and market something of value to the customers. Projects, as building blocks in the design and execution of organizational strategies, provide the means for bringing about realizable changes in products and processes. Senior managers, who have the residual responsibility for the strategic management of the enterprise, can gain valuable insights into both the trajectory of the enterprise and the speed with which the competitive position of the enterprise is being maintained and enhanced.

A belief that projects are building blocks in the design and execution of future strategies for the enterprise means that the organizational planners recognize that preparing for the future based on extrapolations of the past results from a well understood and predictable platform of past experience is not valuable—and can be dangerous to the health of the enterprise. Although planning based on extrapolation of the past has some value for an ongoing business providing routine products and services, it makes little sense when the enterprise's future is dependent on developing and producing new products and services through revised or new organizational processes. All too often people persist in believing that what has gone on in the past will go on into the future—even while the ground is shifting under their feet. If the enterprise is engaged in a business where competition is characterized by the appearance of unknown, uncertain, or not yet obvious new products and services, especially to the competition, then project-driven strategic planning is needed. Project-based strategic planning assumes that:
- Little may be known of the new product or service but much is assumed about potential customer interest in the forthcoming initiative.
- Decision making on the project during its early conceptual phases is based on what information is available. Assumptions concerning the potential future business success of the innovation are an important source of knowledge on which decisions can be made.

• Assumptions concerning the new venture are systematically converted into meaningful databases as new knowledge concerning the innovation evolves through study by the project team.

• Even after the prototype is developed and field tested with customers, uncertainty remains as to how well the product or service will do in the competitive marketplace.

Implications of Technology

Management of an enterprise so that its future is ensured requires that the technology involved in products and/or services and organizational processes be approached from two principal directions: the strategic or long-term perspective and the systems viewpoint. In both these directions, projects play a key role. In this chapter these two directions will be woven into a project management philosophy in which projects are building blocks in the design and execution of organizational strategies. A couple of examples of how contemporary organizations deal with projects make the point:

At Banc One Corporation, one of the fastest-growing and most profitable banks in the United States, 3 percent of the profits has been dedicated to technology R&D. One of the bank's most important technology projects is the development of a new computer system that will dramatically alter the way Banc One branches operate to include the creation of a new credit card processing system. With the assistance of the Dallas-based Electronic Data Systems Corporation, the bank is moving from older mainframe systems to a distributed architecture [2].

Sony, which had nearly $26 billion in sales last year, is the most consistently inventive consumer electronics enterprise in the world. It has had hit after hit of high-technology products. Its products have created billion-dollar markets, designing and producing devices that have altered people's work and leisure. Sony's portfolio of products ranges from semiconductors, batteries, and recording tapes to video and audio gear for consumers, professionals, computers, communications equipment, and factory robots. Last year the company spent $1.5 billion on research and product development projects—roughly 5.6 percent of revenues. Each year the company sends out 1000 new products—an average of almost 4 a day. Some 200 of these new products are aimed at creating whole new markets, such as the Mini Disc portable digital stereo. Sony founder and honorary chairman Masaru says that the key to success at Sony—and to everything in business, science, and technology—is never to follow the others. In other words, innovation—the creation of something that does not currently exist. Product/project ideas come from many different organizational levels in the company, from the senior managers to the young engineers working in the product design department. Some of Sony's key philosophies are

• An emphasis on making something out of nothing

• People who are optimistic, open-minded, and wide-ranging in their interests, who move around a lot among product groups

• A belief that having continuous success in the same area makes you believe too much in your own power, which harms your creativity

• A belief that new products come primarily out of a creator's imagination, not from a marketing study

• Occasional use of a "skunk works" project to circumvent the formal project approval process in the company

- Use of competing project teams to work on promising technologies [3].

Projects are essential to the survival and growth of organizations. Failure in project management in an enterprise can prevent the organization from accomplishing its mission. The greater the use of projects in accomplishing organizational purposes, the more dependent the organization is on the effective and efficient management of those projects. Projects are a direct means of creating value for the customer is terms of future products and services. The pathway to change will be through development and process projects. Future strategies will entail a portfolio of projects, some of which will survive and lead to new products and/or services and the manufacturing and marketing processes that will beat out the competition. With projects playing such a pivotal role in future strategies, senior managers must approve and maintain surveillance over these projects to determine which ones can make a contribution to the strategic survival of the company.

For the last decade or so many managers have been preoccupied with the improvement of operations through remedial strategies involving the use of reengineering, benchmarking, TQM, time-based competition, empowerment, team-based organizational designs, continuous improvement, and the so-called learning organization. The use of outsourcing, greater customer satisfaction, and the "virtual" organization helped to eliminate inefficiencies, improve customer satisfaction, and make the enterprise more competitive. In the short run, these remedial strategies helped to improve organizational efficiency and effectiveness. But survival in the long term requires that the enterprise do something that will establish a difference in its products/services and organizational processes that it can preserve in the marketplace. Although current activities are the basic components of today's competitiveness, overall strategic competitive behavior requires that new initiatives be conceptualized, developed, and implemented that will lead to changes in products/services and organizational processes that will ensure future competitiveness. In many cases this means that these new initiatives have to be different from those of the competitors. Few enterprises are able to survive and compete successfully on the basis of current operational capabilities over an extended period. The reason for this is the simple diffusion of new technologies, practices, and best products/services and supporting organizational processes—expressed in a superior way of meeting and exceeding customer expectations. The more a company benchmarks its competitors, the more likely it is that the enterprise and the competitor will become similar. The more a company uses outsourcing as a competitive thrust, the more likely it is that its competitors will copy its strategies and move to an equitable market position. As rivals imitate each other's operational competitive strategies, the more probable it is that their strategies will converge. Competition becomes a series of behaviors that look similar—and no one competitor can become a big winner. Competition based on operational performance becomes self-defeating, leading to wars of competitive attrition. Unfortunately, many of the "flavors of the year" in the last 10 years have led to diminishing competitive returns. Competition based on continuous improvement reinforced by many of the flavors of reengineering, benchmarking, change management, and so forth have drawn all too many enterprises into a "me too" mentality that has inhibited true creativity and innovation in creating strategic pathways for true competition in *strategic* performance.

The responsibility for allowing companies to degenerate into competition based on operational improvements clearly rests with the company's leaders. Unfortunately, this means that such leaders have failed to recognize their larger role beyond just operational stewardship, viz., a proactive role in selecting and executing the use of resources to provide a competitive, strategic pathway for the enterprise. Enterprise leaders have to work with the creative and innovative talent in the enterprise's pool of people and define and communicate new directions, allocating resources, making tradeoffs through the study of alternatives, and making the hard choices of what to do for the future and—just as important—what not to do by way of committing organizational resources.

A product or process development project is a business venture—the creation of something that does not currently exist but which can provide support to the overall organizational strategy being developed to meet competition. Many projects are found in successful organizations.

A Stream of Projects

An enterprise that is successful has a "stream of projects" flowing through it at all times. When that stream of projects dries up, the organization has reached a stable condition in its competitive environment. In the face of the inevitable change facing the organization, the basis for the firm's decline in its products, services, and processes is laid—and the firm will hobble on but ultimately face liquidation.

In the healthy firm, a variety of different preliminary ideas are fermenting. As these ideas are evaluated, some will fall by the wayside for many reasons: lack of suitable organizational resources, unacceptable development costs, a position too far behind the competition, lack of "strategic fit" with the enterprise's direction, and so on. There is a high mortality rate in these preliminary ideas. Only a small percentage will survive and will be given additional resources for study and evaluation in later stages of their life cycles. Senior managers need to ensure that evaluation techniques are made available and their use known to the people who provide these preliminary innovative ideas. Essentially this means that everyone in the organization needs to know the general basis on which product and process ideas can survive and can be given additional resources for further study. Senior management must create a balance between providing a cultural ambience in the enterprise that encourages people to bring forth innovative product and process ideas and an environment that ensures that rigorous strategic assessment will be done on these emerging ideas to determine their likely strategic fit in the enterprise's future. For example, Elan Corporation, Plc., whose mission is the development of novel drug absorption systems for therapeutic compounds that provide distinctive benefits for the physician and patient—carrying out all the necessary clinical studies and regulatory work prior to market introduction—follows a fundamental strategy called *mind to market*. To implement this strategy which brings their products to market through the formulation, clinical testing, registration, and manufacturing phases, project management is used. In the product development area, the company was committed to 56 active projects, utilizing 9 specialized drug delivery technologies in 18 therapeutic categories which range from cardiovascular and narcotic analgesics to antiemetics and neuropharmacological agents. Research and development is the very essence of the company's business. Its work in R&D ensures a continuing stream of new products and technologies. In the global marketplace, the company currently has new-drug applications or their equivalent filed for 20 products in 30 countries around the world [4].

Kmart Corporation's strategy in assessing strategic opportunities is to jump-start a number of small projects at a relatively low cost and then shift the money into the promising ideas as the development work evolves. One example of such a promising project involves the development of electronic shelf tags which would display pertinent information about a product, including the unit price, price per ounce, sales data, or whatever the company wanted to highlight. No longer would the employees have to change the traditional shelf tags. Another project is under development for a ceiling-mounted scanner to track the number of customers entering and exiting a Kmart store, thus alerting personnel that additional sales assistance is needed in specific departments. Another project borrows from manufacturing just-in-time inventory management concepts and processes. Products are shipped to Kmart distribution centers only when needed, thus reducing inventory requirements. Suppliers under this new procedure would write their own purchase orders by looking into Kmart's inventory databases and would ship products in time to keep Kmart's shelves from becoming bare [5].

When the use of project management is described in an enterprise, it is easy to think of just one project in the organization. Often we think of a large single dedicated project team led by a project manager who has the proper authority and responsibility needed to do the job. What usually exists after the enterprise has experimented with project management for a while is that several and perhaps many projects are under way, each having its own life-cycle phases. Team members may be working on several different small projects. As the use of project management continues to expand, the matrix organizational design emerges, and many projects share common resources provided by the functional entities and appropriate stakeholders. As the growth of project management continues and different projects come and go, there are some unique forces at work. The projects share common resources but will likely have objectives that are not shared with other projects, particularly if a diverse set of customers are involved. As projects start and are closed out or terminated for cause, a new mix in the use of resources comes forth. New projects may have a higher priority than the existing ones. As the competition for resources gets under way in the matrix organization, the opportunities for conflict in the assignment of the resources to the projects will erupt, often requiring senior management to intervene in deciding how the project priorities will impact the priorities for the use of the resources; and the opportunity for gamesmanship emerges. Also, having many projects under way provides the opportunities for politics to enter the picture. Sometimes the enterprise will appoint a "manager of projects" who has jurisdiction over the project managers that are acting as a focal point for the projects.

Strategic Relationship of Projects

Organizational conceptual planning forms the basis for developing a project's scope in supporting the organizational mission. For example, a project plan for facilities design and construction would be a series of engineering documents from which detailed design, estimating, scheduling, cost control, and effective project management will flow. Conceptual planning, while forming the framework of a successful project, is strategic in nature and forms the basis for

• Contributing, through the execution of strategies, to the organizational objectives, goals, and mission

• Standards by which the project can be managed
• Coping with the market and other environmental factors likely to have an impact on the project and the organization.

Senior management deficiencies in the organization using project management will probably be echoed in the management of the projects. For example, an audit conducted in the early 1980s of a gas and electric utility that experienced problems with a major capital project found several key deficiencies in that utility, such as

1. Weak basic management processes
2. No implementation of the project management concept for major facilities
3. Fragmented and overlapping organizational functions
4. No focus on authority and accountability [6].

Ford Motor Company is committed to the use of project management in its corporate strategy. To provide consistency in the use of project management, Ford realized during the 1980s that a *common* project management system was required. To bring about a consistent way to manage projects, a Ford corporate mainframe project management tool selection committee was created. Care was taken to ensure that users would be given a voice in the system selection process. Several key policies were established to both guide and motivate the committee to pursue its work. (1) There was agreement by senior management to accept the recommendations of the committee, assuming that such recommendations were supported by adequate facts. (2) The committee agreed to operate as a cross-functional project team. (3) A schedule was adopted to maintain user interest and enthusiasm; decisions by the committee would be made by consensus. (4) It was recognized that leadership of the committee was an important variable in realizing success of the work under way [7].

Determining Strategic Fit

Projects are essential to the survival and growth of organizations. Failure in the management of projects in an organization will impair the ability of the organization to accomplish its mission in an effective and efficient manner. Projects are a direct means of creating value for customers—both customers in the marketplace and "in-house" customers, who work together in creating value for the ultimate customer in the marketplace. The pathway to change is through the use of projects which support organizational strategies. Future strategies for organizations entail a portfolio of projects, some of which survive during their emerging life cycle and create value for customers. Since projects play such a pivotal role in the future strategies of organizations, senior managers need to become actively involved in the efficiency and effectiveness with which the stream of projects is managed in the organization. Surveillance over these projects must be maintained by senior managers to provide insight into the probable promise or threat that the projects hold for future competition. In considering these projects, senior managers need to find answers to the following questions:

• Will there be a "customer" for the product or process coming out of the project work?
• Will the project results survive in a contest with the competition?
• Will the project results support a recognized need in the design and execution of organizational strategies?
• Can the organization handle the risk and uncertainty likely to be associated with the project?

- What is the probability of the project's being completed on time, within budget, and at the same time satisfying its technical performance objectives?
- Will the project results provide value to a customer?
- Will the project ultimately provide a satisfactory return on investment to the organization?
- Finally, the bottom-line question: Will the project results have a strategic fit in the design and execution of future products and processes?

As senior managers conduct a review of the projects under way in organizations, the above questions can serve to guide the review process. As such questions are asked and the appropriate answers are given during the review process, an important message will be sent throughout the organization: Projects are important in the design and execution of our organizational strategies?

The question of the strategic fit of a project is a key judgment challenge for senior executives. Who should make such decisions? Clearly those executives whose organizational projects and services will be improved by the successful project outcome should be involved. Senior executives of the enterprise should act as a team in the evaluation of the stream of projects that should flow through the top of the enterprise for assessment and determination of future value. Participative decision making concerning the strategic fit of projects is highly desirable. For some senior executives this can be difficult, particularly if they have been the entrepreneurs who conceptualized the company and put it together. Such founding entrepreneurs tend to dominate the strategic decision making of the organization, reflecting their ability in having created the enterprise through their strategic vision in developing a sense of future needs of products and services.

But senior executives, too, can lose their sense of future vision for the enterprise. Or they can become fixated on favorite development projects that may not make any strategic sense to the organizational mission and goals. For example, in a large computer company the founder's dominance of key project decisions drove out people whose perceptions of a project's strategic worth were contrary to that of the CEO. A new-products development group was abruptly disbanded by the CEO, who had sharp differences of opinion with the group executive over several key projects. This group executive had disagreed with the CEO on a key decision involving continuing development of a computer mainframe project whose financial promise was faint—if potentially attainable at all.

The Vision

Projects and organizational strategies start with a vision. A "vision is the art of seeing things invisible to others," according to Jonathan Swift.

The corporate vision statement of Whirlpool Corporation is, "Whirlpool, in its chosen lines of business, will grow with new opportunities and be the leader in an ever-changing global market." Implicit in the statement are commitments to market orientation, leadership, customer satisfaction, and quality.

The CEO of Motorola, Inc., holds the vision of "...a corporation that will look gigantic but have the dynamics of little teams." Motorola calculates that its project teams produce an average of four new or improved products each day. Additional reasons for the success of this company are a nonunion work force and a macho culture

Table 1. A Project Selection Model

Program/project evaluation criteria		Criteria weights	Very good (8)	Good (6)	Fair (4)	Poor (2)	Poor (0)	Expected level weight	Expected weighted score
Fit with mission	Product	10	1.0					8.0	80
	Market	10	1.0					8.0	80
Consistency with objectives	ROI	10	0.2	0.6	0.2			6.0	60
	Dividends	5		0.2	0.6	0.2		4.0	20
	Image	5			0.8	0.2		3.6	18
Consistency with strategy	Stage 1	10					1.0	0	0
	Stage 2	7	1.0					8.0	56
	Stage 3	3					1.0	0	0
Contribution to goals	Goal A	8					1.0	0	0
	Goal B	6	0.8	0.2				7.6	45.6
	Goal C	4		0.8	0.2			5.6	22.4
	Goal D	2					1.0	0	0
Corporate strength base		10				0.8	0.2	1.6	16
Corporate weakness avoidance		10				0.2	0.8	0.4	4
Comparative advantage level		10	0.7	0.3				7.4	74
Internal consistency level		10	1.0					8.0	80
Risk level acceptability		10				0.7	0.3	1.4	14
Policy guideline consistency		10			1.0			4.0	40
								Total score	610

uniquely suitable to its professional class of highly trained engineers. In addition, the company has a huge cash flow to support R&D, capital investment, and training [8].

During the strategic-fit review of organizational projects, insight should be gained into which projects are entitled to continued assignment of resources and which are not. Senior managers need to decide; the project manager is an unlikely person to execute the decision. Most project managers are preoccupied with bringing the project to a successful finish, and they cannot be expected to clearly see the project in an objective manner of supporting the enterprise mission. There is a natural tendency for the project manager to see the termination of the project as a failure in the management of the project. Projects are sometimes continued beyond their value to the strategic direction of the organization. The selection of projects to support corporate strategies is important in developing future direction.

A Project Selection Framework

A project selection framework is shown in Table 1. In the leftmost column is a set of evaluation criteria. The body of the table shows how a proposed new program to begin manufacturing system components in Europe might be evaluated. The "criteria weights" in the second column of the table reflect their relative importance and serve to permit the evaluation of complex project characteristics within a simple framework.

a base weight of 20 is used here for the major criteria related to mission, objectives, strategy, and goals. Weights of 10 are applied to the other criteria.

Within each major category, the 10 "points" are judgmentally distributed to reflect the relative importance of subelements or some other characteristic of the criterion. For instance, the three stages of strategy and the four subgoals are weighted to ensure that earlier stages and goals are treated to be more important than later ones. This implicitly reflects the *time value of money* without requiring a more complex "present value" discounting calculation.

The first criterion in Table 1 is the "fit" with mission. The proposal is evaluated to be consistent with both the "product" and "market" elements of the mission and is thereby rated to be "very good," as shown by the 1.0 probability entries at the upper left.

In terms of "consistency with objectives," the proposal is rated to have a 0.2 (20 percent) chance of being "very good" in contributing to the ROI element of the objectives, a 60 percent chance of being "good," and a 20 percent chance of being only "fair," as indicated by the probabilities entered into the third row of the table. The proposed project is rated more poorly with respect to the "dividends" and "image" elements.

The proposal is also evaluated in terms of its expected contribution to each of the three stages of the strategy. In this case, the proposed project is believed to be one which would principally contribute to stage 2 of the strategy. (Note that only certain assessments may be made in this case, since the stages are mutually exclusive and exhaustive.)

The proposal is similarly evaluated with respect to the other criteria.

The overall evaluation is obtained as a weighted score that represents the sum of products of the likelihoods (probabilities) and the 8, 6, 4, 2, 0 arbitrary level weights that are displayed at the top of the table. For instance, the "Consistency with objectives—ROI" expected level weight is calculated as:

$$0.2(8) + 0/6(6) + 0.2(4) = 6.0$$

This is then multiplied by the criterion weight of 10 to obtain a weighted score of 60. The weighted scores are then summed to obtain an overall evaluation of 610. [9]

Of course, this number in isolation is meaningless. However, when various projects are evaluated in terms of the same criteria, their overall scores provide a reasonable basis for developing the ranking shown on the right side of Table 1. Such a ranking can be the basis for resource allocation, since the top-ranked program is presumed to be the most worthy, the second-ranked is the next most worthy, etc.

It can readily be seen that such a project selection process will enhance the implementation of the choices made in the strategic planning phase of management.

The critical element of the evaluation approaches its use of criteria that ensure that projects will be integrated with the mission, objectives, strategy, and goals of the organization and will reflect critical bases of strategy, such as business strengths, weaknesses, comparative advantages, internal consistency, opportunities, and policies.

Projects and Organizational Management

Projects, goals, and objectives must fit together in a synergistic fashion in supporting the enterprise mission. Project success by itself may not contribute to enterprise success.

11

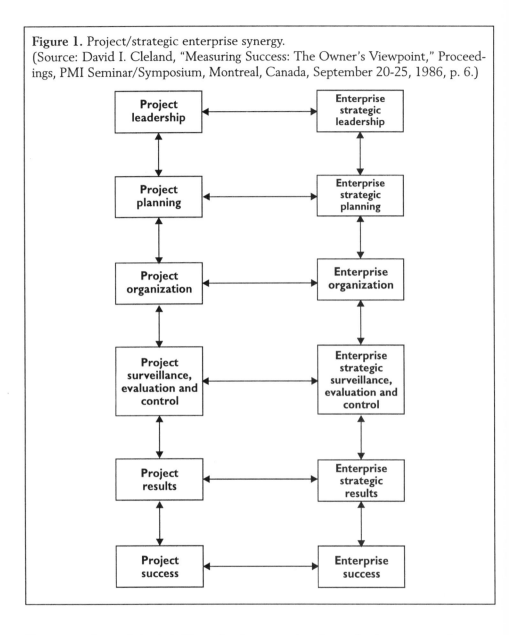

Figure 1. Project/strategic enterprise synergy.
(Source: David I. Cleland, "Measuring Success: The Owner's Viewpoint," Proceedings, PMI Seminar/Symposium, Montreal, Canada, September 20-25, 1986, p. 6.)

Projects might, early in their life cycle, show promise of contributing to enterprise strategy. A project that continues to support that mission should be permitted to grow in its life cycle. If the project does not provide that support, then a strategic decision faces the senior managers: Can the project be reprogrammed, replanned, and redirected to maintain support of the enterprise mission, or should the project be abandoned?

Project managers cannot make such a strategic decision since they are likely to be preoccupied with bringing the project to a successful finish, and project termination is not their responsibility. Such managers may lack an overall perspective of the project's strategic support of the enterprise mission. Therefore, the decision of what to do about the project must remain with the general manager, who is the project "owner" and has residual responsibility and accountability for the project's role in the enterprise mission and usually puts up the money for the project.

Project success is very dependent upon an appropriate synergy with the enterprise's success. The management of the project and the management of the enterprise depend on a synergistic management approach—planning, organizing, evaluation, and control tied together through an appropriate project-enterprise leadership. This synergy is shown in Figure 1.

Projects are designed, developed, and produced or constructed for a customer. This customer or project owner may be an internal customer, such as a business unit manager who pays for product development by the enterprise central laboratory. An external customer might be a utility that has contracted with an architectural and engineering firm to design, engineer, and build an electricity generating plant.

Senior managers, who have the responsibility to sense and set the vision for the enterprise, need a means of marshaling the resources of the organization to seek fulfillment of that vision. By having an active project management activity in the enterprise, an organizational design and a development strategy are available to assist senior managers in bringing about the changes and synergy to realize the organizational mission, objectives, and goals through a creative and innovative strategy. Leadership of a team of people who can bring the changes needed to the enterprise's posture is essential to the attainment of the enterprise's vision. As additional product and/or service and process projects are added to marshal the enterprise's resources, the strategic direction of the enterprise can be guided to the attainment of the vision. When projects are accepted as the building blocks in the design and execution of organizational purposes, a key strategy has been set in motion to keep the enterprise competitive. Such strategies are dependent on the quality of the leadership in the enterprise.

Compaq Computer Corporation CEO Eckhard Pfeiffer has provided the leadership in launching a long-term strategy initiative in that company. This planning effort was launched as soon as the immediate situation at the company was moving adequately toward correction. A comprehensive long-range strategy has been developed and put in place. The CEO has stated that the focus of the company is clearly on future strategy—a means to totally transform the company.

One of the more important strategic decisions made by the Compaq CEO was to launch development efforts into cut-rate personal computers (PCs). An independent business unit was organized into a project team to develop a low-price machine—a real Compaq.

Revised manufacturing strategies were developed to get costs down at plants in Houston, Singapore, and Scotland. The entire manufacturing process strategy was rethought. An entire system is now built on a single assembly line instead of making the motherboard in one building and the chassis in another. Testing of every subassembly was stopped in favor of testing a sample. All finished systems are still fully tested. Compaq leaned on suppliers to cut prices to bring down overall manufacturing costs [10]. Project planning contributed to the overall planning strategy at Compaq.

Project Planning

Why is project planning so important? Simply because decisions made in the early phases of the project set the direction and force with which the project moves forward as well as the boundaries within which the work of the project team is carried out. As the project moves through its life cycle, the ability to influence the outcome of the project declines rapidly. After design of the project done early in the life cycle, the cost of producing the resulting product, as well as the product quality, has been largely determined. Senior managers tend to pay less attention during the early phases of the project than when the product development effort approaches the prototype or market-testing stage. By waiting until later in the life cycle of the project, their influence is limited in the sense that much of the cost of the product has been determined. Design has been completed, and the manufacturing or construction cost has been set early in the project. Senior managers need to become involved as early as possible, and they must be able to intelligently assess the likely market outcome of the product, its development cost, its manufacturing economy, how well it will meet the customers' quality expectations, and the probable strategic fit of the resulting product in the overall strategic management profile of the enterprise. In other words, when senior managers become involved early in the development cycle through regular and intelligent review, they can enjoy the benefits of leverage in the final outcome of the product and its likely acceptance in the marketplace. What happens early in the life cycle of the project essentially lays the basis for what is likely to happen in subsequent phases. Since a development project is taking an important step into the unknown—with the hope of creating something that did not previously exist—as much information as possible is needed to predict the possible and probable outcome. For senior managers to neglect the project early in its life cycle and leave the key decisions solely to the project team is the implicit assumption of a risk that is imprudent from the strategic management perspective of the enterprise.

Flexibility

The leading competitors in the world are moving toward a strategy of *flexibility*. Such strategy involves faster reading of the market. The use of concurrent engineering to commercialize products sooner, plus the use of flexible manufacturing systems to manufacture different products on the same line, switching from on product to another quickly, helps to keep costs down. Developing and using comprehensive just-in-time information systems for planning and control, gaining as much profit from short production runs as from long ones, and commercializing higher-quality products and services faster provide added flexibility.

Baxter Healthcare is testing a modular factory—an intravenous-solutions factory that can be shipped anywhere, set up in a week, and moved again anytime. At Kao Corporation, Japan's biggest soap and cosmetics company and the sixth largest in the world, an information system links everything: sales and shipping, production and purchasing, accounting, R&D, marketing, hundreds of shopkeepers' cash registers, and thousands of salespeople's handheld computers. The information is so complete that year-end financial statements can be turned out by noon of the first day of the new year. Kao can know if a new product will be successful within 2 weeks of launch through the melding of point-of-sale information from 216 retailers with a test-marketing operation called the

Echo System, which uses focus groups and consumers' calls and letters to gauge customer response more quickly than market surveys can. At Fuji Electric, Japan's fourth largest maker of electrical machinery, a flexible manufacturing system using bar codes developed by a project team tells machines what to do. Before the flexible manufacturing system, Fuji filled orders in 3 days; now Fuji needs only 24 hours, using one-third as many workers and almost one-third less inventory, to make about 8000 varieties—3 times more than before [11].

Project planning and organizational renewal are linked through the development of organizational strategy. For example, Lawrence A. Bossidy, now CEO of Allied-Signal Company, upon joining the company established ambitious objectives including:

- An 8 percent annual revenue growth
- A total-immersion total-quality program
- A top-to-bottom change in human resources management.

A statement of corporate vision and values listed these objectives, developed by the company's top twelve executives to include such things as being "one of the world's premier companies, distinctive and successful" and the values of satisfying customers, integrity, and teamwork. The vision helped to galvanize people. In addition, with these objectives as guidelines, Bossidy chopped $225 million from capital spending, reduced the annual dividend to $1 a share from $1.870, put eight small divisions up for sale, cut 6200 jobs, and combined ten data-processing centers into two.

The company formed *commodity teams*—cross-functional project teams of manufacturing, engineering, design, purchasing, and finance in such areas as castings, electronic gears, machine parts, and materials. Each team was responsible for picking the best suppliers in its specialty, with the chosen suppliers getting long-term national contracts. Suppliers were expected to bring down costs for themselves and for Allied-Signal.

Projects are usually paid for by the project owners, key members of project teams. The project owner has the residual responsibility and accountability for managing the project during its life cycle.

The Project Owner's Participation

Project owners cannot leave to others the responsibility for continuously measuring the success of the project, even experienced project management contractors and constructors. Foxhall stated:

> The owner must recognize that he is the key member of the project development team. Only he can select and organize the professional team, define his own needs, set his priorities and make final decisions. He cannot delegate these roles, so he must have a sustained presence in project management [12].

The project owner clearly has responsibility for the efficiency and effectiveness of a contractor involved on the project. This requires a surveillance system to know what the contractor is doing and how well the contractor is performing. For example, one report noted:

> Another essential characteristic of a successful nuclear construction project is a project management approach that shows an understanding and appreciation of the complexities and difficulties of nuclear construction. Such an approach

15

includes adequate financial and staffing support for the project, good planning and scheduling, and close management oversight of the project [13].

In the nuclear power plant construction industry, project owners are taking a more proactive position in managing their projects. Project owners in the utility industry, driven by the need to better manage projects, have responded by building up personnel and developing improved management systems. Such involvement has enabled the owners to obtain better control over projects and reduce risk [14].

Every project has (or should have) its owner: the agency or organization that carries the project on its budget and whose strategic plans include the project as an essential building block for future growth or survival. The project owner has the residual responsibility to approve and maintain oversight of the project during its life cycle. The project owner should be more than a corporation or a government agency. Rather the project owner should be identified by name, an individual recognized as the personal owner who assumes managerial oversight of the project as an element of future strategies.

Project owners can come from within the organization, such as

• A senior manager who budgets for a product or process development project
• A division profit-center manager who funds an R&D project to support a product improvement program
• A manufacturing manager who is converting a traditional factory to an automated, flexible manufacturing system.

Outside project owners usually contract for the project work through architects, engineers, and constructors. The Department of Defense contracts for substantially all the work involved in designing, engineering, and manufacturing weapon systems. In the electric utility industry, many investor-owned utilities do not design and construct their own generating facilities but hire architects, engineers, and constructors to perform most of the work. However, other utilities, such as Duke Power and Pacific Gas & Electric, perform a substantial portion of the design and construction for major projects in-house.

To put it simply, the project owner is the one who puts up the money to fund the project. On such a project funder rests the responsibility to see that those funds are used in a prudent and reasonable fashion. This requires adequate assessment of the project risk, project plans, and ongoing monitoring, evaluation, and control of the resources used on the project. Furthermore, an owner's decision to fund a project affects a variety of "stakeholders" who have, or believe they have, a stake in the project and its outcome. In some cases some of these stakeholders will seek legal redress if the project does not meet their particular expectations. Emerging case law establishes that project managers have the legal responsibility for the strategic management of projects [15].

Project owners' involvement on large construction contracts can range from total divestiture to total internal control of a project. One of the major growth areas of large international contractors such as Fluor, Bechtel, and Parsons has been the implementation of large projects on behalf of an owner. [16] Blanchard suggests some broad generalities to define the responsibilities of the contractor, manager, and owner, as shown in Table 2.

Table 2. Contractor, Manager, and Owner Responsibilities
(Source: F.L. Blanchard, "Contracted Management—Clarifying the Roles of Owner
and Manager," *Project Management Quarterly*, June 1983, pp. 42-43.)

Contractor

Engineering	1. Prepare detailed design drawings. 2. Prepare fabrication drawings for piping, structural steel, and concrete reinforcing. 3. Prepare purchase specifications. 4. Review vendor shop drawings. 5. Prepare as-built drawings. 6. Provide drawings and sketches as required for field crews.
Finance/ procurement	1. Prepare progress invoices. 2. Purchase materials and supplies. 3. Maintain payrolls and records. 4. Develop and submit changes as appropriate.
Construction	1. Plan and schedule plant and personnel. 2. Supervise craft and labor crews. 3. Operate and maintain construction equipment. 4. Resolve labor disputes. 5. Maintain clean and safe worksite.

Manager

Engineering	1. Review contractor drawings for conformance to standards and job specifications. 2. Interpret standards and specifications. 3. Review vendor technical proposals for conformance to standards and specifications. 4. Review and approve contractor quality assurance and quality control program. 5. Inspect vendor-supplied material.
Finance/ procurement	1. Review and approve contractor progress payments. 2. Review change requests. Prepare estimates and negotiate change settlements. 3. Review and approve contractor and subcontractor financial qualifications. 4. Prepare expenditures forecasts and other financial statements of job condition.
Construction	1. Inspect workmanship for conformance to drawings and specifications. 2. Interpret specifications. 3. Review contractor progress. 4. Monitor contractor performance against contract requirements.

Owner

Engineering	1. Provide design basis and establish standards. 2. Provide soil and other data. 3. Resolve conflicts in interpretation of standards and specifications.
Finance/ procurement	1. Provide funds for the work. 2. Identify any special material requirements or preferred equipment or vendors. 3. Provide owner-required insurance and indemnity. 4. Approve changes.
Construction	1. Provide site and access. 2. Obtain permits. 3. Arrange utilities.

Hansen describes several reasons for the success of a project for the construction of a facility for Republic Steel Corporation in Cleveland, Ohio:
• The intimate involvement of the owner with the planning and execution of the project
• A comprehensive feasibility study of the project during the strategic planning phase
• Ongoing project planning, coordination, and review
• The teamwork resulting from focusing on one clear-cut objective
• Commitment by the owner to support technical design decisions, project management objectives, and modern project management techniques [17].
Hansen's concluding comment charges project owners with a key responsibility: to make sure that the project will be managed by a solid team and that project management principles are known by all members on the project team [18].

A landmark study of the design and construction of nuclear power plants found that deep involvement by utilities (owners) in cost, schedule, productivity, and quality considerations contributed to project success as much as close management oversight of the project and the project's contractors [19].

Project success depends on a commitment by the owner to use contemporaneous project management theory and practice. Support of the enterprise mission comes about through the project owner's effective discharge of her or his strategic planning and management responsibility.

Successful project management depends on senior enterprise management for authority, strategic guidance, and support. Senior managers in turn depend on project managers for timely, cost-effective achievement of project results to support corporate strategy. Project management is a form of "strategic delegation" whereby senior managers delegate to project managers the authority and responsibility to do such things as building capital facilities, introducing new products, conducting research and development, and creating new marketing and production opportunities.

Project management also is a type of strategic management control. Senior managers can use project management as a way to ensure that key strategies are accomplished in an effective manner. A senior manager oversees the strategic direction of the enterprise by providing resources to accomplish the mission, objectives, goals, and strategies. By determining the success or failure of a project, senior management ensures that control systems are instituted to track strategic progress of the enterprise. As project managers make and execute key decisions, these key decisions should be reviewed by senior managers to determine if the decisions are consistent with corporate strategy. Senior enterprise managers commit a serious breach of responsibility and accountability for the management of the enterprise when they ignore or accept key project decisions without review. When adequate project evaluation is carried out to determine project success, senior managers get information on how effectively enterprise strategies are being implemented.

In order for the owner to do a credible job of measuring project success, several conditions must exist:
• An appropriate organizational design is in place which delineates the formal authority, responsibility, and accountability relationships among the enterprise corporate senior managers, project manager, functional manager, and work package managers.
• Adequate strategic and project planning has been carried out within the enterprise

- Relevant and timely information is available that gives insight into the project status
- Adequate management monitoring, evaluation, and control systems exist
- Contemporary state-of-the-art management techniques are used in the management of the project
- A supportive cultural ambience exists that facilitates the successful management of projects.

An important part of the strategic management of a project is to carry out such management in the context of a project management system.

Project Management System

Once the mission of the enterprise is established through the operation of a strategic planning system, planning can be extended to select and develop organizational objectives, goals, and strategies. Projects are planned for and implemented through a *project management system* composed of the following subsystems [20].

The *facilitative organizational subsystem* is the organizational arrangement that is used to superimpose the project teams on the functional structure. The resulting "matrix" organization portrays the formal authority and responsibility patterns and the personal reporting relationships, with the goal of providing an organizational focal point for starting and completing specific projects. Two complementary organizational units tend to emerge in such an organizational context: the project team and the functional units. The *project control subsystem* provides for the selection of performance standards for the project schedule, budget, and technical performance. The subsystem compares actual progress with planned progress, with the initiation of corrective action as required. The rationale for a control subsystem arises out of the need to monitor the various organizational units that are performing work on the project in order to deliver results on time and within budget.

The *project management information subsystem* contains the information essential to effective control of the projects. This subsystem may be informal in nature, consisting of periodic meetings with the project participants who report information on the status of their project work, or a formal information retrieval system that provides frequent printouts of what is going on. This subsystem provides the data to enable the project team members to make and implement decisions in the management of the project.

Techniques and methodology is not really a subsystem in the sense that the term is used here. This subsystem is merely a set of techniques and methodologies, such as PERT, CPM, PERT-Cost, and related scheduling techniques, as well as other management science techniques which can be used to evaluate the risk and uncertainty factors in making project decisions.

The *cultural ambience subsystem* is the subsystem in which project management is practiced in the organization. Much of the nature of the cultural ambience can be described in how the people—the social groups—feel about the way in which project management is being carried out in the organization. The emotional patterns of the social groups, their perceptions, attitudes, prejudices, assumptions, experiences, and values, all go to develop the organization's cultural ambience. This ambience influences how people act and react, how they think and feel, and what they say in the organization, all of which ultimately determines what is taken for socially acceptable behavior in the organization.

19

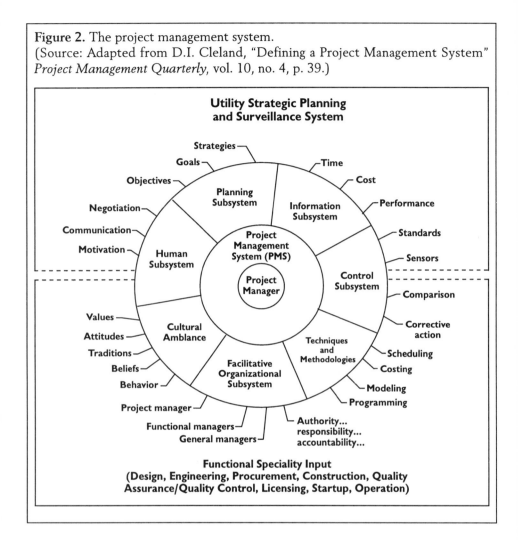

Figure 2. The project management system.
(Source: Adapted from D.I. Cleland, "Defining a Project Management System" *Project Management Quarterly*, vol. 10, no. 4, p. 39.)

The *planning subsystem* recognizes that project control starts with project planning, since the project plan provides the standards against which control procedures and mechanisms are measured. Project planning starts with the development of a *work breakdown structure* which shows how the total project is broken down into its component parts. Project schedules and budgets are developed, technical performance goals are selected, and organizational authority and responsibility are established for members of the project team. Project planning also involves identifying the material resources needed to support the project during its life cycle.

The *human subsystem* involves just about everything associated with the human element. An understanding of the human subsystem requires some knowledge of sociology, psychology, anthropology, communications, semantics, decision theory, philosophy, leadership, and so on. Motivation is an important consideration in the management of the project team. Project management means working with people to accomplish project objectives and goals. Project managers must find ways of putting themselves into the human subsystem of the project so that the members of the project team trust and are loyal in supporting project purposes. The artful management style that project managers develop and encourage within the peer group in the project may very well determine the success or failure of the project. Leadership is the most important role played by the project manager.

Figure 2 depicts the project management system in the context of a public utility commission with all its subsystems. The utility owners responsible and accountable for the effective management of the project work through their boards of directors and senior management with the project manager, functional managers, and functional specialists.

Two authors have suggested that three paths to market leadership can be realized by focusing on three *value* disciplines: (1) operational excellence—providing customers with reliable products or services at competitive prices and delivered with minimal inconvenience; (2) customer intimacy—targeting markets precisely and then providing offerings that match these niches; and (3) product leadership—offering customers leading-edge products and services that constantly enhance the customer's use or application of the product [21]. Of these three value disciplines, product leadership is directly related to how well the company uses a *project management system* to manage its product development activities through a project management philosophy.

References

1. Portions of this chapter have been taken from D.I. Cleland, "Measuring Success: The Owner's Viewpoint," *Proceedings*, PMI Seminar/Symposium, Montreal, Canada, September 20-25, 1986, and D.I. Cleland, "Project Owners Beware," *Project Management Journal*, December 1986, pp. 83-93.

2. Alice LaPlante, "Shared Destinies: CEOs and CIOs," *Forbes ASAP*, December 7, 1992, pp. 32-42.

3. Brenton R. Schlender, "How Sony Keeps the Magic Going," *Fortune*, February 24, 1992, pp. 75-82.

4. *Annual Report*, Elan Corporation, Plc., 1992.

5. LaPlante, op.cit.

6. Cresap, McCormick, and Paget, Inc., *An Operational and Management Audit of PG&E: Executive Summary*, June 1980.

7. Paraphrased from "Using a Cross-Functional Team at Ford to Select a Corporate PM System," *PM Network*, August 1990, pp. 35-59.

8. G. Christian Hill and Ken Yamada, "Staying Power," *The Wall Street Journal*, December 12, 1992.

9. Adapted from D.I. Cleland and W.R. King, *Systems Analysis and Project Management*, 3d ed. (New York: McGraw-Hill, 1983), pp. 68-70.

10. Catherine Arnst et al., "Compaq," *Business Week*, November 2, 1992.

11. Thomas A. Steward, "Brace for Japan's Hot New Strategy," *Fortune*, September 21, 1992, pp. 62-74.

12. William B. Foxhall, "Professional Construction Management and Project Administration," *Architectural Record*, March 1972, pp. 57-58.

13. *Improving Quality and the Assurance of Quality in the Design and Construction of Nuclear Power Plants*, NUREG-1055, U.S. Nuclear Regulatory Commission, Washington, D.C., May 1984, pp. 2-17. (Emphasis added.)

14. Theodore Barry & Associates, *A Survey of Organizational and Contractual Trends in Power Plant Construction*, Washington, D.C., March 1979.

15. For a more thorough analysis see Randall L. Speck, "The Buck Stops Here: The Owner's Legal and Practical Responsibility for Strategic Project Management," *Project Management Journal*, September 1988, pp. 45-52.

16. F.L. Blanchard, "Contracted Management—Clarifying the Roles of Owner and Manager," *Project Management Quarterly*, June 1983, pp. 41-46.

17. Soren Hansen, "An Owner's Perception of Project Management," *Proceedings*, PMI Seminar/Symposium, 1982, III-J.1 to J.9.

18. Ibid., III-J.9.

19. *Improving Quality and the Assurance of Quality in the Design and Construction of Nuclear Power Plants*, NUREG-1055, U.S. Nuclear Regulatory Commission, Washington, D.C., May 1984, pp. 2-17.

20. David I. Cleland, "Defining a Project Management System," *Project Management Quarterly*, vol. 10, no. 4, 1977, pp. 37-40.

21. Michael Treacy and Fred Wiersema, "Customer Intimacy and Other Value Disciplines," *Harvard Business Review*, January-February 1993, pp. 84-93.

Portfolio Management in New Product Development: Lessons From the Leaders, Phase II

Robert G. Cooper, Scott J. Edgett and Elko J. Kleinschmidt

Strategy and new-product resource allocation must be intimately connected. Strategy, agreed the managements of several of the companies we investigated (2), begins when you start spending money! Until one begins allocating resources—for example, to specific development projects—strategy is just words in the strategy document.

The mission, vision and strategy of a business is made operational through the decisions that the business makes on where to spend money. For example, if a business's strategic mission is "to grow via leading edge product development," then this must be reflected in the number of new-product projects underway—projects that will lead to growth (rather than simply defend) and projects that really are innovative. Similarly, if the strategy is to focus on certain markets, products or technology types, then the majority of R&D spending must be focused on such markets, products or technologies.

Not every company we studied had achieved proficiency in this respect. For example, one business unit's senior executive claimed that, "My SBU's strategy is to achieve rapid growth through product leadership"; however, when we examined his SBU's breakdown of R&D spending, the great majority of resources was going to maintenance projects, product modifications and extensions. Clearly, this was a case of a disconnect between *stated strategy* and *where the money is spent*. His business was not alone!

Linking Strategy to the Portfolio

Two broad questions arise from the desire to achieve strategic alignment in the portfolio of projects:

1. *Strategic fit.* Are all your projects consistent with your business's strategy? For example, if you have defined certain technologies or markets as key areas to focus on, do your projects fit into these areas; are they in bounds or out of bounds?

2. *Spending breakdown.* Does the breakdown of your spending reflect your strategic priorities? That is, if you say you are a growth business, then the majority of your R&D spending ought to be for projects that are designed to grow the business. In

---

How the Study Was Done

Interviews were conducted in 35 leading firms in various industries. Five companies were singled out for in-depth and detailed interviews, on the basis of the uniqueness and proficiency of their portfolio approach. The companies, although quite willing to share the details of the portfolio approaches with us, were promised anonymity in some cases. Also, in no way do we reveal any details on any project under development—all illustrations use disguised projects. These leading firms included:

• The U.S. arm of the world's largest chemical company (Hoechst).
• A major industrial materials supplier—the number one in its industry in the world (English China Clay).
• A major high-technology materials producer.
• A major financial institution (Royal Bank of Canada), among the top five in North America.
• A multinational consumer goods company (Reckitt & Colman, U.K.).

Three of the five were in the United States. Additionally, another 30 companies provided data on their portfolio methods, experiences and outcomes (most were from North America). Note that the method of sample selection was purposeful (not random); we deliberately selected firms according to their experience, proficiency and ability to provide insights regarding portfolio management. During the interviews, the details of the portfolio approaches used, the rationale, problems faced and issues raised were all investigated (1).

The study is a two-part study: Phase I has been completed and is reported here; Phase II is underway in cooperation with the Industrial Research Institute, and involves a much larger sample size.—R.G.C., S.J.E., and E.J.K.

---

short, when you add up the areas in which you are spending money, are these totally consistent with your stated strategy?

Two general approaches to achieving strategic alignment were observed in some companies we studied:

1. *Building strategic criteria into project selection tools.* Here, strategic fit was achieved simply by incorporating numerous strategic criteria into the Go/Kill and prioritization models.

2. *Top-down strategy models.* These began with the business's strategy and then moved to setting aside funds—envelopes or buckets of money—destined for different types of projects.

Not only are scoring models effective ways of maximizing the value of the portfolio, but they can also be used to ensure strategic fit. One of the multiple objectives considered in a scoring model, along with profitability or likelihood of success, can be to *maximize strategic fit,* simply by building into the scoring model a number of strategic questions. For example:

• In the scoring model used by Hoechst (1), two major factors out of five are strategic, and of the 19 criteria used to prioritize projects, six deal with strategic issues.

Thus, projects that fit the firm's strategy and boast strategic leverage are likely to rise to the top of the list. Indeed, it is inconceivable that any "off-strategy" projects could make the active list at all; the scoring model weeds them out naturally.

• Reckitt & Colman subjects all projects at gate meetings to a list of "must" criteria before any prioritization consideration is given. At the top of this "must meet" list is *strategic fit;* projects that fail this criterion are knocked out immediately. Next, a set of "should meet" criteria is used via a scoring model: unless the project scores a certain minimum point count, again it is knocked out. Embedded within this scoring model are several strategic direction criteria. Finally, in R&C's bubble diagram, where *concept attractiveness* is plotted versus *ease of implementation* (see Fig. 4 in Ref. 1), of the six parameters that make up *concept attractiveness*, two capture important strategic directions: ability to build the brand and franchise, and geographic scope. Thus, R&C builds in strategic fit and direction throughout its scoring and bubble diagram portfolio approaches.

Top-down Strategic Approaches

While strategic fit could be achieved via a scoring model, a top-down approach is the only method we observed designed to ensure that the eventual portfolio of projects truly reflects the stated strategy for the business: Where the money is spent mirrors the business's strategy. There were two variations of this approach:

1. *Strategic Buckets Model.* This top-down method operates from the simple principle that *implementing strategy equates to spending money on specific projects.* Thus, setting portfolio requirements really means setting spending targets. A number of firms studied used bits and pieces of this approach, and what we describe next is a composite across several companies.

The method begins with the business's strategy, and requires the senior management of the business to make forced choices along each of several dimensions—choices about how they wish to allocate their scarce money resources. This enables the creation of "envelopes of money" or "buckets." Existing projects are categorized into buckets; then, one determines whether actual spending is consistent with desired spending for each bucket. Finally, projects are prioritized within buckets to arrive at the ultimate portfolio of projects, one that mirrors management's strategy.

Here are the details: Management first develops the vision and strategy for the business (or SBU). This includes defining strategic goals and the general plan of attack to achieve these goals—a fairly standard business strategy exercise. Next, it makes forced choices across key strategic dimensions; that is, based on this strategy, management allocates R&D resources (either in dollars or as a percent) across categories on each dimension. Some dimensions that we witnessed included:

• *Strategic goals:* Management is required to split resources across specified strategic goals. For example, what percent (or how many dollars) should be spent on Defending the Base, on Diversifying, on Extending the Base? and so on.

• *Product lines:* Resources are split across product lines; for example, how much to spend on Product Line A? On Product Line B? On C? One firm plots product line locations on the product life cycle curve to help determine this split. Rhode & Schwarz, a sizable German electronics and instruments firm, uses a scoring model to allocate resources across product lines.

Table 1. Projects Prioritized Within Strategic Buckets

New Products Product Line A Target Spend: $8.7 M		New Products Product Line B Target Spend: $8.7 M		Maintenance of Business: Product Lines A & B Target Spend: $8.7 M		Cost Reductions: All Products Target Spend: $8.7 M	
Project A	4.1	Project B	2.2	Project E	1.2	Project I	1.9
Project C	2.1	Project D	4.5	Project G	0.8	Project M	2.4
Project F	1.7	Project K	2.3	Project H	0.7	Project N	0.7
Project L	0.5	Project T	3.7	Project J	1.5	Project P	1.4
Project X	1.7	**Gap =**	**5.8**	Project Q	4.8	Project S	1.6
Project Y	2.9			Project R	1.5	Project U	1.0
Project Z	4.5			Project V	2.5	Project AA	1.2
Project BB	2.6			Project W	2.1		

Projects rank-ordered within columns according to a financial criterion: NPV * Probability of Success, or ECV, or a scoring model.

• *Project type:* What percent of resources should go to new product developments? To maintenance projects? To process improvements? To fundamental research? etc. One SBU within Exxon Chemicals used the standard *product/market newness* matrix proposed by Booz-Allen to visualize this split (3). Here, the six different types of projects defined on this matrix each receive a certain percentage of the total budget.

• *Familiarity Matrix:* What should be the split of resources to different types of markets and to different technology types in terms of their *familiarity to the business?* Both Dow Corning and Eastman Chemical use variants of the "familiarity matrix" proposed by Roberts—technology newness versus market newness—to help allocate resources (4).

• *Geography:* What proportion of resources should be spent on projects aimed largely at North America, at Latin America, at Europe, at the Pacific? Or at global?

Next, management develops *strategic buckets*. Here, the various strategic dimensions (above) are collapsed into a convenient handful of buckets. For example, buckets might be:

• Product development projects for product lines A and B.
• Cost reduction projects for all products.
• Product renewal projects for product lines C and D; and so on (see Table 1).

Next, the desired spending by bucket is determined: the "what should be." This involves a consolidation of desired spending splits from the strategic allocation exercise above.

Following this comes a gap analysis. Existing projects are categorized by bucket and the total current spending by bucket is added up (the "what is"). Spending gaps are then identified between the "what should be" and "what is" for each bucket.

Finally, projects within each bucket are rank-ordered. Companies used either scoring models or financial criteria to do this ranking within buckets. Portfolio adjustments are then made, either by immediately pruning projects, or by adjusting the approval process for future projects.

The major strength of the Strategic Buckets Model is that it firmly links spending to the business's strategy. Over time, the portfolio of projects, and the spending across strategic buckets, will equal management's desired spending levels across buckets. At this point, the portfolio of projects truly mirrors the strategy for the business. Another positive facet of the strategic buckets model is the recognition that *all development projects that compete for the same resources* should be considered in the portfolio approach. For example, product development projects must compete against cost reduction projects, because both utilize R&D resources.

Also, different criteria can be used for different types of projects; that is, one is not faced with comparing and ranking very different types of projects against one another—for example, major new-product projects versus minor modifications. Because this is a two-step approach—first allocate money to buckets, then prioritize like projects within a bucket—it is not necessary to arrive at a universal list of scoring or ranking criteria that fits all projects. (See Table 1.)

The major weakness of the approach is the burden this very time-consuming, arduous exercise places on senior management. Further, making forced choices on resource splits, in the absence of consideration of specific projects, may be a somewhat hypothetical exercise.

2. *StratPlan or Strategic Check.* This method is similar in that it begins with the business's strategy and then develops a strategic mission for each business. But it tends to be more of an "after-the-fact" model—a check or correction designed to bring the portfolio back closer to the strategic ideal. Thus, instead of deliberately setting up buckets of resources, as in the Strategic Buckets Model above, this method simply begins by developing a complete portfolio ranking of all projects; for example, using a traditional maximization method (scoring model or financial criteria). It then *checks* to see that the resulting list of projects is indeed consistent with the business's strategy. The method is similar to the Strategic Buckets Model, except that it reverses the order of steps.

The strategic planning exercise used within one division of Royal Bank (RBC) is fairly typical. Like Hoechst, RBC uses a scoring model to rate and rank projects. One check the firm has built into its scoring technique to ensure that project spending is linked to strategy is its "StratPlan" exercise.

StratPlan is a macro-level, *strategic planning exercise* whereby the 12 product groups in RBC are analyzed via a strategic portfolio exercise, resulting in missions and macrostrategies for each of the groups. StratPlan scores these 12 product groups and classifies them according to a McKinsey-style grid. This macrostrategic exercise is fairly traditional, but worth mentioning here because of the way in which it is tied into new product spending and RBC's scoring model.

Independently, new-product projects are scored and rank-ordered via a scoring model, much like Hoechst's method. The cutoff on the rank-ordered list is the point where total spending equals the total budget: All projects above this cutoff line are a "first-cut Go." This list of Go projects is then broken down by product group, and the total proposed expenditures by product group are determined.

These totals, as a percentage of revenue, are next compared across groups, seeking inconsistencies with each product group's macrostrategy. Gaps are identified between new-product spending levels per product group versus the desired spending. For example, if a product group was classified as a "maintain and defend" business, yet received a rather large percentage of product development spending via the scoring model, a gap exists.

A second round of project prioritization ensues, with some projects that originally had been "Go" now removed from the list. This moves the portfolio closer to the one dictated by the StratPlan exercise. Several rounds are required before the final list of Go projects is agreed to. At this point, the prioritized list contains good projects, according to the scoring model, and the spending allocations correctly reflect the various strategies and missions of each product group.

This StratPlan exercise resembles the Strategic Buckets Model in that desired spending levels per area (in this case, by product line group) are decided, gaps identified, and the portfolio of projects arranged accordingly. However, the method reverses the order of steps (projects are prioritized first, and then checked for consistency with strategy after), is easier to implement, and is less demanding on management.

Where We Stand

After 30 years of development, are we any further ahead? The answer is clearly yes! At worst, we have discovered what *does not work* in portfolio management. More positively, some companies are close to a solution that works for them. But there remain many unresolved issues and barriers yet to be overcome in portfolio management, which we discuss now.

1. *Portfolio management is a vital issue.* The portfolio management question is an important one, perhaps more important than we had previously judged. If the amount of time and money that these and other companies have spent on the problem is any indication, then portfolio management and project selection is likely the *number-one issue* in new product development and technology management for the next decade, and may even be among the top three strategic issues faced by today's executives.

Portfolio management is critical for at least three reasons, according to companies interviewed:

• First, a successful new product effort is *fundamental to corporate success* as we move into the next century. More than ever, senior management recognizes the need for new products—especially the right new products. This logically translates into portfolio management: the ability to select today's projects that will become tomorrow's new product winners.

• Second, new product development is the *manifestation of the business's strategy.* One of the most important ways you operationalize strategy is through the new products you develop. If your new product initiatives are wrong—the wrong projects, or the wrong balance—then you fail at implementing your business strategy.

• Third, portfolio management is about *resource allocation.* In a business world preoccupied with value to the shareholder and doing more with less, technology and marketing resources are simply too scarce to allocate to the wrong projects. The consequences of poor portfolio management are evident: You squander scarce resources on the wrong projects, and as a result, starve the truly meritorious ones.

2. *There is no magic solution.* There is no magic answer or black box model to overcome the portfolio management challenge. Indeed, despite expensive and extensive attempts to develop such portfolio models, the firms we studied were quick to admit that there was no single right answer, and that they were actively seeking solutions and making improvements to their own approaches.

Not only is there no magic answer, there isn't even a *dominant* approach! Despite the fact that many of these managements had read the same reports, articles and books, had benchmarked against the same firms, and had even hired the same consultants, the approaches they arrived at for their own companies were quite different. There is no universal method, dominant theme or generic model here; rather, the models and approaches employed were quite firm-specific.

A great variety of concepts, tools and approaches were employed by these leading firms. The most popular were sophisticated variants on scoring models and financial value models, and also various portfolio mapping approaches, such as bubble diagrams. Some progressive firms used a hybrid approach—a combination of approaches that looked at both the issues of balancing the portfolio as well as maximizing its value against certain objectives.

There was no evidence of the use of (or interest in) mathematical programming and optimization techniques. Interestingly, such models are common in the literature, but have rarely been implemented or tested in industry. Indeed, the notion of a "black box decision model" that would yield a prioritized list of projects had been rejected by all firms studied; rather, a *decision tool* or *decision support system* designed to help managers make the decision was the preferred route.

3. *There are no "flavor of the month" solutions.* The problem is far from solved. Many of the models we observed in companies, although elegant and comprehensive, were as yet relatively untested. These are largely new approaches being implemented only now in these firms. No doubt there remain years of work before well-accepted portfolio models and methods become commonplace in industry.

Observations and Questions

1. *Portfolio management has three main goals:*
• *Maximizing the value of the portfolio* against an objective, such as profitability. Here, financially based methods (such as ECV or the Productivity Index) and scoring models (which build the desired objectives into the criteria list) were most effective.
• *Balance in the portfolio.* Portfolios can be balanced in many dimensions; the most popular were risk versus reward, ease versus attractiveness, and breakdown by project type, market and product line. Visual models, especially bubble diagrams, were thought most appropriate to portray balance.
• *Link to strategy.* Strategic fit and resource allocation which reflects the business's strategy were the key issues here. Scoring models, strategic buckets and strategic checks are appropriate techniques. Of the three, no one goal seemed to dominate; moreover, no one portfolio model or approach seemed capable of achieving all three goals.

2. *There is a need to integrate gate decisions and portfolio decisions.*
Every company we studied relied on some type of new product process model, such as Stage-Gate™, to drive new products from idea through to market. Embedded within these processes are gates or Go/Kill decision points, where the project is reviewed before moving to the next stage. The gates are where the senior decision makers or "gatekeepers" make Go/Kill and prioritization decisions on individual projects.

The potential for conflict exists between this gating decision process and portfolio reviews, namely: real time decisions made on individual projects at gates, versus portfolio decisions made periodically but on all projects together. These are two different decision processes (and in some firms, even involve different people and somewhat different criteria!); yet, both purport to select projects and allocate resources, hence the potential for conflict. For example:

• Portfolio decisions consider all projects together—a comparison against one another. This holistic view is healthy, but it does limit the amount of time the decision makers can spend on any one project. By contrast, gate decisions tend to focus on one project; that one project receives a thorough management review, but in relative isolation from the other projects.

• Gate decisions occur in real time, as the project moves from one stage to the next; by contrast, portfolio review meetings are held in calendar time, perhaps annually, semi-annually or quarterly.

Given these two different decision processes, it is essential that *both processes be functioning well*, and most important, that they be *integrated and harmonized*. We saw many instances in which only one process was working; for example, no kill decisions were ever made at the gates, so the company relied too heavily on portfolio review meetings to weed out poor projects. In other firms, the gates were effective, but rarely was the entire list of projects reviewed to prioritize projects against each other, check for balance, and check for strategic alignment. Neither situation is desirable.

3. *Portfolio models suffer from imaginary precision.*
A universal weakness is that virtually every portfolio model we studied *implied a degree of precision far beyond people s ability to provide reliable data;* that is, the model's sophistication far exceeded the quality of the input data. Ironically, some managements confessed to being mesmerized by their models into believing that the data were quite accurate; the various financial models, rank-ordered lists and bubble diagrams appear so elegant that one sometimes forgets how imprecise are the data upon which these diagrams or charts are constructed. Clearly, before one proceeds to develop even more sophisticated portfolio approaches, there is a great need to bring the quality of the data up to the levels needed in the current models.

4. *Variable resource commitments is a problem.*
Should viable and active projects be killed or de-prioritized, simply because a better one comes along? We encountered two very different philosophies:

• Resource commitments to projects *are not firm*. Rather, they are infinitely flexible; resources should be moved at will from one active project to another project. For example, even though one project has been given a Go, and resources have been committed—and even if it remains a positive one—when a better project comes along, then resources can be stripped from the first project to feed the second. The argument here is that management must have the flexibility to optimally allocate resources, regardless of commitments previously made to project teams-survival of the fittest!

• Resource commitments *are quite firm*. That is, resource commitments made to project teams must be kept, for the sake of continuity and morale, even though a more attractive project comes along. The notion here is that while it may be desirable to have resource flexibility in order to allocate resources optimally, the human side—team morale, commitments, and not "jerking around" project teams and leaders—is more important. Further, if projects are "on again, off again," there is a great waste of resources and time; shifting resources from one project to the next is not seamless, and there are start-up and shut-down costs and times. Finally, newer projects always look better than ones that are part-way through development (warts always seem to appear as time passes!), so that the inevitable outcome is that resources are stripped from projects in their later phases to support new ones; taken to an extreme, no project ever is completed!

Generally, companies with a longer-term perspective, and with considerable experience in major new product projects, embraced the more stable, second view: that resources committed are firm, while firms in shorter-term projects and dynamic markets leaned more to the flexible resource model.

5. Too many projects are "on hold."

More projects pass the gate criteria than have resources to fund them. This places even greater pressure on the prioritization process. In some firms interviewed, the list of projects "on hold" was far longer than the list of active projects!

The problem here is that no one, especially some senior managements, wants to kill potentially good projects, even when it is recognized that there are likely a number of other projects better than this one, and prioritization decisions are essential to achieving focus—this means killing projects. Consequently, it becomes much more convenient to start a Hold Tank, and dump good projects into it.

The implicit argument is this: A Kill decision is averted—*No one's feelings are hurt;* besides, someday there may even be resources available to do some of the projects in the Hold Tank (often wishful thinking on the part of the senior gatekeepers).

When it first implemented its Stage-Gate™ new product process, English China Clay (ECC) encountered this "on hold" problem, and a log-jam of projects awaiting entry to Development occurred. When the "hold list" exceeded the active project list, management knew it was in trouble. A new decision rule was instituted: a project could remain on hold for no longer than three months. After that, it is "up or out"—either it becomes an active and resourced project or it is killed. Brutal perhaps, but at least the rule forces the gatekeepers to be more discriminating and make tough decisions. Further, it has made gatekeepers search for additional resources for meritorious projects that are in danger of being killed.

6. Why have a prioritized or rank-ordered list at all?

According to management in one leading firm, there are only three classes of projects: 1) funded and active projects, with people assigned; 2) good projects, but with no one working on them (currently unfunded—these are the on-hold projects; and 3) dead projects.

If there are only three types, why the need for rank-ordered lists? In short, management here believed there was no great need for a prioritization or scoring method, or any other model that led to a rank-ordered list. All that was needed was a *triage:* active, hold or dead!

A contrary opinion expressed at many other firms is that a rank-ordered list is not only important but necessary. For example, even though a project is Go, there are *varying degrees of Go*, depending on the project's importance, payoffs and priority. As an illustration, management at Hoechst regularly selects a subset of active projects, and performs a *full court press* on these; that is, it resources these chosen projects to the maximum, ensuring that they are done as quickly as possible. Given that different levels of resource commitment can be made to any project, logic dictates that not only must projects be separated into Go and Hold categories, but that Go projects themselves must be prioritized. Those top-priority projects receive maximum resources for a timely completion.

7. Portfolio management must consider all types of R&D projects.

All projects that compete for the same resources ought to be considered in the portfolio approach. This includes new-product projects as well as process improvements, cost reductions, fundamental research, and so on. Conceptually, this is quite correct, but it does increase the magnitude of the portfolio problem: Rather than simply comparing one new-product project to another, now management must deal with a myriad of different types of projects—a much more complex decision situation.

This issue of whether or not all projects should be compared against one another has proponents on both sides of the argument. Some firms studied simply set aside envelopes of money for different types of projects; within each envelope, projects were then rated and ranked against each other. The Strategic Buckets Model outlined above is an example of this, and solves two thorny problems:

First, the Strategic Buckets Model obviates the task of comparing and ranking unlike projects against one another—projects that may have a different nature and quality of information (for example, a process improvement project is likely to have fairly predictable cost and benefit estimates, while a new-product project does not, especially early in the project).

Second, by setting aside buckets of money or resources, one is assured that spending and resource allocation mirrors the business's strategy. Recall that this is the major strength of the Strategic Buckets Model: it forces resources to be allocated into buckets *a priori*.

The opposing viewpoint is that *all projects should compete against one another;* and that no pool of money or resources should be set aside for any particular type of project. For example, if all the cost-reduction projects are superior to all the new-product projects, then all the resources *ought to go to the process improvement projects!* In short, the merits of each project should decide the total split of resources, rather than having some artificial and *a priori* split in resources.

8. Should portfolio management models focus on information display or be decision models?

Should the portfolio model merely *display information* to managers in a useful way (as bubble diagrams do), or should it produce a *prioritized list of projects* (as a scoring model does)? The display approach means that management must review the various maps and charts, integrate the information, and then arrive at a prioritized list itself. By contrast, the prioritized list approach provides management with a "first cut" list of projects, prioritized according to certain criteria; management then reviews and adjusts the list as needed.

9. Many portfolio models yield information overload.

One deficiency with certain mapping approaches is the large number of possible maps. Admittedly, portfolio selection is a complex problem, and hence one is tempted to plot everything versus everything. As noted above, there are many possible parameters to consider; indeed, the permutations of X-Y plots, histograms and pie charts are almost endless.

Are managers overwhelmed with all the information and plots? Experience in some firms suggests they are. For example, when first conceived, Reckitt & Colman's portfolio method contained far more maps and charts than the final version now in use. What managers quickly realize is that they must simplify the problem, and boil the decision down to a few key parameters and hence a few important charts. Some of the more useful maps and charts from among the many we saw in companies: The Reward versus Risk bubble diagram or map (NPV versus Probability of Success).

• A non-financial version of the Risk/Reward bubble diagram (in which the two axes are scored indices, derived from the gate scoring model).

• The Concept Attractiveness versus Ease-of-Implementation bubble diagram.

• The timing histogram (where resources are being spent, projects by year of launch.)

• Various pie chart breakdowns: project types, and across markets, technologies and product lines.

10. Financial analysis methods pose problems.

For most firms, strict reliance on financial methods and criteria in order to prioritize projects was considered inappropriate; financial data are simply too unreliable during the course of a project, especially in the earlier phases when prioritization decisions are most needed. Postproject reviews suggested that estimates made on key variables, such as expected revenues and profits at the Goto-Development decision point, are highly inaccurate. Yet this is the point where serious resource commitments are made and the project must be in the portfolio model.

A second problem is that sophisticated financial models and spreadsheets often implied a level of reliability beyond the facts on which the data were based. Computer-based spreadsheets in some firms had become quite complex, and produced best case and worst case scenarios, sensitivity analyses, and so on. So impressive were these financial models that managers actually began to believe the financial projections!

Even when valid financial data were available and reasonably reliable, there were still problems. Here are three that we heard:

• How does one deal with the possible *cannibalization of other products* already in the product line? Often negative interrelationships among products—especially between new and existing products—are complex; hence, quantitative estimates are difficult to arrive at. For example, a new product might be expected to cannibalize the sales of an old product in the company's lineup. But at how fast a rate? Reliable estimates are difficult to make. And the argument that, "If we don't cannibalize our own products, a competitor surely will; thus, no cannibalization cost effects should be borne by the new product" was often heard. The issue is difficult to resolve.

• How does one treat *capital cost requirements in the case of shared or idle facilities?* For example, one capital-intensive product developer always faced the problem of determining the cost of spare production capacity on capital equipment: How much cost should the new-product project bear? Some pundits in the company argued "none"; after all, the equipment is idle, so there is no opportunity or incremental capital cost. Others in that company made a case that the new product should bear a "fair share" of the equipment capital costs, even when equipment was otherwise idle. Finally, the argument often was that the equipment may be idle this year but may not be next year, so there really is an opportunity cost.

• How does one treat *terminal values* of projects? That is, what is the project "worth" at the end of the five-or ten-year projection considered in the cash flow analysis. Assuming that the project is worth nothing after, say, ten years, could penalize a project severely, especially in the case of projects where the internal rate of return (ROI or IRR) is low and close to the hurdle rate (5).

The Portfolio Management Process

Which portfolio management process is right for your organization? This is not an easy question, as there is no single right answer. But here are some recommendations based on our study of what appeared to work, and managers' comments about the various methods.

Four decision processes are at play in deciding the business's portfolio:

1. *Corporate Planning.* This is the well-known process whereby a company's resources are allocated among business units, each with its own mission and strategy. Here, for example, the BU's total R&D, marketing and capital budgets may be decided.

Comment: Corporate planning and resource allocation across business units is a well-documented process, and has had many models proposed over the years; for example, the Boston Consulting Group 4-quadrant model and the GE/McKinsey 9-cell model (6, 7), and is beyond the scope of this article.

2. *Strategy development at the business unit level.* Ideally, the BU's business strategy also includes a new product stategy, which specifies new product goals (e.g., percentage of sales to be derived from new products), arenas of focus (e.g., those markets, technologies and product areas where new products will be developed), and even attack plans and relative priorities (e.g., the desired breakdown of spending across markets, technologies, product categories, and project types [2]).

Suggestion: If your business unit lacks such a business and new product strategy, consider developing one. This is the domain of the BU leadership team. Without such a business and new product strategy in place, portfolio management becomes next to impossible.

3. *The BU's new product process.* This is the formal process or road map that drives new-product projects from idea to new product launch (e.g., a Stage-Gate™ process). This process typically has multiple stages, steps or phases, and most important, gates or decision points. The gates are where Go/Kill decisions are made on individual projects, and hence where resources are allocated.

Suggestion: The new product process must have tough gates, complete with rigorous criteria, where mediocre projects are weeded out. Given that multiple criteria are often required to select projects, we recommend the use of a *scoring model*, much like Hoechst's model. Moreover, many managements are reluctant to place too much emphasis on a strictly financial method to rate projects, given the inaccuracy of such data, especially pre-development.

Prioritization should also take place at gates, as resources must be allocated (companies can no longer wait for semi-annual reviews to make these resource allocation decisions, given the desire for cycle time reduction!). Resources are allocated by comparing the project score of the proposed project to the active projects already in the pipeline, as well as to those "on hold" awaiting resources.

4. *The portfolio review.* This is the periodic review of the portfolio of *all projects.* It is here when all projects—active projects as well as those on hold—are reviewed and compared against one another. The vital question here is: Do we have the right set of active projects? Is this really where we want to spend our money?

Suggestion: The portfolio review should be a periodic check on the decisions made via the gating process, and held semi-annually or quarterly. If the gates are working well, the portfolio review should be merely a course correction; if too many Go and Kill decisions are made at this portfolio review, then look hard at your gating process—something is wrong here!

The portfolio review must consider all projects together; it is holistic. Think of the gate decisions, which deal with individual projects, as the fingers, and the portfolio review as the fist. Be sure to check that the projects in the portfolio meet the three goals of portfolio management: maximum value to the business balance and strategic link. We recommend the following portfolio models for use at the portfolio review:

• *Maximum Value:* The gate scoring model, suggested above, can also be used to rate and rank projects at the portfolio review, yielding a prioritized list of the best projects, much like Hoechst does.

• *Balance:* This is best portrayed by the various charts:

• If your business is very financially driven, and if financial projections for new products are quite predictable, then we suggest using an NPV versus Probability of Technical Success bubble diagram, as described in Part I (1). If there are goals in addition to financial ones, and if financial estimates are uncertain, place less reliance on these financial numbers, and utilize a bubble diagram whose axes are derived from the scoring model factors (as does Specialty Minerals).

• Standard pie charts and histograms that capture split in spending across markets, product categories, technologies, project types, and launch timing.

• *Strategic Alignment:* Consider using the Strategic Buckets approach in order to preallocate funds to various buckets; for example, across project types or across markets, technologies or product lines. Alternatively, use the strategic check approach to ensure that the spending breakdown at least mirrors strategic priorities. Additionally, build strategic criteria—fit and importance—into your scoring model in order to drive on-strategy projects toward the top of the list.

Your company should have all four of these processes in place and working properly in order for there to be effective portfolio management. Three of these occur within the business unit and comprise what we call the Portfolio Management Process: business unit strategy development, the new product process with its gates, and the portfolio review (see Figure 1).

The three decision models ideally are integrated, in harmony and feed each other. For example, the business's strategy (top) drives the gating method by providing key criteria for the scoring model; it also provides key criteria for the portfolio review,

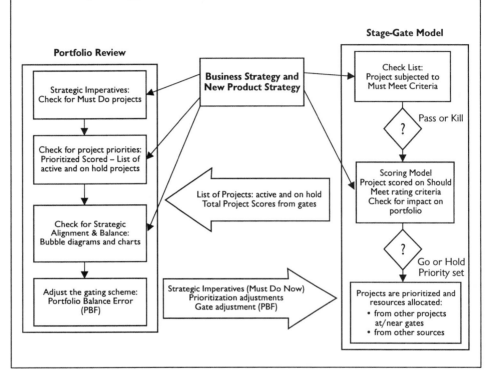

Figure 1. In the total Portfolio Management Process, the portfolio review feeds the stage-gate model, which in turn feeds the portfolio review. Both models are in sync and driven by strategy.

helps to establish the targets for various spending breakdowns or buckets (for balance), and identifies strategic imperatives ("must do now" projects).

Similarly, the gating process (at illustration's right) feeds the gate decisions and project scores to the portfolio review (horizontal arrow, heading left).

Finally the portfolio review (left) feeds strategic project decisions (imperatives) and gate adjustments to the gating process (horizontal arrow, heading right in the diagram). These gate adjustments simply adjust the gate criteria or scoring model to favor project types which are deemed "desirable but under-represented" in the portfolio, and moves the project portfolio toward the ideal balance.

If all three elements of the Portfolio Management Process are in place—the business's strategy, the new product process, and the portfolio review (with its various models and tools)—then a harmonized system should yield excellent portfolio choices: projects that deliver economic payoffs to the business, that mirror the business's strategy and direction, and that realize the BU's goals for new products. But if any piece of the illustrated process is not working—for example, if there is no clearly defined BU strategy, or if the new product process and gating process is broken-the results are less than satisfactory.

Make the Right Choices

New products are the leading edge of your business strategy. The product choices you make today determine what your business's product offerings and market position will be in five years. Making the right choices today is paramount. Portfolio management and new-product project selection is fundamental to business success. Make sure that you have the tools you need to make these right choices—an effective Portfolio Management Process (2)—in your business!

Acknowledgement

The research reported in this article was generously supported by grants from Esso Chemical Canada (Exxon in Canada) and the Innovation Research Centre at the Michael G. DeGroote School of Business, McMaster University.

References and Notes

1. Cooper, R. G., S. J. Edgett and E. J. Kleinschmidt. "Portfolio Management in New Product Development: Lessons from the Leaders-I" *Research Technology Management*, Sept.-Oct. 1997, pp. 16-28.

2. The entire study and full results are available in detail in the authors' report: *Portfolio Management for New Products*, McMaster University, Hamilton, Ontario, Canada, 1997. It may be ordered for $30.00 (Visa card only) from Edgett at (905) 525-9140, ext. 27437.

3. *New Product Management for the 1980s.* New York: Booz, Allen & Hamilton. 1982.

4. Roberts, E. and C. Berry. "Entering New Businesses: Selecting Strategies for Success." *Sloan Management Review.* Spring 1983, pp. 3-17.

5. Heldey, B. "Strategy for the Business Portfolio." *Long Range Planning.* Vol. 10, No. 1 Feb. 1997, pp. 9-15.

6. Day, G. *Analysis for Strategic Marketing Decisions.* St. Paul, MN: West Publishing, 1986.

7. Cooper, R. and E. Kleinschmidt, "Winning Businesses in Product Development: Critical Success Factors." *Research Technology Management*, July-Aug. 1996, pp. 18-29.

Project Portfolio Management: A Song Without Words?

Harvey A. Levine

I am about to shoot holes in the gospel of project management. Not that what we are preaching is wrong. But it confuses the means to an end with the end itself.

Read PMI's *A Guide to the Project Management Body of Knowledge (PMBOK™ Guide)*. Read just about anything else on measurements of project success. They all dwell on the four pillars of success: scope, time, cost and quality. We are taught to identify the goals for success in each of these areas and then to create plans that balance these objectives. Then we implement practices and utilize computer-based tools to measure how well we are accomplishing these objectives.

But talk to almost any executive in the firm and you will find that he or she will not be interested in this area of measurement. What do these executives talk about? They respond to measurements of profitability, return on investment, delivery of content, and taking advantage of windows of opportunity. We used to say that executives are interested in just two things about projects: when they will finish and what they will cost. Not anymore. Now they ask: What mix of potential projects will provide the best utilization of human and cash resources to maximize long-range growth and ROI for the firm?

Perhaps this is an oversimplification. However, if we start with this premise and examine its meaning, we can begin to realize the tremendous impact of this observation on the way that we conduct project management and especially in the way that we select and implement project management tools.

The Emergence of Project Portfolio Management

Certainly, it is not news to anyone that the basic concept of project management has evolved to what we call "enterprise project management." At first, we thought that this shift was more of a way of aggrandizing project management—sort of a pompous raising of project management to a higher level of importance. Later, we came to realize that enterprise project management was a reflection of the importance of consolidating and integrating all of the firm's projects for universal access and evaluation. Now, we come to find that enterprise project management entails consideration of potential projects as well as approved projects. We also find that the emphasis has shifted from traditional project-centric objectives to higher-level operational objectives.

Executives have come to realize that projects are the basis for future profitability of the firm. Hence, there is rising interest on the part of executives in how projects are managed. They are precipitating a growing demand for more standardization and automation of project management. But what they are asking for is different than the requests from traditional project management sources.

And what they are calling this emerging project management protocol has also changed. It is no longer just project management, or even enterprise project management. It is now called "Project Portfolio Management."

But is Project Portfolio Management for real? Or is it just a nice-sounding phrase, without real substance? I get the idea that it's just a lingering melody—a song without words. It's a pretty tune, and, with the right lyrics, it might be a big hit. But for the moment, I don't see a consensus as to how this emerging concept will play out.

But don't mistake my skepticism for a lack of support for the concept. My concern is not whether Project Portfolio Management is worthwhile. It is with how to integrate the concepts of Project Portfolio Management with traditional project management that requires attention.

Effect on Tool Selection

We can trace the shifting project management emphasis on the patterns of project management tools. First there were the project-oriented tools. These provided support for detailed planning and control of individual projects. With the shift to enterprise project management, we saw a change in the project management tools to support multiple projects and multiple users. In some cases, these tools were designed to allow use of the traditional desktop, single-project products, by providing a repository-based, client/server environment that consolidated individual projects and added multiproject, multiuser time entry, cross-project resource loading and analysis, and cross-project roll-up and reporting. In parallel with that trend, we saw the development of full-featured enterprise project management tools using built-in multiproject scheduling engines and time entry capabilities.

For Project Portfolio Management, additional attributes are required. The ability to add or extract projects for "what if" analyses is important. Executives also want to place some value criteria on the projects so that they can evaluate the relative benefits of adding a project to the mix. Resource and cost impacts of projects will have to be defined at higher than normal levels (because the details might not yet be available or practical to define). Somehow, these executives will expect that the new Project Portfolio Management systems will be able to support ROI calculations (but I don't think that they have yet defined how this would be done).

The ability to slice-and-dice large repositories of project information becomes paramount in these systems. The data must be able to be rolled up and expanded, and must be able to be viewed from several dimensions. As the volume of data increases, we will need more sophisticated ways of manipulating the data so that we don't have to wait for the analyses. OLAP (online analytical processing) is but one of the ways to do this.

Misconceptions and Conceptual Gaps

While the overall concept of Project Portfolio Management makes a lot of sense, there remains a tremendous gap between perceived applications and practical realities. I know of at least one instance where senior management expressed a desire to implement a Project Portfolio Management capability (and backed it up with funding). Yet they had little interest in project management itself. It was as if the firm's project mix could be managed and manipulated without management of the projects themselves. Is this possible?

There is an increasing interest in knowing where the firm's resources are committed and what the firm is getting for their resource investment. Again, I have to ask: How can this be satisfied without knowing to what work the resources have been assigned and how well that work is going? We might, at the higher level, have built a plan that models resource allocation vs. time, but if 40 percent of the way into the project only 20 percent of the work has been accomplished, then that situation has to be factored into the portfolio analysis?

One of the ways to do this is to use the Earned Value Analysis (EVA) capabilities of our project management software. This simple and effective protocol can provide important schedule and cost variance data. This is important not only as a way of remodeling the resource demand for the project(s) but also as a measurement of how well the project is meeting its objectives. Yet, when we mention EVA to the very people who are asking for Project Portfolio Management, they shudder. EVA is assumed to be "too technical" for the high-level view they seek.

Nothing can be further from the truth. I don't see how a Project Portfolio Management system can be put in place without using EVA as part of the performance analysis approach. The resource and cost commitments may have been reasonable (as measured against the expected gains) but there has to be a point where deteriorating performance (increasing investment or time-to-market) crosses the (profitability) line. More on this latter.

What is the "Value" of a Project?

Another thing that puzzles me about the emerging concepts of Project Portfolio Management is how to fix a value on the project. For instance, under the concept of Project Portfolio Management I have seen requests for the following types of information:

• Find out which proposed projects have the highest value to the organization and therefore should receive priority in resource allocation.

• Evaluate proposed projects in terms of their impact on the overall portfolio, specifically with regard to resource availability and the performance of other projects.

• Identify which projects are 25 percent or more behind schedule, and analyze the impact to the overall portfolio of canceling those projects, again in terms of resource availability and performance of other projects.

These requests seem a bit vague to me. How is "value" being defined? How is "impact" being defined? I understand the importance of being able to get answers here, but has anyone thought about just what data is required to provide the answers?

Project Portfolio Management and Strategic Planning

We have fought a battle, for years now, to convince senior management that they can't implement project management capability by just bringing in project management tools. This holds true for Project Portfolio Management as well. The tools process information; they don't generate knowledge that isn't there. If management cannot describe the aspects of "value," the system will not know what to do.

This brings us to the realization that the true strategic value of a proposed project must be determined and quantified before it can be placed into the project mix. And this step cannot be executed by the supporting enterprise project management software.

I would hate to think that Project Portfolio Management will be used as an excuse for lack of good strategic thinking. The fact is that Project Portfolio Management is part of the normal strategic planning process. We wouldn't have the problem of so many failed and aborted projects if the people who authorized these projects were more organized and diligent about their decisions to proceed. How many times have you seen a business case presented, with most-likely, best-case and worst-case scenarios, then the presenter says that "the downside will never happen," and the execs buy it. No wonder projects fail!

Practical Project Portfolio Management and Risk Assessment

So, in order for this modern Project Portfolio Management to work, we need to get back to the sound basics of identifying a range of satisfactory performance for any project. We have to have a predetermination of acceptable performance so that we can set alarms and alerts within the Project Portfolio Management system to advise us of out-of-tolerance conditions. The ROI analysis can't assume just a single result. It must consider a spread of possible scope, time, cost and quality conditions and identify what values (limits) reduce the ROI to an unacceptable number. When does an increase in time-to-market make the project significantly less attractive? How much of a cost overrun can be tolerated before it blows the projected profit? When does the scope reduction reduce the expected benefits of the project?

We must consider if the project is worth the risk. This means conducting a thorough risk assessment, identifying both the potential for risk and the impact of risk events. We must consider risk mitigation actions. And then we must evaluate whether the project is still worthwhile after factoring in the costs of risk mitigation.

The New Project Portfolio Team

To make this whole thing work, we have to have specialists who are responsible for evaluating and communicating these essential business/project data. We are already getting management to accept the necessity of the Project Office. Next, we have to expand this to include people who will be responsible for portfolio and risk management. Why not a CRO—Chief Risk Officer? How about a PPM—Project Portfolio Manager? And, with the increased concern for resource availability and utilization, perhaps a CHRO—Chief Human Resource Officer—could be justified.

In this enlightened environment, no project should be considered without review by the CRO. No resources should be allocated without review by the CHRO. And no project should be added or removed from the portfolio without review by the PPM. I can see an advisory committee made up of these three managers plus the CPO—Chief Project Officer (or head of the Project Office) and the CFO to decide on project viability and management of the portfolio. It is these leaders who would use and support the tools that would provide essential information and analyses in support of the projects.

Implementing Project Portfolio Management

I am convinced that Project Portfolio Management is the way to go. I am equally convinced that the success of a Project Portfolio Management initiative is dependent on how the organization develops and supports an environment for Project Portfolio Management, rather than just on tool selection. However, once the decision is made to implement Project Portfolio Management, and once the support structure is in place, the team will want to find tools that adequately support their new way of life. This tool set must include the following capabilities and features, over and above traditional project management software functions:

• Electronic time sheets, supporting the collection of actual time spent on project tasks and auxiliary work. These must allow the posting of time to all projects in the system, and should support various means of remote entry. These tools should also provide for management review and control of time reporting. In some environments, the time entry tools must also support progressing of the work, including revised estimate-to-complete data.

• Posting and retention of project data in an open, SQL-type database. This database acts as a repository for the data produced by various project management tools, as well as connectivity to other data of the enterprise.

• (For some applications) integration with corporate accounting systems. For seamless integration, look for "Projects" modules provided by ERP vendors as part of their financial packages, coupled with integration engines provided by your project management software vendor.

• When projects and operations data is integrated it often become voluminous. In order to interrogate the data and reduce it to meaningful information, look for OLAP-based slice-and-dice analysis engines or other means of prearranging the data for rapid access. Also, for the slice-and-dice capabilities, the enterprise project management software must have robust project classification systems (coding) with support for hierarchical structures.

• Earned value computation to support schedule and cost variance analysis.

• Mid- and high-level resource loading and budgeting, with discrete spreading capabilities, to allow analysis of proposed projects without requiring planning at the detailed level.

• Risk assessment, including ranking of project risks, determination of risk possibility and impact of the risk event. Good risk management practice supports the inclusion of proposed mitigation plans and the appraisal of the cost effect of taking mitigation action as opposed to experiencing the effect of the risk event.

Project Portfolio Management is the bridge between traditional operations management and project management. For organizations that will be depending on project success for success of the overall enterprise, a well-structured bridge, built on a good foundation, is the preferred way to overcome the tradional gap between operations and projects management.

This article is reprinted from the July 1999 *PM Network* with permission of the Project Management Institute Headquarters, Four Campus Boulevard, Newtown Square, PA 19073-3299 USA, Phone: (610) 356-4600 Fax: (610) 356-4647. Project Management Institute (PMI) is the world's leading project management association with over 40,000 members worldwide. For further information contact PMI Headquarters at (610) 356-4600 or visit the web site at www.pmi.org.

Project Portfolio Management: Ideas and Practices

Dianne N. Bridges

The formal practice of portfolio management is becoming more common place in today's business environment. Organization's find themselves juggling traditional research and new product development projects with information technology enhancements and internal business improvements. No doubt, there are different investment paths to take; and with so much at stake, businesses are making every attempt to wisely select the best route.

Even after selecting the route, it is easy to get distracted along the way: things may not unfold as originally planned, a competitor introduces a new product, the chief scientist makes a key breakthrough elsewhere, legislation is enacted causing industry-wide upheaval, or technology advances and matures. Your original selection is no longer the best. So, an adjustment is made and a better path for the future is selected.

This is the art of portfolio management—doing the right thing, selecting the right mix of projects and adjusting as time evolves and circumstances unfold. Although the practice of portfolio management is becoming commonplace, there is no single approach that works in every organization, industry, or culture. Over the last several years, more and more information has circulated proposing different methods and citing specific organizational experiences. This article provides ideas to establish or fine tune portfolio management activities. Many ideas are demonstrated with specific industry examples. The reader will benefit by having a list of ideas with specific industry experiences to adopt, as appropriate.

The Larger Picture

Simply selecting the right portfolio is only one element of being successful. First, the organization needs to focus. Second, the right projects need to be selected. Third, after selection, the projects need to be managed well. (See Figure 1)

Focus the organization (strategic planning). The organization needs to define the overall reason for their existence. This is generally captured in a vision statement, mission statement, statement of principles, organization objectives, and/or strategic plan(s). Commonly known as strategic planning, the organization and individual business units determine their direction and identify key objectives and goals. The strategic

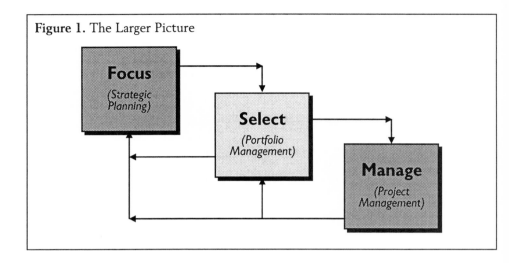

Figure 1. The Larger Picture

focus of the organization becomes the foundation for selecting research, new product development, information technology, and business improvement projects.

Select the right projects (portfolio management). After the organization's focus is established and understood, projects are selected and resources are placed where it matters. The selection process is called portfolio management and involves identifying opportunities; assessing the organizational fit; analyzing the costs, benefits, and risks; and developing and selecting a portfolio. Portfolio management is concerned with *fit, utility, and balance.*

Fit. What is the project? Does the project fit within the focus of the organization and the business strategy and goals? This is where opportunities are identified and the fit is assessed.

Utility. Why should this project be pursued? What is the usefulness and value of the project? This is where the costs, benefits, and risks are identified and analyzed.

Balance. Which projects should be selected? How does the project relate to the entire portfolio and how can the project mix be optimized? This is where the portfolio is developed and selected.

If done effectively, portfolio management will ensure optimum use of people and resources. The secret is to be efficient and effective.

Manage the projects well (project management). After the portfolio of projects is selected, the organization needs to do the work—they need to conduct the research, develop the new product, design and implement the new information architecture, or develop the new business process. The organization will now apply its knowledge, skills, tools, and techniques to create the product or service [1]. Simply selecting the right projects is not enough; the business needs to manage project execution and practice sound project management.

It is this three-pronged effort—focus, select, and manage—that must be synchronized. The overriding goal is to do the right thing, then to do the right things right (and quickly). Doing the right thing starts with focus and ends with project selection. Doing the right things right (and quickly) is project management. The elements outside of

Figure 2. The Fit, Utility and Balance Paradigm.

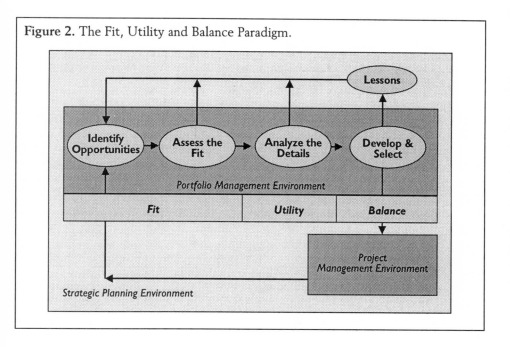

portfolio management are exciting and important, but they are out of the scope of this article.

Ideas and Practices

Figure 2 provides a visual snapshot of the *fit, utility, and balance* paradigm. Almost every organization will flow through this thought process to build a portfolio of projects. The organization may first identify opportunities; then assess the organizational fit; analyze the costs, benefits, and risks; and finally develop and select a portfolio. It is the methods and techniques employed that differ. Invariably, at some level of sophistication, all organizations will understand the fit and utility of their projects and make some attempt to establish a mix of projects.

The Fit (Identify Opportunities and Assess the Fit): The first major element of portfolio management is to identify opportunities and determine if those opportunities are in line with the corporate strategic direction. In a sense, this may be the identification and initial screening of projects before more in-depth analysis is conducted. The questions to ask are: What is the project? Does the project fit within the focus of your organization and the business strategy and goals? Several things to consider:

• *Develop a process to identify opportunities and make it easy to follow.* Many individuals have an aversion to complex processes and bureaucratic paperwork. Establish an avenue for communicating ideas versus a paperwork nightmare that is impossible to wade through. Make the process simple and easy to use all of the time. Identify a team to review the opportunities and assess the fit within the strategic direction and business goals.

• As part of the process, *establish a template for project justification.* The ideas need to have some substance and content; otherwise it will be difficult to screen the projects.

The template may include things such as a description of the project, what will be done, the project's sponsor, the link to organizational direction and business goals, and a top-level description of the project's costs, benefit, and risks.

• As part of the process, *establish minimal acceptance criteria.* The individuals submitting ideas and the review team should understand the minimal acceptance criteria. There should be basic requirements a project must meet before they are considered for further analysis and funding. Such requirements may include the link to strategic direction, business threshold minimums (e.g., return-on-investment or cost/benefit ratio minimums), compliance with organizational constraints (e.g., existing technology architecture), and completion of the project justification paperwork.

• *Reward ideas and suggestions…give credit where credit is due.* Most employees love recognition for their ideas and suggestions. Take the time and interest to formally acknowledge ideas that meet the "fit" test. Always give credit where credit is due.

• Last but not least, *make sure clear strategic direction and business goals have been established.* Since strategic focus becomes the foundation for selecting projects, the strategic direction and business goals should have been clearly established. These may be reflected in the vision statement, mission statement, statement of principles, organization objectives, and/or strategic plan(s).

The Utility (Analyze the Details): The second major element of portfolio management is to further define the project (if needed) and to analyze the details surrounding its utility. The utility of a project captures the usefulness of the project, its value, and is typically defined by costs, benefits, and associated risks. The questions to ask are: Why should this project be pursued? What is the usefulness and value of the project? Several things to consider:

Establish criteria and develop a model to support decision making. Multiple projects vie for resources and funding, and somehow a decision has to be made on which ones to select. To help in the decision-making process, establish common decision criteria and measure each project against the criteria. Since most decisions are based upon multiple factors, weight each criterion to establish the relative importance of each item. This will identify what is most significant to the organization and each project can be measured against the criteria that are important.

A typical approach to analyzing the details is to 1) establish the common decision criteria, 2) assign relative weights to each criteria, 3) determine the project's value in meeting the criteria (determine it's utility), and 4) calculate a score for each project using its value for each criterion and applying the relative weights.

The criteria and weights an organization selects is dependent upon its strategic plans and its vision, guiding principles, capabilities, and limitations. The decision criteria vary by organization. Following are some industry examples to consider:

1. **New Product Development Criteria for Hoechst-AG Chemical, Corporate Research & Technology Unit.** Hoechst-AG, one of the largest chemical companies in the world, uses a scoring portfolio model with 19 questions within five major categories to rate projects. The five categories are probability of technical success, probability of commercial success, reward to the company, business strategy fit, and strategic leverage (ability of the project to leverage company resources and skills). Within each of these five factors are a number of specific characteristics or measures which are scored on 1-10 scales by management

(e.g., strategic leverage, synergy with other operations within the corporation, absolute contributions to profitability). The criteria and scoring approach is a particularly effective model and purported to be one of the best [2].

2. **Research & Development (R&D) Criteria for Weyerhaeuser Corporate Research and Development.** Starting in 1990, the mission of Corporate R&D was refocused to help core business areas succeed over the long run (core areas include Timberland; Pulp, Paper and Packaging; and Wood Building Products). The Corporate R&D program was modified and new processes were put into place to align and prioritize R&D projects. The Corporate R&D program is broken down into three types of activities: technology assessment (changes in external environment and impact to the company); research (building knowledge base and competencies in core technical areas); and development (development of specific commercial opportunities). Four key inputs are considered when establishing priorities: significant changes in the external environment; long-term future needs of lead customers; business strategies, priorities and technology needs; and corporate strategic direction. Their lessons learned are: be patient, it takes time to engage company business leaders, get the project leaders involved so they understand the criteria and rationale, and put processes in place that encourage staff across technical areas to be involved [3].

3. **Information Technology (IT) Criteria.** A construct was developed to help organizations choose between IT projects. The criteria centers around four areas: customer (commitment in terms of need); strategy (alignment with company goals and objectives); technology (ability to meet technical requirements); and delivery (ability to successfully deliver the project). Strategy is further broken down into profitability (measuring the IT project's cost savings), process improvement (ability to improve business processes—time), and employee satisfaction (satisfaction of employees working the IT project). Technology is broken down into core competency (organization capability to perform the project), cost competitiveness (ability to provide a competitive solution), and integration (with existing technology). Delivery is broken down into schedule, budget, and quality reflecting the organization's ability to complete on schedule, within budget, and deliver a quality solution. The relative importance of each criterion is determined using a simple spreadsheet or the pair-wise comparisons of the Analytical Hierarchy Process (AHP). It is recommended to establish twelve to fifteen criteria to support IT decision-making [4].

4. **Three Predominant Themes of Importance in Industry Portfolios.** As shown, organizations establish different sets of criteria and varying importance for each criterion. Although the specifics may be different, there is a tendency within industry to place emphasis on one or more of three specific goals when selecting project portfolios. The three goals are: maximization of value, development of a balanced portfolio, and alignment with strategic objectives [5]. The point is that the criteria and weights will help in the selection of project portfolios and typically industry selects a method that emphasizes one of these predominant themes.

• *Make sure accurate data is available to make decisions.* In addition to establishing criteria and developing a decision support model, ensure the data used to value each project is accurate and current. The organization should have a reliable accounting system that collects and accounts for resources (expenditures, revenues, and manpower). Information from the accounting system may be necessary to forecast project costs and benefits. The organization should have reliable, up-to-date market, technical, and manufacturing information. Since project portfolios are made up of both new projects and on-going projects, the organization should have a system to track the status of on going project activity.

• *Establish a process to analyze the project information.* Establish a process that will validate project information and compare the information against the common decision criteria. The purpose of this process is to analyze the project information to ensure data validity and consistent application of the decision criteria. It is important to go through this process before selecting the portfolio to eliminate any controversy over the data and key assumptions while in the midst of developing the portfolio (the next area).

For example, in 1993, SmithKline Beecham—a pharmaceuticals company—was spending more than a half a billion dollars per year on R&D. Concerned about the effectiveness of their resource allocation process, SmithKline Beecham designed a better decision-making process that would, among other things, establish a consistent valuation method and engage peers/management in the analysis to ensure credibility to the overall process. The company instituted a process where peers and management first discussed and agreed upon the project descriptions (the "what"). Following agreement, the peers and management discussed and agreed upon the calculated value of each project (the "utility"). With these reviews the company made a conscious effort to understand the underlying assumptions and information before they selected a portfolio of projects. This approach added an element of credibility and fairness to the decision process and involved individuals from all parts of the organization [6].

• *Uniformly apply the methodology across the organization.* Finally, the approach and methodology used to analyze a project's utility must be uniformly applied across the organization, regardless what criteria is used to capture utility. Although this seems a little stifling, the criteria and weights should be identified, defined, and completely documented. The process established should ensure project teams consistently interpret the criteria and its related measures and/or probabilities. An analogy can be made to performance reviews and the use of criteria and performance scales. For example, different managers may have different definitions of an "excellent" rating. In order to ensure fairness for all employees, it is imperative the organization clearly defines all performance levels so managers consistently interpret and apply the scales. If this doesn't happen, employees may be unfairly evaluated and rewarded—just like projects may be unfairly evaluated and rewarded. If the cost, benefits, and risks are identified for one project, they should be identified for all.

The Balance (Develop and Select the Portfolio): The third and last major area of portfolio management is the development and selection of the project portfolio. The questions to ask are: Which projects should be selected? How does the project relate to the entire portfolio, and how can the project mix be optimized? Several things to consider.

Establish a process that will help *optimize the portfolio—not just the individual projects.* Industry approaches for developing portfolios range from simple ranking based on individual project financial returns to more complex methodologies that take into account the inter-relationships between projects. Regardless of the chosen method, the objective should be to optimize the portfolio, not necessarily the individual projects (assuming you have more than one project opportunity). The appropriate method is dependent upon an organization's strategic direction, guiding principles, capabilities, limitations, and complexities. When developing and selecting the portfolio, the organization needs to consider all types of projects such as research, new product development, information technology, and business improvement. Remember that relative comparisons are being made, not specific comparisons. Following are some industry examples:

Use of Strategy Tables for R&D Portfolio Management at Eli Lilly and Company. Strategy tables are being introduced at Eli Lilly to develop alternative portfolios and compare alternative strategies. The strategy table represents different combinations of projects and different courses of action for each project; thus providing an array of portfolios for selection. The benefits of examining multiple portfolios vs. simply ranking projects are: 1) the focus is on the portfolio of opportunities vs. individual opportunities, 2) relationships between opportunities are considered, and 3) alternative courses of action are determined and evaluated [7].

Use of Project Alternatives to Understand the Full Range of Alternatives at SmithKline Beecham. SmithKline Beecham examines a range of alternatives for each candidate project before they assess the value of each project. In doing so, the organization has gone away from a single plan of action with one viable option to four project alternatives with four viable options. Each project team must develop at least four alternatives: the current plan (follow existing activity), a "buy-up" option (have more to spend); a "buy-down" option (have less to spend); and a minimal plan (abandon project but preserve as much as possible). The approach has been beneficial to the company citing an experience in finding a new alternative that could create more value for less money. The benefits to creating project alternatives include 1) the formation of new ideas, 2) the creation of new chances for projects that would not survive under their current plans, and 3) the help to teams to understand the elements of their development plans (they have to think it through to determine options) [8].

Use of Risk-Reward Bubble Diagrams at 3M. Bubble diagrams are visual depictions of project portfolios. Generally two axes are drawn dividing the space into four quadrants. Each axis stands for a key characteristic that describes the portfolio. The most popular diagram is a risk-return diagram (such as the probability of technical success and reward). In this case, the separate quadrants stand for different combinations of the risk-return (low-risk, low-return; high-risk, high-return; low-risk, high-return; high-risk, low-return). Each project is assessed and placed within a quadrant, resulting in a visual depiction of the portfolio. There is really no prioritization of projects—but more a display of information to help in the portfolio decision. 3M uses bubble diagrams and adds another level of complexity to portray uncertainty and probabilities. The size and shape of each "bubble" on the diagram is adjusted to reflect project uncertainties. The bubble diagrams help decision-makers visualize the total portfolio [9].

Use of Real Options vs. Static Cash Flows for Portfolio Development. Option Space Analysis employs a more dynamic approach to portfolio management vs. following a predetermined plan, regardless of what happens. In theory, this analysis approach takes into account uncertainty in business and active strategic planning. The method uses a volatility metric and a value-to-cost-metric vs. the conventional discounted cash flow. The volatility metric measures how much things can change before an investment decision is made and the value-to-cost metric measures the value of what's being built with the costs needed to build them. Using the metrics, opportunities can be categorized into invest now, maybe now, probably later, maybe later, probably never, and invest never [10].

There are many mathematical decision methods and tools to help organizations compare a project against the decision criteria, develop a relative score for comparison against other projects, and build a portfolio. Jack R. Meredith and Samuel J. Mantel, Jr., in their book *Project Management: A Managerial Approach* discuss the different types of models, provide a variety of mathematical techniques, and make references to other books on decision making to help individuals master the fundamentals of decision making [11].

• *Establish Portfolio Decision meetings to make decisions.* The idea of establishing a process to analyze the project information was discussed above. The purpose of the process was to validate project information and ensure consistent application of the decision criteria. For portfolio decisions, separate decision meetings and teams should be established to make portfolio decisions using the validated project information. Typically, senior leadership makes the portfolio decisions. The meetings and reviews are normally held in conjunction with the corporate planning schedule.

The portfolio management process used by Weyerhaeuser Corporate Research and Development (mentioned earlier) also includes a logical hierarchy of groups in defining research priorities across core-competency areas. Project Advisory Groups conduct technical reviews of projects and focus on tactical issues (the project level). Review Boards provide guidance for on-going projects, represent the needs and priorities of core-competency areas, ensure alignment with the needs, and take a broad view (the core competency level). The Technology Strategy & Research Council decides on strategic research priorities, provides guidance on alignment, and approves project portfolios (the corporate R&D level) [12].

About the Process

An organization may have the best ideas and methods; but, if the process is not structured or implemented correctly, there will be difficulties in obtaining widespread acceptance of the new process. It is important to think through the process and the implementation plan before establishing the new practice. If the organization is planning to develop or enhance a portfolio management process, there are key points to keep in mind from a process perspective. Most of these points are self-explanatory, but still worth serious consideration.

• Make the process easy to follow—keep it simple.

• Make the process known throughout the organization—ensure employees and management understand the objective of the process, key steps, and points of contact.

• Make the process iterative and structured—quite often it ("it" being what we are making) is not done right the first time. Build a process that allows for reviews, discussions, and re-reviews.

• Include utility triggers for on-going projects—remember portfolios are composed of new projects and existing projects. As time passes, existing projects may cost more,

52

take more time, or change technically. Build a process that puts existing projects back in the review process, especially if they go over original cost and time estimates.
• Make someone responsible for the process—typically things don't get done unless someone is responsible.
• Establish appropriate review and decision levels—put in place a logical hierarchy of reviews and decision points.
• Periodically assess how well things are doing—ask key individuals how the process is working; normally the opinions are invaluable.
• Establish a historical database to capture progress—keep records and establish metrics for how well things are doing (metrics such as number of projects in the queue, types of projects, number of successes, number of missed opportunities).
• Pilot test the process before implementing it corporate-wide—it is *extremely* important to test the process before full implementation.

Summary

There is a lot of merit to wisely managing a portfolio of projects. Obviously, resources need to be allocated where they'll be effective—pursuing projects that offer little benefit to the organization is a waste. Project opportunities need to be identified, their fit to the organization needs to be assessed, their utility and value analyzed, and then, finally, the right mix of projects to pursue needs to be determined. Use the portfolio management ideas from this article to help implement or enhance a portfolio management effort.

The benefits of portfolio management are tremendous. After establishing their new portfolio process, top management at SmithKline Beechman felt their new portfolio was 30% more valuable than the old one, without any additional investment. They saw the marginal return on additional investment triple from 5:1 to 15:1. These achievements prompted the company to eventually increase development spending by more than 50% [13].

All organizations and employees can benefit by implementing project portfolio management. These benefits include:
• having a structure in place to select the right projects and immediately remove the wrong projects
• placing resources where it matters, reducing wasteful spending
• linking portfolio decisions to strategic direction and business goals
• establishing logic, reasoning, and a sense of fairness behind portfolio decisions
• establishing ownership amongst the staff by involvement at the right levels
• providing avenues for individuals to identify opportunities and obtain support
• helping project teams understand the value of their contributions.
It's worth it!

Notes

1. Project Management Institute Standards Committee, *A Guide to the Project Management Body of Knowledge*, Upper Darby, PA: Project Management Institute, 1996, p. 167.

2. Robert G. Cooper, Scott J. Edgett, and Elko J. Kleinschmidt, *Portfolio Management for New Products*, Reading, MA: Perseus Books, 1998, p. 37.

3. Gilbert L. Comstock and Danny E. Sjolseth, "Aligning and Prioritizing Corporate R&D," *Research Technology Management*, May-June 1999, p. 20.

4. Bruce Miller, "Linking Corporate Strategy to the Selection of IT Projects," *Project Management Institute 28th Annual Seminars & Symposium Proceedings*, 1997, p. 56.

5. Robert G. Cooper, et al., pp. 19-20.

6. Paul Sharpe and Tom Keelin, "How SmithKline Beecham Makes Better Resource-Allocation Decisions," *Harvard Business Review*, March-April 1998, pp. 5-10.

7. C. Thomas Spradlin and David M. Kutoloski, "Action-Oriented Portfolio Management," *Research Technology Management*, March-April 1999, p. 27.

8. Paul Sharpe, et al., pp. 4-5.

9. Robert G. Cooper, et al., p. 60.

10. Timothy A. Luehrman, "Strategy as a Portfolio of Real Options," *Harvard Business Review*, September-October 1998, pp. 91-93.

11. Jack R. Meredith and Samuel J. Mantel, Jr., *Project Management: A Managerial Approach*, New York: John Wiley & Sons, 1995, pp. 39-80.

12. Gilbert L. Comstock, et al., p. 21.

13. Paul Sharpe, et al., p. 10.

Portfolio Management for Projects: A New Paradigm

Renee J. Sommer

In any organization where projects are competing for resources, funding, and priority status, significant controversy can occur. Each business unit has its own, individual list of important projects that may or may not be corporately shared. Which projects will truly support the business needs and objectives? How can you ensure that the projects chosen for completion align with corporate objectives? More importantly, how can you continue to ensure that you're working on the right projects as things change from day to day and new business opportunities arise?

The concept of portfolio project management refers to organizations managing their composite group of projects with the same rigor, balance, executive leadership, and decision-making involvement as the company's financial portfolio. In a project-driven organization, projects are the single, most significant investment made. Investments of this nature must be managed from a corporate, strategic-planning perspective, not merely administratively.

Your Organization Already Has a Project Portfolio

A project portfolio is simply this—organizational assets applied to more than one project initiative for a particular organizational outcome or objective. If your organization funds, manages, and allocates resources or time to more than one project, you already have a project portfolio. You may not know what the portfolio comprehensively looks like, how it is strategically invested, or be managing it proactively, but it does exist.

Portfolio Management Is a Process

Portfolio Management is an ongoing process that includes decision-making, prioritization, review, realignment, and reprioritization.

Let's say that you are taking a direct flight from Miami to San Francisco, which is scheduled to be a five-hour flight. Once you've reached cruising altitude, the pilot sets the heading coordinates to San Francisco, engages auto pilot, and decides not to change the heading coordinates again until he's ready to request landing in San Francisco. At the five-hour mark, the pilot and passengers may be shocked to find that the plane is seriously off course and most definitely not in San Francisco. Does it mean

55

that the coordinates set over Miami were wrong? Of course not, but changing flight and weather conditions required realignment of the coordinates *while in progress* to ensure success. It is a *process* not a static, finite task.

Similarly, this is true of investments. If you gave all of your retirement funds to an investment professional for management today, would you wait until just before retirement to check on progress or to reevaluate how your investments are doing? Would you wait for a year? What if a new great investment surfaced, which promised significant return on investment?

As with financial investments, the organizational goals, objectives, and resulting tactical strategies are evolving on a daily basis. The competitive markets continually challenge our plans and demand redirection and realignment of organizational focus. The first area of project misalignment is in the area of fiscal planning and budgeting. Most organizations do fiscal planning and budgets on an annual basis. Optimistically, these plans are reviewed quarterly for accuracy or revision, usually only to review actual budget against planned. This type of planning may seem "top-down" and organization-objectives focussed. However, it does not balance the evolving business dynamics and allow for much needed fine tuning.

Setting a Project Investment Strategy and Objectives

Before an organization invests capital in any project, it should first establish an appropriate strategy for measuring project proposals against the corporate objectives, as well as other proposed projects. To create a truly effective mix of projects, the organization must consider a wide range of factors that include the mission, vision, objectives, short-, mid-, and long-term goals of the organization, in addition to the size of the proposed project portfolio and funding guidelines.

Additionally, organizations must establish an unbiased mechanism for monitoring projects for continued investment, how to measure the individual project return on investment, how to weight multiple projects appropriately within the project portfolio, and how to ensure continued alignment with overall corporate objectives. It is essential to have an agreed-upon, unbiased prioritization process. Once the organization has established its overall objectives and project investment strategy, it must create the optimal group of projects, or mix, to implement its strategy and achieve the objectives.

Classification of Project Investments

The highest level of analysis for your project portfolio is project classification. This is necessary to decide where discretionary funding choices may be made versus non-discretionary. There are two primary categories that all projects fall into: *Survival* and *Growth*. If a proposed project does not fall into one of these two categories, the business should immediately question the validity of investment funding.

Survival

These are the *must-do* projects. A project falls into this category if, and only if, the project must be completed for the health of the business. In other words, if you don't do this project during this fiscal planning period, your business will fail or suffer irreparable damage. Projects in the Survival category must be included as part of the project portfolio and should be viewed as an existing, nondiscretionary investment.

Growth

All other projects fall into the growth category. Contrary to what the word *growth* implies, a growth project does not necessarily mean that it produces revenue (directly or indirectly). Growth projects may be exclusively internal and support oriented or external and financially based. The real qualifier for a project in this category is that it is discretionary and has business value for the organization to excel and prosper.

Constructing a Project Portfolio

Once you've identified the list of *survival* and prospective *growth* projects, there are two main components in the construction of a project portfolio:

1. *Project Allocation*—how the project portfolio is spread among all of its project types such as infrastructure, new projects, research and development, etc.

2. *Project Selection*—the selection of the best individual projects for investment within each project type.

Top-Down and Bottom-Up Project Allocation and Selection

Top-down analysis looks at the big picture economic themes and trends and how they affect the overall organization's growth, rather than analyzing, validating, and approving individual projects.

By contrast, the bottom-up approach is driven by the "project benefits," as defined by the individual business units or project advocates, and is based on the individual project's return-on-investment to the business unit and organization. This approach concentrates first on the likely out-performance of individual projects, and thus the project portfolio is constructed from the bottom up.

A combination of both allocation and selection analysis is required to formulate the appropriate project *mix* for the organization with corresponding importance weightings and prioritization.

The Appropriate Project Mix for Your Organization

One of the most important decisions that any project organization must make is the selection of the appropriate project mix for the portfolio. Why is this so important? One answer is that for most project-driven businesses, the projects included in the portfolio are the single most important determinant of organizational success. Historically, project mix decisions have tended to be unstructured without reference to a quantitative, analytical framework. A new method is required to emphasize business assumptions, goals, and objectives in all project decisions, including:

• some statement of the business objectives and constraints that will be used to select the appropriate mix (Constraints include time horizons, market windows, financial budgets, resource utilization and availability, and technology drivers.)
• forecasts on return for each project
• estimates of risk for each project
• weighting and prioritization techniques for ordering projects.

Who Should Make the Project Mix Decision

Since business objectives and constraints are such key considerations, the business must provide input to the decisions at a corporate level. The common practice at one time was for the organization to allocate project funds among the various business units and let the individual business units decide how to prioritize project spending. Of course, each business unit has its unique priority list and, for the information systems (IS) group in particular, this has became a significant problem. As a central support organization with conflicting priorities, IS has been put in a no-win situation with infinite work possibilities and finite, many times overallocated, resource pools. For any internal support organization to be successful, it must have a method for connecting daily project decisions to the overall corporate perspective, prioritizing, and escalating conflicting project priorities for corporate reevaluation. This means letting the *investor* (collectively) control the investment decisions. The individual business units are contributors to the process but do not make decisions on their own without balance across organizational boundaries.

Elements for Weighting and Prioritizing Projects

Risk and Return
Unlike financial investments, higher project risk is not necessarily correlated with higher potential project return. Measuring project risk and return is much more complex, and while some of the criteria are generic across all industries and organizations, much of the measurement is unique to the specific business. Generally speaking, risk is represented by the tangible and intangible impediments that may potentially cause the project to fail. Once the individual risk factors for each project are identified, the project may be weighted against the other projects for a relative comparison. Return on investment (ROI) is quantified by the tangible and intangible benefits, or returns, to the business.

Other Key Weighting Criteria
In addition to Risk and Return weightings, several other inputs are key to choosing the right mix of projects for your organization. Some of these items include:
- project's success potential—specific measurement for probability of project success
- degree of correlation to business plans
- degree of correlation to market position
- degree of correlation to competitive pressures
- degree of correlation to financial objectives.

Bringing It All Together
The above criteria can be measured, consolidated, weighted, and compared by project for a complete portfolio perspective. Once a prioritized list of projects is corporately agreed upon, across business units and organizational boundaries, the project portfolio is in place, and measurement can begin, as well as rebalancing if new priorities are introduced. Rebalancing is the process by which new projects enter the queue and are assessed against the current portfolio of project investments. The decision to change the portfolio by increasing project investment or replacing a project is made using the same weighting criteria.

Managing for Results
By taking a proactive approach to the selection of projects and managing actual performance against planned, organizations can dramatically improve the timeliness,

quality, and completeness of their projects, as well as ensure that all projects enable overall business success.

References

Champy, J. 1997. It Pays To Think Big. *Computerworld* (August 25).

Comaford, C. 1997. Getting Net Projects Into the Pearly Gates of ROI. *PC Week* (March 10).

Conway, B., R. Hunter, M. Light. 1995. Strategic Analysis Report. The AD Management Continuum: Integrated Methods, Process and Project Management. Gartner Group (September 27).

Feiler, P.H., and W.S. Humphrey. 1992. Software Process Development and Enactment: Concepts and Definitions. CMU/SEI-92- TR-4, ADA258465 (March).

Fowler, P., and S. Rifkin. 1990. Software Engineering Process Group Guide. Software Engineering Institute, CMU/SEI-90-TR-24, ADA235784 (September).

Freedman, D.P., and G.M. Weinberg. 1990. *Handbook of Walkthroughs, Inspections, and Technical Reviews.* 3d ed. New York, NY: Dorset House.

Grochow, J.M. 1996. Chaos Theory and Project Estimates. *PC Week* (August 5).

King, J. 1997. Project Management Ills Cost Businesses Plenty. *Computerworld* (September 22).

Kitson, D.H., and S. Masters. 1992. An Analysis of SEI Software Process Assessment Results: 1987–1991. Software Engineering Institute, CMU/SEI-92-TR-24 (July).

Paulk, M.C., B. Curtis, M.B. Chrissis, et al. 1991. Capability Maturity Model for Software. Software Engineering Institute, CMU/SEI-91-TR-24, ADA240603 (August).

Paulk, M.C., B. Curtis, M.B. Chrissis, and Charles V. Weber. 1993. Capability Maturity Model for Software, Version 1.1. Software Engineering Institute, CMU/SEI-93-TR-24 (February).

Paulk, M.C., C.V. Weber, S. Garcia, M.B. Chrissis, and M. Bush. 1993. Key Practices of the Capability Maturity Model, Version 1.1. Software Engineering Institute, CMU/SEI-93-TR-25 (February).

Smith, H. 1996. Hitting the Project Mark. *InfoWorld* (December 2).

Weber, C.V., M.C. Paulk, C.J. Wise, and J.V. Withey. 1991. Key Practices of the Capability Maturity Model. Software Engineering Institute, CMU/SEI-91-TR-25, ADA240604 (August).

Zells, L. 1996. Practical Strategic I/S Planning. *Application Development Trends* (April).

———. 1997. The Project Office Answer. *Application Development Trends* (April).

This article is reprinted from *1998 Proceedings of the Annual Project Management Institute Seminars & Symposium* with permission of the Project Management Institute Headquarters, Four Campus Boulevard, Newtown Square, PA 19073-3299 USA, Phone: (610) 356-4600 Fax: (610) 356-4647, Project Management Institute (PMI) is the world's leading project management association with over 40,000 members worldwide. For further information contact PMI Headquarters at (610) 356-4600 or visit the web site at www.pmi.org.

Using Decision Quality Principles To Balance Your R&D Portfolio

James E. Matheson and Michael M. Menke

Researchers at a large U.S. chemical company recently developed a new product that was scientifically very impressive. Designed to solve a long-time problem faced by a sizable group of industrial users, the product had proven to be extremely effective in initial bench-scale testing. The project team was enthusiastic and was proceeding to commercialize what it considered a breakthrough product.

However, the new formulation turned out to have a shelf-life of only a few days. Even with a significant amount of additional R&D, it was highly unlikely the shelf-life could be extended to more than one-quarter of what the users' customary practices required. Moreover, market research and customer interviews revealed that the need for the product was not so great—nor the product so revolutionary—that users would be willing to redesign their production systems to accommodate the shorter shelf-life.

Applying the same decision quality principles used to evaluate individual projects, Strategic Decisions Group (SDG) demonstrated that the new product was not the breakthrough the project team had hoped for and, as a result, did not justify the considerable resources earmarked for investment in it. This allowed the company to immediately reallocate several million dollars of R&D funding to other projects within the portfolio that had a higher probability of generating substantial returns.

The Industrial Research Institute has estimated that it is possible to improve return on R&D investment by as much as 100 percent through actions that enhance decision quality. In SDG's experience, clients have achieved gains of 30 to 100 percent or higher in their portfolios. Whether you are spending $10 million or $100 million annually, that's a significant improvement.

Balancing Risk and Return
Balancing high-risk, breakthrough R&D with projects that produce near-term returns through incremental improvements to existing products and processes is one of the most difficult, yet critical, components of R&D portfolio decision-making.

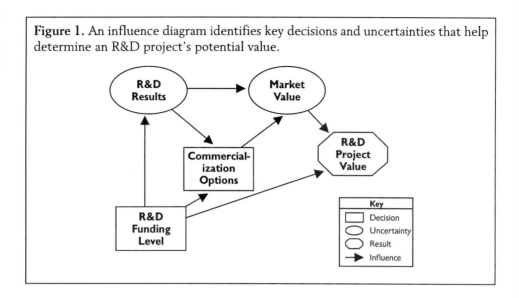

Figure 1. An influence diagram identifies key decisions and uncertainties that help determine an R&D project's potential value.

To achieve the appropriate balance of risk and return in your R&D portfolio, you need to evaluate each project for two characteristics: technical difficulty and commercial value. The secret to successful R&D management is understanding the critical relationship between the probability of success and the value of a project given its success. This provides a solid platform for making quality decision about your entire R&D portfolio.

Most portfolio decisions are complicated by the long time horizons, high uncertainty, and wide number of variables affecting each individual project. At SDG, we use a number of proven tools such as influence diagrams, sensitivity analyses, and decision trees to develop a business model that forecasts a project's potential value. For example, an influence diagram (Figure 1) enables us to graphically depict the decisions and uncertainties regarding technology options, technical hurdles, regulatory constraints, market considerations, and other factors.

In its simplest form, an influence diagram shows the relationships between decisions, uncertainties, and results, and clearly illustrates which parts of the process directly influence other parts. For example, an influence diagram can help you to assess the pros and cons of undertaking parallel projects using different technologies to increase the probability of success, or to determine whether a joint venture or licensing agreement might be more attractive than trying to introduce a new product into a highly competitive market.

But influence diagrams are more than just conceptual aids. Figure 2 demonstrates how, after numerical probabilities are assigned to each component of a diagram, these values can be multiplied together to determine the likelihood of a project's ultimate success.

Completing our evaluation requires the use of other influence diagrams to assess the commercial potential of the project, the creation of charts and graphs to illustrate the expected value from commercialization balanced against the degree of uncertainty, and the development of a simplified decision tree that aids in making quality decisions.

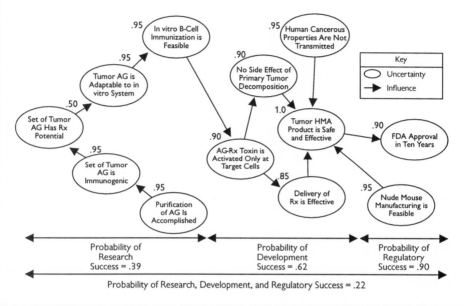

Figure 2. Numerical probabilities representing the best judgment of knowledgeable scientists in an organization are assigned to each step of the R&D process. When multiplied together, these values provide an accurate assessment of a project's chances for success.

The Importance of Decision Quality

Quality decision-making is the cornerstone of developing an effective portfolio strategy. Yet defining decision quality as it applied to R&D—where the outcome of many decisions will not be known for years—is a difficult proposition.

In evaluating the quality of one of your company's products, you would be likely to compare specific, quantifiable characteristics—such as performance, defect rate, useful life, and overall customer satisfaction—against those of a competitor's product. To help assess the value of projects in an R&D portfolio, we use a six-step process that provides the basis for quality decisions: Identifying the appropriate frame; generating creative, achievable alternatives; developing meaningful, reliable information; establishing clear values and trade-offs; applying logically correct reasoning; and building a commitment to action.

• *Identify the appropriate frame*—The frame is the window through which one views a problem. The proper frame focuses attention on the unique context and critical elements that must be considered for a particular decision. One of the keys to good R&D decision-making is to frame the problem at the appropriate level—viewing it in light of your technology, portfolio, or project strategy. If the frame is wrong, you may make a sound decision about the wrong problem.

• *Generate creative, achievable alternatives*—A good strategy development process consciously creates more than one attractive, achievable option that links R&D with

63

Figure 3. This spider diagram depicts the relationship among six requirements for quality R&D decision-making.

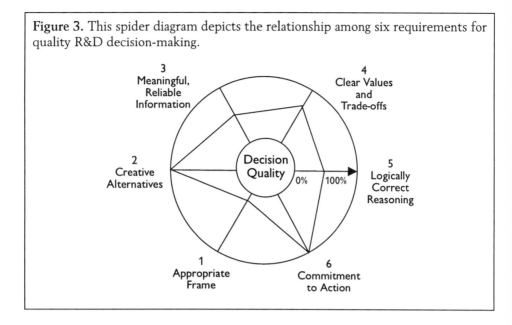

business strategy. This allows senior executives to use their broad experience and distant perspective to add value to the ultimate decision.

• *Develop meaningful, reliable information*—In gathering information, it is critical that it be important, relevant and accurate, and that the uncertainty associated with particular data be presented and discussed as well. Pertinent information typically includes technical, business and legal considerations, as well as environmental and regulatory issues.

• *Establish clear values and trade-offs*—Two common trade-offs for R&D are time and risk. Decisions often high on evaluating long-term versus short-term results and risk versus reward. Establishing clear values and trade-offs at the start allows you to avoid confusion later.

• *Apply logically correct reasoning*—At this stage, the information is ready to be analyzed, using solid logic and consistent reasoning to explore how the alternatives will create business value. Decision analysis is one of the most reliable quantitative approaches for dealing with the uncertainty and complexity of major R&D decisions—enabling you to get the clear results and insights you need.

• *Build a commitment to action*—The objective of all R&D decision-making should not only be to reach the "right" decision, but to involve and empower the right groups of people to carry out the decision efficiently and effectively. Obtaining the appropriate level of participation among cross-functional teams ensures a constructive dialogue between decision-makers and implementers, leading to a commitment to definitive action once the process is complete.

In evaluating the quality of a decision, SDG plots scores for each of the six elements using a "spider diagram" (Figure 3). Points on the rim indicate "perfection" in a specific area. In this case, perfection is defined as having done everything that is

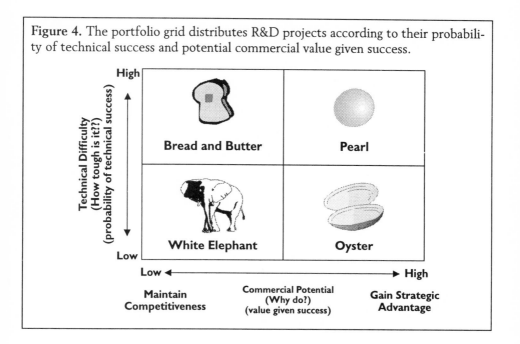

Figure 4. The portfolio grid distributes R&D projects according to their probability of technical success and potential commercial value given success.

worth doing, given the economics and urgency of the decision at hand. For example, a decision that has been framed with an unambiguous purpose, perfectly defined scope, and conscious perspective would be plotted on the outer circle. Points on the hub indicate the absence of quality in an area—for instance, no plan of action.

The best decisions will always be characterized by points on or near the rim for all six elements, creating a web of balance and beauty.

The Portfolio Grid
Once you have completed a high-quality analysis of each project, you can view the projects on a portfolio grid (Figure 4). Again, the projects are plotted according to their technical difficulty (probability of success) and commercial potential (value given success).

By examining the distribution of the projects in the grid's quadrants, you can more easily visualize the strengths and weaknesses of your R&D portfolio. At SDG, we have labeled the four quadrants as follows:

• *Bread and Butter*—Projects in the upper left-hand quadrant have a high probability of technical success but relatively low commercial value. These are typically incremental improvements to a product or process—a consumer product that's "new and improved," a manufacturing enhancement that cuts costs by a few percent. You need bread-and-butter projects to maintain or improve near-term performance, but you can't build your future on them.

• *Oysters*—The opposite of bread-and-butter projects, oysters are your long shots—scientific research with a low probability of technical success, but with exceptional commercial value. Oysters must be patiently cultivated over long periods in hopes of obtaining breakthrough products and processes. Sometimes, all you end up with is oyster stew. But once in a while, you get...

• *Pearls*—The handful of projects in the upper right-hand quadrant are what you build future business success on. Typically, reaching this position only after years of experimentation and considerable investment to clear key hurdles, pearls have a high probability of technical success and high commercial value.

• *White Elephants*—Legend has it that the King of Siam gave disagreeable courtiers white elephants. Because these animals were considered holy and could not be disposed of, their upkeep often caused financial ruin. The same thing can happen to your business if you don't terminate these low-potential long shots.

Most R&D efforts begin as either bread-and-butter or oyster projects. For example, many bread-and-butter projects probably are requested by managers who seek to address market opportunities or increase company profits through product or process improvements.

Oysters, on the other hand, grow out of peoples' vision for the future. These projects can be driven by a recognized market opportunity or a single researcher's creativity, or they may be sparked by the acquisition of innovative technology that opens the door to a new line of products. Business success requires strategically balancing bread-and-butter and oyster projects to fit the changing needs of your company, capitalizing on pearls when you find them and transforming or eliminating white elephants.

Managing Different Categories of R&D

Once you have segmented your R&D projects into different categories, you have the opportunity to do what you've probably intended to do for some time—selectively manage each project to achieve its highest potential and reward the people who are working on them.

For example, when you are working on a bread-and-butter project, a business unit is most likely counting on you to help them make their plan. So, with these projects, you use typical project-management techniques: setting firm deadlines, establishing budget parameters, and developing traditional performance incentives.

In the bread-and-butter category, the question of whether you can complete the task has already been answered—it's only a question of when and what you will deliver. Therefore, incentives should be tied directly to the outcome: quality products or process improvements that are finished on time and on budget. The management concepts found in the current quality movement work very well with bread-and-butter projects.

Oysters require a strategy that's completely different from bread-and-butter projects. The first thing to recognize is that it takes many oysters to produce a pearl. It is surprising how many R&D organizations seem to overlook this basic principle. And this leads to the "liar's game," in which people put a positive spin on everything. Asked to analyze a project, they underestimate the technical risk and overestimate the market potential. In life, a positive attitude is good but when making strategic R&D decisions, you want the truth.

So, realizing that you need to fund a number of oysters at the same time, your management objective is not only to find out what ones are going to produce a pearl, but to do this as quickly as possible (much better to fail when you have invested $3 million and 5 person-years than after $50 million and 100 person-years).

To accomplish this—and this, too, probably goes against natural instincts—you want to work on the most difficult challenges first. These include not only the most imposing technical constraints, but anything that might destroy or diminish a product's commercial potential. These are often the most overlooked steps in the R&D process.

To avoid wasting valuable time and money, it is important to continually focus on the long-term commercial prospects of each oyster while overcoming technical hurdles. For instance, a medical equipment manufacturer had invested millions of dollars in developing a sophisticated new testing device with tremendous market potential. Although the machine performed well, the R&D team wanted to delay its production until it could reduce from five to two minutes the time the machine required to deliver results to the doctor. This would give the device a clear competitive advantage in the marketplace.

However, when SDG analyzed the market for the company, we learned that hospitals wanted reliability more than faster performance. So the R&D team replaced the machine's computer system with one that relied on parallel processors for failsafe operation and successfully launched the product—saving precious time and millions of dollars in additional, unnecessary R&D funding.

What incentives do you offer researchers working on oysters? You need a system that rewards people for professionally completing each stage of a project. And here is something else that is countercultural to almost every company we consult with—it is critical to reward the researcher who proves something can not be done just as highly as you reward the individual who discoveries a way to do something. Halting a doomed project is worth as much or more to a company as continuing to pursue one that has a chance to succeed. Yet even the most progressive companies have difficulty doing this. They may not punish technical failure, but they still tend to reward only those who succeed.

The third type of R&D project is the pearl. A handful of pearls can provide your company with long-term strategic advantages. What is most important is to avoid managing pearls too narrowly, and this is precisely what happens it you apply the same management-by-objective techniques you use with bread-and-butter projects.

Successful management of pearls requires more of an entrepreneurial approach. Budgets shouldn't be a key issue, because a pearl's high payoff makes almost any additional investment worth it. The project team needs the flexibility to explore other ways to commercialize a pearl once a capability exists or to take more time to perfect a product if market conditions require it.

Sometimes the best thing to do with a pearl is to get the simplest version of a new product into the market as soon as possible. Apple's Macintosh computer is a perfect illustration of this. Even in its flawed, early form, the Macintosh found a niche, and as each new generation met more of the market's requirements, the computer's acceptance—and Apple's success as a company—soared.

With pearls, then, you make development time your top priority. You target the best markets for the technology. And you work closely with the project team to strategize the full range of commercial applications and future generations of the product before introducing the first version to the marketplace.

Incentives for pearls should be structured similarly to those in a start-up company—stock options and the like. You may even want to establish a subsidiary to develop and market the new technology. This raises another issue: When do you add entrepreneurial managers to the equation to complement the abilities of the scientists and researchers? This decision is never easy, but it's often the key to transforming a promising pearl into a successful business venture.

Finally, there are the white elephants—big, slow and expensive. These are technically complex projects aimed at markets or opportunities too small to justify the time and expense they require. In some instances, white elephants may have once been oysters that simply developed too slowly. The secret to managing white elephants is to put them into Chapter 11, thereby beginning a process that will determine whether it's worth saving and, if so, what form the new company should take when it emerges.

If, after analyzing the white elephant, the opportunity remains interesting, perhaps you can find a simpler way to implement it—for example, using off-the-shelf technology rather than developing costly new technology. Or perhaps you can expand the scope and time horizon of the project. If the technology is really promising, you may be working on an oyster instead of a white elephant, and you need to treat it as such.

So, a white elephant may come out of Chapter 11 as a completely new project, revitalized and with the potential to contribute to company profits. Or it may not come out at all. In any case, staff members working on what you've identified as white elephants should be rewarded for resolving or repositioning the project quickly and efficiently.

Using decision quality principles to evaluate and manage the projects in your R&D portfolio can significantly increase profitability and productivity. But other factors beyond those we have discussed add complexity to the balancing process.

One of the most important is the interaction of the projects in the portfolio. Rather than being an independent undertaking, each project is part of an overlapping, interconnected whole—with a variety of critical dependencies. To form a true picture of the balance in your portfolio, you must analyze these dependencies to determine whether they offer risk compensation (less risk in the result) or risk concentration (greater risk).

For example, several of your R&D projects may be targeted at a common market. Will this prove to be an advantage, by allowing the use of a common sales force, or a disadvantage, by competing for the same customers? Similarly, will common resources enable you to efficiently share costs, or will they result in a shortage of key resources needed by both products?

SDG has developed tools to help accurately assess the balance of risk and return in an R&D portfolio. These include tools for analyzing the aggregate risk and net present value of a portfolio, for evaluating the efficiency of R&D investment based on funding levels, and for determining the number of new products one can expect from a portfolio over time.

One client had adopted a strategy of simultaneously pursuing three or four R&D projects targeted at the same market. The company liked this "insurance" against missed opportunities. Unfortunately, exceptionally high expenses were seriously hurting portfolio returns. By adopting decision quality principles (and in fact, establishing a significant in-house capability), the company terminated several white-elephant projects, reallocated its R&D investments according to each project's potential, and entered into negotiations to acquire a new technology at less cost than developing it. The combined savings for the client amounted to more than $50 million.

An effective R&D strategy requires the proper balance between risk and return. Applying decision quality principles at the portfolio level can help to achieve this balance, resulting in improved performance and playing a key role in sustaining and enhancing your company's long-term success.

Reprinted from "Using Decision Quality Principles To Balance Your R&D Portfolio" by James E. Matheson and Michael M. Menke. *Research Technology Management*, May-June 1994, pp. 38-43, by permission of publisher. Copyright 1994 by Industrial Research Institute. All rights reserved.

Strategy as a
Portfolio of Real Options

Timothy A. Luehrman

When executives create strategy, they project themselves and their organizations into the future, creating a path from where they are now to where they want to be some years down the road. In competitive markets, though, no one expects to formulate a detailed long-term plan and follow it mindlessly. As soon as we start down the path, we begin learning—about business conditions, competitors' actions, the quality of our preparations, and so forth—and we need to respond flexibly to what we learn. Unfortunately, the financial tool most widely relied on to estimate the value of strategy—discounted-cash-flow (DCF) valuation—assumes that we will follow a predetermined plan, regardless of how events unfold.

A better approach to valuation would incorporate both the uncertainty inherent in business and the active decision making required for a strategy to succeed. It would help executives think strategically on their feet by capturing the value of doing just that—of managing actively rather than passively. Options can deliver that extra insight. Advances in both computing power and our understanding of option pricing over the last 20 years make it feasible now to begin analyzing business strategies as chains of real options. As a result, the creative activity of strategy formulation can be informed by valuation analyses sooner rather than later. Financial insight may actually contribute to shaping strategy, rather than being relegated to an after-the-fact exercise of "checking the numbers."

In financial terms, a business strategy is much more like a series of options than a series of static cash flows. Executing a strategy almost always involves making a *sequence* of major decisions. Some actions are taken immediately, while others are deliberately deferred, so managers can optimize as circumstances evolve. The strategy sets the framework within which future decisions will be made, but at the same time it leaves room for learning from ongoing developments and for discretion to act based on what is learned.

To consider strategies as portfolios of related real options, this article exploits a framework presented in "Investment Opportunities as Real Options: Getting Started on the Numbers" (*HBR*, July-August 1998). That article explains how to get from conventional DCF value to option value for a typical project—in other words, it is about how to get a number. This article extends that framework, exploring how option pricing can be used to improve decision making about the sequence and timing of a portfolio of strategic investments.

A Gardening Metaphor: Options as Tomatoes

Managing a portfolio of strategic options is like growing a garden of tomatoes in an unpredictable climate. Walk into the garden on a given day in August, and you will find that some tomatoes are ripe and perfect. Any gardener would know to pick and eat those immediately. Other tomatoes are rotten; no gardener would ever bother to pick them. These cases at the extremes—now and never—are easy decisions for the gardener to make.

In between are tomatoes with varying prospects. Some are edible and could be picked now but would benefit from more time on the vine. The experienced gardener picks them early only if squirrels or other competitors are likely to get them. Other tomatoes are not yet edible, and there's no point in picking them now, even if the squirrels do get them. However, they are sufficiently far along, and there is enough time left in the season, that many will ripen unharmed and eventually be picked. Still others look less promising and may not ripen before the season ends. But with more sun or water, fewer weeds, or just good luck, even some of these tomatoes may make it. Finally, there are small green tomatoes and late blossoms that have little likelihood of growing and ripening before the season ends. There is no value in picking them, and they might just as well be left on the vine.

Most experienced gardeners are able to classify the tomatoes in their gardens at any given time. Beyond that, however good gardeners also understand how the garden changes over time. Early in the season, none of the fruit falls into the "now" or "never" categories. By the last day, all of it falls into one or the other because time has run out. The interesting question is, What can the gardener do during the season, while things are changing week to week?

A purely passive gardener visits the garden on the last day of the season, picks the ripe tomatoes, and goes home. The weekend gardener visits frequently and picks ripe fruit before it rots or the squirrels get it. Active gardeners do much more. Not only do they watch the garden but, based on what they see, they also cultivate it: watering, fertilizing, and weeding, trying to get more of those in-between tomatoes to grow and ripen before time runs out. Of course, the weather is always a question, and not all the tomatoes will make it. Still, we'd expect the active gardener to enjoy a higher yield in most years that the passive gardener.

In option terminology, active gardeners are doing more than merely making exercise decisions (pick or don't pick). They are monitoring the options and looking for ways to influence the underlying variables that determine option value and, ultimately, outcomes.

Option pricing can help us become more effective, active gardeners in several ways. It allows us to estimate the value of the entire year's crop (or even the value of a single tomato) before the season actually ends. It also helps us assess each tomato's prospects as the season progresses and tells us along the way which to pick and which to leave on the vine. Finally it can suggest what to do to help those in-between tomatoes ripen before the season ends.

Figure 1. Option Space is Defined by Two Option-Value Metrics

We can use the two option-value metrics to locate projects in option space. Moving to the right and/or downward corresponds to higher option value.

value-to-cost

0.0 lower   1.0   higher

lower

European call-option value increases in these directions.

volatility

higher

Value-to-cost metric = **NPVq** = $S \div PV(X)$
Volatility metric = $\sigma\sqrt{t}$

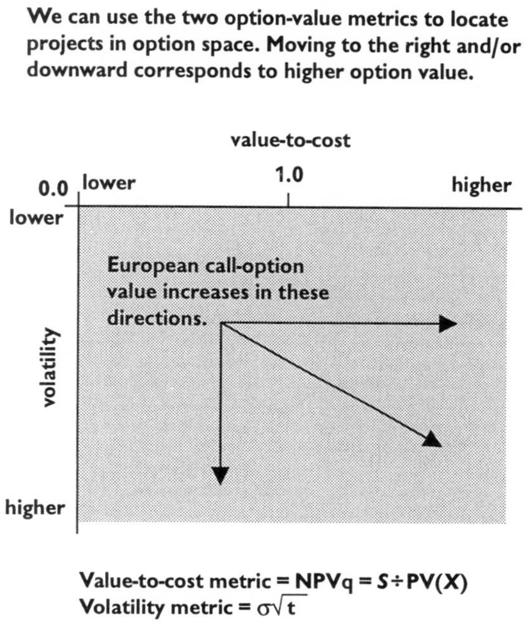

A Tour of Option Space

Instead of a garden plot, visualize a rectangle we'll call *option space*. Option space is defined by two option-value metrics, each of which captures a different part of the value associated with being able to defer an investment. Option space can help address the issues an active gardener will care about: whether to invest or not (that is, whether to pick), when to invest, and what to do in the meantime.

Let's briefly review the two metrics, which were developed in "Investment Opportunities as Real Options." The first metric contains all the usual data captured in net present value (NPV) but adds the time value of being able to defer the investment. We called that metric NPV_q and defined it as the value of the underlying assets we intend to build or acquire divided by the present value of the expenditure required to build or buy them. Put simply, this is a ratio of value to cost. For convenience, here, we'll call it our *value-to-cost* metric instead of NPV_q, but bear in mind that *value* and *cost* refer to the project's assets, not to the option on those assets.

When the value-to-cost metric is between zero and one, we have a project worth less than it costs; when the metric is greater than one, the project is worth more than the present value of what it costs.

The second metric we'll call our *volatility* metric. It measures how much things can change before an investment decision must finally be made. That depends both on how uncertain, or risky, the future value of the assets in question is and on how long we can defer a decision. The former is captured by the *variance per period of*

73

Figure 2. Dividing Option Space into Regions

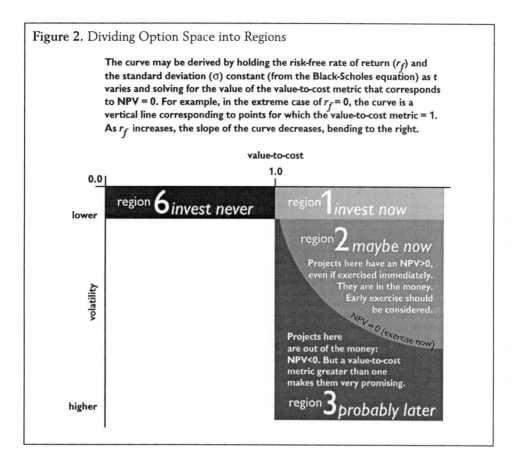

The curve may be derived by holding the risk-free rate of return (r_f) and the standard deviation (σ) constant (from the Black-Scholes equation) as t varies and solving for the value of the value-to-cost metric that corresponds to NPV = 0. For example, in the extreme case of r_f = 0, the curve is a vertical line corresponding to points for which the value-to-cost metric = 1. As r_f increases, the slope of the curve decreases, bending to the right.

value-to-cost

0.0   1.0

lower

region **6** *invest never*   region **1** *invest now*

region **2** *maybe now*

Projects here have an NPV>0, even if exercised immediately. They are in the money. Early exercise should be considered.

$NPV = 0$ (exercise now)

Projects here are out of the money: NPV<0. But a value-to-cost metric greater than one makes them very promising.

volatility

higher

region **3** *probably later*

asset returns; the latter is the options' *time to expiration*. In the previous article, this second metric was called *cumulative volatility*.

Option space is defined by these two metrics, with value-to-cost on the horizontal axis and volatility on the vertical axis. See the graph, "Option Space Is Defined by Two Option-Value Metrics." The usual convention is to draw the space as a rectangle, with the value-to-cost increasing from left to right (its minimum value is zero), and the volatility metric increasing from top to bottom (its minimum value also is zero). Within the interior of the rectangle, option value increases as the value of either metric increases; that is, from any point in the space, if you move down, to the right, or in both directions simultaneously, option value rises.

How does option space help us with strategy? A business strategy is a series of related options; it is as though the condition of one tomato actually affected the size or ripeness of another one nearby. That obviously makes things more complicated. Before we analyze a strategy, let's first consider the simpler circumstance in which the tomatoes growing in the garden don't affect one another. To do that, we need to explore the option space further.

In a real garden, good, bad, and in-between tomatoes can turn up anywhere. Not so in option space, where there are six separate regions, each of which contains a distinct type of option and corresponding managerial prescription. We carve up the space into distinct regions by using what we know about the value-to-cost volatility metrics, along with conventional NPV.

What's the added value of dividing option space in this fashion? Traditional corporate finance gives us one metric—NPV—for evaluating projects, and only two possible actions: invest or don't invest. In option space, we have NPV, two extra metrics, and six possible actions that reflect not only where a project is now but also the likelihood of it ending up somewhere better in the future. When we return to assessing strategies, this forward-looking judgment will be especially useful.

Top of the Space: *Now* and *Never*. At the top of our option space, the volatility metric is zero. That's so either because all uncertainty has been resolved or because time has run out. With business projects, the latter is far more likely. So projects that end up here differ from one another only according to their value-to-cost metrics, and it's easy to see what to do with them. If the value-to-cost metric is greater than one, we go ahead and invest now. If it's less than one, we invest never. Once time has run out, "now or never" completely describes our choices. It will be convenient to refer to regions by number, so let's number these extremes 1 and 6. Region 1 contains the perfectly ripe tomatoes; it is the *invest now* region. Region 6 contains the rotten ones; the prescription there is *invest never*.

Right Side of the Space: *Maybe Now* and *Probably Later*. What about projects whose value-to-cost metric is greater than one but whose time has not yet run out? All such properties fall somewhere in the right half of our option space but below the top. Projects here are very promising because the underlying assets are worth more than the present value of the required investment. Does that mean we should go ahead and invest right away? In some instances, the answer is clearly no, while in other cases, it's maybe. We want to be able to distinguish between those cases. The key to doing so is not option pricing but conventional NPV.

In terms of the tomato analogy, we are looking at a lot of promising tomatoes, none of which is perfectly ripe. We want to distinguish between those that, if picked right away, are edible (NPV > 0) and those that are inedible (NPV < 0). The distinction matters because there is no point in picking the inedible ones. Conventional NPV tells us the value of investing immediately despite the fact that time has not yet run out. If NPV is negative, immediate exercise is unambiguously suboptimal. In option terminology, we say that such an option is *out of the money*: it costs more to exercise it than the assets are worth. The exercise price (X) is greater than the underlying asset value (S), therefore NPV = $S - X < 0$.

The curve in our diagram separates options that are out of the money from those that are in the money. For points above the curve in the diagram, NPV is positive; for those below the curve, NPV is negative. For points actually on the curve itself, NPV = 0.

Projects below the curve, which we'll call region 3, are like the inedible tomatoes that we clearly do not want to pick right away. Even so, they are very promising because their value-to-cost metric is positive and time has not yet run out. I call this region *probably later*, because, even though we should not invest yet, we expect to invest eventually for a relative high fraction of these projects. In the meantime, they should be cultivated.

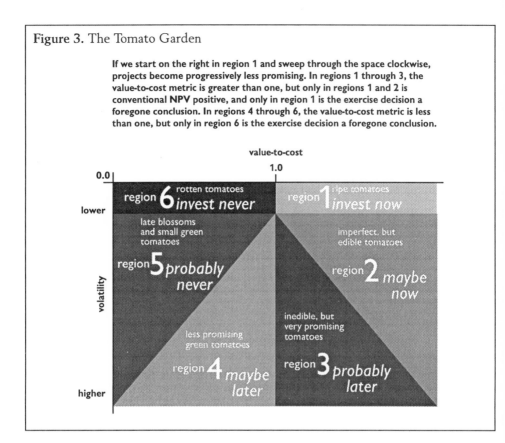

Figure 3. The Tomato Garden

If we start on the right in region 1 and sweep through the space clockwise, projects become progressively less promising. In regions 1 through 3, the value-to-cost metric is greater than one, but only in regions 1 and 2 is conventional **NPV** positive, and only in region 1 is the exercise decision a foregone conclusion. In regions 4 through 6, the value-to-cost metric is less than one, but only in region 6 is the exercise decision a foregone conclusion.

Projects that fall above the NPV = 0 curve are even more interesting. These options are in the money. They are like tomatoes that even though not perfectly ripe are nevertheless edible. We should be considering whether to pick them early.

It may seem contradictory to consider exercising an option early when all along I've argued in "Investment Opportunities as Real Options" that it is valuable to be able to defer the investment—to wait, see what happens, and then make an optimal choice at the last possible moment. If there is value associated with deferring, why would we ever do otherwise? Sometimes, especially with real options, value may be lost as well as gained by deferring, and the proper decision depends on which effect dominates.

The financial analog to such a real option is a call option on a share of stock. If the stock pays a large dividend, the shareholder receives value that the option holder does not. The option holder may wish to become a shareholder simply to participate in the dividend, which otherwise would be for-gone. Think of the dividend as value lost by deferring the exercise decision.

In the case of real options, where the underlying asset is some set of business cash flows, any *predictable* loss of value associated with deferring the investment is like the dividend in our stock example. Phenomena like pending changes in regulations, a predictable loss of market share, or preemption by a competitor are all costs associated

Figure 4. Vital Statistics for Six Independent Projects

Variable		A	B	C	D	E	F	Portfolio
S	Underlying asset value ($ millions)	$100.00	$100.00	$100.00	$100.00	$100.00	$100.00	Value
X	Exercise price ($ millions)	$90.00	$90.00	$110.00	$110.00	$110.00	$110.00	
t	Time to expiration (years)	0.00	2.00	0.00	0.50	1.00	2.00	
σ	Standard deviation (per year)	0.30	0.30	0.30	0.20	0.30	0.40	
r_f	Risk-free rate of return (% per year)	0.06	0.06	0.06	0.06	0.06	0.06	
NPVq	Value-to-cost metric	1.11	1.248	0.909	0.936	0.964	1.021	
$\sigma\sqrt{t}$	Volatility metric	0.000	0.424	0.000	0.141	0.300	0.566	
	Call value ($ millions)	$10.00	$27.23	$0.00	$3.06	$10.42	$23.24	$73.95
S–X	Conventional NPV ($ millions)	$10.00	$10.00	-$10.00	-$10.00	-$10.00	-$10.00	$20.00
	Region	1	2	6	5	4	3	
	Exercise decision	now	maybe now	never	probably never	maybe never	probably later	

with investing later rather than sooner and might cause us to exercise an option early. Or, to use the tomato analogy, we might pick an edible tomato early if we can predict that squirrels will get it otherwise. *Unpredictable* gains and losses, however, would not lead us to exercise our options early.

Options that are in the money (that is, those for which NPV>0) should be evaluated to if they ought to be exercised early. Immediate investment will not always be the optimal course of action because by investing early the company loses the advantages of deferring, which also are real. Deciding whether to invest early requires a case-by-case comparison of the value of waiting a bit long—that is, of continuing to hold the project as an option. I refer to that part of the option space as *maybe now* because we might decide to invest right away. Let's label it region 2.

Left Side of the Space: *Maybe Later* and *Probably Never.* All options that fall in the left half of the space are less promising because the value-to-cost metric is everywhere less than one, and conventional NPV is everywhere less than zero. But even here we can separate the more valuable from the less valuable. The upper left is unpromising territory because both the value-to-cost and volatility metrics are low. These are the late blossoms and the small green tomatoes that are unlikely to ripen before the season ends. I call this part of the option space *probably never*, and we can label it region 5.

In contrast, the lower section (of this left half of the space) has better prospects because at least one of the two metrics is reasonably high. I call it *maybe later*, and we can label it region 4. The diagram "The Tomato Garden" dispenses with fancy curves and simply divides the option space roughly into the six regions.

When to Harvest

As an example of what we learn from the tomato garden, consider six hypothetical projects that are entirely unrelated to one another. The table "Vital Statistics for Six Independent Projects" shows the relevant data for these projects, which have been labeled A through F. Note that each of them involves assets worth $100 million. Two of them (A and B) require capital expenditures of $90 million; the other four require expenditures of $110 million. So A and B each has a positive NPV of $10 million.

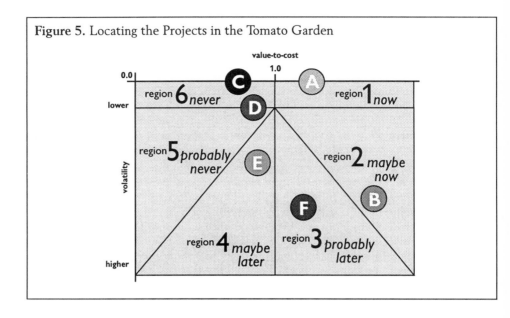

Figure 5. Locating the Projects in the Tomato Garden

Each of the other four has a NPV of negative $10 million. The NPV of the entire portfolio is negative $20 million or, more reasonably, positive $20 million, since the four projects with negative NPVs can be included at a value of zero. Conventional capital budgeting offers only two prescriptions—invest or don't invest. Following those rules, we'd accept projects A and B and reject all the others.

Although their NPVs are tightly clustered, the six projects have different time and volatility profiles, and hence different values for their value-to-cost and volatility metrics. Consequently, each is located in a different region of the option space. (See the diagram "Locating the Projects in the Tomato Garden.")

A is a *now* project that falls in region 1; C is a *never* project in region 6. Project B is very promising: its NPV is positive, and its value-to-cost metric is greater than one. B plots in region 2, and we should consider whether we ought to exercise our option on this project early. However, unless there is some predictable loss in future value (either a rise in cost or a fall in value), then early exercise is not only unnecessary but also suboptimal. Project F's value-to-cost metric is greater than one, but its NPV is less than zero. It falls in region 3 and is very valuable as an option, despite its negative NPV. That's because it will not expire for two years and has the highest volatility of the whole group. Hence, project F's prognosis is *probably later*.

Project E has less going for it than project F. It is in region 4 and deserves some attention because, with a year to go and the moderate standard deviation of its underlying asset return ($\sigma = 9.3$ per year), it just might make it. That's why it is classified as *maybe later*. Project D is much less promising (a *probably never*) because a decision must be made in only six months and, with a low volatility, there's not much likelihood that D will pop into the money before times runs out.

Because it can account for flexibility and uncertainty, the options-based framework produces a different assessment of this portfolio than the conventional DCF approach would. Most obviously, where DCF methods give the portfolio a value of $20 million, option pricing gives it a value of about $74 million, more than three times greater. Just as important, locating these projects in the tomato garden yields notably different exercise decisions. Instead of accepting two projects and rejecting four, our option analysis leads us to accept one, reject one, and wait and see about the other four. And as we wait, we know how each project's prospects differ. Moreover, we don't wait passively. Having only limited resources to devote to the portfolio, we realize that some wait-and-see projects are more likely to reward our active cultivation than others. In particular, we can see that projects E and F together are worth about $34 million (not negative $20 million or even $0) and should be actively cultivated rather than abandoned. At the very least, they could be sold to some other gardener.

A Dynamic Approach
Cultivation is intended to improve the crop, but it has to work within boundaries set by nature. In option space, as in nature, there are basic laws of time and motion. The most basic is that options tend to move upward and to the left in the option space as time passes. Upward, because the volatility metric decreases as time runs out. To the left, because, as a present-value calculation, the value-to-cost metric also decreases over time if its other constituent variables remain constant.

To illustrate, consider project F. Its volatility metric is 0.566, and its value-to-cost metric is 1.021. Now let a year pass, and suppose none of project F's variables changes except for t, which is now one year instead of two. Were we to recompute the metrics, we would discover that both have declined. The volatility metric falls from 0.566 to 0.400, which moves F upward in option space. And its value-to-cost metric declines from 1.021 to 0.964—that is, $100 \div [110 \div (1+0.06)^1]$—which moves F to the left. In fact, project F moves from region 3 (*probably later*) to the less promising region 4 (*maybe later*). Despite its initial promise, the only way project F is going to wind up in the money (that is, in region 1 or 2) and eventually get funded is if some force pushes it to the right, overcoming the natural tug to the left, before time runs out. Only two forces push in that direction: good luck and active management.

Neither force should be ignored. Sometimes we succeed by putting ourselves squarely in the way of good fortune. Other times we have to work at it. Managers actively cultivating a portfolio of opportunities are, in effect, working to push options as far as possible to the right in the space before they float all the way to the top. How is that done? By taking some action that increases either or both of our option-value metrics. Of the two, the value-to-cost metric is perhaps the more obvious one to work on first because managers are more accustomed to managing revenues, costs, and capital expenditures than volatility or time to expiration.

Anything managers can do to increase value or reduce cost will move the option to the right in our space. For example, price or volume increases, tax savings, or lower capital requirements, as well as any cost savings, will help. Such enhancements to value are obvious either with or without a real-options framework. What the framework provides is a way to incorporate them visually and quantitatively into option value through the value-to-cost metric.

The real world seldom gives managers the luxury of isolating one variable and holding all others constant. Managers cannot simply declare, "Let's raise prices to increase the value of our project." More likely, they will invent and evaluate complex proposal modifications driven or constrained by technology, demographics, regulations, and so on. For example, one way to cultivate a market-entry option might be to add a new product feature. That may entail extra investment (raising X), but it will also help differentiate the product in the local market, permitting higher prices (raising S) but also adding extra manufacturing costs (lowering S), some of which are fixed. The net effect on the value-to-cost metric is what counts, and the net effect is unclear without further analysis.

Evaluating the project as an option means there is more, not less, to analyze, but the framework tells us what to analyze, gives us a way to organize the effects, and offers a visual interpretation. Observing the change in the option's location in our space tells us both whether its value is risen or fallen and whether it has migrated to a different region of the tomato garden.

There are still more considerations even in this simple example of adding a product feature. Extra fixed costs mean greater risk, which might lower the value of the project (due to the need to discount future cash flows at a higher risk adjusted rate) and cause its value-to-cost metric to drop further. But the extra fixed costs also represent operating leverage that raises the volatility metric. That augments option value. We could hypothesize further that adding an extra feature will stimulate a competitor to match it. We, in turn, might be forced to introduce the next generation of our product (on which we hold a different option) earlier than we otherwise would have.

In general, actions taken by managers can affect not only the value-to-cost measure but also the volatility metric. In this example, both elements of the volatility metric—risk and time to expiration—are affected. And for more than one option. There is a spillover from one option to another: adding a feature reduces the length of time a subsequent decision can be deferred. For other situations, there are a myriad of possible spillover effects.

Nested Options in a Business Strategy

Once we allow options in a portfolio to directly influence other options, we are ready to consider strategies: a series of options explicitly *designed* to affect one another. We can use "nests" of options upon options to represent the sequence of contingencies designed into a business, as in the following simplified and hypothetical example.

Three years ago, the WeatherIze Corporation bought an exclusive license to a technology for treating fabric to retard its breakdown in extreme weather conditions. The idea was to develop a new line of fabric especially suitable for outdoor commercial awnings, a market the company already serves with a less durable product. Now WeatherIze's engineers have developed their first treated fabric, and the company is considering making the expenditures required to roll it out commercially. If the product is well received by awning manufacturers, WeatherIze will have to expand capacity within three years of introduction just to serve awning producers.

The vice president for business development is ebullient. He anticipates that success in awnings will be followed within another two years by product extensions—similar treatment of different fabrics designed for such consumer goods as tents, umbrellas, and patio furniture. At that time, WeatherIze would expand capacity yet again. The company envisions trademarking its fabrics, expanding its sales force, and supporting the consumer products made from these fabrics with cooperative advertising.

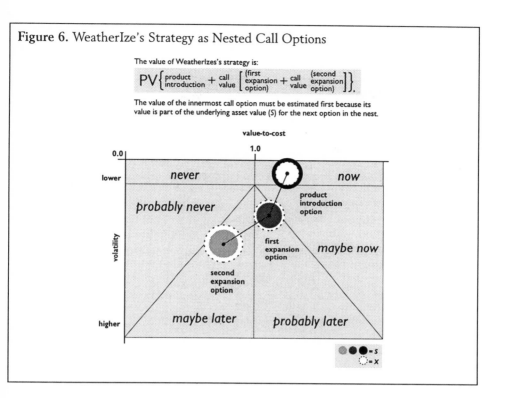

Figure 6. WeatherIze's Strategy as Nested Call Options

The value of WeatherIzes's strategy is:

$$PV\left\{ \substack{\text{product} \\ \text{introduction}} + \substack{\text{call} \\ \text{value}} \left[\substack{\text{(first} \\ \text{expansion} \\ \text{option)}} + \substack{\text{call} \\ \text{value}} \substack{\text{(second} \\ \text{expansion} \\ \text{option)}} \right] \right\}.$$

The value of the innermost call option must be estimated first because its value is part of the underlying asset value (S) for the next option in the nest.

WeatherIze's strategy for exploiting the treatment technology is pretty straightforward. It consists of a particular sequence of decision opportunities. The first step of the execution was to purchase the license. By doing so, the company acquired a sequence of nested options: to develop the product; to introduce the product; to expand capacity for manufacturing awning fabric; and to expand again to make related, branded fabrics. Just now, having developed the product, WeatherIze is part way through the strategy and is considering its next step: spending on the product introduction. That is, it's time to exercise (or not) the next real option in the chain.

WeatherIze's strategy, at this point in time, is depicted in option space in the diagram "WeatherIze's Strategy as Nested Call Options." Each circle represents an option whose location in space is determined by its value-to-cost and volatility metrics. The size of each solid circle is proportionate to the underlying asset value (S) for each option. The area within each dashed circle is proportionate to required expenditures (X). Thus a dashed circle inside a solid one represents an option that is in the money (S>X). A dashed circle outside a solid circle shows an option that is out of the money.

The line segments in the diagram indicate that the options are nested. The option to expand for awning production is acquired if and only if the option to introduce is exercised. As such, the underlying asset for the introduction option includes both the value of the operating cash flows associated with the product itself *and* the present value of the option to expand. Likewise, the option to expand a second time for commercial product production is acquired only if WeatherIze decides to exercise its first expansion option. The value of the whole strategy at this point is:

$$
PV\left\{ \begin{array}{l} \text{product} \\ \text{introduction} \end{array} + \begin{array}{l} \text{call} \\ \text{value} \end{array} \left[\begin{array}{l} \text{(first} \\ \text{expansion} \\ \text{option)} \end{array} + \begin{array}{l} \text{call} \\ \text{value} \end{array} \begin{array}{l} \text{(second} \\ \text{expansion} \\ \text{option)} \end{array} \right] \right\}.
$$

In effect, WeatherIze owns a call on a call.

The option to introduce the new awning fabric is in the money and about to expire. (WeatherIze will forfeit its license if it does not go ahead with the introductions.) As soon as this option is exercised, the picture changes. The top circle goes away; the bottom two remain linked and begin drifting upward. One of the most important factors determining whether they move right or left on their way up is how well the awning fabric does in the marketplace. But there are other factors as well. Anything that enhances the value of the second expansion option enhances the value of the first, too, because the value of the second option forms part of the value of the underlying asset value for the first option.

Suppose, for example, the risks associated with the consumer-product fabric's assets increase. Let's trace the effects in the diagram "What Happens If the Consumer Fabric Opportunity Becomes Riskier?" The most direct effect is on the second expansion option, which moves down in the space because its volatility metric rises. The second expansion option becomes more valuable. But the increased risk also affects the first expansion option for awning fabric. Its value-to-cost metric rises because the second expansion option is part of the underlying assets (S) of the first. In fact, a change in either metric for the second option must also change the value-to-cost metric (at least) of the first.

As another example, suppose a competitor introduces a substitute fabric in the consumer goods markets that WeatherIze had planned to target. Try to visualize what will happen. Not only will the location of the options change but so will the sizes of the circles. The solid circle, or asset value (S), of WeatherIze's second expansion option will shrink, and both the first and second expansion options will move to the left. Further, the first expansion option's underlying assets value also should shrink.

Drawing simple circles in the option space also lets us compare strategies. For example, we have been assuming that WeatherIze would not introduce branded fabrics without first expanding its awning fabric capacity. Now suppose the company could do either first, or both simultaneously, but that a larger investment would be required to make branded fabrics if the awning expansion weren't accomplished first. We could also assume that profit margins on the branded goods would be higher if the company first gained more experience with awning fabric.

These options in WeatherIze's alternative strategy are not nested, and they are no longer in the same locations. The diagram "Call Options in WeatherIze's Alternative Strategy" depicts the new strategy. Not that the second option, the branded-fabric option, is now farther left, its solid circle, or asset value (S), is smaller, and its dashed circle, or expenditures (X), is larger than it was originally. It is further out of the money but is now linked directly to the product introduction option. Given that the branded-fabric option is father left under this new strategy and its solid circle is smaller, could we possibly prefer it? Yes, actually, provided it also moves down the space—that is, if its volatility metric has increased. The pricing table in the real-options

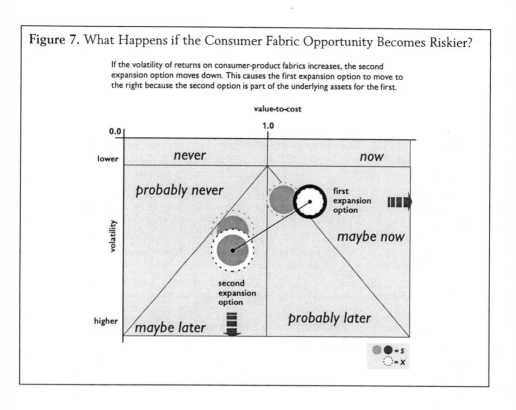

Figure 7. What Happens if the Consumer Fabric Opportunity Becomes Riskier?

If the volatility of returns on consumer-product fabrics increases, the second expansion option moves down. This causes the first expansion option to move to the right because the second option is part of the underlying assets for the first.

framework can tell us how far down it would have to go to compensate for any given move to the left. Finally, note that for the nonnested strategy, the value of both options directly enhances the value of the underlying assets associated with the initial product introduction. But it is no longer the case that any change in the second expansion option must affect the location of the first expansion option: each could, in fact, move around independently.

Although the options are not nested, they are very much related. Suppose, for example, that the awning expansion option pops into the money and is indeed exercised first, before the consumer fabric option. The value of the latter would be enhanced because the underlying assets associated with it would be expected to produce better margins—the value-to-cost metric for the consumer fabric option rises.

To compare WeatherIze's alternative strategies, we compute the value of each strategy's introduction option. We can do that quantitatively using the real-options framework. In visual terms, we prefer the introduction option to be farther to the right and to have a larger solid circle. Whichever strategy accomplishes that is more valuable.

Learning to Garden

I argued in "Investment Opportunities as Real Options" that companies should adopt option-pricing techniques as adjuncts to their existing system, not as replacements. If WeatherIze takes that approach there is a good chance that the "tomato garden" will help the company create and execute a superior strategy.

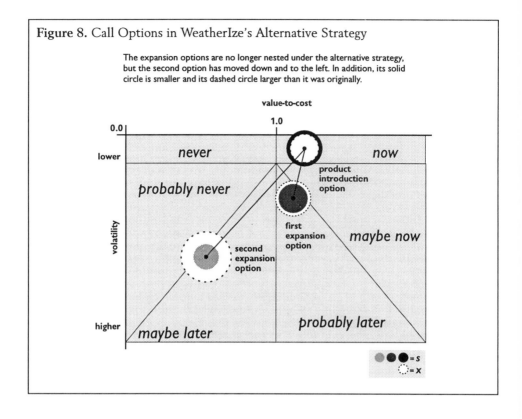

Figure 8. Call Options in WeatherIze's Alternative Strategy

The expansion options are no longer nested under the alternative strategy, but the second option has moved down and to the left. In addition, its solid circle is smaller and its dashed circle larger than it was originally.

Strategists at WeatherIze already were thinking several moves ahead when they purchased the license. They don't need to tomato garden to tell them merely to think ahead. But option pricing quantifies the value of the all-important follow-on opportunities much better than standard DCF-valuation techniques do. And the tomato garden adds a simple but versatile picture that reveals important insights into both the value and the timing of the exercise decisions. It gives managers a way to "draw" a strategy in terms that are neither wholly strategic nor wholly financial but some of both. Managers can play with the pictures much as they might with a physical model built of Lego's or Tinker Toys. Some of us are most creative while at play.

As executives at WeatherIze experiment with circles in option space, it is important that they preserve the link between the pictures they draw and the disciplined financial projections required by the real-options framework. They need to remember that the circles occupy a certain part of the space because the numbers—the value-to-cost and volatility metrics—put them there. At the same time, they need to prevent the exercise from becoming just another variation on "valuation as usual." This is the well-worn rut in which valuation analysis is used primarily to check numbers and as due diligence documentation for investments. Instead, the purpose should be to incorporate financial insights at the stage when projects and strategies are actually being created.

How does one become a good gardener? Practice, practice. I recommend starting by drawing simple combinations of projects to learn some common forms. What are the different ways you can depict a pair of nested call options? How can the pair move into the space? What are the ways to transform their configuration by changing the variables? Then move on to simple generic strategies. What does a given strategy look like when drawn in the option space? How does the picture change over time? How does it change when an option is exercised?

Next, practice translating real business phenomena into visual effects to update pictures. For example, how will the picture change if you add a direct mail campaign to your product introduction? Or how will the picture change if your competitor cuts prices when you enter a market?

Finally, try drawing your strategy and your competitors' side by side: How does the value and location of your options affect the value and location of theirs? How will they move over time?

In most companies, strategy formulation and business development are not located in the finance bailiwick. Nevertheless, both activities raise important financial questions almost right away. Although the questions arise early, answers typically do not. For finance to play an important creative role, it must be able to contribute insightful interpretive analyses of sequences of decisions that are purely hypothetical—that is, while they are still mere possibilities. By building option pricing into a framework designed to evaluate not only hard assets but also opportunities (and multiple, related opportunities at that), we can add financial insight earlier rather than later to the creative work of strategy.

Building on the Stage/Gate: An Enterprise-wide Architecture for New Product Development

Beebe Nelson, Bob Gill, and Steve Spring

The Stage/Gate Process: A Foundation

The foundation for managing and executing individual product development projects in today's corporation is the stage/gate process. This important process was first defined as a repeatable corporate process about ten years ago (Cooper 1993). Before that, new products were developed chiefly in an "over the wall" way, with each function handing its work on to the next. Increased competition and more demanding customers pushed companies to find ways to reduce cycle time and new product failure rate. They identified the sequence of activities required to develop products and defined these as a process—usually called the *stage/gate* or *phase/review* process—which was carried out by a team comprised of members of the key functional organizations, and which was reviewed by management at specified intervals.

The focus in the stage/gate process is on the execution of individual projects or programs. By specifying clear stage-by-stage deliverables and clear check points—gates, or management reviews—the use of stage/gate processes brought product development activities and decision making under closer scrutiny and better control. As they clarified the process, companies were able to introduce good project management techniques and concurrent engineering practices, and many were able also to achieve cycle time reduction. They also improved their ability to manage risk by making key project parameters more certain, thus allowing them to weed out less promising programs earlier in the development process.

From Stage/Gate to Aggregate Product Planning

The stage/gate process, however, leaves some important issues unaddressed. It focuses on individual projects, and can become bureaucratic if applied in a "one size fits all" way. More important, decisions on which programs to continue are made at the review gates in the context of a single program with no clear way to compare benefits from program to program. When limited resources have to be deployed, the stage/gate decision making process does not provide reviewers with the information they need to make decisions across programs. And perhaps most important, there is no clear way to decide what programs will be included in the development portfolio. It is this last stage/gate shortcoming that this paper addresses.

Choosing the best portfolio of programs for development, and managing that portfolio over time, requires that management consider the *aggregate* of possible development programs in the context of its business strategies and objectives, and also in the context of the other corporate processes involved in product development (Crawford 1996; Souder and Mandakovic 1986). Several things become clear as we "chunk up" to the aggregate or portfolio level of new product decision making.

First, we get a very different view of the role of strategy in product development decision making. In stage/gate decision making fit with strategy is an important criterion for moving a program through the gates. However, if we are looking at one project at a time there is no way of telling whether the aggregate of projects fulfills the strategy. When we ask the question of strategic fit about the portfolio of programs, we can begin to select a combination of programs which together forward the strategy, and we can look for portfolio balance around such issues as risk/return, markets addressed, and technology leverage.

Second, we are better equipped to consider individual new products in the context of enhancing technology capabilities, platforms, product lines, and product families (McGrath 1995). This allows for better long range product planning, including the intentional development of line extensions and derivatives from initial products, as well as planned platform regeneration and replacement. For example, this way of thinking can show that it is desirable to resource a program with low initial ROI because it provides downstream advantages as part of a product family.

Third, we can begin to address the all-important issue of technology management as we see the portfolio of programs drawing on and developing different aspects of the corporation's technology capability (Roussel et al 1991). An understanding of the product portfolio in relation to the technology of the corporation permits management to make decisions based on broad business objectives. This in turn enables management to address the question of what they are getting for their research and development investment.

Fourth, by thinking of the programs in aggregate, we can identify and act on opportunities with greater flexibility, and can link product lines and technologies to meet customer needs and competitor threats. Real innovation does not come in neat boxes: corporations whose development efforts are driven by customer needs are often pushed to develop products outside their traditional offerings, which in turn can lead to whole new platforms or product lines. But when development teams are held to thinking in terms of a single product, they are not in a position to act on a deep understanding of customer needs.

Finally, when the portfolio of programs is managed in the aggregate, corporations are better able to manage resources across programs, better able to avoid having programs compete for finite resources in the development pipeline.

As Kent Crawford has pointed out (Crawford 1996, 1), "effective product development necessitates a much broader view of organization management. Product development processes must encompass the entire business planning, administering, directing,

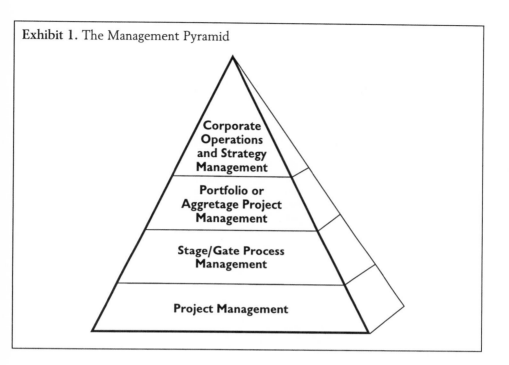

Exhibit 1. The Management Pyramid

Corporate Operations and Strategy Management

Portfolio or Aggretage Project Management

Stage/Gate Process Management

Project Management

and controlling functions, in addition to the traditional areas of project management. A holistic approach to project management is required where organizations have a need to more effectively manage multiple product development efforts."

In Exhibit 1, we see *project management* as the ground level set of practices for product development; the *stage/gate* process requires good project management practices for successful implementation. Moving up a level, the practices and disciplines of *portfolio* or *aggregate* project management allow the product development effort to respond to the complexities of managing multiple projects over time; this multiple and complex view, finally, provides the discipline needed to link product development to the organization's processes and strategies. Reading down, the top of the pyramid provides direction for aggregate product management; the stage/gate process provides the discipline for translating the strategic objectives of the corporation into manageable projects; and project management provides the discipline for successful stage/gate implementation.

To achieve holistic, integrated new product management, we have been working with companies who are beginning to think in terms of an *Expanded Product Development Process*. The expanded process begins not with an identifiable program or product concept but in the broader arena of strategic goal setting and opportunity identification, and it ends not with a successful product launch but with successful integration of new products into the ongoing business. This expanded product development process includes three subprocesses.

• the Innovation Subprocess, sometimes called the "Fuzzy Front End," is characterized by openness and the nurturing of new ideas and opportunities. Project boundaries

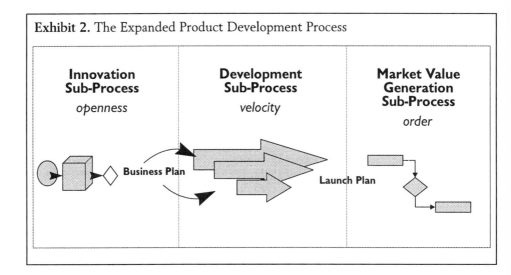

Exhibit 2. The Expanded Product Development Process

may be fluid, and screens and filters have low thresholds to encourage experimentation and exploration.

• the Development Subprocess is characterized by velocity of execution and speed to market. It is in this subprocess that a corporation can achieve cycle time reduction and process repeatability, particularly when clear customer requirements, clear product definition, and clear link to strategy are achieved in the upstream process.

• the Market Value Generation Subprocess is characterized by order and integration of new products into the existing product line. It includes post launch reviews and the planning of product ramp up and decline (product life cycle planning).

These three subprocesses are tied together by systematic reviews and metrics.

Strategic portfolio management reviews make decisions about the selection and resourcing of the portfolio of products. These reviews are held in the context of the corporation's overall planning calendar.

Operational reviews support ongoing decision making about projects in the development pipeline. These reviews are held regularly by the functions responsible for this aspect of the development process.

Stage/gate reviews are focused on individual programs, and are held as appropriate in terms of the program's timetable and milestones.

Distinguishing between these different kinds of reviews allows product development decision makers to address issues dealing with both individual programs (risk/return, strategic fit, competitive advantage) and with the portfolio of programs (portfolio balance, resourcing). This clarification of reviews and decision making encourages senior management to focus on strategic decision making, and encourages teams to focus on speedy implementation.

Managing the Product Development Process Enterprise Wide

An understanding of the expanded product development process leads us to ask how product development links to the key business processes enterprise wide. Hammer

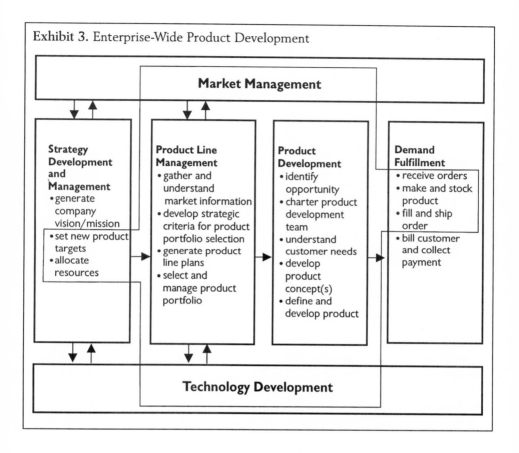

Exhibit 3. Enterprise-Wide Product Development

and Champy (1993) propose that to understand the enterprise as *process* rather than *function* amounts to a revolution. Unfortunately, the work of transforming the modern corporation from a functional organization to a process organization produced, in many cases, only downsizing. Functionally organized corporations simply did more with less and called it reengineering.

Nonetheless, an understanding of the corporation as composed of a small number of key processes (usually about seven) can help us identify the connections that must be managed in order for product development to be successful. Exhibit 4 shows a typical process map, to which the supporting processes of Human Relations, Finance, and Information Management are often added. In this map, Product Development is shown as one of six processes. The process detail indicates the steps that a corporation might include, both at the management level (*identify opportunity, charter product development team*) and at the team level (*understand customer needs, develop product concept, define and develop product*), in specifying its product development process. The other business processes, however, include activities and areas of concern that are key to successful product development. At Polaroid Corporation, for instance, the *Product Development Process (PDP)*, which is their stage/gate process, is differentiated from *New Product Delivery (NPD)*. PDP outlines deliverables, activities,

Exhibit 4. Seven Steps: Linking Product Development and Strategy

- Setting new product targets
- Gathering strategic information
- Creating a list of new product options
- Setting criteria
- Mapping the strategic geography
- Creating the portfolio
- Managing the portfolio

The Seven Steps to Strategic New Product Development are Seldom in a Straight Line

© Product Development Partners, Inc. 1997

gates, and metrics for teams and reviewers. NPD, which has never been as fully articulated, expresses the understanding of the corporation that to be successful PDP must be linked to many other business processes.

In working with clients we follow seven steps which provide a roadmap for managing the enterprise wide product delivery process (Gill, Nelson, Spring 1996). These seven steps begin with *setting new product targets*, a function of the Strategy Development and Management Process. Without clear targets and the allocation of resources to meet those targets, the product development effort will lack support from upper management. The next steps in the enterprise wide product delivery process comprise the activities under the Product Line Management Process. The corporation must *gather and understand market information* (steps 2 and 3), including customer and competition, and this information must be integrated with an understanding of the technology and process capabilities of the corporation. It is at this point that the Market Management Process and the Technology Development Process will be integrated into the product delivery process. In fact, we have found that it is often the people responsible for the Technology Development Process who push the corporations to articulate product/technology/customer linkages through the use of product/technology roadmaps (Willyard and McClees 1987) and variations on QFD (Quality Function Deployment; Griffin 1992) so that technology resources can be deployed effectively.

Step 4 is simply to list all of the product and opportunity options that are available to the product delivery process. Often this information is scattered throughout the corporation: Market Management is in close contact with the customer, Technology Development is working on numbers of technology advances, and others in the company have good ideas which they are either working on or have shelved because they can't get resources. Before any selection of a product portfolio can be undertaken, the corporation needs to have a way of gathering together all these sources of possible products and listing them in comparable form. This deceptively simple step can be a difficult one to accomplish because of the territorial boundaries it needs to cross.

Developing strategic criteria for product portfolio selection is step 5 in the process. Although this step is the responsibility of the Product Line Management Process, it calls upon the work of the Strategy Development and Management Process to articulate a strategy for the corporation from which new product strategy can be understood. A constant failure of product development is the shifting of strategic priorities, which keeps teams from being able to move quickly from identified opportunity to product. Unless the product delivery process is thought of as enterprise wide, executives are prone to involve themselves during the Product Development Process itself, where their influence is historically more distracting than helpful (Wheelwright and Clark 1992).

Selecting the product portfolio depends on the accomplishment of the earlier steps. We have found that many companies still use a linear planning process which compares product to product and results in a prioritized list. The processes which result in good portfolio planning involve iterative multidimensional (matrixed) displays of information which move decision making from linear to strategic, from implicit to explicit, and from individual to collaborative (Gill, Nelson, Spring 1996). This kind of decision making requires supporting tools to help management compare and contrast a lot of different information while engaging in discussions that result in collaborative decision making. We have found that displaying information in "bubble charts," which allow for up to seven or eight variables to be displayed in one frame, provides an excellent and flexible methodology to promote portfolio decision making. Commercially available software analysis tools provide databases that can keep track of product information and display it against comparable and strategically relevant criteria, thus generating multiple scenarios which display the portfolio candidates against different criteria. Such tools enable the corporation to keep ongoing track of its product options and to support decision making by generating portfolio scenarios for use at reviews.

Step 7 is managing the portfolio. In most product development stage/gate processes, individual projects are managed as they move through the pipeline. In making our view enterprise wide, we see that what must be managed is the aggregate product portfolio as it promises collectively to deliver on strategic goals and as it collectively draws on the corporation's finite resources (Harris and McKay 1996). This seventh step also links the product delivery process to the Demand Fulfillment Process. Too often, product development fails to make a clear connection with the supply side of the corporation. New products are seen by that process as competing with existing products, and lack of planning and integration means that even a potentially successful product is under-marketed or poorly distributed, and so fails to meet its potential. Further, the product lifecycle is often not managed, and so existing product information is not fed back to Product Line Management for optimal planning.

These steps are seldom if ever followed linearly: rather, the corporation will find itself moving from one step to another iteratively, developing information as best it can in one step, returning to that step when the information can be more fully developed. The steps enable the corporation to act out of an understanding of its enterprise wide product delivery process. When the corporation takes on the practices of the Seven Steps, linking its product development efforts to corporate strategy and thus making optimal use of its product development resources, it is able to make portfolio decisions that create balance and synergy through involving the cooperative participation of management

The expanded view of product development, and the recognition of its fit within the key business processes of the corporation, will allow corporations to bring discipline to the management of product development and aggregate product planning. The management of the new product portfolio will be to the next decade of new product program management what the stage/gate was to the decade of the mid 1980's to the mid 1990's. Managing across programs increases the complexity of program management, and it requires new project management tools and new ways of thinking.

References

Cooper, Robert G. *Winning at New Products: Accelerating the Process from Idea to Launch.* 2nd ed. Reading, MA: Addison-Wesley, 1993.

Crawford, J. Kent. "Effective Product Development Through Holistic Project Management." *Project Management Institute 27th Annual Seminar/Symposium.* Boston, 1996.

Gill, Bob, Beebe Nelson, and Steve Spring. "Seven Steps to Strategic New Product Development." *The PDMA Handbook of New Product Development.* New York: Wiley, 1996.

Griffin, Abbie. "Evaluating QFD's Use in U.S. Firms as a Process for Developing Products." *Journal of Product Innovation Management.* 9:171-187 (March 1992)

Hammer, Michael, and James Champy. *Reengineering the Corporation. A Manifesto for Business Revolution.* New York: HarperCollins, 1993.

Harris, John R, and Jonathan C. McKay. ""Optimizing Product Development Through Pipeline Management." *The PDMA Handbook of New Product Development.* New York: Wiley, 1996.

McGrath, Michael E. *Product Strategy for High-Technology Companies: How to Achieve Growth, Competitive Advantage, and Increased Profits.* New York: Irwin. 1995.

Roussel, Philip A., Kamal N. Saad, and Tamara J. Erickson. *Third Generation R&D: Managing the Link to Corporate Strategy.* Boston: Harvard Business School Press, 1991.

Souder, W. E., and T. Mandakovic. "R&D Project Selection Models." *Research Management.* 1986.

Wheelwright, S. C. and K. B. Clark. Revolutionizing Product Development: Quantum Leaps in Speed, Efficiency, and Quality. New York: Free Press, 1992.

Willyard, C. W., and C. W. McClees. "Motorola's Technology Roadmap Process." *Harvard Business Review.* 1987.

This article is reprinted from *1997 Proceedings of the Annual Project Management Institute Seminars & Symposium* with permission of the Project Management Institute Headquarters, Four Campus Boulevard, Newtown Square, PA 19073-3299 USA, Phone: (610) 356-4600 Fax: (610) 356-4647, Project Management Institute (PMI) is the world's leading project management association with over 40,000 members worldwide. For further information contact PMI Headquarters at (610) 356-4600 or visit the web site at www.pmi.org.

Part 2:

Selection and Prioritization

Portfolio Management in New Product Development: Lessons from the Leaders, Phase I

Robert G. Cooper, Scott J. Edgett and Elko J. Kleinschmidt

How can a company most effectively invest its R&D and new product resources? Answering this question is what portfolio management is all about: resource allocation to achieve corporate new product objectives. Much like stock portfolio managers, those senior managers who succeed at optimizing their R&D investments, who define the right new-product strategy for their firm, select the winning new-product projects, and achieve the ideal balance of projects—will win in the long run.

This article reports the results of an exploratory investigation into portfolio practices (see "How the Study Was Done"). It tells how leading firms manage their R&D portfolios, and offers insights and recommendations to help your company achieve a greater return from its R&D investment (1).

Understanding Portfolio Management

Portfolio management and the prioritization of new product projects is a critical management task. Roussel, Saad and Erikson in their widely-read book claim that "... new product portfolio analysis and planning will grow in the 1990s to become the powerful tool that business portfolio planning became in the 1970s and 1980s" (2).

Portfolio management and project prioritization is about resource allocation in the firm; that is, which new-product projects shall the corporation fund from the many opportunities it faces? And, which ones shall receive top priority and be accelerated to market? It is also about corporate strategy, because today's new-product projects decide tomorrow's product/market profile of the firm. An estimated 50 percent of firms' sales today come from new products introduced within the last five years (3,4). Finally, it is about balance; namely, the optimal investment mix between risk versus return, maintenance versus growth, and short-term versus long-term new product projects.

We define portfolio management as a dynamic decision process, whereby a business's list of active new product (and R&D) projects is constantly updated and revised. In this process, new projects are evaluated, selected and prioritized; existing projects may be accelerated, killed or de-prioritized; and resources are allocated and reallocated to the active projects.

The portfolio decision process is characterized by uncertain and changing information, dynamic opportunities, multiple goals and strategic considerations, interdependence among projects, and multiple decision makers and locations. The process encompasses or overlaps a number of decision-making processes within the business, including periodic reviews of the total portfolio of all projects (looking at the entire set of projects, all projects against each other), making Go/Kill decisions on individual projects on an on-going basis, and developing a new product strategy for the business, complete with strategic resource allocation decisions.

New product portfolio management sounds like a mechanistic exercise of decision making and resource allocation. But there are many unique facets of the problem that make it perhaps the most challenging decision-making faced by the modern business. First, new-product portfolio management deals with *future events* and opportunities; thus, much of the information required to make project selection decisions is at best, uncertain, and at worst, highly unreliable. Second, the decision environment is a *dynamic* one; the status and prospects for projects in the portfolio are continually changing as new information becomes available. Next, projects in the portfolio are at *different stages* of completion, yet all projects compete against each other for resources; consequently, comparisons must be made between projects with different amounts and "goodness" of information. Finally, *resources* to be allocated across projects are limited; a decision to fund one project may require taking resources away from another, and resource transfers between projects are not totally seamless.

The challenge of portfolio management in product development is not new. Over the decades, the topic has surfaced under various guises including "R&D project selection," "R&D resource allocation," "project prioritization," and "portfolio management." By the early 1970s, dozens of articles had appeared on the topic, with most authors only making one stab at it before moving on to more fruitful fields.

The majority of these early proposed methods were management science optimization techniques. To the management scientist, this portfolio management problem is one of constrained optimization under conditions of uncertainty: a multi-project, multi-stage decision model solved by mathematical programming. The original portfolio selection models were thus highly mathematical, and employed techniques such as linear, dynamic and integer programming. The objective was to develop a portfolio of new and existing projects to maximize some objective function (for example, the expected profits), subject to a set of resource constraints.

Anyone familiar with these programming techniques will immediately recognize the hurdles that the mathematician and management scientist would face in solving this portfolio problem. Further, despite the many methods proposed in the early days, there was a remarkable lack of follow-up; few authors ever described attempts to actually implement their methods and to gauge their feasibility. Indeed, the articles in the 1960s and 1970s appear to be largely the result of academics writing to and for one another. In spite of the importance of the topic, no guru or "dominant school of thought" ever emerged here, perhaps an indication of the frustrations encountered when seeking solutions (5-9).

How the Study Was Done

Interviews were conducted in 35 leading firms in various industries. Five companies were singled out for in-depth and detailed interviews, on the basis of the uniqueness and proficiency of their portfolio approach. The companies, although quite willing to share the details of the portfolio approaches with us, were promised anonymity in some cases. Also, in no way do we reveal any details on any project under development—all illustrations use disguised projects. These leading firms included:

• The U.S. arm of the world's largest chemical company (Hoechst).

• A major industrial materials supplier—the number one in its industry in the world (English China Clay).

• A major high-technology materials producer.

• A major financial institution (Royal Bank of Canada), among the top five in North America.

• A multinational consumer goods company (Reckitt & Colman, U.K.).

Three of the five were in the United States. Additionally, another 30 companies provided data on their portfolio methods, experiences and outcomes (most were from North America). Note that the method of sample selection was purposeful (not random); we deliberately selected firms according to their experience, proficiency and ability to provide insights regarding portfolio management. During the interviews, the details of the portfolio approaches used, the rationale, problems faced and issues raised were all investigated (1).

The study is a two-part study: Phase I has been completed and is reported here; Phase II is underway in cooperation with the Industrial Research Institute, and involves a much larger sample size.—R.G.C., S.J.E. and E.J.K.

Portfolio Methods in Practice

How are leading firms handling portfolio management? Here we outline the portfolio methods used by a selection of companies known to be actively using or developing and implementing a portfolio management process. Before we delve into the details of these processes, consider some of the study's key findings which became evident immediately:

First, every company we interviewed believed the portfolio management, project selection and resource allocation problem to be critical to new product success.

However, virtually all companies had experienced problems with project selection. And with resources tighter than ever, the issue of proper resource allocation and picking the right projects was paramount. Further, the desire to see the business's strategy reflected in its portfolio of R&D investments was another driver of improved portfolio management techniques.

Second, the problems the companies faced in project selection and portfolio management that were creating the sense of urgency for better portfolio management are familiar ones:

• *Does not reflect strategy*—Many businesses or SBUs studied had enunciated business strategies; in some cases, they even had developed new product strategies for the business. These strategies defined the goals for new products (e.g., by year five, 32 percent of sales revenue will be generated by products we do not now have), the role that product development will play in achieving overall business goals, and even strategic arenas of focus—which product types, markets and technologies (or platforms) will generate these new products. The problem lay in linking these strategies—business and new product—to spending on R&D projects. A breakdown of R&D spending by project types often revealed serious disconnects between goals/strategies of the business and where the money was spent.

• *Poor quality portfolios*—Managers were generally displeased with, or at best doubtful about, their firm's current portfolio of projects. Many new-product projects were thought to be weak or mediocre; others were considered unfit for commercialization; and success rates in the marketplace were less than adequate. As one manager put it: "We implemented our portfolio management approach [a risk/reward bubble diagram], and the first thing that became evident was that half our projects were in the wrong quadrants, including some of our big ones! By the end of the year, the list of projects had been cut in half." Similar audits had resulted in similar cuts in other firms, leading one to doubt the quality of current portfolios.

• *Tunnels, not funnels*—A related problem is that Go/Kill decision points—the gates in new product processes—were often perceived to be ineffective. In too many companies, projects tended to get a life of their own, and little could stop them once they gained momentum. In one large consumer firm, an internal audit of 60 current projects revealed that 88 percent resembled an express train ... "slowing down at stations [project reviews], but never with the intention of being stopped!" Only 12 percent were handled thoughtfully with rigorous Go/Kill decision points. Even when killed, the complaint in some firms was that projects had a habit of being resurrected, perhaps under a new name.

• We observed that criteria for making Go/Kill decisions were inadequate or not used, and that often a mechanism for rating, prioritizing or even killing projects was lacking. As one frustrated manager exclaimed: "We talk about having a funnelling process that weeds out poor projects; heck, we don't have a funnel—we have a tunnel ... ten projects enter the process, ten go into Development, ten go to Launch ... and one succeeds!"

• *Scarce resources, a lack of focus*—Resources are too scarce to waste on the wrong projects. Indeed, a common complaint was that product development was suffering from too-lean resources, especially in marketing and manufacturing/operations. Most firms confessed to having far too many projects for the limited resources available. The result was that resources were spread very thinly across new-product projects, so that even the best projects were starved for people, time and money. As a result, projects were taking too long to reach the market, and such key activities as up-front homework, getting sharp, early product definition, and building in the voice of the customer were not being executed as well or consistently as they should be.

• *Trivialization of product development*—The quest for cycle-time reduction, together with the desire for more new products than ever, when coupled with resource constraints, led many firms to do the obvious: pick "low hanging fruit"—projects that could be done quickly, easily and cheaply. Often these projects were trivial ones—modifications, extensions and up-dates—while the significant products, which were

---

Key Problems in Portfolio Management and Project Selection

Portfolio management, project selection and resource allocation were deemed critical to new product success by all firms in the study. But every firm faced problems in this respect:

1. The portfolio of projects does not reflect the business's strategy: Too many projects are "off strategy," and there are disconnects between spending breakdowns on projects and the strategic priorities of the business.

2. The portfolio's quality is poor: There are too many unfit, weak and mediocre projects; success rates at launch are inadequate.

3. Firms' new product processes are tunnels when they should be funnels. The Go/Kill decision points are weak; projects tend to take on a life of their own; poor projects are often not killed.

4. Resources are scarce, and there is a lack of focus: Most firms confess to having far too many projects for the limited resources available; cycle times and success rates are suffering as a result.

5. Some firms admitted to having too many trivial projects in their new product pipeline—modifications, up-dates and extensions—and too few of the projects needed to yield major breakthroughs and real competitive advantage. This is the result of the quest for cycle time reductions, coupled with insufficient resources.

---

the ones needed to yield real competitive advantage and major breakthroughs, were often placed on the back burner. The result was a portfolio of short-term projects, with projects designed to create tomorrow's big winners, such as technology platforms, missing.

Many of the portfolio techniques presented below are new to the companies involved. For example, a major consumer goods company and a materials firm had set up task forces to deal with the portfolio problem one year before our interviews and were only in the early stages of implementation at the time of the interviews. We saw new, relatively untried methodologies being implemented in other firms as well. Thus, the reader should treat some of the techniques described as "exploratory" and "experimental" rather than tried-and-proven methods.

Portfolio Management Goals

While the portfolio methods employed in these firms varied greatly, the common denominator across firms was the goals management was trying to achieve. One or more of three high-level or macro goals dominated the thinking of each firm we studied, either implicitly or explicitly. Which goal was most emphasized by the firm in turn seemed to influence the choice of portfolio method. These three broad or macro goals were:

• *Value Maximization*—In some firms, the preoccupation was to allocate resources so as to maximize the value of the portfolio in terms of some company objective (such as long-term profitability, return-on-investment, likelihood of success, or some other strategic objective).

• *Balance*—Here the principal concern was to achieve a balance of projects in terms of a number of parameters; for example, the right balance of long-term projects versus short ones; or high-risk versus lower-risk, sure bets; and across various markets, technologies, product categories, and project types (e.g., new products, improvements, cost reductions, maintenance and fixes, and fundamental research) (10).

• *Strategic Direction*—The main focus here was to ensure that, regardless of all other considerations, the final portfolio of projects truly reflected the business's strategy—that the breakdown of spending across projects, areas, markets, etc., was directly tied to the business strategy (e.g., to previously delineated areas of strategic focus), and that all projects were "on strategy."

What becomes clear is the potential for conflict between these three high-level goals. For example, the portfolio that yields the greatest NPV or IRR may not be a balanced one (it might contain a majority of short-term, low-risk projects, or be overly focused on one market). Similarly, a portfolio that is primarily strategic may sacrifice other goals (such as short-term profitability).

Our interviews also revealed that although managers did not explicitly state that one of the above goals took precedence over the other two, the nature of the portfolio management tool elected by that firm certainly indicated a hierarchy of goals. This was because certain portfolio approaches were more applicable to some goals than others; for example, the visual models (such as portfolio bubble diagrams) were most amenable to achieving a balance of projects (visual charts being an excellent way of demonstrating balance), whereas scoring models tended to be very poor for achieving or even showing balance but most effective if the goal was maximization against an objective. Thus, the choice of the "right" portfolio approach depends on which goal management explicitly or implicitly focuses on.

Which methods did firms find most effective for achieving the three portfolio goals? The next sections outline the methods, complete with strengths and weaknesses, beginning with the goal of maximizing portfolio value.

Maximizing the Value of the Portfolio

A variety of methods were used to achieve this goal, ranging from financial models to scoring models. Each has its strengths and weaknesses. The end result of each method is a rank-ordered list of "go" and "hold" projects, with those at the top scoring highest in terms of achieving the desired objective(s); the value in terms of that objective is thus maximized.

Expected Commercial Value

This method seeks to maximize the "value" or commercial worth of the portfolio, subject to certain budget constraints.

It is one of the better-thought-out financial models, featuring several new twists that make it particularly appropriate to portfolio management. We found it in use at English China Clay (ECC), a major materials producer with U.S. headquarters in Atlanta, Georgia.

The ECV method determines the commercial worth of each project to the corporation; namely, its expected commercial value. This calculation, shown in Figure 1, is based on a decision tree analysis, and considers the future stream of earnings from the

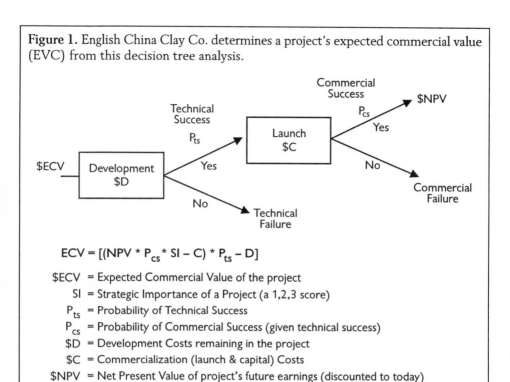

Figure 1. English China Clay Co. determines a project's expected commercial value (EVC) from this decision tree analysis.

$$ECV = [(NPV * P_{cs} * SI - C) * P_{ts} - D]$$

ECV = Expected Commercial Value of the project

SI = Strategic Importance of a Project (a 1,2,3 score)

P_{ts} = Probability of Technical Success

P_{cs} = Probability of Commercial Success (given technical success)

D = Development Costs remaining in the project

C = Commercialization (launch & capital) Costs

NPV = Net Present Value of project's future earnings (discounted to today)

project, the probabilities of both commercial success and technical success, along with both commercialization costs and development costs. It also incorporates the strategic importance of the project.

In order to arrive at a prioritized list of projects, ECC considers scarce resources. In ECC's case, capital resources are thought to be the constraining or scarce resource (note that many of ECC's projects are very capital-intensive). Other companies may choose to use R&D people or work-months, or R&D dollars, as the constraining resource. ECC takes the ratio of what it is trying to maximize—namely the ECV—divided by the constraining resource, namely the capital cost per project. Projects are rank-ordered according to this ratio, thereby ensuring the greatest "bang for buck"; that is, the ECV is maximized, for a given capital budget (11).

This ECV model has a number of attractive features. Because it is based on a decision tree approach, it recognizes that if the project is halted partway through, certain expenses are not incurred, and that the Go/Kill decision process is a step-wise or incremental one. (For example, the simplistic route adopted by some—namely, multiplying the NPV of a project by its probability of success—fails to capture this subtlety). A second feature is that all dollar amounts are discounted to today (not just to the launch date), thereby appropriately penalizing projects that are years away from launch. A third benefit is that the ECV, although largely financially-based, does consider the strategic importance of projects. Finally, the model recognizes the issue of

Table 1. Dynamic Rank-Ordered List, as Used by Company G

Project	IRR*PTS	NPV*PTS	Strategic Importance	Ranking Score*
Alpha	16.0 (2)	8.0 (2)	5 (1)	1.67 (1)
Epsilon	10.8 (4)	18.0 (1)	4 (2)	2.33 (2)
Delta	11.1 (3)	7.8 (3)	2 (4)	3.33 (3)
Omega	18.7 (3)	5.1 (4)	1 (6)	3.67 (4)
Gamma	9.0 (6)	4.5 (5)	3 (3)	4.67 (5)
Beta	10.5 (5)	1.4 (6)	2 (4)	5.00 (6)

Notes: Both IRR and NPV are multiplied by Probability of Technical Success. Projects are then ranked according to the three criteria; numbers in parentheses show the ranking in each column. Projects are rank-ordered until there are no more resources.

*The final column is the mean across these three rankings. This is the score on which the six projects are finally ranked. Project Alpha is number 1; Project Beta is last.

constrained resources and attempts to maximize in light of this constraint; in other words, it strives for "maximum bang for buck" rather than just "maximum bang."

The major weakness of the method is the dependence on financial and other quantitative data. Accurate estimates on all projects' future stream of earnings, on their commercialization (and capital) expenditures, on their development costs, and on probabilities of success are model inputs—estimates that are often unreliable, or at best, simply not available early in the life of a project. For example, one seasoned executive took great exception to multiplying two very uncertain probability figures together: "This will always unfairly punish the more venturesome projects!"

A second weakness is that the method does not look at the balance of the portfolio—at whether the portfolio has the right balance between high- and low-risk projects, or across markets and technologies. A third weakness is that the method considers only a single criterion—the ECV—for maximization (although admittedly, this ECV is composed of a number of parameters).

Productivity Index
The PI is similar to the ECV method described above, and shares many of its strengths and weaknesses: the PI also tries to maximize the financial value of the portfolio for a given resource constraint. We saw the method in use in two firms: a medical products firm in the U.S. and a nuclear firm in the U.K. The method is one advocated by the Strategic Decisions Group (12).

The Productivity Index = $[ECV * P_{ts} - R\&D]/R\&D$

Here, *expected commercial value* (ECV) is a probability-weighted stream of cash flows from the project, discounted to the present, and assuming technical success. Note that the definition of ECV here is different from that used by English China

Clay (Figure 1). P_{ts} is the probability of technical success, while *R&D* is the R&D expenditure remaining in the project (R&D monies already spent on the project are sunk costs and hence not relevant to the decision). Projects are rank-ordered according to this index in order to arrive at the preferred portfolio.

Dynamic Rank Ordered List

The next method overcomes the limitation of relying on only a single criterion to rank projects, such as ECV or PI shown above. We call it the Dynamic Rank Ordered List approach, although Company G, a telecommunications hardware supplier, simply called it their "portfolio model." This method has the advantage that it can rank-order according to several criteria concurrently, without becoming as complex and time-consuming as the use of a full-fledged, multiple-criteria scoring model. These criteria can include, for example: profitability and return measures, strategic importance, ease and speed to do, and other desirable characteristics of a high-priority project. The four criteria used by Company G are (see Table 1):

• *Strategic importance* of the project; namely, how important and how aligned the project is with the business's strategy. It is gauged on a 1-5 scale, where 5 = critically important.

• *NPV* (net present value) of the future earnings of projects, less all expenditures remaining to be spent on the project. Here, the NPV has built into it probabilities of commercial success. (In calculating the NPV, sales revenues, margins, etc. have all been multiplied by probabilities to account for uncertainties.) NPV was considered to be an important criterion because it captures the "bang" or financial impact of projects.

• *IRR* (internal rate of return), calculated using the same data as the NPV, gives the percent return. Management here considered IRR also to be important, capturing "bang for buck."

• *Probability of technical success* as a percentage. Some projects were very speculative technically.

How are projects prioritized or ranked on four criteria simultaneously? Simple: First, the probability of technical success is multiplied by each of the IRR and NPV to yield an adjusted IRR and NPV. Next, projects are ranked independently on each criterion: adjusted IRR, adjusted NPV, and strategic importance (see numbers in parentheses in Table 1). The final, overall ranking—the far right column in Table 1—is determined by calculating the mean of the three rankings. For example, Project Alpha scored first on strategic importance and second on each of IRR and NPV; the mean of these three rankings is 1.67, which places Alpha at the top of the list. Simple perhaps, but consider the list of projects in Table 1 and try to arrive at a better ranking yourself—one that maximizes against all three criteria!

The major strength of this dynamic list is its simplicity: Rank-order your projects on each of several criteria and take the mean of the rankings! Another strength is that the model can handle several criteria concurrently, without becoming overly complex. Its major weakness is that the model does not consider constrained resources (as did the ECV or PI methods above, although conceivably Company G could build this into its rank-ordering model), and like the ECV and PI models, it is largely based on uncertain, often unreliable, financial data. Finally, it fails to consider the balance of projects.

Table 2. Hoechst's 19-Question Scoring Model

Reward
- Absolute contribution to profitability (5-year cash flow: cumulative cash flows less all cash costs, before interest and taxes).
- Technological payback: the number of years for the cumulative cash flow to equal all cash costs expended prior to the start-up date.
- Time to commercial start-up.

Business Strategy Fit
- Congruence: how well the program fits with the strategy (stated or implied) for the product line, business and/or company
- Impact: the financial and strategic impact of the program on the product line, business and/or company (scored from "minimal" to "critical").

Strategic Leverage
- Proprietary position.
- Platform for growth (from "one of a kind" to "opens up new technical and commercial fields").
- Durability: the life of the product in the marketplace (years).
- Synergy with other operations/businesses within the corporation.

Probability of Commercial Success
- Existence of a market need.
- Market maturity (from "declining" to "rapid growth").
- Competitive intensity: how tough or intense the competition is.
- Existence of commercial application development skills from "new" to "already in place").
- Commercial assumptions (from "low probability" to "highly predictable").
- Regulatory/social/political impact (from "negative" to "positive").

Probability of Technical Success
- Technical gap (from "large gap" to "incremental improvement").
- Program complexity.
- Existence of technological skill base (from "new to us" to "widely practiced in company").
- Availability of people and facilities (from "must hire/build" to "immediately available").

Each criterion (question) is scored 1–10; 1, 4, 7, and 10 are "anchored."
The five factors are calculated via weightings × ratings, and added in a weighted fashion to yield a project score.
Projects are ranked by project score until there are no more resources!

Scoring models

Scoring models have long been used to make Go/Kill decisions at individual project reviews or gates, but they are also applicable to project prioritization and portfolio management. Here, a list of criteria is developed to rate projects—criteria believed to discriminate between high- and low-priority projects. Projects are then rated by evaluators on each criterion, typically on 1—5 or 0—10 scales with anchor phrases. Next, these scores are multiplied by weightings, and summed across all criteria to yield a *project score* for each project.

Although many firms we interviewed professed to use such scoring models, either they were poorly crafted models (for example, inappropriate criteria), or there were serious problems in the actual use of the model at management decision meetings. Consequently, such models often fell into disuse. The key seemed to be the construction of an appropriate list of scoring criteria-ones that really do separate winners from losers—and a procedure to gather the data and use the model at a management meeting.

Hoechst-U.S. had constructed one of the best scoring models we have seen. It took several years of refinement, but the eventual model is so well-conceived that we report it here. Each question or criterion (Table 2) had been carefully selected and worded, operationally defined, and tested for validity and reliability over some years.

The five major factors considered in prioritizing Hoechst's projects are:

- Reward (to the company).
- Business strategy fit (fit with the business unit's strategy).
- Strategic leverage (ability of the project to leverage company resources and skills).
- Probability of commercial success.
- Probability of technical success.

Within each of these five factors are a number of specific characteristics or measures (19 in total), which are scored on 1—10 scales by management. The 19 scales are anchored (scale points 1, 4, 7, and 10 are defined) to facilitate discussion. Simple addition of the items within each factor yields the five factor scores, which are added together in a weighted fashion to yield an overall program attractiveness score for the project. This final score is used for two purposes:

1. *Go/Kill decisions at gates*—The program attractiveness score is one input to the Go/Kill decisions made by senior management at each gate in Hoechst's Stage—Gate trademark new product process; a score of 50 percent of maximum is the cut-off or hurdle.

2. *Prioritization*—Immediately following the gate meeting, a portfolio review occurs, prioritization of "Go" projects from the gate takes place, and resources may be allocated to the approved projects. Here, the program attractiveness scores for the new projects are compared to the scores of active projects (previously resourced) in order to determine the relative prioritization of the new projects.

Managers at Hoechst and other firms were generally pleased with scoring models, but all confessed that some rough edges remained to be ironed out:

- *Imaginary precision:* Using a scoring model imputed a degree of precision that simply did not exist; as one Hoechst executive exclaimed, "They're trying to measure a [soft] banana with a micrometer!"

- *Halo effect:* This was a concern at the Royal Bank of Canada (RBC), which over the years had cut its list of multiple criteria in its scoring model down to five key criteria. Why? Management argued that if a project scores high on one criterion, it tends to score high on many of the rest—a halo effect.

- *Efficiency of allocation of scarce resources:* Missing from the scoring models was a means of ensuring that the resulting list of Go projects actually achieved the highest

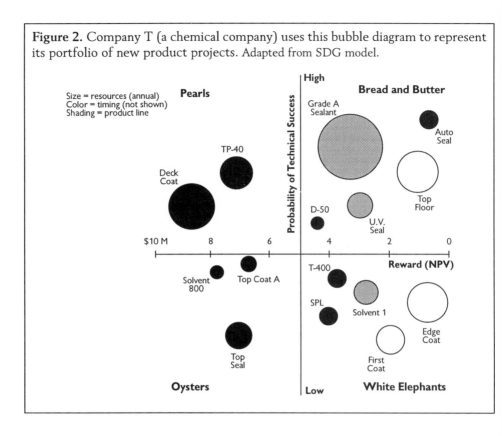

Figure 2. Company T (a chemical company) uses this bubble diagram to represent its portfolio of new product projects. Adapted from SDG model.

possible score for a given total R&D expenditure. For example, an artifact of one firm's scoring model was that much larger projects tended to rise to the top of the list; however, if the ranking criterion had been "Project Score/R&D Spend" instead of just "Project Score," then some smaller but efficient projects—ones that required; less R&D resources—would have risen to the top.

Greatest Weakness
Although the value maximization methods outlined above have much to commend them, their greatest weakness as a group is that they fail to ensure that the portfolio is strategically aligned and optimally balanced. For example, the resulting portfolio of projects generated via any of the above methods might maximize profits or some project score, but yield an unbalanced list of projects (for example, too many short-term ones) or fail to mirror the strategic direction of the business. These goals—balance and strategic alignment—are discussed below.

In spite of these weaknesses, maximization of the portfolio's value is still a worthwhile objective. We can argue about balance, and philosophize about strategic direction of the portfolio, but if the projects in the portfolio are poor ones—poor profitability, low likelihood of success or poor attractiveness scores—then the portfolio exercise is academic. First and foremost, a portfolio must contain "good" projects, and that is where the maximization methods outlined above excel. One cannot ignore these methods; they must be part of your portfolio-building repertoire.

A Balanced Portfolio

The second major goal sought by some firms is a balanced portfolio—a balanced set of development projects in terms of a number of key parameters. The analogy is an investment fund, where the fund manager seeks balance in terms of high-risk versus blue-chip stocks, domestic versus foreign investments, and balance across industries, in order to arrive at an optimum investment portfolio.

Visual charts were favored for displaying balance in new-product project portfolios. These visual representations include the portfolio maps or bubble diagrams (Figure 2) which are an adaptation of the four-quadrant BCG (star, cash cow, dog, wildcat) diagrams, as well as more traditional pie charts and histograms.

A casual review of portfolio bubble diagrams will lead some to conclude that these new models are nothing more than the old strategy bubble diagrams of the '70s! *Not so*. Recall that the BCG strategy model, and others like it (such as the McKinsey/GE model), plotted SBUs on a market attractiveness versus business position grid. The key here is that the unit of analysis was the SBU—an existing business, and whose performance, strengths and weaknesses are all known. By contrast, although today's new-product portfolio bubble diagrams may appear similar, they plot individual new-product projects—future businesses, or *what might* be as opposed to *what is*. As for the dimensions of the grid, there too the "market attractiveness versus business position" dimensions used for existing SBUs may not be appropriate for new products; consequently, we saw other dimensions or axes being used extensively.

Dimensions To Consider

Which parameters do companies plot on these bubble diagrams in order to achieve balance? Pundits recommend various parameters and lists, and even suggest the "best plots" to use. Here is a sample list of possible parameters to consider; any pair can be the X- and Y-axes for a bubble plot (2):
- Fit with business or corporate strategy.
- Inventive merit and strategic importance to the business.
- Durability of the competitive advantage.
- Reward, based on financial expectations.
- Competitive impact of technologies (base, key, pacing, and embryonic technologies).
- Probabilities of success (technical and commercial success).
- R&D costs to completion.
- Time to completion.
- Capital and marketing investment required to exploit.

Risk-Reward Bubble Diagrams

Perhaps the most popular bubble diagram is a variant of the *risk/return diagram*. Here, one axis is some measure of the reward to the company; the other is a success probability:
- Some firms use a *qualitative estimate* of reward, ranging from "modest" to "excellent" (2). Management points out that too heavy an emphasis on financial analysis can

do serous damage, notably in the early stages of a project. The other axis is the probability of overall success (probability of *commercial* success multiplied by probability of *technical* success).

• In contrast, other firms rely on quantitative and financial gauges of reward; namely, the risk-adjusted NPV of the project (13,14). The NPV is adjusted for risk by means of a risk-adjusted discount rate to determine the NPV, applying probabilities to uncertain estimates in calculating the NPV, or via Monte Carlo simulation to determine NPV. The probability of *technical* success is the vertical axis, as probability of commercial success has already been built into the NPV calculation.

Figure 2 shows a bubble diagram for a division of a major chemical company, Company T. The size of each bubble shows the annual resources spent on each project (in Company T's case, this is dollars per year; it could also be people or work-months allocated to the project).

The four quadrants of the portfolio model are:

• *Pearls* (upper left quadrant): These are the potential star products—projects with a high likelihood of success, and which are also expected to yield a very high reward. Most firms wished they had more of these. Company T has two such Pearl projects, and one of them has been allocated considerable resources (denoted by the size of the circles).

• *Oysters* (lower left): These are the *long-shot* projects—projects with a high expected payoff, but with low likelihood of technical success. They are the projects where technical breakthroughs will pave the way for solid payoffs. Company T has three of these; none receives many resources.

• *Bread and Butter* (upper right): These are small, "no-brainer" projects—high likelihood of success but low reward. They include the many fixes, extensions, modifications, and up-dating projects of which most companies have too many. Company T has a typical over-abundance of such projects (note that the large circle here is actually a cluster of related renewal projects). More than 50 percent of spending goes to these "bread and butter" projects in Company T's case.

• *White Elephants* (lower right): These are the low-probability and low-reward projects. Every business has a few white elephants—they are inevitably difficult to kill, but Company T has far too many. One-third of the projects and about 25 percent of Company T's spending falls in the lower right White Elephant quadrant.

One attraction of this bubble diagram model is that it forces management to deal with the resource issue. Given finite resources (e.g., a limited number of people or money), *the sum of the areas of the circles must be a constant*. That is, if you add one project to the diagram, you must subtract another; alternatively, you can shrink the size of several circles. The elegance here is that the model forces management to consider the resource implications of adding one more project to the list—that some other projects must pay the price!

Also shown in this bubble diagram is the product line with which each project is associated (via the shading or cross-hatching). A final breakdown which Company T reveals via color is timing (not shown). Here, hot red means "imminent launch" while blue is cold and means "an early-stage project." Thus, this apparently simple risk/reward diagram shows a lot more than simply risk and profitability data; it also conveys resource allocation, timing, and spending breakdowns across product lines.

Figure 3. 3M Co. uses this bubble diagram to make uncertain estimates visible. Larger ellipses signify greater uncertainty.

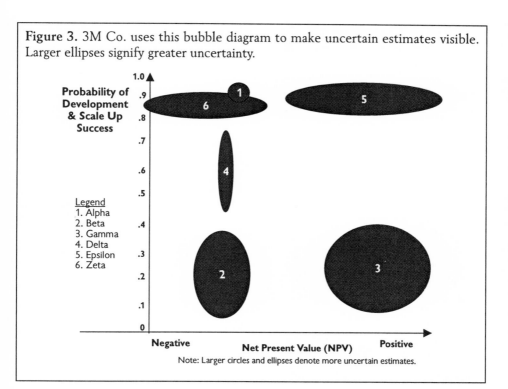

Note: Larger circles and ellipses denote more uncertain estimates.

Dealing with Uncertainties

• *3M's ellipses:* One problem with Company T's bubble diagram is that it requires a point estimate of both the reward, namely the likely or probable NPV, as well as the probability of success. Some 3M businesses use a variant of the bubble diagram to effectively portray uncertain estimates. In calculating the NPV, optimistic and pessimistic estimates are made for uncertain variables, leading to a range of NPV values for each project. Similarly low, high and likely estimates are made for the probability of technical success. The result is Figure 3, in which the size and shape of the bubbles reveal the uncertainty of projects; small bubbles mean highly certain estimates on each dimension, whereas large ellipses mean considerable uncertainty (a high spread between worst case and best case) for that project.

• *Monte Carlo simulation:* Procter & Gamble and Company M (a U.S. medical products firm) use Monte Carlo simulation to handle probabilities. P&G's portfolio model is a three-dimensional portfolio model created by three-dimensional CAD software; the three axes are NPV, time to launch, and probability of commercial success (15). Similarly, Company M uses a portfolio model similar to Company T's in Figure 3. In both firms, in order to account for commercial uncertainty, every variable—revenue, cost, launch timing, and so on—requires three estimates: a high, low and likely estimate. From these three estimates, a *probability distribution curve* is calculated for each variable. Next, random scenarios are generated for the project using these probability curves as variable inputs. Thousands of scenarios are computer-generated

Figure 4. Reckitt & Colman considers an "ease vs. attrativeness" chart to be the most useful portfolio map. Both axes are based on a weighted addition of multiple items (much like a scoring model). Solid circles represent new-product projects.

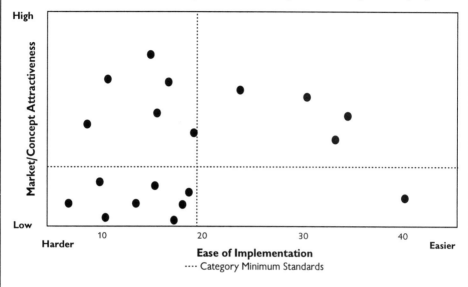

(hence, the name Monte Carlo, for thousands of spins of the wheel), and the result is a distribution of financial outcomes. From this, the expected NPV and its range is determined—an NPV figure in which all commercial outcomes and their probabilities are figured. P&G shows this range of NPVs as simply an I-beam drawn through the spheres (in P&G's three-dimensional bubble diagram, the bubbles become spheres).

Portfolio Maps Derived From Scoring Models

Reckitt & Colman uses a simpler risk-reward diagram, one of the many visual charts that comprise R&C's portfolio method (16). The most useful portfolio map, in management's view, is their "ease versus attractiveness" chart. Here, the axes are "concept attractiveness" and "ease of implementation" (Figure 4). Both axes are constructed from multi-item scored scales (scoring models).

Concept attractiveness is made up of scores on six items, including, for example, purchase intent, product advantage, sustainability of advantage, and international scope. Similarly, *ease of implementation*, the second axis, is composed of scored items, including the firms' technological strengths and the expected absence of problems in terms of development, registration, packaging, manufacturing, and distribution. Thus, R&C uses a scoring model, but in this case to construct the axes of the two-dimensional portfolio bubble diagram.

A variant on this scoring approach is employed by Speciality Minerals (17). A scoring model is used to make Go/Kill decisions at gates and also to rank-order projects

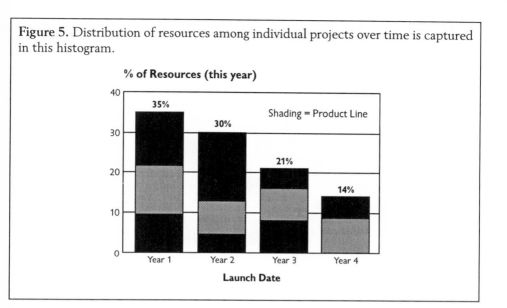

Figure 5. Distribution of resources among individual projects over time is captured in this histogram.

on a prioritization list. Seven factors are considered in the firm's scoring model: business-unit interest, customer interest, sustainability of competitive advantage, technical feasibility, credibility of the business case, fit with technical/manufacturing capabilities, and financial attractiveness. These *same factors* then provide the input data to construct the bubble diagram (not shown). For example:

• The vertical axis, labelled "value to the corporation," is composed of the financial attractiveness and competitive advantage factors, added together in a weighted fashion.

• The horizontal axis is "probability of success" and is made up of three factors: customer interest, technical feasibility, and fit with technical/manufacturing capabilities (again, a weighted addition). The unique feature here is that this company's seven-factor scoring model does double duty: It is the basis for Go/Kill decisions at gate reviews, and it provides five factors (and data) to construct the two axes of the portfolio bubble diagram. The gate decisions are thus closely linked to portfolio reviews.

Traditional Charts

There are numerous parameters, dimensions or variables across which one might wish to seek a balance of projects. As a result, we witnessed an endless variety of histograms and pie charts which help to portray portfolio balance. Some examples:

Timing is a key issue in the quest for balance. One does not wish to invest strictly in short-term projects, nor totally in long-term ones. Another timing goal is for a steady stream of new-product launches spread out over the years—constant "new news," with no sudden log-jam of product launches in any one year. The histogram in Figure 5 captures the issue of timing and portrays the distribution of resources to specific projects according to year of launch. For example, Company T allocates 35 percent of monies to four projects, all due to be launched within year 1. Another 30 percent of resources is being spent on four projects whose projected launch date is year 2, and so on.

Another timing issue is *cash flow*. Here, the desire is to balance one's projects in such a way that cash inflows are reasonably balanced with cash outflows in the business. R&C thus produces a timing histogram that portrays the total cash flow per year from all projects in the portfolio over the next few years (not shown).

Project types is yet another vital concern. What is your spending on genuine new products versus product renewals (improvements and replacements), product extensions product maintenance, cost reduction of process improvements? And what should it be? Pie charts that capture the spending split across project types are common and were found in just about every company we studied.

Market, products and technologies provide another set of dimensions across which managers sought balance. The question faced is: Do you have the appropriate split in R&D spending across your various product lines? Or across the markets or market segments in which you operate? Or across the technologies you possess? Pie charts are appropriate for capturing and displaying this type of data.

The Issue of Portfolio Balance

There is much to be said for achieving the right balance of projects in a portfolio; that is, there is more to life than simply achieving a high-value portfolio—balance is also an issue. The trouble is that achieving balance—or selecting an appropriate tool to help achieve balance—is easier conceptually than in practice.

What impressed us was how many intricate and ingenious methods and diagrams companies had invented to deal with balance. We could have filled an entire book with the maps, bubble diagrams and pie charts that we discovered. In spite of all this cleverness, however, there remain problems with the quest for balance:

1. Some of the more popular bubble diagrams suffered the same fate as the maximization models previously outlined; namely, they rely on substantial financial data when often these data are either unavailable or, at best, uncertain. Witness the popular risk-reward bubble diagrams (Figures 2 and 3) in which NPV is one of the axes.

2. There is the problem of information overload. "Maps, endless maps!" was the complaint of one exasperated executive as he leafed through more than a dozen maps plotting everything versus everything in his firm's portfolio method. Very few companies had even attempted to use all the maps and charts recommended.

3. These methods are information display, not decision models *per se*. Unlike the value maximization methods, the result is not a convenient rank-ordered list of preferred projects. Rather, these charts and maps are only a starting point for discussion. Management still has to translate the data into prioritization decisions. Some failed; too many maps, or the wrong maps, may have contributed.

4. It was not clear what the "right balance" of projects was. Managers could stare all they wanted at various charts, but unless a portfolio was obviously and extremely out of balance (as in Company T's Figure 2), how does one know whether or not one has the right balance? If one lacks an idea of what the right balance is in the first place—the *what should be*—then all these balance maps and charts—the *what is*—are meaningless: What is one comparing the existing balance against? A portfolio manager at Hewlett-Packard mused about the possibility of "having rules of thumb for optimal portfolio balance," much like the stock market portfolio manager has.

5. Finally, it wasn't clear in every case what one did with the charts and maps. At R&C, the initial inclination was to make these maps part of the gate meeting. After a few attempts, this practice was halted, as it merely added to the confusion (the company has since worked out a better method of integrating portfolio and gate decisions). At R&C, electronic portfolio maps were also used at gate meetings, but only a few times before they, too, gave up. Company G uses the maps as an after-the-fact course correction—"to make sure we have the right balance." But it was never clear what would happen if the "wrong balance" ever occurred; would management immediately start canceling projects, and approving others in the queue?

The fact that portfolio balance methods are far from perfect does not mean they should be dismissed outright. Certainly not! But such approaches should be used with care; the choice of maps (which axes to use in the plots, for example) and charts (which parameters to show) must be well thought out. Avoid the temptation to portray too many maps and charts, and be sure to test their use in portfolio reviews or gate meetings before adopting them.

Acknowledgement

The research reported in this article was generously supported by grants from: Esso Chemical Canada (Exxon in Canada) and the Innovation Research Centre at the Michael G. DeGroote School of Business, McMaster University.

References and Notes

1. The entire study and full results are available in detail in the authors' report *Portfolio Management for New Products*, McMaster University, Hamilton, Ontario, Canada, 1997. It may be ordered for $30.00 (Visa Card only) from Edgett at (905) 525-9140, ext. 27437.

2. Roussel, P., K. Saad and T. Erickson. *Third Generation R&D: Managing the Link to Corporate Strategy*. Boston, Massachusetts: Harvard Business School Press and Arthur D. Little Inc., 1991.

3. Griffin, A. and A. Page. "An Interim Report on Measuring Product Development Success and Failure." *Journal of Product Innovation Management* 9, 1 (1993): pp. 291-308.

4. Page, Albert L. "Assessing New Product Development Practices and Performance: Establishing Crucial Norms." *Journal of Product Innovation Management* 10, 4 (1993): pp. 273-290.

5. Archer, N.P. and F. Ghasemzadeh. "Project Portfolio Selection Techniques: A Review and a Suggested Integrated Approach." Innovation Research Centre Working Paper No. 46, McMaster University, 1996.

6. Baker, N.R. "R&D Project Selection Models: An Assessment." *IEEE Transactions on Engineering Management*. EM-21, 4 (1974): pp. 165-170.

7. Baker, N.R. and W.H. Pound. "R&D Project Selection: Where We Stand." *IEEE Transactions on Engineering Management*. EM-11, 4 (1964): pp. 124-134.

8. Danila, N. "Strategic Evaluation and Selection of R&D Projects." *R&D Management* 19, 1 (1989): pp. 47-62.

9. Liberatore, M.J. "A Decision Support System Linking Research and Development Project Selection with Business Strategy." *Project Management Journal* 19, 5 (1988): pp. 14-21.

10. Although we were principally interested in portfolio management for new products, to the extent that technology resources used in new products are also required for other types of projects, portfolio management must consider the fact that new-product projects compete against process developments, product maintenance projects and even fundamental research projects.

11. This decision rule of rank order according to the ratio of what one is trying to maximize divided by the constraining resource seems to be an effective one. We did simulations with a number of random sets of projects, and found that this decision rule worked very well—truly giving "maximum bang for buck"!

12. Taken from internal documents and discussions with Patricia Evans of Strategic Decisions Group.

13. Matheson, D., J. Matheson and M. Menke. "Making Excellent R&D Decisions." *Research Technology Management* (November-December 1994): pp. 21-24.

14. P. Evans. "Streamlining Formal Portfolio Management." *Scrip Magazine* (February 1996).

15. This unique three-dimensional portfolio diagram is still experimental at P&G, and is being developed by Corporate New Ventures.

16. R&C is a major multinational consumer goods firm, headquartered in the United Kingdom. In North America, familiar brands sold by R&C include Easy-Off oven cleaner, Air Wick air freshener, Lysol disinfectant cleaners, and Woolite fabric wash.

17. Specialty Minerals, a spin-off company from Pfizer, produces specialized industrial mineral products.

Reprinted from "Portfolio Management in New Product Development: Lessons from the Leaders-I" by Robert G. Cooper, Scott J. Edgett and Elko J. Kleinschmidt. *Research Technology Management*, September–October 1997, pp. 16-19, by permission of publisher. Copyright 1997 by Industrial Research Institute. All rights reserved.

An Integrated Framework for Project Portfolio Selection

Norman P. Archer and Fereidoun Ghasemzadeh

Project portfolio selection and the associated activity of managing selected projects throughout their life cycles are important activities in many organizations [1-3], since project management approaches are so commonly used in many industries for activities such as research and development of new products, implementing new systems and processes in manufacturing and information systems, and contracting engineering and construction projects. But there are usually more projects available for selection than can be undertaken within the physical and financial constraints of a firm, so choices must be made in making up a suitable project portfolio.

There are many relatively divergent techniques that can be used to estimate, evaluate, and choose project portfolios [4]. Many of these techniques are not widely used because they are too complex and require too much input data, they provide an inadequate treatment of risk and uncertainty, they fail to recognize interrelationships and interrelated criteria, they may just be too difficult to understand and use, or they may not be used in the form of an organized process [1]. But because of growing competitive pressures in the global economy, it has been suggested [5] that project portfolio analysis and planning will grow in the 1990s to become as important as business portfolio planning became in the 1970s and 1980s. Firms that wish to be competitive by selecting the most appropriate projects must therefore use techniques and procedures for portfolio selection that are based on the most critical project measures, but these techniques will not be used if they cannot be understood readily by managerial decision makers. Although there is no lack of techniques for project evaluation and portfolio selection, there is a total lack of a framework for organizing these techniques logically in a flexible process which supports the project portfolio selection process.

The objectives of this paper are to (a) evaluate briefly the current state of the art in project portfolio selection methods and to develop a number of related propositions for effective portfolio selection, based on the literature, (b) suggest an integrated framework to provide decision support for portfolio selection, allowing decision makers to utilize a desired subset of available methodologies in a flexible and logical manner and (c) describe a decision support system which can embody this framework in the support of portfolio selection activities.

Tools for *decision support*, not *decision making* tools, are emphasized in this discussion, since the thought processes in decision making should be supported and not supplanted by the tools used. This support is provided through techniques or models, data, and management of large amounts of information, so decision makers can make informed decisions based on the most important facts. To bring these points forward we examine the literature and develop a series of propositions that must be met if a framework is to be developed that will succeed in practice. Then an integrated framework is proposed which allows decision makers to choose from a variety of techniques or models, based on these propositions. This integrated approach can help decision maker(s) to select a project portfolio that maximizes the criteria of interest, suitably balanced on both quantitative and qualitative measures they choose. The approach also has provision for built-in assistance to account for different types of resource limitations and project interdependencies. Finally, a prototype decision support system is described for modeling, managing, and displaying project and portfolio information during portfolio selection.

Propositions for Project Portfolio Selection

A *project* can be defined as "a complex effort, usually less than three years in duration, made up of interrelated tasks, performed by various organizations, with a well-defined objective, schedule, and budget" [6]. A *project portfolio* is a group of projects that are carried out under the sponsorship and/or management of a particular organization. These projects must compete for scarce resources (people, finances, time, etc.) available from the sponsor, since there are usually not enough resources to carry out every proposed project which meets the organization's minimum requirements on certain criteria such as potential profitability, etc. *Project portfolio selection* is the periodic activity involved in selecting a portfolio, from available project proposals and projects currently underway, that meets the organization's stated objectives in a desirable manner without exceeding available resources or violating other constraints.

There have been many published articles and books on the subject of project evaluation and selection, discussing well over 100 different techniques [1]. Certain taxonomies of these techniques have appeared in the literature [2,7], but for the purposes of our discussion the process of portfolio selection uses project evaluation and selection techniques in a progression of three phases: *strategic considerations, individual project evaluation,* and *portfolio selection*. Techniques used in the first phase can assist in the determination of a strategic focus and overall budget allocation for the portfolio, while those in the second can be used to evaluate a project independently of other projects. The third phase deals with the selection of portfolios based on candidate project parameters, including their interactions with other projects through resource constraints or other interdependencies. In the following, each phase is considered separately. The techniques applicable to each phase are described first, followed by a series of propositions that specify requirements dealing with that phase's impact in a suitable portfolio selection framework, which will be described in a following section.

Strategic Considerations Phase

The strategic implications of portfolio selection are complex and varied [8,9] and involve considerations of factors both external and internal to the firm, including the marketplace and the company's strengths and weaknesses. These considerations can be used to build a broad perspective of strategic direction and focus, and specific initiatives for competitive advantage. This strategy can be used to develop a focused objective for a project portfolio and the level of resources needed for its support. Project portfolio matrices have been used [9] to evaluate the strategic positioning of the firm, where various criteria for a firm's position are shown on one or more displays on two descriptive dimensions. These displays can be used by decision makers to evaluate their current position and where they would like the firm to be in the future. Wheelwright and Clark [10] discuss a project mapping approach which develops a strategic direction for the firm, but Khurana and Rosenthal [11] discovered that the front end planning process is often done poorly. it is clear that the strategic direction of the firm must be determined before individual projects can be considered for a project portfolio: many firms do extensive preparation and planning of strategy before considering individual projects [12].

Proposition 1.

Strategic decisions concerning portfolio focus and overall budget considerations should be made in a broader context that takes into account both external and internal business factors, before the project portfolio is selected.

An important operational consideration is that while there are many possible methodologies that can be used in selecting a portfolio, there is no consensus on which are the most effective. As a consequence each organization tends to choose, for the project class(es) being considered, the methodologies that suit its culture and that allow it to consider the project attributes it believes are the most important [1,7,13,14]. Also, the methodologies most useful in developing a portfolio for one class of projects may not be the best for another (e.g. good estimates of quantitative values such as costs and time may be readily available for certain construction projects, but qualitative judgment is more likely to be used for development of advanced new products).

Proposition 2.

A project selection framework should be flexible enough so that stakeholders can choose in advance the particular techniques or methodologies with which they are comfortable, in analyzing relevant data and making choices of the type of projects at hand.

A major concern with most of the models for choosing project portfolios is that they are complex and difficult to use, and they require large amounts of input data [1,12]. To alleviate these problems, the portfolio selection process should be organized in a logical manner so each step moves from either a top-down (strategic considerations) or bottom-up (individual project considerations) perspective towards an integrated consideration of the projects most likely to be selected. However, each step should have a sound theoretical basis in modeling, and should generate suitable data to feed the following step. Users need access to data underlying the models, with 'drill-down' capability to develop confidence in the data being used and the decisions being made. At the same time, users should not be overloaded with unneeded data; it should be available only when needed and requested. Users also need training in the use of techniques that specify project parameters to be used in making decisions [15].

An overall balance must be achieved between the need to simplify and the need to generate well-founded and logical solutions.

Proposition 3.
To simplify the portfolio selection process, it should be organized into a number of stages, allowing decision makers to move logically towards an integrated consideration of projects most likely to be selected, based on sound theoretical models.

Proposition 4.
Users should not be overloaded with unneeded data, but should be able to access relevant data when it is needed.

Project Evaluation Phase
The benefit derived through project evaluation methods is measured in terms of each project's individual contribution to one or more portfolio objectives (e.g. return on investment). Evaluation on an individual project basis includes such methods as:
• *Economic return* [2,16]. This includes Net Present Value (NPV), Internal Rate of Return (IRR), Return on Original Investment (ROI), Return on Average Investment (RAI), PayBack Period (PBP), and Expected Value (EV). The latter allows a consideration of risk at various project stages, usually based on either IRR or NPV. These techniques include time dependency consideration of investment and income flows. The Capital Asset Pricing Model (CAPM) can also be used [17,18]. A 1991 industry survey of the use of the above techniques (not including CAPM) indicated a movement towards the use of NPV, a moderate reduction in use of IRR, and a significant reduction in the use of PBP [16] when compared to a 1978 survey.
• *Benefit/cost techniques* [19] involve the calculation of a ratio of benefits to costs, where inputs may be derived from present value calculations of both benefits and costs, to transform them to the same time basis.
• *Risk* is a combination of the probability of an event (usually an undesirable occurrence) and the consequences associated with that event. Every project has some risk associated with not meeting the objectives specified for the project. To analyze project risk, a project is first decomposed into component activities, forming the project's work breakdown structure (WBS). Depending on the depth of analysis appropriate at the point in the project's life cycle, the WBS can range from relatively simple (e.g. development and market activities during early feasibility analysis of a new product) to complex (e.g. detailed breakdown of activities for the business plan prior to commitment for full scale development). Risk events relating to each activity are then identified, and their probabilities and consequences estimated. Information used in estimating risk can be derived from expert opinion, technical data, or previous experience with similar projects. A model which combines the risks from each activity, including interdependent events, can then be used to estimate overall project risk. Models used in analyzing risk include Monte Carlo simulation, decision theory and Bayesian statistical theory [2,19,21], and decision theory combined with influence diagram approaches [13,22]. Risk is important when considering the inclusion of a project in a portfolio, and a portfolio should be 'balanced' by avoiding an over-commitment to high risk projects that may jeopardize the future of the organization.

- *Market research* approaches can be used to collect data for forecasting the demand for new products or services, based on concepts or prototypes presented to potential customers, to gauge the potential market. Techniques used include consumer panels, focus groups, perceptual maps, and preference mapping, among many others [23].

The use of specific project evaluation techniques is situation dependent. For example, a product development organization may use market research, economic return, and risk analysis to develop project characteristics that can be useful in selection exercises. Or a government agency may use economic and cost benefit measures. Measures used may be qualitative or quantitative, but regardless of which techniques are used to derive them, a set of common measures should be used so projects can be compared equitably during portfolio selection.

Proposition 5.

Common measures should be chosen which can be calculated separately for each project under consideration. These will allow an equitable comparison of projects during the portfolio selection process.

Selection of, or adjustments to, a project portfolio is a process which recurs. Existing projects require resources from the available pool, and therefore their schedules and resource requirements interact with potential new projects. It is common practice to re-evaluate at major 'milestones' [3] or 'gates' [1] to determine whether they merit continuing development.

Proposition 6.

Current projects that have reached major milestones or gates should be re-evaluated at the same time as new projects being considered for selection. This allows a combined portfolio to be generated within available resource constraints at regular intervals due to (a) project completion or abandonment, (b) new project proposals, (c) changes in strategic focus, (d) revisions to available resources, and (e) changes in the environment.

The number of projects which may be proposed for the portfolio may be quite large [12], and the complexity of the decision process and the amount of time required to choose the portfolio increases geometrically with the number of projects to be considered. In addition, the likelihood of making sound business choices may be compromised if large numbers of projects must be considered unnecessarily. For this reason, screening processes should be used to eliminate projects in advance that are clearly deficient, before the portfolio selection stage of the process begins. For example, screening may be used to eliminate projects which do not match the strategic focus of the firm, do not yet have sufficient information upon which to base a logical decision, do not meet a marginal requirement such as minimum internal rate of return, etc.

Proposition 7.

Screening should be used, based on carefully specified criteria, to eliminate projects from consideration before the portfolio selection process is undertaken.

Portfolio Selection Phase

Portfolio selection involves the simultaneous comparison of a number of projects on particular dimensions, in order to arrive at a desirability ranking of the projects. The most highly ranked projects under the evaluation criteria are than selected for the portfolio, subject to resource availability. Classes of available portfolio selection techniques include:

• *Ad hoc approaches* such as (a) Profiles [2], a crude form of scoring model, where limits are set for the various attribute levels of a project, and any projects which fail to meet these limits are eliminated (study of the human-computer interface aspects of such approaches have shown [24] that users prefer these minimum effort approaches, whether or not they give an optimal solution), and (b) Interactive selection [7], involving an interactive and iterative process between project champions and responsible decision maker(s) until a choice of the best projects is made.

• *Comparative approaches* include Q-Sort [25], pairwise comparison [2], the Analytic Hierarchy Procedure (AHP) [26], dollar metric, standard gamble, and successive comparison [27,28]. Q-Sort is the most adaptable of these in achieving group consensus. In these methods, first the weights of different objectives are determined, then alternatives are compared on the basis of their contributions to these objectives, and finally a set of project benefit measures is computed. Once the projects have been arranged on a comparative scale, the decision maker(s) can proceed from the top of the list, selecting projects until available resources are exhausted. With these techniques, both quantitative and qualitative and/or judgment criteria can be considered. A major disadvantage of Q-sort, pairwise comparison and AHP is the large number of comparisons involved, making them difficult to use for comparing large numbers of projects. Also, any time a project is added or deleted from the list, the process must be repeated.

• *Scoring models* [2] use a relatively small number of decision criteria, such as cost, work force availability, probability of technical success, etc., to specify project desirability. The merit of each project is determined with respect to each criterion. Scores are then combined (when different weights are used for each criterion, the technique is called 'Weighted Factor Scoring') to yield an overall benefit measure for each project. A major advantage is that projects can be added or deleted without re-calculating the merit of other projects.

• *Portfolio matrices* [5,9] can be used as strategic decision making tools. They can also be used to prioritize and allocate resources among competing projects [29]. This technique relies on graphical representations of the projects under consideration, on two dimensions such as the likelihood of success and expected economic value. This allows a representative mix of projects on the dimensions represented to be selected.

• *Optimization models* select from the list of candidate projects a set that provides maximum benefit (e.g. maximum net present value). These models are generally based on some form of mathematical programming, to support the optimization process and to include project interactions such as resource dependencies and constraints, technical and market interactions, or program considerations [2,30]. Some of these models also support sensitivity analysis [19], but most do not seem to be used extensively in practice [31]. Probable reasons for disuse include the need to collect large amounts of input data, the inability of most such models to include risk considerations, and model complexity. Optimization models may also be used with other approaches which calculate project benefit values. For example, 0-1 integer linear programming can be used in conjunction with AHP to handle qualitative measures and multiple objectives, while applying resource utilization, project interaction, and other constraints [32].

Multiple and often conflicting objectives (or criteria) may be associated with portfolio selection, and projects may be highly interdependent. This could be due to value contribution, resource utilization, or mutual exclusion. For example, before project C can be undertaken, projects A and B must be completed, since their outputs feed project C. In addition, resource constraints such as available capital and technical workforce over the planning horizon should be considered, including resource time dependencies.

Proposition 8.
Project interactions through direct dependencies or resource competition must be considered in portfolio selection.

Many portfolio selection techniques do not consider the time-dependent resource requirements of projects [2], and most implicitly assume that all projects selected will start immediately. This does not fit the reality of project management, where projects compete for limited resources, should be scheduled to use resources as smoothly as possible in time, and should be completed within some planned interval.

Proposition 9.
Portfolio selection should take into account the time-dependent nature of project resource consumption.

One of the drawbacks of model-based optimal portfolio selection methods [2,30] is that they may proceed to portfolio selection without intervention by decision maker(s) who may wish to make desirable adjustments to the selected portfolio [29]. If the emphasis of a system is to be on decision support rather than decision making, decision makers must be able to make adjustments, but they should receive feedback on the resulting consequences, in terms of optimality changes and effects on resources.

Proposition 10.
Decision makers should be provided with interactive mechanisms for controlling and overriding portfolio selections generated by any algorithms or models, and they should also receive feedback on the consequences of such changes.

Portfolio selection is usually a committee process, where objective criteria such as predicted rate of return and expected project cost are mingled with subjective criteria relating to the needs of the different organizations represented on the project selection committee. All committee members should have access to information with which project inter-comparisons are made, as well as information on the project portfolio as a whole. Decision making environments for group decision support are available, which allow interactions among the decision makers as well as between decision makers and the support system [33]. This allows portfolio selection decisions to be made that more closely meet the overall objectives of the organization.

Proposition 11.
Project portfolio selection must be adaptable to group decision support environments.

Project Portfolio Selection Framework
Among published methodologies for project portfolio selection, there has been little progress towards achieving an integrated framework that decomposes the process into

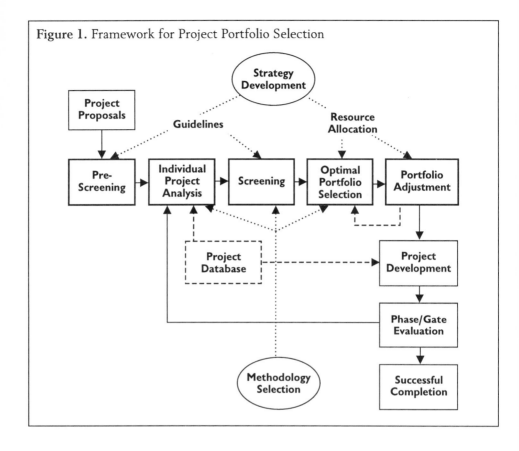

Figure 1. Framework for Project Portfolio Selection

a flexible and logical series of activities that involve full participation by the selection committee. Such an approach could take advantage of the best characteristics of a combination of existing methods well grounded in theory. Other attempts to build integrated support for portfolio selection have been reported [7,34,35]. However, these have been limited and specific to the methods used, rather than providing flexible choices of techniques and interactive system support for users. Based on the propositions outlined in the foregoing discussion, an integrated framework for project portfolio selection suited to decision support system (DSS) application is described in the following (relevant propositions are abbreviated as P*x*, where *x* is the number of the proposition indicated in the previous section).

Stages in the Project Portfolio Selection Framework
In line with considerations of simplification (P3), we decomposed the selection process into a series of discrete stages which progress from initial broad strategy considerations towards the final solution. This is depicted in *Figure 1*, where the major stages are represented by the heavy outlined boxes. The ovals in the diagram represent pre-process activities, which we also discuss. Post-process stages (that follow the portfolio selection process) are also shown in the lightly outlined boxes for completeness, since these may

result in data generation and project evaluation during development that may also affect portfolio selection at some future time. We now consider the sequential activities that go into developing the portfolio. Since we know the desired end result, which is an optimal or near-optimal portfolio that satisfies the constraints placed on it by the selection committee, it is best to analyze the process from end to beginning, to show how information needed for models/techniques used at each stage is made available from previous stages.

Portfolio adjustment. The end result is to be a portfolio which meets the objectives of the organization optimally or near-optimally, but with provisions (P10) for final judgmental adjustments which are difficult to anticipate and include in a model. Selecting a project portfolio is a strategic decision, and the relevant information must be presented so it allows decision makers to evaluate the portfolio without being overloaded with unnecessary information (P4). The final stage is a portfolio adjustment stage which provides an overall view, where the characteristics of projects of critical importance in an optimized portfolio (e.g. risk, net present value, time-to-complete, etc.) can be represented, using matrix-type displays, along with the impact of any suggested changes on resources or selected projects. It is important to use only a limited number of such displays, to avoid confusion (cognitive overload) while the final decisions are being made. Users should be able to make changes at this stage and, if these changes are substantially different from the optimal portfolio developed in the previous stage, it may be necessary to re-cycle back to re-calculate portfolio parameters such as project schedules and time-dependent resource requirements. In addition, sensitivity analysis should be available to predict and display the impact of change (addition or deletion of projects) on resources and portfolio optimality (P10).

An important aspect of portfolio adjustment is achieving some form of balance among the projects selected, again through user interaction (P10). This will require interactive displays on certain portfolio dimensions, such as risk, size of project, and short term vs. long term projects while adjustments are being made.

For example, the proposition of high risk projects should not be too high due to the fact that failures of several of these projects could be dangerous to the future of the company. On the other hand, low risk projects may not carry the high return that is often typical of risky projects, so the expected return from the portfolio may be too low if project selection is too conservative on the risk dimension. Balance on project size is also important, because the commitment of a high proportion of resources to a few large projects can be catastrophic if more than one fails. And too many long term projects, no matter how promising they are, may cause financing or cash flow problems.

Optimal portfolio selection. Performed in the second-last stage. Here, interactions among the various projects are considered, including interdependencies, competition for resources, and timing (P8,P9), with the value of each project determined from a common set of parameters that were estimated for each project in the previous stage. AHP, scoring models, and portfolio matrices are popular among decision makers for portfolio selection, because they allow users to consider a broad range of quantitative and qualitative characteristics as well as multiple objectives. However, none of these techniques consider multiple resource constraints and project interdependence. AHP, pairwise comparison, and Q-sort also become cumbersome and unwieldy for larger numbers of projects. A serious drawback of portfolio matrices is that they do not appear to meet stated objectives such as profit maximization [36], so this approach should not be considered for the portfolio selection stage.

We suggest a two-step process for the portfolio selection stage. In the first step, the relative total benefit is determined for each project. A comparative approach such as Q-Sort, pairwise comparison, or AHP, may be used in this step for smaller sets of projects, allowing qualitative as well as quantitative measures to be considered. This may involve extensive work by committee members in comparing potential project pairs. For large sets of projects, scoring models are more suitable as these do not involve comparison of large numbers of project pairs. The result of either of these approaches would be to establish the relative worth of the projects.

In the second step of this stage, all project interactions, resource limitations, and other constraints should be included in an optimization of the overall portfolio, based on the relative worth of each proposed project. If all the project measures could be expressed quantitatively, the foregoing step could be omitted since optimization could be performed directly in a mathematical program in the second step. In the unusual case where interdependence and timing constraints were not important, and there is only one resource that is binding, it might be tempting in the second step to simply select the highest valued projects until available resources were used up. However, this does not necessarily select an optimal portfolio (combinations of certain projects may produce a higher total benefit than individual projects with higher individual benefits). The relative worth of each project should therefore be input to a computerized process, which can be a 0-1 integer linear programming model that applies resource, timing, interdependence, and other constraints to maximize total benefit (P8, P9) [32]. Goal programming [30] may be used for multiple objectives in this step, if more than one objective is explicitly identified.

Screening. Shown in *Figure 1* following the individual project analysis stage. Screening may use such techniques as Profiles. Here, project attributes from the previous stage are examined in advance of the regular selection process (P6, P7), to eliminate any projects or inter-related families of projects which do not meet pre-set criteria such as estimated rate of return, except for those projects which are mandatory or required to support other projects still being considered. The intent is to eliminate any non-starters and reduce the number of projects to be considered simultaneously in the Portfolio Selection stage (P7). Care should be taken to avoid setting thresholds which are too arbitrary, to prevent the elimination of projects which may otherwise be very promising.

Individual project analysis. The fourth from last stage, where a common set of parameters required for the next stage is calculated separately for each project, based on estimates available from feasibility studies and/or from a database of previously completed projects. Such techniques were discussed previously. For example, project risk, net present worth, return on investment, etc. can be calculated at this point, including estimated uncertainty in each of the parameter estimates (P5). Scoring, benefit contribution, risk analysis, market research, or checklists may also be used. Note that current projects which have reached certain milestones may also be re-evaluated at this time, but estimates related to such projects will tend to have less uncertainty than those projects which are proposed but not yet underway. The output from this stage is a common set of parameter estimates for each project. For example, if the method to be used were a combination of net present value combined with risk analysis, data required would include estimates of costs and returns at each development stage of a product or service, including the risks. Uncertainty could be in the form of likely ranges for the uncertain parameters. Other data needed could include qualitative variables such as policy or political measures. Quantitative output could be each project's expected net value, risk, and resource requirements over the project's time frame, including calculated uncertainties in these parameters (P5).

Pre-screening. Precedes portfolio calculations. It uses manually applied guidelines developed in the strategy development stage, and ensures that any project being considered for the portfolio fits the strategic focus of the portfolio (P1,P7). Essential requirements before the project passes this stage should also include a feasibility analysis and estimates of parameters needed to evaluate each project, as well as a project champion who will be a source of further information. Mandatory projects are also identified at this point, since they will be included in the remainder of the portfolio selection process. Mandatory projects are projects agreed upon for inclusion, including improvements to existing products no longer competitive, projects without which the organization could not function adequately, etc.

A pre-process stage provides high level guidance to the portfolio selection process. Activities in this stage appear in ovals in *Figure 1*. These include 'Strategy Development' (P1) (determination of strategic focus and setting resource constraints), and 'Methodology Selection' (P2, P5) (choosing the techniques the organization wishes to use for portfolio selection). Determination of strategic focus may be carried out at higher managerial levels than the portfolio selection committee, because it very much involves the firm's strategic direction. Strategy development is an unstructured process which can consume a great deal of managerial time [12], but is critical if the portfolio selected is to promote the business objectives of the firm. Only occasional adjustments will be needed for strategic guidelines developed at this point in the process, although the portfolio selection process itself recurs at regular planning intervals.

Resource allocation to different project categories also involves high level decisions which must be made before the portfolio selection process (P1). Choosing and implementing techniques suitable to the project class at hand, the organization's culture, problem solving style, and project environment may also depend upon previous experience. Methodology selection (P2, P5) should be based on committee understanding of, and experience with, the candidate methodologies, or their willingness to learn new approaches. The methodology selection stage would not normally be repeated, unless the committee found other methodologies which were better matches to · their preferences.

Stages in the project portfolio selection framework (*Figure 1*) are organized logically, in a manner which allows decision makers to work through the portfolio selection process logically (P3). Each stage involves methodology choices which are at the discretion of users (P2), in order to gain maximum acceptance and cooperation of decision makers with the portfolio selection process. *Table 1* summarizes the stages in the framework, the associated activities, and some of the potential methodologies previously mentioned, for each stage.

Table 1. Activities and Methodologies in the Portfolio Selection Framework

Process Stage	Selection Stage	Activity	Potential Methodologies
Pre-process	Strategy development, methodology selection, development of strategic focus, resource constraints, choice of model techniques	Strategic mapping, portfolio matrices, cluster analysis, etc.	
Portfolio selection process	Pre-screening	Rejection of projects which do not meet portfolio criteria	Manually applied criteria, strategic focus, champion, feasibility study available
	Individual project anaylsis	Calculation of common parameters for each project	Decision trees, uncertainty est., NPV, ROI, etc., resource requirements est., etc.
	Screening	Rejecting non-viable projects	Ad hoc techniques (e.g., profiles)
	Portfolio selection	Integrated consideration of project attributes, resource constraints, interactions	AHP, constrained option, scoring models, sensitivity analysis
	Portfolio adjustment	User-directed adjustments	Matrix displays, sensitivity analysis
Post-process	Final portfolio	Project development	Project management techniques, data collection

Decision Support Systems Considerations

The framework we have outlined can be used for project portfolio selection in an environment which is only partially supported by computerized modeling and databases, since users are given the flexibility of choosing their own techniques or models at each stage. However, the set of main stages (heavy outlined boxes) in the framework (*Figure 1*) can be integrated into a Decision Support System (DSS) including a carefully designed model management module that handles models of the many different types which may be chosen. These models require a common interface through which data may be interchanged. The system involves considerations of model representation and integration [37,40].

Integrated modeling approaches which have been suggested include *process integration* [37]. Process integration is useful when heterogeneous models (models from different paradigms) are to be integrated, as in our framework. The major issues that arise during process integration are *synchronization* and *variable correspondence*. Synchronization deals with the order in which models must be executed, and timing of dynamic interactions among the models. Variable correspondence deals with input/output relationships among the component variables in the various models being

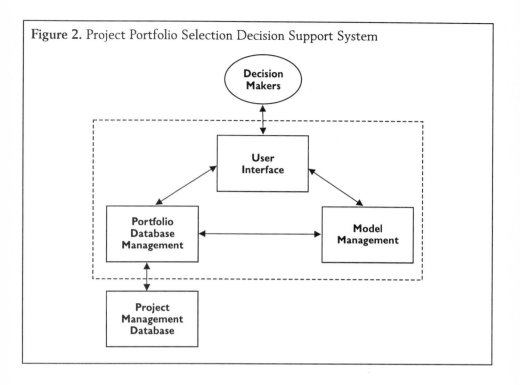

Figure 2. Project Portfolio Selection Decision Support System

used, and assuring dimensional consistency among these variables. In our proposed framework, models are not executed in parallel. They typically terminate after transferring their outputs for use by subsequent models, so synchronization in this case is not a critical issue. To handle variable correspondence, a central database can be used. This can act first as a data repository which is open to inspection by users during the portfolio selection process, and secondly as a transfer site to provide matched data for the input and output variables of the various models being used.

Decision Support System Application

From the foregoing and from *Figure 1*, in all process stages the decision makers would interact with the proposed system, which provides supporting models and data. Data could either be input directly, generated by models as they are used, or extracted from existing project management databases containing information useful to the analysis of the candidate projects (see *Figure 1*). Provision for continuous interaction between system and decision makers is required because: (a) it is extremely difficult to formulate explicitly in advance all of the preferences of the decision makers, (b) involvement of decision makers in the solution process indirectly motivates successful implementation of the selected projects, and (c) interactive decision making (P10) has been accepted as the most appropriate way to obtain correct preferences [14]. If this interaction is to be supported by a computer-based system, a module is required to manage the related techniques/models, and another module to support data needs. This is shown in *Figure 2* as a Decision Support System [33].

Published work on group attempts to reach consensus on portfolios includes work by Souder [41], who explored combinations of paired comparisons, group discussions, and member interactions in decision making of this type. Group Decision Support Systems (GDSS) are DSS which facilitate the solution of unstructured problems by groups of decision makers. A GDSS provides support for the exchange of ideas, opinions, and preferences [42], and is clearly a requirement of a portfolio selection DSS (P11). A GDSS may be implemented at one location, or it may involve simultaneous communication among decision makers at different sites. It can be a simple computer-projected display on a large screen visible to committee members, or a system where each committee member sees a separate display with which he or she interacts, using computer-based models and data independently of others. These results are shared through a common system and display [33], to aid in developing a consensus.

Prototype interface

As shown in *Figure 2*, a DSS for project portfolio selection includes the following modules:

1. Project portfolio database management.
2. A model management module to support the techniques or models to be used.
3. A user interface to the model management and database management modules.
4. Not shown here are GDSS extensions to allow individual private work spaces in the database during committee portfolio selection activities.

An additional link is included to the project management database, a useful source of information for project attribute estimation and decision making, based on previous project results.

We have developed a PC Windows-based prototype interface, for experimental studies of the portfolio adjustment stage of the proposed framework, which is the stage where user-system interactions are most critical to the successful use of the DSS. This interface includes a link to database management software to support the portfolio database [43].

Features included in the interface include a list of currently selected projects, which can be shown as a window overlay of the interface. A graphical display is used to display projects as circles on a two-dimensional presentation, where the dimensions can be chosen to represent project parameters such as risk level, project time span, estimated market, etc. Projects currently selected are shown as dark hatched circles, where the area of the circle is proportional to the benefit (e.g. net present value) available from that project. Projects not selected are shown as open circles. Interdependencies of projects with certain other projects are shown by arrows between the corresponding circles on the display. An arrow to a circle representing another project indicates that this project must precede the other project (P8).

More information about each project can be displayed simply by pressing the right mouse button on the relevant circle (P4). The percentage of resources still available and unassigned from the total budget are also shown as sidebars in the display. Also shown are the percentage of committed resources allocated to projects on each dimension of the display. A project's status may be changed between 'selected' and 'de-selected' simply by moving the cursor to the corresponding circle and clicking on it (P10). Changes to resource consumption due to such a change are displayed immediately. Users are not allowed to de-select projects upon which another selected project depends. Modifications may be made to this interface according to user requirements (P2), including the choice of project dimensions displayed, the dimension related to circle size, resources displayed, etc.

Discussion

The framework we propose is basically an attempt to simplify and organize the project portfolio selection process. It matches considerations which are important to decision makers who need to make portfolio selection decisions. Since decision makers should be directly involved with the selection process at each of its stages, support tools (either manual or computer-based) will be essential to implement each technique used, and the framework leaves the choice of specific techniques up to the decision makers. This generic approach also allows each technique chosen to be integrated into a decision support system which provides far better and more acceptable project portfolios than those which can be generated by any single technique we have discussed. Because of the staging concept, it is possible to eliminate certain stages if the organization finds it more efficient to do so. After the first application of the framework, strategy development and methodology selection need only be reviewed as required, and not every time the portfolio is reconsidered. Also, for example, screening is discretionary since it is used only to reduce the number of projects (and therefore complexity) in the portfolio selection stage. This may not be needed if the number of projects is small or if there are interdependencies among all the projects being considered. And in the portfolio selection stage, the optimization process may be simplified in various ways, depending on the circumstances.

An integrated DSS can support these activities, first as a model management system, and second as a repository of data related to all the projects being considered. This is clearly adaptable to a group support system, which is essential if the system is to be used in the real world of business, where most such decisions are made by committees. The prototype described here is a demonstration of the major interactive components of such a system.

Based on the results we have obtained, an extensive development effort is underway to implement the suggested framework as an integrated decision support system, and to test it in real decision-making situations. This system will include a powerful linear programming package to generate optimal solutions, a database management system as a data repository, modeling packages which interface with the data repository, and a highly interactive and user-friendly interface, programmed through a rapid application development environment. An initial testing phase will be to evaluate the usability and usefulness of the system in a laboratory environment, in order to eliminate flaws in the interface design. A second phase will be to demonstrate the system to users in real application environments, to get feedback on further refinements to the system's modeling capabilities. A third phase will be to implement the system in several corporate environments, and determine which refinements are needed to tailor it to company use. Included in this phase will be an evaluation of the system in a group decision environment.

From the framework we have established, it is also clear that further research is needed into the generic requirements for decision support in project portfolio selection, including: (a) determining which modeling techniques are preferred by decision makers, and how to simplify some of the more useful techniques to make them more acceptable, (b) finding in which situations input information requirements can be supported by data gathered from existing projects, and which inputs can be provided by estimates or values generated from economic models, and (c) examining the scope of strategic decisions which are made outside the purview of the portfolio selection process, to ease the process of portfolio selection.

Acknowledgements
This research was supported by a grant from the Innovation Research Centre, Michael G. DeGroote School of Business, McMaster University.

References
1. Cooper, Robert G., *Winning At New Products*, 2nd edn. Addison-Wesley, Reading, MA, 1993.
2. Martino, Joseph P., *R&D Project Selection*. Wiley, New York, NY, 1995
3. Meredith, Jack R. and Mantel, Samuel J., Jr., *Project Management: A Managerial Approach*, 3rd edn. Wiley, New York, 1995.
4. Santos, B.L., Selecting information system projects: problems, solutions and challenges. *Hawaii Conference on System Sciences*, 1989, pp. 1131-1140.
5. Roussel, P. Saad, K. and Erickson, T., *Third Generation R&D: Managing the Link to Corporate Strategy*. Harvard Business School Press, Cambridge, MA, 1991.
6. Archibald, Russell D., *Managing High-Technology Programs and Projects*, 2nd edn. Wiley, New York, 1992.
7. Hall, D.L. and Nauda, A., An interactive approach for selecting IR&D projects. *IEEE Trans. Eng. Management*, 1990, 37(2), 126-133.
8. Hax, Arnoldo C. and Majluf, Nicolas S., *Strategic Management: An Integrative Perspective*. Prentice-Hall, Englewood Cliffs, NJ, 1984.
9. Hax, Arnoldo and Majluf, Nicolas S., *The Strategy Concept and Process: A Pragmatic Approach*, 3nd edn. Prentice-Hall, Upper Saddle River, NJ, 1996.
10. Wheelwright, Steven C. and Clark, Kim B., Creating project plans to focus product development. *Harvard Business Review*, 1992, 70(2), 70-82.
11. Khurana, Anil and Rosenthal, Stephen R., Integrating the fuzzy front end of new product development. *Sloan Management Review*, 1997, 38, 103-120.
12. Cooper, R.G., Edgett, S.J. and Kleinschmidt, E.J., *Portfolio Management for New Products*, Innovation Research Centre, McMaster School of Business, Hamilton, ON, 1997.
13. Krumm, F. and Rolle, C.F., Management and application of decision and risk analysis in Du Pont. *Interfaces*, 1992, 22(6), 84-93.
14. Mukherjee, Kampan, Application of an interactive method for MOLIP in project selection decision: case from Indian coal mining industry. *Int. J. Prod. Econ.*, 1994, 36, 203-211.
15. Kao, Diana and Archer, Norman P., Abstraction in conceptual model design. *Int. J. Human Computer Systems*, 1997, 46, 125-150.
16. Remer, Donald S., Stokdyk, Scott B. and Van Driel, Mike. Survey of project evaluation techniques currently used in industry. *Int. J. Prod. Econ.*, 1993, 32, 103-115.
17. Khan, Arshad M. and Fiorino, Donald P., The capital asset pricing model in project selection: a case study. *The Engineering Economist*, 1992, 37(2), 145-159.
18. Sharpe, W.F., Capital asset prices: a theory of market equilibrium under conditions of risk. *J. Finance*, 1964, 425-442.
19. Canada, John R. and White, John A., *Capital Investment Decision Analysis for Management and Engineering*. Prentice-Hall, Englewood Cliffs, NJ, 1980.
20. Hess, Sidney W., Swinging on the branch of a tree: project selection applications. *Interfaces*, 1993, 23(6), 5-12.
21. Riggs, Jeffrey L., Brown, Sheila B. and Trueblood, Robert P., Integration of technical, cost, and schedule risks in project management. *Comp. and Oper. Res.*, 1994, 21(5), 521-533.

22. Rzasa, Philip V., Faulkner, Terrence W. and Sousa, Nancy L., Analyzing R&D portfolios at Eastman Kodak. *Res. Tech. Management*, 1990, Jan-Feb, 27-32.

23. Wind, Yoram, Mahajan, Vijay and Cardozo, Richard N., *New Product Forecasting*. Lexington Books, Lexington, MA, 1981.

24. Todd, Peter and Benbasat, Izak, An experimental investigation of the relationship between decision makers, decision aids, and decision making effort. *INFOR.*, 1993, 31(2), 80-100.

25. Souder, William E., *Project Selection and Economic Appraisal*. Van Nostrand Reinhold, New York, NY, 1984.

26. Saaty, Thomas L., Rogers, Paul C. and Pell, Ricardo, Portfolio selection through hierarchies. *J. Portfolio Management*, 1980, 6(3), 16-21.

27. Churchman, C.W. and Ackoff, R.L. An approximate measure of value. *Operations Res.* 2, 1954.

28. Pessemier, E.A. and Baker, N.R., Project and program decisions in research and development. *R&D Management*, Vol. 2, No. 1, 1971.

29. Morison, A. and Wensley, R., Boxing up or boxed in? A short history of the Boston Consulting Group share growth matrix. *J. Marketing Management*, 1991, 7, 105-129.

30. Santhanam, R., Muralidhar, K. and Schniederjans, M., A zero-one programming approach for information system project selection. *OMEGA, 1989*, 17(6), 583-593.

31. Souder, W.E. Analytical effectiveness of mathematical models for R&D project selection. *Management Science*, 1973, 19(8), 907-923.

32. Ghasemzadeh, F., Iyogun, P. and Archer, N., A zero-one ILP model for project portfolio selection. *Innovation Research Centre Working Paper*, Michael G. DeGroote School of Business, McMaster University, Hamilton, ON, 1996.

33. Turban, Efraim, *Decision Support and Expert Systems*, 4th edn. Prentice-Hall, Englewood Cliffs, NJ, 1995.

34. De Maio, Adriano, Verganti, Roberto and Corso, Mariano, A multi-project management framework for new product development. *Eur. J. Oper. Res.*, 1994, 78, 178-191.

35. Kira, Dennis S., Kusy, Martin I., Murray, David H. and Goranson, Barbara J., A specific decision support system (SDS) to develop an optimal project portfolio mix under uncertainty. *IEEE Trans. Eng. Management*, 1990, 37(3), 213-221.

36. Armstrong, J. Scott and Brodie, Roderick J. Effects of portfolio planning methods on decision making: experimental results. *Int. J. Res. Marketing*, 1994, 11, 73-84.

37. Dolk, Daniel R. and Kottemann, Jeffrey E., Model integration and a theory of models. *Decision Support Systems*, 1993, 9, 51-63.

38. Geoffrion, A.M., An introduction to structured modeling. *Management Science*, 1987, 33(5), 547-588.

39. Kottemann, Jeffrey E. and Dolk, Daniel R., Model integration and modeling languages: a process perspective. *Inf. Systems Res.*, 1992, 3(1), 1-16.

40. Muhanna, Waleed A. and Pick, Roger A., Meta-modeling concepts and tools for model management: a systems approach. *Management Science*, 1994, 40(9), 1093-1123.

41. Souder, William E., Achieving organizational consensus with respect to R&D project selection criteria. *Management Science*, 1975, 21(6), 669-681.

42. Finholt, T. and Sproull, L.S., Electronic groups at work. *Org. Sci.* Vol. 1. No. 1, 1990.

43. Archer, N.P. and Ghasemzadeh, F., Project portfolio selection management through decision support: a system prototype. *Innovation Research Centre Working Paper No. 49*, School of Business, McMaster University, Hamilton, ON, 1996.

Reprinted from *International Journal of Project Management*, Vol. 17, No. 4, pp. 207-216, by N.P. Archer and F. Ghasemzadeh, Copyright 1999, with permission from Elsevier Science.

Project Selection

Jack R. Meredith and Samuel J. Mantel, Jr.

Project selection is the process of evaluating individual projects or groups of projects, and then choosing to implement some set of them so that the objectives of the parent organization will be achieved. This same systematic process can be applied to any area of the organization's business in which choices must be made between competing alternatives. For example, a manufacturing firm can use evaluation/selection techniques to choose which machine to adopt in a part-fabrication process; a TV station can pick out which of several syndicated comedy shows to rerun in its 7:30 PM weekday time-slot; a trucking firm can use these methods to decide which of several tractors to purchase; a construction firm can select the best subset of a large group of potential projects on which to bid; a hospital can find the best mix of psychiatric, orthopedic, obstetric, pediatric, and other beds for a new wing; or a research lab can choose the set of R&D projects that holds the best promise of reaching a technological goal.

Realists cannot solve problems, only idealists can do that. Reality is far too complex to deal with in its entirety. The reality of this page, for instance, includes the weight of ink imprinted on it as well as the number of atoms in the period at the end of this sentence. Those aspects of reality are not relevant to a decision about the proper width of the left margin or the precise position of the page number. An "idealist" is needed to strip away almost all the reality from a problem, leaving only the aspects of the "real" situation with which he or she wishes to deal. This process of carving away the unwanted reality from the bones of a problem is called *modeling the problem*. The idealized version of the problem that results is called a *model*.

The model represents the problem's *structure*, its form. Every problem has a form, though often we may not understand a problem well enough to describe its structure. Several different types of models are available to make the job of modeling the problem easier. *Iconic* models are physical representations of systems. The category includes everything from teddy bears to the dowel rod and styrofoam model of an atom hanging from the ceiling of a high school chemistry lab. *Analog* models are similar to reality in some respects and different in others. Traditionally, every student of elementary physics was exposed to the hydraulic analogy to explain electricity. This model emphasized the similarities between water pressure and voltage, between the flow of water and the flow of electrical current, between the reservoir and the capacitor. *Verbal* models use words to describe systems—George Orwell's novel *Animal Farm*, for example. *Diagrammatic* models may be used to explain the hierarchical command structure of an army battalion or a business firm, just as *graphic* models may be used to illustrate the equilibrium solution to problems of supply and demand. We will use all these models in this book, as well as *flow graph* and *network* models to help solve scheduling problems, *matrix* models to aid in project evaluation, and *symbolic* (mathematical) models for a number of purposes.

This wide variety of models allows the decision maker considerable choice. Most problems can be modeled in several different ways, and it is often not difficult to transform a problem from one model to another—the transformation from matrix to network to mathematical models, for instance, is usually straightforward. The decision maker usually has some leeway in selecting the model form.

Models may be quite simple to understand, or they may be extremely complex. In general, introducing more reality into a model tends to make the model more difficult to manipulate. If the input data for a model are not known precisely, we often use probabilistic information; that is, the model is said to be *stochastic* rather than *deterministic*. Again, in general, stochastic models are more difficult to manipulate. (Readers who are not familiar with the fundamentals of decision making might find a book such as *The New Science of Management Decisions* [57] or *Fundamentals of Management Science* [65] useful.) A few of the models we discuss employ mathematical programming techniques for solution. These procedures are rarely used, but they illustrate a logic that can be useful; and it is not necessary to understand mathematical programming to profit from the discussion.

Criteria for Project Selection Models

We live in the midst of what has been called the "knowledge explosion." We frequently hear such comments as "90 percent of all we know about physics has been discovered since Albert Einstein published his original work on special relativity"; and "80 percent of what we know about the human body has been discovered in the past 50 years." In addition, evidence is cited to show that knowledge is growing exponentially. Such statements emphasize the importance of the *management of change*. To survive, firms must develop strategies for assessing and reassessing the use of their resources. Every allocation of resources is an investment in the future. Because of the complex nature of most strategies, many of these investments are in projects.

To cite one of many possible examples, special visual effects accomplished through computer animation are common in the movies and television shows we watch daily. A few years ago they were unknown. When the capability was in its idea stage, computer companies as well as the firms producing movies and TV shows faced the decision whether or not to invest in the development of these techniques. Obviously valuable as the idea seems today, the choice was not quite so clear a decade ago when an entertainment company compared investment in computer animation to alternative investments in a new star, a new rock group, or a new theme part—or when the computer firm considered alternative investments in a new business software package, a higher resolution color monitor, or a faster processor.

The proper choice of investment projects is crucial to the long-run survival of every firm. Daily we witness the results of both good and bad investment choices. In our daily newspapers we read of Ashland Oil's decision to reformulate its automotive fuel in order to lower pollution at a cost of \$0.03 to \$0.05 per gallon—at the same time that British Petroleum decides to lower the volatility of its automotive fuel to lower pollution at a cost of $0.01 per gallon. We read of Chrysler's decision to make a major alteration in its passenger car line, of IBM's decision to make significant cuts in the prices of its personal computers, and of the United States congressional decision to withdraw funding from the Super Conducting Super Collider project. But can such important choices be made rationally? Once made, do they ever change, and if so, how? These questions reflect the need for effective selection models.

Within the limits of their capabilities, such models can be used to increase profits, to select investments for limited capital resources, or to improve the competitive position of the organization. They can be used for ongoing evaluation as well as initial selection, and thus are a key to the allocation and reallocation of the organization's scarce resources.

When a firm chooses a project selection model, the following criteria, based on Souder [60], are most important.

1. *Realism.* The model should reflect the reality of the manager's decision situation, including the multiple objectives of both the firm and its managers. Without a common measurement system, direct comparison of different projects is impossible. For example, Project A may strengthen a firm's market share by extending its facilities, and Project B might improve its competitive position by strengthening its technical staff. Other things being equal, which is better? The model should take into account the realities of the firm's limitations on facilities, capital, personnel, etc. The model should also include factors for risk—both the technical risks of performance, cost, and time and the market risk of customer rejection.

2. *Capability.* The model should be sophisticated enough to deal with multiple time periods, simulate various situations both internal and external to the project (e.g., strikes, interest rate changes, etc.), and *optimize* the decision. An optimizing model will make the comparisons that management deems important, consider major risks and constraints on the projects, and then select the best overall project or set of projects.

3. *Flexibility.* The model should give valid results within the range of conditions that the firm might experience. It should have the ability to be easily modified, or to be self-adjusting in response to changes in the firm's environment; for example, tax laws change, new technological advancements alter risk levels, and, above all, the organization's goals change.

4. *Ease of Use.* The model should be reasonably convenient, not take a long time to execute, and be easy to use and understand. It should not require special interpretation, data that are hard to acquire, excessive personnel, or unavailable equipment. The model's variables should also relate one to one with those real-world parameters the managers believe significant to the project. Finally, it should be easy to simulate the expected outcomes associated with investments in different project portfolios.

5. *Cost.* Data-gathering and modeling costs should be low relative to the cost of the project and must surely be less then the potential benefits of the project. All costs should be considered, including the costs of data management and of running the model.

We would add a sixth criterion:

6. *Easy Computerization.* It must be easy and convenient to gather and store the information in a computer data base, and to manipulate data in the model through use of a widely available, standard computer package such as Lotus 1-2-3®, Quattro Pro®, Excel®, and like programs.

The Nature of Project Selection Models

There are two basic types of project selection models, numeric and nonnumeric. Both are widely used. Many organizations use both at the same time, or they use models that are combinations of the two. Nonnumeric models, as the name implies, do not use numbers as inputs. Numeric models do, but the criteria being measured may be either objective or subjective. It is important to remember that the *qualities* of a project may be represented by numbers, and that *subjective* measures are not necessarily less useful or reliable than so-called *objective* measures. (We will discuss these matters in more detail later.)

Before examining specific kinds of models within the two basic types, let us consider just what we wish the model to do for us, never forgetting two critically important, but often overlooked, facts.

• Models do not make decisions; people do. The manager, not the model, bears responsibility for the decision. The manager may "delegate" the task of making the decision to a model, but the responsibility cannot be abdicated.

• All models, however sophisticated, are only partial representations of the reality they are mean to reflect. Reality is far too complex for us to capture more than a small fraction of it in any model. Therefore, no model can yield an optimal decision except within its own, possibly inadequate, framework.

We seek a model to assist us in making project selection decisions. This model should possess the characteristics discussed previously: ease of use, flexibility, low cost, and so on. Above all, it must evaluate potential projects by the degree to which they will meet the firm's objectives. (In general, we will not differentiate between such terms as *goals*, *objectives*, *aims*, etc.) To construct a selection/evaluation model, therefore, it is necessary to develop a list of the firm's objectives.

Such a list should be generated by the organization's top management. It is a direct expression of organizational philosophy and policy. The list should go beyond the typical clichés about "survival" and "maximizing profits," which are certainly real goals but are just as certainly not the only goals of the firm. Others might include maintenance of share of specific markets, development of an improved image with specific clients or competitors, expansion into a new line of business, decrease in sensitivity to business cycles, maintenance of employment for specific categories of workers, and maintenance of system loading at or above some percent of capacity, just to mention a few.

A model of some sort is implied by any conscious decision. The choice between two or more alternative courses of action requires reference to some objective(s), and the choice is thus made in accord with some, possibly subjective, "model."

In the past two or three decades, largely since the development of computers and the establishment of operations research as an academic subject area, the use of formal, numeric models to assist in decision making has expanded. A large majority of such models use financial measures of the "goodness" of a decision. Project selection decisions are no exception, being based primarily on the degree to which the financial goals of the organization are met [35]. As we will see later, this stress on financial goals, largely to the exclusion of other criteria, raises some serious problems for the firm, irrespective of whether the firm is for-profit or not-for-profit.

When the list of objectives has been developed, an additional refinement is recommended. The elements in the list should be weighted. Each item is added to the list because it represents a contribution to the success of the organization, but each item does not make an equal contribution. The weights reflect the different degree of contribution of each element in the set of goals.

Once the list of goals has been developed, one more task remains. A project is selected or rejected because it is predicted to have certain outcomes if implemented. These outcomes are expected to contribute to goals achievement. If the estimated level of goal achievement is sufficiently large, the project is selected. If not, it is rejected. The relationship between the project's expected results and the organization's goals must be understood. In general, the kinds of information required to evaluate a project can be listed under production, marketing, financial, personnel, administrative, and other such categories.

The following is a list of factors that contribute, positively or negatively, to these categories. In order to give focus to this list, we assume that the projects in question involve the possible substitution of a new production process for an existing one. The list is meant to be illustrative. It certainly is not exhaustive.

Production Factors
1. Time until ready to install
2. Length of disruption during installation
3. Degree of disruption during installation
4. Learning curve-time until operating as desired
5. Effects on waste and rejects
6. Energy requirements
7. Facility and other equipment requirements
8. Safety of process
9. Other applications of technology
10. Consistency with current technological know-how
11. Change in cost to produce a unit output
12. Change in time to produce a unit output
13. Change in raw material usage
14. Availability of raw materials
15. Required development time and cost
16. Impact on current suppliers
17. Change in quality of output
18. Change in quality control procedures

Marketing Factors
1. Size of potential market for output
2. Probably market share of output
3. Time until market share is acquired
4. Impact on current product line
5. Ability to control quality
6. Consumer acceptance
7. Impact on consumer safety
8. Estimated life of output
9. Share of output life cycle curve
10. Spin-off project possibilities

Financial Factors
1. Profitability, net present value of the investment
2. Impact on cash flows
3. Payout period
4. Cash requirements
5. Time until break-even
6. Size of investment required
7. Impact on seasonal and cyclical fluctuations
8. Cost of getting system up to speed
9. Level of financial risk

Personnel Factors
1. Training requirements
2. Labor skill requirements
3. Availability of required labor skills
4. Level of resistance from current work force
5. Other worker reactions
6. Change in size of labor force
7. Change in sex, age, or racial distribution of labor force
8. Inter- and intra-group communication requirements
9. Support labor requirements
10. Impact on working conditions

Administrative and Miscellaneous Factors
1. Meet government safety standards
2. Meet government environmental standards
3. Impact on information system
4. Impact on computer usage
5. Need for consulting help, inside and outside
6. Reaction of stockholders and securities markets
7. Patent and trade secret protection
8. Impact on image with customers, suppliers, and competitors
9. Cost of maintaining skill in new technology
10. Vulnerability to single supplier
11. Degree to which we understand new technology
12. Elegance of new process
13. Degree to which new process differs from current process
14. Managerial capacity to direct and control new process

Some factors in this list have a one-time impact and some recur. Some are difficult to estimate and may be subject to considerable error. For these, it is helpful to identify a *range of uncertainty*. In addition, the factors may occur at different times. And some factors may have *thresholds*, critical values above or below which we might wish to reject the project.

Clearly, no single project decision need include all these factors. Moreover, not only is the list incomplete, but it contains redundant items. Perhaps more important, the factors are not at the same level of generality: *profitability* and *impact on organiza-tional image* both affect the overall organization, but *impact on working conditions* is more oriented to the production system. Nor are all elements of equal importance. *Change in production cost* is usually considered more important than *impact on com-puter usage.* Later in this chapter we will deal with the problem of generating an acceptable list of factors and measuring their relative importance. At that time we will discuss the creation of a DSS (Decision Support System) for project evaluation and selection.

Although the process of evaluating a potential project is time-consuming and dif-ficult, its importance cannot be overstated. A major consulting firm has argued [37] that the primary cause for the failure of R&D projects is insufficient care in evaluat-ing the proposal before the expenditure of funds. What is true of R&D projects also appears to be true for other kinds of projects. Careful analysis of a potential project is a *sine qua non* for profitability in the construction business. There are many horror stories [43] about firms that undertook projects for the installation of a computer sys-tem without sufficient analysis of the time, cost, and disruption involved.

Later in this chapter we will consider the problem of conducting an evaluation under conditions of uncertainty about the outcomes associated with a project. Before dealing with this problem, however, it helps to examine several different evaluation/selection models and consider their strengths and weaknesses. Recall that the problem of choos-ing the project selection model itself will be discussed later.

Types of Project Selection Models

Of the two basic types of selection models, numeric and nonnumeric, nonnumeric models are older and simpler and have only a few subtypes to consider. We examine them first.

Nonnumeric Models

The Sacred Cow. The project is suggested by a senior and powerful official in the organization. Often the project is initiated with a simple comment such as, "If you have the change, why don't you look into...," and there follows an undeveloped idea for a new product, for the development of a new market, for the installation of a new decision support system, for the adoption of Material Requirements Planning, or for some other project requiring an investment of the firm's resources. The immediate result of this bland statement is the creation of a "project" to investigate whatever the boss has suggested. The project is "sacred" in the sense that it will be maintained until successfully concluded, or until the boss, personally, recognizes the idea as a failure and terminates it.

The Operating Necessity. If a flood is threatening the plant, a project to build a protective dike does not require much formal evaluation. Republic Steel corporation (now a part of LTV Corp.) has used this criterion (and the following criterion also) in evaluating potential projects. If the project is required in order to keep the system operating, the primary question becomes: Is the system worth saving at the estimat-ed cost of the project? If the answer is yes, project costs will be examined to make sure they are kept as low as is consistent with project success, but the project will be funded.

The Competitive Necessity. Using this criterion, Republic Steel undertook a major plant rebuilding project in the late 1960s in its steel-bar-manufacturing facilities near Chicago. It had become apparent to Republic's management that the company's bar mill needed modernization if the firm was to maintain its competitive position in the Chicago market area. Although the planning process for the project was quite sophisticated, the decision to undertake the project was based on a desire to maintain the company's competitive position in that market.

In a similar manner, many business schools are restructuring their undergraduate and MBA programs to stay competitive with the more forward-looking schools. In large part, this action is driven by declining numbers of tuition-paying students and the stronger competition to attract them.

Investment in an *operating necessity* project takes precedence over a *competitive necessity* project, but both types of projects may bypass the more careful numeric analysis used for projects deemed to be less urgent or less important to the survival of the firm.

The Product Line Extension. A project to develop and distribute new products would be judged on the degree to which it fits the firm's existing product line, fills a gap, strengthens a weak link, or extends the line in a new, desirable direction. Sometimes careful calculations of profitability are not required. Decision makers can act on their beliefs about what will be the likely impact on the total system performance if the new product is added to the line.

Comparative Benefit Model. Assume that an organization has many projects to consider, perhaps several dozen. Senior management would like to select a subset of the projects that would most benefit the firm, but the projects do not seem to be easily comparable. For example, some projects concern potential new products, some concern changes in production methods, others concern computerization of certain records, and still others cover a variety of subjects not easily categorized (e.g., a proposal to set up a daycare center for employees with small children). The organization has no formal method of selecting projects, but members of the Selection Committee do think that some projects will benefit the firm more than others, even if they have no precise way to define or measure "benefit."

The concept of comparative benefits, if not a formal model, is widely adopted for selection decisions on all sorts of projects. Most United Way organizations use the concept to make decisions about which of several social programs to fund. The comparative benefit concept is also commonly used when making funding decisions on fundamental research projects. Organizations such as the National Science Foundation, the Office of Naval Research, and a great many other governmental, private, and university sponsors of research usually send project proposals to outside experts in the relevant areas who serve as "referees," a process known as *peer review*. The proposal is evaluated according to the referee's technical criteria, and a recommendation is submitted. Senior management of the funding organization then examines all projects with positive recommendations and attempts to construct a portfolio that best fits the organization's aims and its budget.

Of the several techniques for ordering projects, the *Q-Sort* [26] is one of the most straightforward. First, the projects are divided into three groups—*good*, *fair*, and *poor*—according to their relative merits. If any group has more than eight members, it is

Figure 1. The Q-sort method. *Source:* [61].

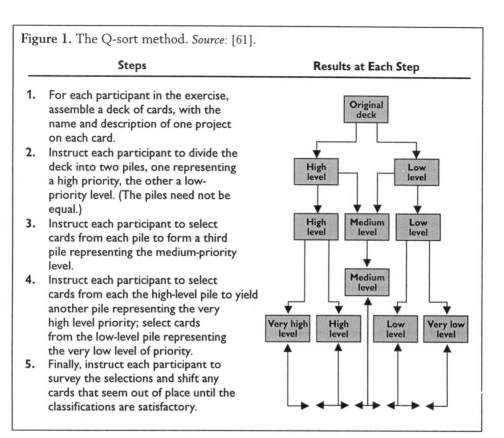

| Steps | Results at Each Step |

1. For each participant in the exercise, assemble a deck of cards, with the name and description of one project on each card.
2. Instruct each participant to divide the deck into two piles, one representing a high priority, the other a low-priority level. (The piles need not be equal.)
3. Instruct each participant to select cards from each pile to form a third pile representing the medium-priority level.
4. Instruct each participant to select cards from each the high-level pile to yield another pile representing the very high level priority; select cards from the low-level pile representing the very low level of priority.
5. Finally, instruct each participant to survey the selections and shift any cards that seem out of place until the classifications are satisfactory.

subdivided into two categories, such as *fair-plus* and *fair-minus*. When all categories have eight or fewer members, the projects within each category are ordered from best to worst. Again, the order is determined on the basis of relative merit. The rater may use specific criteria to rank each project, or may simply use general overall judgment. See Figure 1 for an example of a Q-Sort.

The process described may be carried out by one person who is responsible for evaluation and selection, or it may be performed by a committee charged with the responsibility. If a committee handles the task, the individual rankings can be developed anonymously, and the set of anonymous rankings can be examined by the committee itself for consensus. It is common for such rankings to differ somewhat from rater to rater, but they do not often vary strikingly because the individuals chosen for such committees rarely differ widely on what they feel to be appropriate for the parent organization. Projects can then be selected in the order of preference, though they are usually evaluated financially before final selection.

There are other, similar nonnumeric models for accepting or rejecting projects. Although it is easy to dismiss such models as unscientific, they should not be discounted casually. These models are clearly goal-oriented and directly reflect the primary concerns of the organization. The sacred cow model, in particular, has an added feature; sacred cow projects are visibly supported by "the powers that be." Full support by top management is certainly an important contributor to project success [43]. Without such support, the probability of project success is sharply lowered.

Numeric Models: Profit/Profitability

As noted earlier, a large majority of all firms using project evaluation and selection models use profit/profitability as the sole measure of acceptability. We will consider these models first, and then discuss models that go well beyond the profit test for acceptance.

Payback Period. The payback period for a project is the initial fixed investment in the project divided by the estimated annual cash inflows from the project. The ratio of these quantities is the number of years required for the project to repay its initial fixed investment. For example, assume a project costs $100,000 to implement and has annual cash inflows of $25,000. Then

Payback period = $100,000/$25,000 = 4 years

This method assumes that the cash inflows will persist at least long enough to pay back the investment, and it ignores any cash inflows beyond the payback period. The method also serves as an inadequate proxy for risk. The faster the investment is recovered, the less the risk to which the firm is exposed.

Average Rate of Return. Often mistakenly taken to the reciprocal of the payback period, the average rate of return is the ratio of the average annual profit (either before or after taxes) to the initial or average investment in the project. Because average annual profits are not equivalent to net cash inflows, the average rate of return does not equal the reciprocal of the payback period. Assume, in the example just given, that the average annual profits are $15,000:

Average rate of return = $15,000/$100,000 = 0.15

Neither of these evaluation methods is recommended for project selection, though payback period is widely used and does have a legitimate value for cash budgeting decisions. The major advantage of these models is their simplicity, but neither takes into account the time value of money. Unless interest rates are extremely low and the rate of inflation is nil, the failure to reduce future cash flows or profits to their present value will result in serious evaluation errors.

Discounted Cash Flow. Also referred to as the present value method, the discounted cash flow method determines the net present value of all cash flows by discounting them by the required rate of return (also known as the *hurdle rate, cutoff rate,* and similar terms) as follows,

$$\text{NPV (project)} = A_0 + \sum_{t=1}^{n} \frac{F_t}{(1+k)^t}$$

where

F_t = the net cash flow in period t,
K = the required rate of return, and
A_0 = initial cash investment (because this is an outflow, it will be negative).

To include the impact of inflation (or deflation) where p_t is the predicted rate of inflation during period t, we have

$$\text{NPV (project)} = A_0 + \sum_{t=1}^{n} \frac{F_t}{(1+k+p_t)^t}$$

Early in the life of a project, net cash flow is likely to be negative, the major outflow being the initial investment in the project, A_0. If the project is successful, however, cash flows will become positive. The project is *acceptable* if the sum of the net present values of all estimated cash flows over the life of the project is positive. A simple example will suffice. Using our $100,000 investment with a net cash inflow of $25,000 per year for a period of eight years, a required rate of return of 15 percent and an inflation rate of 3 percent per year, we have

$$\text{NPV (project)} = -\$100,000 + \sum_{t=1}^{8} \frac{\$25,000}{(1+0.15+0.03)^t}$$

$$= \$1939$$

Because the present value of the inflows is greater than the present value of the outflow—that is, the net present value is positive—the project is deemed acceptable.

Internal Rate of Return. If we have a set of expected cash inflows and cash outflows, the internal rate of return is the discount rate that equates the present values of the two sets of flows. If A_t is an expected cash outflow in the period t and R_t is the expected inflow for the period t, the internal rate of return is the value of k that satisfies the following equation (note that the A_0 will be positive in this formulation of the problem):

$$A_0 + A_1/(1+k) + A_2/(1+k)^2 + ... + A_n/(1+k)^n = R_1/(1+k) + R_2/(1+k)^2$$
$$+ ... + R_n/(1+k)^n \quad t = 1,2,3,...,n$$

The value of k is found by trial and error.

Profitability Index. Also known as the benefit-cost ratio, the profitability index is the net present value of all future expected cash flows divided by the initial cash investment. (Some firms do not discount the cash flows in making this calculation.) If this ratio is greater than 1.0, the project may be accepted.

Other Profitability Models. There are a great many variations of the models just described. These variations fall into three general categories: (1) those that subdivide net cash flow into the elements that comprise the net flow, (2) those that include specific terms to introduce risk (or uncertainty, which is treated as risk) into the evaluation, and (3) those that extend the analysis to consider effects that the project might have on other projects or activities in the organization. Two product line extension models, taken from Dean [16], will illustrate these methods.

Pacifico's Method. PI is the profitability index of acceptability where

$$\text{PI} = rdpc \ SP \ \sqrt{L}/C,$$

r = probability of research success,
d = probability of development success, given research success,
p = probability of process success, given development success, and
c = probability of commercial success, given process success.

The investment, C, is the estimated total cost of the R&D effort for the project. Risk is incorporated in the *rdpc* term.

The cash flow is $SP\sqrt{L}$ where
S = estimated average annual sales volume in units of product,
P = estimated average annual profit per unit, and
L = estimated life of the product extension in years. (Note that although the profits are not formally discounted, they are "devalued" over time by multiplying them by $\sqrt{L}$ rather than by L.)

Dean's Profitability Method. Dean's model contains a term that subtracts the unit manufacturing cost and the unit selling and administrative costs from the unit price, multiplies the remainder by the expected number of units sold per year, and then subtracts tooling and development costs (a project risk factor is also included). All costs and revenues are time-indexed and discounted to the present. Dean modifies his model to deal with three distinct cases: (1) where the product extension has no significant impact on the existing system, (2) where the product extension may affect the profitability or the sales of existing products, or both, and (3) where the product extension is a replacement for an existing product.

Several comments are in order about all the profit-profitability numeric models. First, let us consider their advantages.

1. The undiscounted models are simple to use and understand.
2. All use readily available accounting data to determine the cash flows.
3. Model output is in terms familiar to business decision makers.
4. With a few exceptions, model output is on an "absolute" profit/profitability scale and allows "absolute" go/no-go decisions.
5. Some profit models account for project risk.
6. Dean's model includes the impact of the project on the rest of the organization.

The disadvantages of these models are the following.
1. These models ignore all nonmonetary factors except risk.
2. Models that do not include discounting ignore the timing of the cash flows and the time value of money.
3. Models that reduce cash flows to their present value are strongly biased toward the short run.
4. Payback-type models ignore cash flows beyond the payback period.
5. The IRR model can result in multiple solutions.
6. All are sensitive to errors in the input data for the early years of the project.
7. All discounting models are nonlinear, and the effects of changes (or errors) in the variables or parameters are generally not obvious to most decision makers.
8. Those models incorporating the risks of research and/or development and/or process (the commercial success risk factor is excluded from this comment) mislead the decision maker. It is not so much that the research-development-process success is risky as it is that the time and cost required to ensure project

Figure 2. Sample project evaluation form.

Project _____

Rater _____ Date _____

	Qualifies	Does Not Qualify
No increase in energy requirements	X	
Potential market size, dollars	X	
Potential market size, percent	X	
No new facility required	X	
No new technical expertise required		X
No decrease in quality of final product	X	
Ability to manage project with current personnel		X
No requirement for reorganization	X	
Impact on work force safety	X	
Impact on environmental standards	X	
Profitability		
Rate of return more than 15% after tax	X	
Estimated annual profits more than $250,000	X	
Time to break-even less than 3 years	X	
Need for external consultants		X
Consistency with current lines of business		X
Impact on company image	X	
With customers	X	
With our industry		X
Totals	**12**	**5**

success is uncertain. The application of these risk terms applies mainly to R&D projects.

9. Some models, Dean's and Pacifico's, for example, are oriented only toward evaluation of projects that result in new products.

10. All these models depend for input on a determination of cash flows, but it is not clear exactly how the concept of cash flow is properly defined for the purpose of evaluating projects. (This problem is discussed later.)

A complete discussion of profit/profitability models can be found in any standard work on financial management—see [1, 9, 67] for example. In general, the net present value models are preferred to the internal rate of return models.

In our experience the payback period model, occasionally using discounted cash flows, is one of the most commonly used models for evaluating projects and other investment opportunities. Managers generally feel that insistence on short payout periods tends to minimize the uncertainties associated with the passage of time. While this is certainly logical, we prefer evaluation methods that discount cash flows and deal with uncertainty more directly by considering specific risks. Using the payout period as a cash-budgeting tool aside, *its only virtue is simplicity*, a dubious virtue at best.

Numeric Models: Scoring

In an attempt to overcome some of the disadvantages of profitability models, particularly their focus on a single decision criterion, a number of evaluation/selection models that use multiple criteria to evaluate a project have been developed. Such models vary widely in their complexity and information requirements. The examples discussed illustrate some of the different types.

Unweighted 0-1 Factor Model. A set of relevant factors is selected by management. These are usually listed in a preprinted form, and one or more raters score the project on each factor depending on whether or not it qualifies for that individual criterion. The raters are chosen by senior managers, for the most part from the rolls of senior management. The criteria for choice are a clear understanding of organizational goals and a good knowledge of the firm's potential project *portfolio*. Figure 2 shows an example of the rating sheet for an unweighted, 0-1 factor model.

The columns of Figure 2 are summed and those projects with a sufficient number of qualifying factors may be selected. The main advantage of such a model is that it uses several criteria in the decision process. The major disadvantages are that it assumes all criteria are of equal importance and it allows for no gradation of the degree to which a specific project meets the various criteria.

Unweighted Factor Scoring Model. The second disadvantage of the 0-1 factor model can be dealt with by constructing a simple linear measure of the degree to which the project being evaluated meets each of the criteria contained in the list. The *x* marks in Figure 2 would be replaced by numbers. Often a five-point scale is used, where 5 is very good, 4 is good, 3 is fair, 2 is poor, 1 is very poor. (Three-, seven-, and 10-point scales are also common.) The second column of Figure 2 would not be needed. The column of scores is summed, and those projects with a total score exceeding some critical value are selected. A variant of this selection process might select the highest-scoring projects (still assuming they are all above some critical score) until the estimated costs of the set of projects equaled the resource limit. The criticism that the criteria are all assumed to be of equal importance still holds.

The use of a discrete numeric scale to represent the degree to which a criterion is satisfied is widely accepted. To construct such measures for project evaluation, we proceed in the following manner. Select a criterion, say, "estimated annual profits in dollars." For this criterion, determine five ranges of performance so that a typical project, chosen at random, would have a roughly equal chance of being in any one of the five performance ranges. (Another way of describing this condition is: Take a large number of projects that were selected for support in the past, regardless of whether they were actually successful or not, and create five levels of predicted performance so that about one-fifth of the projects fall into each level.) This procedure will usually create unequal ranges, which may offend our sense of symmetry but need not concern us otherwise. It ensures that each criterion performance measure utilizes the full scale of possible values, a desirable characteristic for performance measures.

Consider the following two simple examples. Using the criterion just mentioned, "estimated annual profits in dollars," we might construct the following scale:

Score	Performance Level
5	Above $1,100,000
4	$750,001 to $1,100,000
3	$500,001 to $750,000
2	$200,000 to $500,000
1	Less than $200,000

As suggested, these ranges might have been chosen so that about 20 percent of the projects considered for funding would fall into each of the five ranges.

The criterion "no decrease in quality of the final product" would have to be restated to be scored on a five-point scale, perhaps as follows:

Score	Performance Level
	The quality of the final product is:
5	significantly and visibly improved
4	significantly improved, but not visible to buyer
3	not significantly changed
2	significantly lowered, but not visible to buyer
1	significantly and visibly lowered

This scale is an example of scoring cells that represent opinion rather than objective (even if "estimated") fact, as was the case in the profit scale.

Weighted Factor Scoring Model. When numeric weights reflecting the relative importance of each individual factor are added, we have a weighted factor scoring model. In general, it takes the form

$$S_i = \sum_{j=1}^{n} s_{ij} w_j \quad j = 1, 2, 3, \ldots, n$$

where

S_i = the total score of the *i*th project,

s_{ij} = the score of the *i*th project on the *j*th criterion, and

w_j = the weight of the *j*th criterion.

The weights, w_j, may be generated by any technique that is acceptable to the organization's policy makers. There are several techniques available to generate such numbers, but the most effective and most widely used is the Delphi technique. The Delphi technique was developed by Brown and Dalkey of the Rand Corporation during the 1950s and 1960s [15]. It is a technique for developing numeric values that are equivalent to subjective, verbal measures of relative value. (The method is also useful for developing technological forecasts. The method of successive comparisons (or pairwise comparisons) may also be used for the same purpose. Originally described by Churchman, Ackoff, and Arnoff in their classic text on operations research [10], this technique asks the decision maker to make a series of choices between several different sets of alternatives. A set of numbers is then found that is consistent with the choices. These numbers can serve as weights in the scoring model. For an example of the use of this method, see [18]. Another popular and quite similar approach is the Analytic Hierarchy Process, developed by Saaty, see [54, 65] for details.

When numeric weights have been generated, it is helpful (but not necessary) to scale the weights so that

$$0 \leq w_j \leq 1 \quad j = 1,2,3,\ldots,n$$

$$\sum_{j=1}^{n} w_j = 1$$

The weight of each criterion can be interpreted as the "percent of the total weight accorded to that particular criterion."

A special caveat is in order. It is quite possible with this type of model to include a large number of criteria. It is not particularly difficult to develop scoring scales and weights, and the ease of gathering and processing the required information makes it tempting to include marginally relevant criteria along with the obviously important items. Resist this temptation! After the important factors have been weighted, there usually is little residual weight to be distributed among the remaining elements. The result is that the evaluation is simply insensitive to major differences in the scores on trivial criteria. A good rule of thumb is to discard elements with weights less than 0.02 or 0.03. (If elements are discarded, and if you wish $\sum wj = 1$, the weights must be rescaled to 1.0.) As with any linear model, the user should be aware that the elements in the model are assumed to be independent. This presents no particular problems for these scoring models because they are used to make estimates in a "steady state" system, and we are not concerned with transitions between states.

It is useful to note that if one uses a weighted scoring model to aid in project selection, the model can also serve as an aid to project *improvement*. For any given criterion, the difference between the criterion's score and the highest possible score on that criterion, multiplied by the weight of the criterion, is a measure of the potential improvement in the project score that would result were the project's performance on that criterion sufficiently improved. It may be that such improvement is not feasible, or is more costly than the improvement warrants. On the other hand, such an analysis of each project yields a valuable statement of the comparative benefits of project improvements. Viewing a project in this way is a type of *sensitivity analysis*. We examine the degree to which a project's score is sensitive to attempts to improve it— usually by adding resources. We will use sensitivity analysis several times in this book. It is a powerful managerial technique.

It is not particularly difficult to computerize a weighted scoring model by creating a template on Lotus 1-2-3 or one of the other standard computer spreadsheets. In *Project Management: A Managerial Approach* we discuss an example of a computerized scoring model used for the project termination decision. The model is, in fact, a project selection model. The logic of using a "selection" model for the termination decision is straightforward: Given the time and resources required to take a project form its current state to completion, should we make the investment? A "Yes" answer to that question "selects" for funding the partially completed project from the set of all partially finished and not-yet-started projects.

Constrained Weighted Factor Scoring Model. The temptation to include marginal criteria can be partially overcome by allowing additional criteria to enter the model as constraints rather than weighted factors. These constraints represent project characteristics that *must* be present or absent in order for the project to be acceptable. In our example concerning a product, we might have specified that we would not undertake any project that would significantly lower the quality of the final product (visible to the buyer or not).

We would amend the weighted scoring model to take the form:

$$S_i = \sum_{j=1}^{n} s_{ij} w_j \prod_{k=1}^{v} c_{ik}$$

where $c_{ik} = 1$ if the ith project satisfies the kth of v constraints, and 0 if it does not. Other elements in the model are as defined earlier.

Although this model is analytically tidy, in practice we would not bother to evaluate projects that are so unsuitable in some ways that we would not consider supporting them regardless of their expected performance against other criteria. For example, except under extraordinary circumstances, Procter & Gamble would not consider a project for adding a new consumer product or product line:

• that cannot be marketed nationally,
• that cannot be distributed through mass outlets (grocery stores, drugstores)
• that will not generate gross revenues in excess of $———million,
• for which Procter & Gamble's potential market share is not at least 50 percent,
• that does not utilize Procter & Gamble's scientific expertise, manufacturing expertise, advertising expertise, or packaging and distribution expertise.

Again, a caveat is in order. Exercise care when adopting constraints. It may seem obvious that we should not consider any project if it has no reasonable assurance of long-run profitability. But such a constraint can force us to overlook a project that, though unprofitable itself, might have a strong, positive impact on the profitability of other projects in which we are interested.

Dean and Nishry's Model. Beginning with the weighted factor scoring model, Dean and Nishry [16] cast the project selection decision in the form of an integer programming problem. In the problem

$$S_i = \sum_{j=1}^{n} w_j s_{ij}$$

such that

$$x_i = 0 \text{ or } 1$$

and

$$\sum_{i=1}^{n} x_i m_i \leq M$$

where m_i is the resource (labor, capital, etc.) requirement for the ith project, and M is the total amount of the resource available for use. The value of $x_i = 0$ or 1 depends on whether or not the ith project is selected.

In essence, the Dean and Nishry approach selects the highest-scoring project candidates from the scoring model, and selects them one after another until the available resources have been depleted. If there are several scarce resources, the selection problem can be recast and solved by dynamic programming methods. There are several other R&D project evaluation/selection models described in this excellent work [16]. Many are adaptable to a wide variety of project types.

Goal Programming with Multiple Objectives. Goal programming is a variation of the general linear programming method that can optimize an objective function with multiple objectives. In order to apply this method to project selection, we adopt a linear, 0-1 goal program.

First, establish a set of objectives such as "maximize equipment utilization," "minimize idle labor crews," "maximize profits," and "satisfy investment budget constraints." Alternative sets of projects are adopted or rejected based on their impact on goal achievement. A detailed discussion of goal programming is beyond the scope of this book. The interested reader should consult any modern text on management science, for example, [63, 65].

Because most real-world problems are too large for analytic solutions, heuristic solutions are necessary. Ignizio [30, pp. 202-206] has developed a heuristic approach that is easily applied to project selection.

As was the case with profitability models, scoring models have their own characteristic advantages and disadvantages. These are the advantages.

1. These models allow multiple criteria to be used for evaluation and decision, including profit/profitability models and both tangible and intangible criteria.
2. They are structurally simple and therefore easy to understand and use.
3. They are a direct reflection of managerial policy.
4. They are easily altered to accommodate changes in the environment or managerial policy.
5. Weighted scoring models allow for the fact that some criteria are more important than others.
6. These models allow easy sensitivity analysis. The trade-offs between the several criteria are readily observable.

The disadvantages are the following.

1. The output of a scoring model is strictly a relative measure. Project scores do not represent the value or "utility" associated with a project and thus do not directly indicate whether or not the project should be supported.
2. In general, scoring models are linear in form and the elements of such models are assumed to be independent.
3. The ease of use of these models is conducive to the inclusion of a large number of criteria, most of which have such small weights that they have little impact on the total project score.

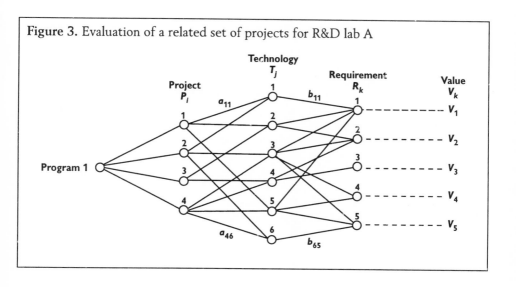

Figure 3. Evaluation of a related set of projects for R&D lab A

4. Unweighted scoring models assume all criteria are of equal importance, which is almost certainly contrary to fact.

5. To the extent that profit/profitability is included as an element in the scoring model, this element has the advantages and disadvantages noted earlier for the profitability models themselves.

Selecting Projects within a Program

This project selection technique is a special type of weighted scoring model. Let us pose a more complex selection problem. Presume that one of a drug firm's three R&D laboratories has adopted a research program aimed at the development of a family of compounds for the treatment of a related set of diseases. An individual project is created for each compound in the family in order to test the compound's efficacy, to test for side effects, to find and install efficient methods for producing the compound in quantity, and to develop marketing strategies for each separate member of the drug family. Assume further that many aspects of the research work on any one compound both profits from and contributes to the work done on other members of the family. In such a case, how does one evaluate a project associated with any given member of the family"? *One doesn't!*

To evaluate each project-drug family combination would require a separation of costs and revenues that would be quite impossible except when based on the most arbitrary allocations. Instead of inviting the political bloodletting that would inevitably accompany any such approach, let us attempt to evaluate the performance of *all* the projects as well as the laboratory that directed and carried out the entire program— and that may be conducting other programs at the same time.

B. V. Dean has developed an ingenious technique for accomplishing such an evaluation [17]. This tool not only helps identify the most desirable projects but can also be used as a planning tool to identify resource needs, especially for *large* projects. Consider Figure 3. R&D Laboratory A is conducting a set of interrelated projects in

Program 1. Project i contributes to technology j, one of a set of desirable technologies that, in turn, makes a contribution to requirement k, one of a desired set of end requirements with some value V_k, the sum of all values being 1.0.

Now consider the set of projects P_i, and the technologies, T_j. We can form the transfer matrix

$$\mathbf{A} = \left[a_{ij} \right]$$

composed of ones and zeros as follows:

$$a_{ij} = \begin{cases} 1, \text{ if } P_i \text{ contributes to } T_j \\ 0, \text{ if } P_i \text{ does not contribute to } T_j \end{cases}$$

Similarly, we form the transfer matrix

$$\mathbf{B} = \left[b_{jk} \right]$$

composed of ones and zeros as follows:

$$b_{jk} = \begin{cases} 1, \text{ if } T_j \text{ contributes to } R_k \\ 0, \text{ if not} \end{cases}$$

Now find

$$\mathbf{C} = \left[c_{jk} \right]$$

where

$$\mathbf{C} = \mathbf{AB}$$

The resultant matrix will link P_i directly to R_k, thus indicating which projects contribute to which requirements.

Now consider the value set V_k. "Normalize" V_k so that

$$\sum_k V_k = 1$$

Each normalized V_k will represent the *relative* value of R_k in the set $\{R_k\}$. The values can be written as a column matrix

$$\mathbf{V} = [V_k]$$

Note that a project, Pi, that contributes to a requirement, Rk, in cjk ways will have a value

$$c_{ik} V_k$$

and that the *total* value of P_i is thus

$$e_i = \sum_k c_{ik} V_k$$

The column matrix $E = [e_i]$ is the set of values for all projects in the laboratory, and the sum of all project values,

$$E = \sum_k e_i = JE$$

where J is a row matrix consisting of ones.

$$E = JE$$
$$ = JCV$$
$$ = JABV$$

Example. An R&D program consists of two projects, four technologies, and three requirements. Project 1 contributes to technologies 1 and 4 only but project 2 contributes to technologies 2, 3, and 4. Technology 1 contributes to requirement 2 only and technology 4 contributes to requirement 1 only. Technologies 2 and 3 contribute to requirements 1 and 3 and requirements 1 and 2, respectively. Requirements 1, 2, and 3 have relative values of 0.2, 0.5, and 0.3, respectively. What is the overall value of the program and which project is most important?

$$A = \begin{bmatrix} 1001 \\ 0111 \end{bmatrix} \quad B = \begin{bmatrix} 010 \\ 101 \\ 110 \\ 100 \end{bmatrix} \quad V = \begin{bmatrix} .02 \\ .05 \\ 0.3 \end{bmatrix}$$

The contribution of each project to each requirement is

$$C = AB = \begin{bmatrix} 110 \\ 311 \end{bmatrix}$$

The value of each project is

$$E = CV = \begin{bmatrix} .7 \\ 1.4 \end{bmatrix}$$

The value of the program is

$$E = JE = 2.1$$

Thus, project 2 is twice as important (valuable) as project 1.

If, in the preparation of matrix A, it seems desirable to differentiate between the different degrees by which a project contributes to a technology or a technology to a requirement, this is easily accomplished. Instead of a one-zero measure of contribution, one might use the following:

$$a = \begin{cases} 2, \text{ if } P_i \text{ makes a major contribution to } T_j; \\ 1, \text{ if } P_i \text{ makes a minor contribution to } T_j; \\ 0, \text{ if } P_i \text{ makes none} \end{cases}$$

Matrix **B** could also accommodate a more sensitive measure of the contributions of a technology to a requirement if the evaluator wishes.

Dean's method has wide applicability for evaluation of programs composed of multiple interdependent projects. Scores can be compared for several programs. When program life is extended over several time periods and generates outputs in these successive time periods, program performance can be compared between periods.

Choosing a Project Selection Model

Selecting the type of model to aid the evaluation/selection process depends on the philosophy and wishes of management. Liberatore and Titus [35] conducted a survey of 40 high-level staff persons from 29 *Fortune 500* firms. Eighty percent of their respondents report the use of one or more financial models for R&D project decision making. Although their sample is small and nonrandom, their findings are quite consistent with the present authors' experience. None of the respondent firms used mathematical programming techniques for project selection or resource allocation.

We strongly favor weighted scoring models for three fundamental reasons. First, they allow the multiple objectives of all organizations to be reflected in the important decision about which projects will be supported and which will be rejected. Second, scoring models are easily adapted to changes in managerial philosophy or changes in the environment. Third, they do not suffer from the bias toward the short run that is inherent in profitability models that discount future cash flows. This is not a prejudice against discounting and most certainly does not argue against the inclusion of profits/profitability as an important factor in selection, but rather *it is an argument against the exclusion of nonfinancial factors* that may require a longer-run view of the costs and benefits of a project. For a powerful statement of this point, see [25].

It is also interesting to note that Liberatore and Titus found that firms with a significant amount of contract research funded from outside the organization used scoring models for project screening much more frequently than firms with negligible levels of outside funding. It was also found that firms with significant levels of outside funding were much less likely to use a payback period [35, p. 969].

The structure of a weighted scoring model is quite straightforward. Its virtues are many. Nonetheless, the actual use of scoring models is not as easy as it might seem. Decision makers are forced to make difficult choices and they are not always comfortable doing so. They are forced to reduce often vague feelings to quite specific words or numbers. The Delphi method mentioned above and described in Appendix B is helpful, and is a satisfying process for decision makers. Even so, multiattribute, multiperson decision making is not simple. (For an interesting discussion of this process, see [31].)

Analysis under High Uncertainty

At times an organization may wish to evaluate a project about which there is little information. Research and development projects sometimes fall into this general class. But even in the comparative mysteries of research and development activities, the level of uncertainty about the outcomes of R&D is not beyond analysis. As we noted when discussing Dean's profitability model, there is actually not much uncertainty

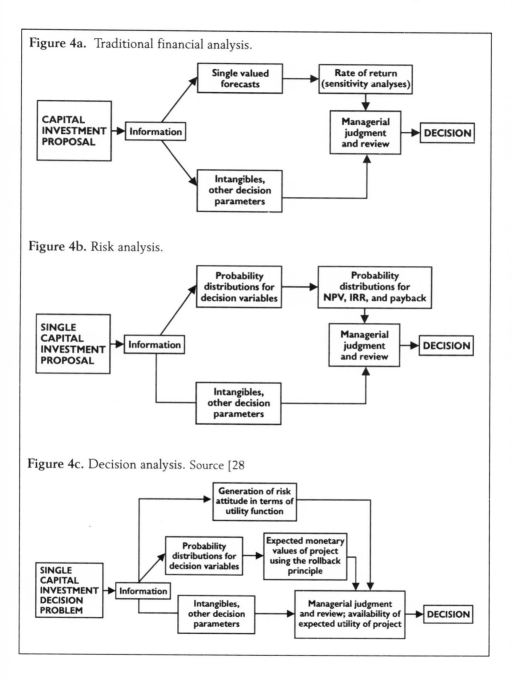

Figure 4a. Traditional financial analysis.

Figure 4b. Risk analysis.

Figure 4c. Decision analysis. Source [28

about whether a product, process, or service can be developed, but there can be considerable uncertainty about *when* it will be developed and at *what* cost.

As they are with R&D projects, time and cost are also often uncertain in other types of projects. When the organization undertakes projects in which it has little or no recent experience—for example, the installation of a new computer, investment in an unfamiliar business, engaging in international trade, and a myriad of other projects common enough to organizations in general but uncommon to any single organization—there are three distinct areas of uncertainty. First, there is uncertainty about the timing of the project and the cash flows it is expected to generate. Second, though not as common as generally believed, there may be uncertainty about the direct outcomes of the project—that is, what it will accomplish. Third, there is uncertainty about the side effects of the project, its unforeseen consequences.

Typically, we try to reduce such uncertainty by the preparation of *pro forma* documents. *Pro forma* profit and loss statements and break-even charts are examples of such documents. The results, however, are not very satisfactory unless the amount of uncertainty is reflected in the data that go into the documents. When relationships between inputs and outputs in the projects are complex, Monte Carlo simulation [34, 65] can handle such uncertainty by exposing the many possible consequences of embarking on a project. *Risk analysis* is a method based on such a procedure. With the great availability of microcomputers and user-friendly software, these procedures are becoming very common.

Risk Analysis

The term risk analysis is generally credited to David Hertz in his classic *Harvard Business Review* article, "Risk Analysis in Capital Investment" [27]. The principal contribution of this procedure is to focus the decision maker's attention on understanding the nature and extent of the uncertainty associated with some variables used in a decision-making process. Although the method can be used with almost any kind of variable and decision problem, risk analysis is usually understood to use financial measures in determining the desirability of an investment project.

Hertz [28] differentiates risk analysis from both traditional financial analysis and more general decision analysis with the diagrams in Figure 4. Figure 4a illustrates traditional financial analysis, Figure 4b risk analysis. The primary difference is that risk analysis incorporates uncertainty in the decision input data. Instead of point estimates of the variables, probability distributions are determined or subjectively estimated for each of the "uncertain" variables. With such inputs, the probability distribution for the rate of return (or NPV) is then usually found by simulation. The decision maker not only has probabilistic information about the rate of return and future cash flows but also gains knowledge about the variability of such estimates as measured by the standard deviation of the financial returns. Both the expectation and its variability are important decision criteria in the evaluation of the project.

When most managers refer to risk analysis, they are usually speaking of what Hertz and Thomas call "decision analysis." As Figure 4c shows, for decision analysis the manager's "utility function" for money must be determined. If the decision maker is seeking a decision that achieves several different objectives simultaneously, this method (utilizing a weighted factor scoring model, for example, rather than simulation) would be appropriate.

This approach is useful for a wide range of project-related decisions. For example, simulation risk analysis was used to select the best method of moving a computer to a new facility [64]. The major task elements and their required sequences were identified. Cost

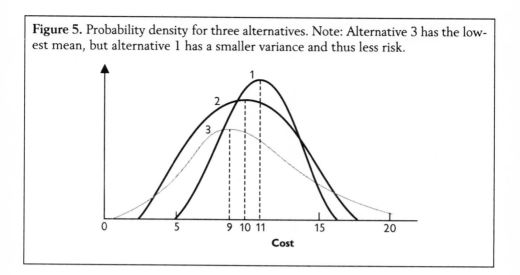

Figure 5. Probability density for three alternatives. Note: Alternative 3 has the lowest mean, but alternative 1 has a smaller variance and thus less risk.

and time distributions were then programmed for analysis and a computer run of 2000 trials was made, simulating various failures and variations in cost and time for each of three methods of moving the computer. A cost-probability distribution was constructed (see Figure 5) to help identify the lowest-cost alternative and also the alternative with the lowest risk of a high cost, alternatives that are often not the same. As seen in the illustration, alternative 3 has the lowest expected cost (or 9) but also has the highest likelihood for a cost of 20 or more.

A public utility faced with deciding between several R&D projects [21] used four separate cost-related distributions in a risk analysis simulation (Figure 6). (Total wage costs required two separate distributions, as shown in the figure.) The distributions were then combined to generate the distribution of a cost overrun for each potential project. In addition, sensitivity analysis was conducted to determine the effect of court rulings and specific task failures on project costs. High-risk projects were identified in this way, and tasks that posed high risk could then be monitored with tight managerial controls. Following the cost analysis, project schedules were analyzed in the same way. Finally, time and cost analyses were combined to determine interactions and overall project effects.

General Simulation Analysis

Simulation combined with sensitivity analysis is also useful for evaluating R&D projects while they are still in the conceptual stage. Using the net present value approach, for example, we would support an R&D project if the net present value of the cash flows (including the initial cash investment) is positive and represents the best available alternative use of the funds. When these flows are estimated for purposes of the analyses, it is well to avoid the *full-cost* philosophy that is usually adopted. The full-cost approach to estimating cash flows forces the inclusion of arbitrarily determined overheads in the calculation—overheads which, by definition, are not affected by the change in product or process and thus are not relevant to the decision. The only relevant

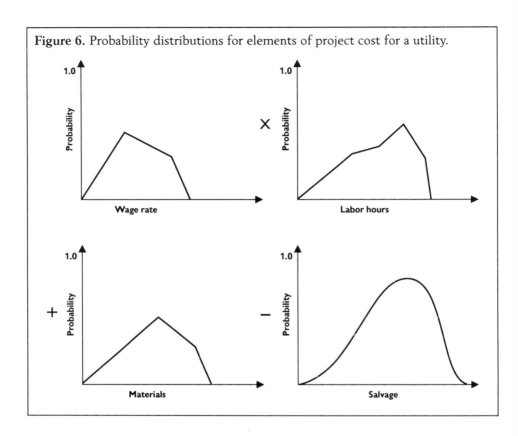

Figure 6. Probability distributions for elements of project cost for a utility.

costs are those that will be changed by the implementation of the new process or product.

The determination of such costs is not simple. If the concept being considered involves a new process, it is necessary to go to the detailed *route sheet*, or *operations sequence sheet*, describing the operation in which the new process would be used. Proceeding systematically through the operating sequence step by step, one asks whether the present time and cost required for this step are likely to be altered if the new process concept is installed. If and only if the answer is yes, three estimates (optimistic, most likely, and pessimistic) are made of the size of the expected change. These individual estimated changes in the production cost and time, together with upstream or downstream time and cost changes that might also result (e.g., a production method change on a part might also alter the cost of inspecting the final product), are used to generate the required cash flow information—presuming that the time savings have been properly costed.

The analysis gives a picture of the proposed change in terms of the costs and times that will be affected. The uncertainty associated with each individual element of the process is included. Simulation runs will then indicate the likelihood of achieving various levels of savings. Note also that investigation of the simulation model will expose the major sources of uncertainty in the final cost distributions. If the project itself is near the margin of acceptability, the uncertainty may be reduced by doing some preliminary research aimed at reducing uncertainty in the areas of project cost estimation where it was highest. This preliminary research can be subjected to a cost-benefit analysis when the benefit is reduced uncertainty. For an example of such an approach see [41].

Comments on the Information Base for Selection

Our bias in favor of weighted scoring models is quite clear, but irrespective of which model is chosen for project selection, an annual or computerized data base must be created and maintained to furnish input data for the model. Directions for the actual construction for the data base go beyond the scope of this article, but some comments about the task are in order.

The use of either scoring models or profit/profitability models assume that the decision-making procedure takes place in a reasonably rational organizational environment. Such is not always the case. In some organizations, project selection seems to be the result of a political process, and sometimes involving questionable ethics, complete with winners and losers. In others, the organization is so rigid in its approach to decision making that it attempts to reduce all decisions to an algorithmic proceeding in which predetermined programs make choices so that humans have minimal involvement—and responsibility. In an interesting paper, Huber examines the impact that the organizational environment has on the design of decision support systems [29].

The remainder of this section deals with three special problems affecting the data used in project selection models.

Comments on Accounting Data

Whether managers are familiar with accounting systems or not, they can find it useful to reflect on the methods and assumptions used in the preparation of accounting data. Among the most crucial are the following.

1. Accountants live in a linear world. With few exceptions, cost and revenue data are assumed to vary linearly with associated changes in inputs and outputs.

2. The accounting system often provides cost-revenue information that is derived from standard cost analyses and equally standardized assumptions regarding revenues. These standards may or may not be accurate representations of the cost-revenue structure of the physical system they purport to represent.

3. As noted in the previous section, the data furnished by the accounting system may or may not include overhead costs. In most cases, the decision made is concerned solely with cost-revenue elements that will be changed as a result of the project under consideration. Incremental analysis is called for, and great care must be exercised when using *pro forma* data in decision problems. Remember that the assignment of overhead cost is always arbitrary. The accounting system is the richest source of information in the organization, and it should be used—but with great care and understanding.

Comment on Measurements

It is common for those who oppose a project, for whatever reason, to complain that information supporting the project is "subjective." This epithet appears to mean that the data are biased and therefore untrustworthy.

To use the scoring methods discussed, we need to *represent* though not necessarily *collect* expected project performance for each criterion in numeric form. If a performance characteristic cannot be measured directly as a number, it may be useful to characterize performance verbally and then, through a word/number equivalency scale, use the numeric equivalents of verbal characterizations as model inputs.

Subjective versus Objective. The distinction between subjective and objective is generally misunderstood. All too often the word *objective* is held to by synonymous with *fact* and *subjective* is taken to by a synonym for *opinion*—where fact = true and opinion = false. The distinction in measurement theory is quite different, referring to the location of the standard for measurement. A measurement taken by reference to an external standard is said to be "objective." Reference to a standard that is internal to the system is said to be "subjective." A yardstick, incorrectly divided into 100 divisions and labeled "meter," would be an objective but inaccurate measure. The eye of an experienced judge is a subjective measure that may be quite accurate.

Quantitative versus Qualitative. The distinction between quantitative and qualitative is also misunderstood. It is not the same as numeric and nonnumeric. Both quantity and quality may be measured numerically. The number of words on this page is a quantity. The color of a red rose is a quality, but it is also a wavelength that can be measured numerically, in terms of microns. The true distinction is that one may apply the law of addition to quantities but not to qualities [66]. Water, for example, has a volumetric measure and a density measure. The former is quantitative and the latter qualitative. Two one-gallon containers of water poured into one container give us two gallons, but the density of the water, before and after joining the two gallons, is still 1.0.

Reliable versus Unreliable. A data source is said to be reliable if repetitions of a measurement produce results that vary from one another by less than a prespecified amount. The distinction is important when we consider the use of statistical data in our selection models.

Valid versus Invalid. Validity measures the extent to which a piece of information means what we believe it to mean. A measure may be reliable but not valid. Consider our mismarked yardstick 36 inches long but pretending to be a meter. It performs consistently, so it is reliable. It does not, however, match up well with other meter rules, so it would not be judged valid.

To be satisfactory when used in the previous project selection models, the measures may be either subjective or objective, quantitative or qualitative, but they must be numeric, reliable, and valid. Avoiding information merely because it is subjective or qualitative is an error and weakens our decisions. On the other hand, including information of questionable reliability or validity in selection models, even thought may be numeric, is dangerous. It is doubly dangerous if decision makers in the organization are comfortable dealing with the selection model but are unaware of the doubtful character of some input data. A condition a colleague has referred to as GIGO—garbage in, *gospel* out—may prevail.

Comment on Technological Shock

If the parent organization is not experienced in the type of project being considered for selection, performance measures such as time to installation, time to achieve 80 percent efficiency, cost to install, and the like are often underestimated. It is interesting to observe that an almost certain, immediate result of installing a new, cost-saving technology is that costs rise. Sometimes we blame the cost increases on resistance to change, but a more sensible explanation is that when we alter a system, we disturb it and it reacts in ways we did not predict. A steelmaker recalling the installation of the then new technology for manufacturing tinplate by electrolysis remarked: "We discovered and installed the world's first electrolytic method for making scrap. It took a year before we had that line running the way it was designed."

Of course, if the organization is experienced, underestimation is not likely to be a serious problem. The Reliance Electric Company undertook several "18-month" plant construction projects that they predicted, accurately, would require 36 months to build from decision to the point when the plant was capable of operating at or above three-fourths capacity. (Note the potential for ethical problems here.)

To the extent possible, past knowledge of system actions and reactions should be built into estimates of future project performance.

The Past and Future of Project Evaluation/Selection Models

In 1964, Baker and Pound [6] surveyed the state of the art of evaluating and selecting R&D projects. Although their investigation focused solely on R&D projects, their findings, and the subsequent findings of Baker and Freeland [4, 5] lead to some tentative conclusions about the past, present, and future use of project selection methods.

The use of formal, numeric procedures for the evaluation and selection of projects is a recent phenomenon, largely post-world War II. At first, payback period (and the related "average annual rate of return") was widely used. It is still used by those who feel that the uncertainties surrounding project selection are so great that a higher level of sophistication is unwarranted.

The use of formal models slowly increased during the 1950s and 1960s, and a large majority of the models employed were strictly profit/profitability models. As we have noted, the emphasis on profitability models tended to shorten the time horizon of project investment decisions. This effect and the results of several studies on the use of project selection models are reported in Mansfield [39, App. A]; also see [40, pp. 15-16].

A similar effect on non-R&D projects is easily observed by noting the sharp decline of investment in long-term projects. The increasing interest rates seen during the 1970s forced cutoff ("hurdle") rates of return higher, which cut back investment in projects for which the time gap between investment and return was more than a very few years. For example, neither new steelmaking capacity nor copper-refining capacity was expanded nearly as rapidly as long-run growth in the demand for steel and copper seemed to justify during this period. Producers tended to blame the lack of investment on foreign competition, but given the aging capacity in the United States, it may well be that the level of foreign competition is as much a result of the lack of growth (that is, our failure to invest in newer technology) as it is a cause. Again, the reader is referred to Hayes and Abernathy [25].

A decade later, Baker [4] and Souder [60] reassessed R&D project selection. In this decade there was considerable growth in the use of formal models, again with great emphasis on profitability models. But Baker reported significant growth in the literature on models that use multiple criteria for decision making. He observed a trend away from decision models *per se*, and toward the use of decision information systems. Among other reasons for this change, he notes [4] that "the decision problem is characterized by multiple criteria, many of which are not easily quantified, and the typical approaches to quantifying subjective preferences are far from satisfactory." He also notes the development of interactive decision systems that allow users to examine the effects of different mixes of possible projects.

More than two decades have passed since Baker's 1974 study. Considerable progress has been made in the development of processes for measuring preferences that yield suitable input data for sophisticated scoring models, models which serve, in turn, as data for goal programming and other resource allocation models. Because it is easy to enter all the parts (data base, decision model, and list of potential projects) in a computer, it is feasible to simulate many solutions to the project selection problem. The decision maker can easily change the criteria being used, as well as the criteria weights. Decision makers can even investigate the sensitivity of their decisions to changes in the estimates of subjective input data, thus directly examining the potential impact of errors in their opinions. In spite of all these capabilities, Liberatore and Titus [35] have found that mathematical programming models are not used for project selection or resource allocation, at least in the firms they interviewed. They did find, however, that scoring models were used for selection—particularly when the firm dealt with outside funding agencies.

We believe that use of these techniques will be extended in the future. As we become more familiar with the construction and use of decision support and expert systems (see [65]), the simulation of project selection decisions will grow in popularity. It seems to us that two concurrent events will support this trend. First is the rapid growth in the ownership and use of microcomputers by organizational executives. The operation of a computer is no longer seen as restricted to computer specialists. Second is the growing realization that profitability alone is not a sufficient test for the quality of an investment.

Almost everyone who has studied project selection in recent years has noted the need for selection processes using multiple criteria. The writings of Michael Porter [47, 48] and others have emphasized the role of innovation in the maintenance or improvement of a competitive position. Indeed, it is now clear that the firm's portfolio of projects is a key element in its competitive strategy. Suresh and Meredith [62] have added a "strategic approach" to the problem of selecting process technologies for implementation. In sum, the methodology and technology for multiple-criteria project selection not only exist but are widely available. Perhaps more important, we are beginning to understand the necessity for using them.

Bibliography

1. Allen, D.E. *Finance: A Theoretical Introduction.* New York: St. Martins Press, 1983.

2. Archibald, R.D. *Managing High Technology Programs and Projects.* New York: Wiley, 1976.

3. Atkinson, A.C., and A.H. Bobis. "A Mathematical Basis for the Selection of Research Projects." *IEEE Transactions on Engineering Management,* Jan. 1969.

4. Baker, N.R. "R&D Project Selection Models: An Assessment." *IEEE Transactions on Engineering Management,* Nov. 1974.

5. Baker, N.R. and J. Freeland. "Recent Advances in R&D Benefit Measurement and Project Selection Models." *Management Science,* June 1975.

6. Baker, N.R., and W.H. Pound. "R&D Project Selection: Where We Stand." *IEEE Transactions on Engineering Management,* Dec. 1964.

7. Beale, P., and M. Freeman. "Successful Project Execution: A Model," *Project Management Journal*, Dec. 1991.

8. Becker, R.H. "Project Selection for Research, Product Development and Process Development." *Research Management*, Sept. 1980.

9. Block S., and G. Hirt. *Foundations of Financial Management*. 5th ed. Homewood, IL: Irwin, 1988.

10. Churchman, C.W., R.L. Ackoff, and E.L. Arnoff. *Introduction to Operations Research*. New York: Wiley, 1957.

11. Clark, P. "A Profitability Project Selection Method." *Research Management*, Nov. 1977.

12. Clayton, R. "A Convergent Approach to R&D Planning and Project Selection." *Research Management*, Sept. 1971.

13. Clifton, D.S., Jr., and D.E. Fyffe. *Project Feasibility Analysis: A Guide to Profitable Ventures*. New York: Wiley, 1977.

14. Cochran, M., E.B. Pyle, III, L.C. Greene, H.A. Clymer, and A.D. Bender. "Investment Model for R&D Project Evaluation and Selection." *IEEE Transactions on Engineering Management*, Aug. 1971.

15. Dalkey, N.C. *The Delphi Method: An Experimental Study of Group Opinion* (RM-5888-PR). Santa Monica, CA: The Rand Corporation, June 1969.

16. Dean, B.V. *Evaluating, Selecting, and Controlling R&D Projects*. New York: American Management Association, 1968.

17. Dean, B.V. "A Research Laboratory Performance Model." In *Quantitative Decision Aiding Techniques for Research and Development*, M.J. Cetron, H. Davidson, and A.H. Rubenstein, eds. New York: Gordon and Breach, 1972.

18. Dean, B.V., and S.J. Mantel, Jr. "A Model for Evaluating Costs of Implementing Community Projects," *Analysis for Planning Programming Budgeting*, M. Alfandary-Alexander, ed. Potomac, Md: Washington Operations Research Council, 1968.

19. Enrick, N.L. "Value Analysis for Priority Setting and Resource Allocation." *Industrial Management*, Sept.-Oct. 1980.

20. European Industrial Research Management Association. "Top-Down and Bottom-Up Approaches to Project Selection." *Research Management*, March 1978.

21. Garcia, A., and W. Cowdrey. "Information Systems: A Long Way from Wall-Carvings to CRTs." *Industrial Engineering*, April 1978.

22. Gee, R.E. "A Survey of Current Project Selection Practices." *Research Management*, Sept. 1971.

23. Golabi, K., G.W. Kirkwood, and A. Sicherman. "Selecting a portfolio of Solar Energy Projects Using Multi-Attribute Preference Theory," *Management Science*, Feb. 1981.

24. Hajek, V.G. *Management of Engineering Projects*, 3rd ed. New York: McGraw-Hill, 1984.

25. Hayes, R., and W.J. Abernathy, "Managing Our Way to Economic Decline." *Harvard Business Review*, July-Aug. 1980.

26. Helin, A.F., and W.E. Souder. "Experimental Test of a Q-Sort Procedure for Prioritizing R&D Projects." *IEEE Transactions on Engineering Management*, Nov. 1974.

27. Hertz, D.B. "Risk Analysis in Capital Investment." *Harvard Business Review*, Sept.-Oct. 1979.

28. Hertz, D.B., and H. Thomas, *Risk Analysis and Its Applications*. New York: Wiley, 1983.

29. Huber, G.P. "The Nature of Organizational Decision Making and the Design of Decision Support Systems," *MIS Quarterly*, June 1981.

30. Ignizio, J.P. *Goal Programming and Extensions*, Lexington, MA: Lexington Books, 1976.

31. Irving, R.H., and D.W. Conrath, "The Social Context of Multiperson, Multiattribute Decision-making." *IEEE Transactions on Systems, Man, and Cybernetics*, May-June 1988.

32. Johnston, R.D. "Project Selection and Evaluating." *Long Range Planning*, Sept. 1972.

33. Khorramshahgol, R., H. Azni, and Y. Gousty. "An Integrated Approach to Project Evaluation and Selection," *IEEE Transactions on Engineering Management*, Nov. 1988.

34. Law, A.M., and W. Kelton. *Simulation Modeling and Analysis*, 2nd ed. New York: McGraw-Hill, 1990.

35. Liberatore, M.J., and G.J. Titus. "The Practice of Management Science in R&D Project Management." *Management Science*, Aug. 1983.

36. Maher, P.M., and A.H. Rubenstein. "Factors Affecting Adoption of a Quantitative Method for R&D Project Selection." *Management Science*, Oct. 1974.

37. *Management of New Products*. New York: Booz, Allen, and Hamilton, Inc., 1966.

38. Mann, G.A. "VERT: A Risk Analysis Tool for Program Management." *Defense Management*, May-June 1979.

39. Mansfield, E. *Industrial Research and Technological Innovation.* New York: Norton, 1968.

40. Mansfield, E., J. Rapoport, J. Schnee, S. Wagner, and M. Hamburger. *Research and Innovation in the Modern Corporation.* New York: Norton, 1971.

41. Mantel, S.J., Jr., J.R. Evans, and V.A. Tipnis. "Decision Analysis for New Process Technology," in B.V. Dean, ed., *Project Management: Methods and Studies.* Amsterdam: North-Holland, 1985.

42. Mason, B.M., W.E. Souder, and E.P. Winkofsky. "R&D Budgeting and Project Selection: A Review of Practices and Models," *ISMS*, 1980.

43. Meredith, J. "The Implementation of Computer Based Systems." *Journal of Operations Management*, Oct. 1981.

44. Merrifield, D.B. "How to Select Successful R&D Projects." *Management Review*, Dec. 1978.

45. Moore, J.R., Jr. and N.R. Baker. "Computational Analysis of Scoring Models for R&D Project Selection." *Management Science*, Dec. 1969.

46. Paolini, A., Jr., and M.A. Glaser. "Project Selection Methods That Pick Winners." *Research Management*, May 1977.

47. Porter, M.E. *Competitive Strategy.* New York: Free Press, 1980.

48. Porter, M.E. *Competitive Advantage.* New York: Free Press, 1985.

49. Ramsey, J.E. "Selecting R&D Projects for Development." *Long Range Planning*, Feb. 1981.

50. Reynard, E.L. "A Method for Relating Research Spending to Net Profit." *Research Management*, Dec. 1979.

51. Robinson, B., and C. Lakhani. "Dynamic Models for New Product Planning." *Management Science*, June 1975.

52. Roman, D.D. *Managing Projects: A Systems Approach.* New York: Elsevier, 1986.

53. Rosenau, M.D., Jr. *Successful Project Management*, 2nd ed. New York: Van Nostrand Reinhold, 1991.

54. Saaty, T.S. *Decision for Leaders: The Analytic Hierarchy Process.* Pittsburgh, PA: University of Pittsburgh, 1990.

55. Schmidt, R.L. "A Model for R&D Project Selection with Combined Benefit, Outcome and Resource Interactions," *IEEE Transactions on Engineering Management*, Nov. 1993.

56. Schwartz, S.L., and I. Vertinsky. "Multi-Attribute Investment Decisions: A Study of R&D Project Selection." *Management Science*, Nov. 1977.

57. Simon, H. *The New Science of Management Decisions*, rev. ed. Englewood Cliffs, NJ: Prentice Hall, 1977.

58. Souder, W.E. "Comparative Analysis of R&D Investment Models." *AIIE Transactions*, April 1972.

59. Souder, W.E. "Analytical Effectiveness of Mathematical Models for R&D Project Selection." *Management Science*, April 1973.

60. Souder, W.E. "Utility and Perceived Acceptability of R&D Project Selection Models." *Management Science*, Aug. 1973.

61. Souder, W.E. "Project Evaluation and Selection," in D.I. Cleland, and W.R. King, eds., *Project Management Handbook*. New York: Van Nostrand Reinhold, 1983.

62. Suresh, N.C., and J.R. Meredith. "Justifying Multimachine Systems: An Integrated Strategic Approach." *Journal of Manufacturing Systems*, Nov. 1985.

63. Thompson, G.E. *Management Science: An Introduction to Modern Quantitative Analysis and Decision Making*. Huntington, NY: Krieger, 1982.

64. Townsend, H.W.R., and G.E. Whitehouse. "We Used Risk Analysis to Move Our Computer." *Industrial Engineering*, May 1977.

65. Turban, E., and J.R. Meredith, *Fundamentals of Management Science*, 6th ed. Homewood, IL: Irwin, 1994.

66. van Gigch, J.P. *Applied General Systems Theory*, 2nd ed. New York: Harper & Row, 1978.

67. Van Horne, J.C. *Fundamentals of Financial Management*. Englewood Cliffs, NJ: Prentice Hall, 1971.

68. Whaley, W.M., and R.A. Williams. "A Profits-Oriented Approach to Project Selection." *Research Management*, Sept. 1971.

69. Williams, D.J. "A Study of a Decision Model for R&D Project Selection," *Operational Research Quarterly*, Sept. 1969.

70. Zaloon, V.A. "Project Selection Methods," *Journal of Systems Management*, Aug. 1973.

Selecting Projects
That Will Lead to Success

J. Davidson Frame

Not so long ago, the common wisdom maintained that the manager's principal jobs were to organize and direct. Such an outlook was appropriate in the hierarchical organizations that dominated Western business life until recently. Today, however, we live in an age of flattened organizations and inverted pyramids. Much of the organization's work is carried on by outsiders through outsourcing arrangements and strategic alliances. Managers are now charged to empower and support their work force rather than to direct them. So much of what was standard managerial fare a decade ago looks positively archaic today.

One thing has still not changed, however. Whatever else they do, managers still have major decision-making responsibilities. This is not to say that they make decisions unilaterally. Now more than ever, in fact, decision making is a cooperative effort between managers, the work force, and customers. In such an environment, the job of managers is not to call the shots independently but to assure that effective decisions are made. They can do this in a number of ways. For example, they can create an environment where they, their work force, and customers can interact productively to arrive at decisions.

Effective decision making does not occur by accident. In this chapter we examine some of its core elements, particularly as they relate to the selection of projects. The discussion can be generalized to cover other selection decisions as well—choosing staff, vendors, designs, and so on.

The Essence of Choice

Rational decision making is fundamentally a process of prioritizing options. The best options go to the top of the list, the worst to the bottom. Consider the choice to buy a car. In this case, buyers consider a number of different selection criteria, including price, performance, styling, safety, and prestige. In the absence of an explicit decision-making methodology such as the analytical hierarchy process, they intuitively assess the performance of the target cars on each of these criteria and then sum up the results. Car A may get top billing on price, performance, and safety but be rated as average on styling and prestige. In contrast, Car B may receive the highest ratings on styling and prestige but middling ratings on price, performance, and safety.

Which car ranks higher? The answer depends on how the buyer grades practical considerations (price, performance, and safety) versus considerations of status (styling and prestige). If practical considerations are paramount, then Car A is chosen. If status considerations dominate, then Car B is chosen.

In view of the fact that decision making entails prioritization, whatever decision-making tools we use should have a built-in capacity to rank order the options. This is precisely what lies at the heart of the specific project selection techniques that we examine in this chapter. What they all have in common is the goal of rank ordering the options.

Benefit-Cost Ratios

The term *benefit-cost analysis* refers to the attempt to systematically weigh the benefits associated with an option against the costs. This can be done in a highly informal manner, as when we divide a page into two columns, labeling one "pros" and the other "cons." It can be done more formally through the creation of sophisticated mathematical models of benefits and costs.

In this section, we discuss one of the more commonly employed approaches to weighing benefits against costs: the benefit-cost ratio. The ratio is created by developing a quantitative estimate of benefits (usually measured in monetary terms), developing an estimate of costs, and dividing the latter into the former. Consider the following primitive example of how a benefit-cost ratio might be created to provide us guidance on what project to select:

$$B/C = \frac{[\text{Estimated Sales}] \quad [\text{Estimated Profit Rate}] \quad [\text{Probability of Success}]}{\text{Estimated Costs}}$$

Let us assume that the estimated sales volume is $100,000, the estimated profit rate is 10 percent, and the probability of success is 80 percent. These three values multiplied together yield the expected value of profit. That is, $100,000 × 10 percent yields a profit of $10,000, we determine that the expected value of profit is $8,000.

Let us further assume that the estimated project costs are $4,000. Our benefit-cost ratio is determined by dividing the expected value of profit by estimated cost, or $8,000 by $4,000. The resulting ratio is 2.0.

It should be noted that this ratio is not an abstract number. A ratio of 2.9 tells us that for every dollar invested in the project, we can anticipate $2.00 in benefits. In other words, the ratio is a measure of "bang for the buck." If this ratio accurately portrays the per-dollar impact of an investment, it can be a valuable tool in our project management toolbox. The relative merits of two or more projects can be established by comparing their benefit-cost ratios.

In finance, the benefit-cost ratio is called the *profitability index* because it tells us whether an option is profitable. When the ratio is greater than 1.0, it is profitable because benefits exceed costs. When it is less than 1.0, it is not profitable because costs are greater then benefits. A ratio of 1.0 indicates that benefits perfectly offset costs—we neither make nor lose money.

Estimating Benefits and Costs

The benefit-cost ratio is a quantitative tool, and as such it requires that the variables being analyzed be quantified. Most typically, benefits are measured in monetary terms.

The example offered above shows how this can be done. In this particular formulation, benefits are measured by estimating profits in the simplest way possible.

Computations of benefits can grow more complex than this. An elaborate modeling of benefits can become quite formidable, filled with exotic integral signs and Greek characters. For example, anticipated benefits might be captured by a mathematical growth function using integral calculus. The effects of depreciation, salvage value, and taxes might be factored out, further complicating the formulation. When all is said and done, the mathematical formula describing benefits might look like something copied from a book on rocket science.

Obtaining data to calculate ratios can be troublesome. Where do the data come from? Ideally, the organization conducting the analysis has been collecting data over a period of time and has developed a historical data base that can be employed. If it is an important project, many departments might contribute to the estimating process: the marketing department might contribute possible sales and price estimates; the manufacturing department, information on projected production runs and costs; and the finance department, data on costs.

It is certain that even the best data will be a bit soft. We are talking, after all, about gazing into a crystal ball to predict the future, and the future is always vague. It is therefore a good idea to establish a range of possible outcomes: a best case, worst case, and most likely scenario. By uncovering the full range of options, decision makers have a better sense of the consequences of their actions.

Unfortunately, the reliability of much of the data being generated through this process may be low because of problems inherent in making estimates. For example, many of the people involved in generating the data may be amateurs in the realm of cost estimating, pulling numbers out of thin air. Or perhaps the optimism of key players makes it impossible to see the downside of certain projects.

Measuring Benefits as Cost Avoidance

Clearly, when one is selling a product or service to an external customer, it is easy to construe benefits as income streams. But what of situations where we do not have income streams? Governments always encounter this situation because they do not operate to generate profits. In the private sector this also occurs, commonly on internal projects designed to improve an organization's operations, as when equipment or information systems are upgraded. For example, it is difficult, if not impossible, to calculate increases in profitability associated with the purchase of a new financial accounting system.

So how can benefits be calculated when there are no income streams associated with an activity? One can measure benefits as *cost avoidance*. That is, one uses benefit-cost ratios to identify options that will save the organization money.

To see how this works, consider the following example. A government scientific laboratory is looking for a way to analyze blood samples more effectively. Currently, their procedures are labor intensive. They seek out modern blood analysis machinery that can automate the process extensively. Three products emerge that can help them carry out their work more effectively. Each of these products meets the lab's technical requirements for blood analysis. The laboratory decides to conduct a benefit-cost analysis to assist it in selecting the proper piece of equipment.

In calculating benefits, the lab first computes the cost of analyzing blood under current procedures. Then, using data supplied to it by the vendor combined with estimates made by its own personnel, the laboratory estimates the cost of analyzing blood for each of the three candidate products (net of the costs of purchasing the equipment in the first place, as well as the cost of a maintenance contract). It determines the annual cost savings associated with each of the products to be $120,000 for Product A, $80,000 for Product B, and $160,000 for Product C. Clearly, Product C will provide the laboratory with the greatest level of cost savings.

These cost savings must be assessed against the purchase price of the equipment plus additional costs, such as the price of a maintenance agreement. Assuming that the equipment has a useful life of five years, the lab divides the total purchase price by five and adds on the annual maintenance fee to derive an estimate of annualized costs for the equipment. The estimated annualized costs are $80,000 for Product A, $60,000 for Product B, and $160,000 for Product C.

In calculating benefit-cost ratios, the laboratory finds that they are 1.5 for Product A, 1.33 for Product B, and 1.0 for Product C. This analysis tells us that from a purely financial point of view, Product A gives the most bang for the buck.

Common Problems with Benefit Cost Ratios

In using benefit-cost ratios, project staff should be aware of a number of common pitfalls.

Focus on the Measurable. Obviously, this approach has a bias toward what is readily measurable. It tends to ignore things that are hard to quantify. However, sometimes the immeasurable can be very important. For example, in calculating benefits, have we taken into account the downstream secondary and tertiary consequences of our project? Possibly a seemingly unimpressive project might be laying the groundwork for major breakthroughs in the future. Have the potential downstream benefits been factored into the benefit-cost ratio for this project?

Other hard-to-quantify factors include the amount of good will generated by the project, its "fit" with corporate goals and the corporate culture, and its contribution to building core competencies in the organization (for example, increasing technological capabilities). If factors such as these are not included in the benefit-cost analysis, the resulting ratio will offer a skewed view of the value of benefits in relation to cost.

Inaccurate Specification of the Benefit-Cost Model. When computing a benefit-cost ratio, an obvious question that arises is: Does the benefit-cost model we have created accurately reflect reality? In statistics, this is called the *specification problem.* There is bound to be some divergence between reality and the model since models are an approximation of reality. The key issue is whether the specified model deviates *dramatically* from reality, providing us with seriously misleading information.

We have just seen that the exclusion of nonmeasurable factors from the model might lead to distortions. But there may be problems even with the measurable factors. For example, our model of benefits may assume that they grow exponentially over the next five years when in fact their growth is linear. Or our model may neglect to take into account the salvage value of a product when this may measurably affect how benefits are calculated.

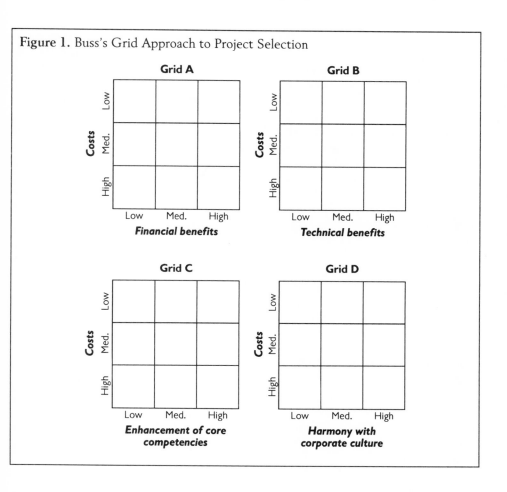

Figure 1. Buss's Grid Approach to Project Selection

To minimize the negative effects of model misspecification, the model should be continually tested against reality and subjected to criticism. Alternative forms of the model should also be explored to determine how sensitive it is to variations of its specifications.

Size-Independent Nature of the Ratios. Given two project options, one whose benefit-cost ratio is 3.22 and the other whose ratio is 2.80, the "obvious" choice is to support the first option. However, consider the data that might have gone into the construction of these two ratio values:

Option A: B/C = ($3,220/$1,000) = 3.22
Option B: B/C = ($2,800,000/$2,000,000) = 2.80

A review of the data underlying the ratios changes our perspective on the relative merits of the two projects. A large company would find Option B more desirable than Option A because it involves larger amounts of payback. The payback of Option A is "chicken feed." Consider that from an investment point of view, Option B is one thousand times larger than Option A (that is, it would take one thousand Option A projects to equal one Option B project because a million dollar investment is a thousand times larger than a thousand dollar investment).

The point here is that benefit-cost ratios are size-independent. They tell us nothing of the dimensions of the underlying investment and payback. There are an infinite number of ways that a ratio of 3.22 can be generated: 0.322/0.100, 3.22/1.00, 32.2/10.00, 322/100, etc. In comparing two benefit-cost ratios, we want to be sure that we are not comparing an elephant with a mouse.

Unknown Payback Periods. If Project Option C has a benefit-cost ratio of 3.22 and Project Option D has a ratio of 2.80, Option C would appear to be more attractive than Option D. However, if the payback period associated with Option C's benefits is longer than that of Option D, Option D may be the more desirable choice. In interpreting benefit-cost ratios, it is generally important to examine the cash inflow and outflow structures associated with benefits and costs respectively. The overall ratio may blur important information contained in the cash flow data.

The Telescope Effect. In Chapter Ten, which covers procedures for estimating project costs and schedules, the telescope effect is described in some detail. Small errors of estimation can telescope into major errors if these errors occur consistently. For example, if an estimator consistently overstates benefits by 10 percent (and understates costs by 10 percent) in the benefit-cost equation shown at the beginning of this chapter, the resulting benefit-cost ratio will overstate benefits by 48 percent. When such an effect takes place, undeserving projects obtain support based on faulty estimates.

Buss's Technique for Rank Ordering Projects

In 1983, an interesting article written by Martin Buss appeared in the *Harvard Business Review*. Entitled "How to Rank Computer Projects," it described a benefit-cost project selection methodology that does not depend on employing quantitative data but that still shares some of the key features of benefit-cost ratios. The following discussion expostulates on Buss's ideas but modifies them slightly in light of my own experience in employing them.

Buss's approach requires that a small project selection team be put together—say, during a quarterly review session—to review at one time a number of project proposals. Ideally, the team members represent different perspectives. For example, a hypothetical team might have the following composition: one member from the marketing department, one from finance, one from production, and one from engineering.

The team members are charged to go through the pile of proposals and to evaluate each of them according to key project selection criteria. Although each organization can create its own specialized criteria, experience shows that four criteria serve the project selection process effectively: financial, technical, developmental, and organizational. Each of these criteria is viewed from the perspective of benefits and is matched against project costs. The matching of costs against benefit for the four selection criteria is pictured in Figure 1. The matching takes the physical form of a three-by-three grid.

Grid A matches costs of the candidate projects against anticipated financial benefits. As the grid illustrates, nine possible scenarios emerge. Project costs can be high while financial benefits are also high; costs can be moderate while benefits are high; costs can be low while benefits are high; and so on.

The team begins the process by evaluating the first proposal according to its relative costs and financial benefits. After some discussion, a team consensus should emerge as to which of the nine cells best captures the essence of the project. In our example, the team determines that Project 1's costs are "medium," as are its financial benefits. This process is repeated with the other proposals. One by one, they are assigned to their appropriate cells in the grid.

Most proposed projects are likely to fall into the cells along the diagonal of the grid. I call the diagonal the "you get what you pay for" cells. Along the diagonal, the relative benefits of a low-cost project are low, the relative benefits of a medium-cost project are medium, and the relative benefits of a high-cost project are high. Projects assigned to these cells are analogous to projects with a benefit-cost ratio of 1.0. They neither make nor lose money. Benefits and costs basically offset each other.

The most desirable cell is found in the top left-hand corner: here projects have high benefits but low costs. The least desirable cell is the one in the bottom right-hand corner: here projects have high costs and low benefits. In general, any projects assigned to the diagonal or to the cells above the diagonal are supportable: they do not lose money. Projects assigned to cells below the diagonal are money losers.

Once all projects have been assigned to their cells in Grid A, attention turns to Grid B. Here project costs are matched against technical benefits arising from the project. A project that leads to a technical breakthrough that can lead to further technical advances would be rated high on the technical benefit scale. One that had no technical benefits would be rated low. As with Grid A, each project is assigned to a cell.

Grid C matches project costs against the contributions that the project might make to nurturing the organization's core competencies. By carrying out a project, is the organization developing the capabilities of its personnel? Is it gaining entry into desirable targeted areas? Is it gaining experience that will serve it well on future projects? If a project is seen to contribute heavily in these areas, it is rated high on the core competency scale.

Finally, Grid D matches project costs against organizational goals and the corporate culture. Key questions addressed here include: Will a project contribute significantly to advancing well-defined organizational goals? Does it reinforce or run against the corporate culture? Projects that go against organizational goals and the corporate culture are doomed to failure and should not be supported.

After all the projects have been assigned to cells in each of the four grids, it is time to make an overall assessment of their value. Buss suggests that the selection team should avoid being too analytical in doing this—for example, by taking a weighted average of each project's "score" for each of the grids. Rather, they should put away the facts and figures and trust in their collective insights. They have spent a substantial amount of time reviewing the proposals and now know each project intimately. As a final step in the selection process, they should assign each project to a cell in a generic "super" benefit-cost grid. When all is said and done, which cell does Project 1 belong in? Project 2? Project 3? And so on.

Buss's approach to rank ordering projects is appealing for at least two reasons. First, it offers a method for conducting a benefit-cost analysis that does not require the

Figure 2. Illustrative Example of the Poor Man's Hierarchy

	Cheap Labor	Transportation	Suppliers	Land Cost	Government Incentives	Tax Policies	Score
Cheap Labor	•••	1	1	1	1	1	5
Transportation	0	•••	0	1	1	0	2
Suppliers	0	1	•••	1	1	0	3
Land Cost	0	0	0	•••	1	0	1
Government Incentives	0	0	0	0	•••	0	0
Tax Policies	0	1	1	1	1	•••	4

organization to develop a quantitative model that might be misspecified. Yet it still shares key features of benefit-cost ratio analysis. For example, the cell to which a project is assigned roughly corresponds to benefit-cost ratios greater than, equal to, or less than zero. In addition, the process is rigorous in that the selection team must be explicit about selection criteria.

Second, the approach depends on the informed collective judgment of the members of the selection team. Because the team members reflect a broad range of perspectives, their decisions are less likely to reflect a narrow outlook. They arrive at their conclusions after measured debate on the merits and shortcomings of different projects in respect to different criteria. Through the process of give-and-take discussion, all features of the project—drawbacks as well as strengths—will have been exposed and reviewed. Because any position can be challenged, project optimists will be forced to justify their rosy projections. The Buss approach is very much a Japanese-style management tool.

Poor Man's Hierarchy

An exciting development in management science in the 1980s was the rapid growth in the popularity of a decision-making tool called the Analytical Hierarchy Process (AHP). This technique was developed in the 1970s by Thomas Saaty. Its applications to management decision making are described in Saaty's book *Decision Making for*

Leaders (1982). AHP has caught people's fancy because it generates quantitative values based on subjective judgments.

A detailed description of this technique lies outside the realm of this book, partly because the mathematics are a bit arcane (they involve the computation of such things as eigenvalues and eigenvectors). However, a pared-down treatment can be offered here. Because it is only a shadow of the full AHP, I call it the "poor man's hierarchy." I developed it as an introduction to AHP concepts for managers lacking a solid mathematical background. After teaching it to many managers and employing it on consulting assignments, I found that it is a good decision-making tool in its own right.

The central objective of the poor man's hierarchy is to enable decision makers to rank order options in a relatively painless fashion. It does this by having managers compare each of the options pairwise. The point is best illustrated by means of an example. Let's say that a small group of managers and technical staff are brought together to select a new site to establish manufacturing operations. In using the poor man's hierarchy, their first task is to identify what criteria should go into the decision-making process. They choose these criteria after give-and-take discussion. They might ultimately decide that the key selection criteria are availability of cheap labor, proximity of the site to a good highway and a major airport, proximity of the site to key suppliers, cost of land, availability of investment incentives from the local government, and tax policies in the region.

After the criteria have been selected, they are rank ordered according to priority by making pairwise comparisons between the criteria. The comparisons are made by addressing the following types of questions: Which is the more desirable criterion, availability of cheap labor or regional tax policies? Proximity to key suppliers or regional tax policies? Availability of cheap labor or proximity to key suppliers? These questions are raised for all possible pairs of questions.

The process of asking questions and tracking the answers is facilitated by the creation of a square grid, as pictured in Figure 2. The selection criteria are listed along the side of the grid as well as across the top. This enables the decision makers to make sure that they address all possible pairwise combinations of criteria.

Cells in the grid are filled in according to the following rule: if the criterion along the side of the grid is preferable to the criterion listed across the top, then a "1" is placed in the cell. If the criterion on top is preferable, then a "0" is placed in the cell. Note that the diagonal cells are blanked out since it does not make sense to compare a criterion to itself. Note additionally that comparisons need only be made for cells above the diagonal. Whatever value is put in a cell above the diagonal, the opposite value will be put into the corresponding cell below the diagonal. For example, the "1" appearing in the cell linking "suppliers" to "land cost" appears as a "0" in the corresponding cell linking "land cost" to "suppliers."

Consider the criterion "suppliers" in Figure 2. The "0" in the cell under "cheap labor" tells us that cheap labor is rated higher than access to suppliers. The "1" in the cell under "transportation" indicates that access to suppliers is deemed more important than access to good roads and an airport. Similarly, the "1" under "land cost" indicates that access to suppliers is more important than the cost of land. And so on.

By adding up the numbers across a row, we obtain a total score. This score signifies the number of times a criterion won its comparisons with other criteria. The higher the score, the higher the number of wins. By implication, the higher the score, the higher the ranking of the criterion. In Figure 2, it is evident that the ranking of criteria is, from highest to lowest, cheap labor (5 points), tax policies (4 points), access to suppliers (3 points), access to good transportation facilities (2 points), land cost (1 point), and government investment incentives (0 points).

In making pairwise comparisons, we may produce logical inconsistencies. For example, we may say that A is preferable to B and B is preferable to C, but in comparing A and C we may say C is preferable to A—a logical inconsistency. In the poor man's hierarchy, inconsistencies will show up as tie scores. For example, "transportation," "suppliers," and "land cost" may all achieve a score of 2. (This will happen if we state that "transportation" is more important than "suppliers" and "transportation" is less important than "land cost.") As Saaty points out in his work, inconsistencies are not inherently bad. They may simply reflect the fact that our model has not taken into account all pertinent decisional dimensions.

The poor man's hierarchy is useful in many contexts. It was noted at the outset of this chapter that the essence of rational decision making is the rank ordering of options. The whole point of this technique is to assist in the rank-ordering process. It is done very simply, by comparing options two at a time. Thus this technique is a generic decision-making tool. It can be employed to rank order projects, vendors, employees, promise dates, and so on. When my daughter Katy was eight years old, she used it to select whom she would invite to her birthday party (she wanted to invite twenty friends, but there was enough room for only twelve).

I used it once in a faculty committee meeting established to identify a suitable commencement speaker. The committee members easily generated a list of about fifteen possible prospects. However, we found it impossible to achieve a consensus on how they should be rank ordered. Finally, I convinced my fellow committee members to rank order the candidates through pairwise comparisons. We had no problem at all choosing one candidate over another in a pairwise mode. The whole process took about ten minutes. At the end of that time, we had our overall rank ordering. Everyone agreed it reflected the consensus of the group. What seemed to be an impossible task when tackled as a whole was easily carried out when reduced to small, workable pieces.

The Murder Board

For project selection to be effective, no proposition should be allowed to go unchallenged. If the project champion states that her project will generate a 20 percent return on investment if supported, she should be prepared to defend that statement rigorously. If the team engineers say that a particular component in their proposed system will outperform existing components by a factor of five, they should be able to back up their projection.

A highly effective project selection methodology has arisen based on the proposition that no idea should go unchallenged. It is given the rather macabre name of *murder board*. It is a simple method, both in concept and execution.

With the murder board approach, a panel of reviewers is put together to review project proposals. The panel is made up of people from different parts of the organization. For example, one member might come from marketing, another from finance, another from engineering, and another from production. The panel is charged to scrutinize the project proposal carefully. In fact, they should tear it apart and try to show how it is not workable.

The project champion is charged to go before the panel and make the best arguments possible in support of the proposal. He should be prepared to field tough questions and to deal with a skeptical audience. Of course, to be effective he should have backup documentation and employ it when necessary.

Effective use of a murder board allows organizations to catch problems during the talking stage, before large sums have been committed and designs have been cast in concrete. This process tempers the unchecked optimism of project champions and makes it less likely that their infectious fervor will lead the organization to support unsound ideas. For this approach to work, all parties in the process must recognize that its objective is not to punish and humiliate the project champion but rather to distinguish between solid and shaky propositions.

An example of a murder board in action has been captured in the *In Search of Excellence* video. It shows a project champion going before a high-level murder board at 3M (which includes the company's CEO) in an attempt to get the organization to support the development of optical disk production capabilities. The project champion is subjected to intense questioning and is clearly rattled. His defense is good, however, and in the end he receives support to go ahead with his project.

The murder board approach likely will be used in conjunction with other approaches. For example, the project champion may be required to develop a benefit-cost ratio to support her arguments. In the final analysis, the murder board serves the function of "reality check," an attempt to make sure that arguments in support of project ideas do not have built into them the seeds of their own destruction.

Peer Review

The dominant form of project selection in scientific areas is called *peer review*. This approach is employed to select billions of dollars of research projects each year under the auspices of government agencies such as the National Science Foundation, the National Institutes of Health, and the National Institute of Standards and Technology. In addition, it is employed to select projects in industrial labs such as Bell Labs and IBM's assorted laboratories.

With peer review, projects are evaluated by "peers," individuals who are technically competent to assess the technical merits of a proposal. Typically, three or more peers receive a copy of a proposal. They are asked to review the proposal independently. After examining it, they are asked to assess its merits according to a number of criteria. The National Science Foundation criteria, for example, ask for an assessment of such things as the project's technical merits, the competence of key players (in particular, the principal investigator), and the value of the management plan. The assessment is usually noted on a scoring sheet, where each criterion is given a score ranging from 1 (low score) to 5 (high score).

After the reviewers have all had a chance to score the proposed project, their assessments are collected and examined jointly. If all three reviewers give the project a low score, it will certainly be rejected. If it receives mixed reviews, it is not likely to be funded in this era of tight budgets. Even the enthusiastic support of all the reviewers is no guarantee of funding.

Peer review has long been criticized as a highly subjective approach that is susceptible to distortions, such as bias in favor of an old boy network. One study by Jonathan and Stephen Cole found that peer review is only marginally better than coin flipping in identifying wining projects. So why is it employed?

The answer to this question is more closely tied to the science of politics than to rational decision making. The scientific community is reluctant to be reviewed by nonscientists and to be accountable to nonscientific selection criteria. It will be interesting to see whether this outlook will be able to survive the tight budgets and societal demands for accountability that we will encounter in the upcoming decades.

General Rules for Selecting Projects

This chapter has focused on a handful of rational techniques that can be helpful for decision making. Clearly, there is more to project selection than technique. Before concluding the chapter, I would like to put these techniques into a broader decision-making context. Following are some general rules for project selection that, if followed, will lead to better choices.

Rule 1: Be Explicit About What Is Important in Choosing Projects. Project selection should occur in accordance with clearly defined selection criteria. These criteria should be written in large, boldface type. They should be taped onto the walls in the room where selection decisions are being made. They should be ritualistically recited at the outset of each selection meeting. During the selection process, people should not be distracted by the wealth of interesting possibilities that the organization can pursue—rather, they should focus on what the organization needs to pursue, as captured in the selection criteria.

Rule 2: Identify Explicit Procedures for Choosing Projects, then Stick to Them. Project selection should not occur by accident. An approach to choosing projects should be developed and rigorously adhered to. Even powerful players in the organization should be required to stick to the procedures. In this way, decisions become less arbitrary. Also, a check can be placed on those powerful players who irresponsibly push for a particular project "because it seemed like a good idea at the time."

Rule 3: Be Prepared to Rigorously Challenge All Assertions. No statement about possible benefits or costs associated with a project should be immune from challenge. Project champions tend to lose sight of possible problems. The picture they paint of project benefits is typically rosy. By the same token, project critics often picture a proposed project in the worst possible light, adducing all manner of facts to back up their position. The most effective way to temper excessive optimism or pessimism is to question the veracity of key assertions made by project champions and critics.

Rule 4: Constitute a Project Selection Team Whose Members Represent a Broad Array of Stakeholders. All projects serve multiple purposes and have multiple impacts. Clearly, the project selection team should be made up of individuals who represent a broad array of perspectives. A typical selection team for a private sector project should have members who reflect the varying perspectives of engineering, marketing, finance, and production.

Rule 5: Involve Key Project Personnel in the Selection Process. In a survey I conducted of a sizable number of project managers, I found that only 20 percent reported being involved in the selection of the projects they work on. For most project managers, the selection decision is made without their input. They are given project management responsibilities after the decision has been made. There are at least two good reasons for including key project personnel in the project selection decision. First, if these people have a role in choosing a project, they will automatically have a stake in it. They will be more energetic in pursuing project goals because they had a role in establishing them. Second, if they are part of the project selection process, they will understand the rationale for conducting a project. In this way, continuity can be maintained between the project selection and project execution phases in the project life cycle. Too often, when key personnel do not understand the original rationale of a project, they redefine this rationale to suit their outlook, and this leads to problems of continuity.

Conclusions

The selection of projects is serious business. It should not be carried out in an offhand manner. Too often, insufficient attention is given to whether a particular project idea has real merit. Thus projects may be selected to satisfy the hunches of powerful players. Or they may be selected simply to keep staff busy or to spend end-of-the-year money.

A big problem with offhand project selection is that it leads to the ineffective use of resources. Support of a project to satisfy short-term exigencies may lead to long-term fiascoes. Those making the decisions often forget that by committing resources to a poorly conceived project idea, they are tying up those resources. They have not taken into account the opportunity costs of their decision. If a truly good project prospect arises in the future, they may no longer have the resources to pursue it because their resources are tied up in marginal undertakings.

How to Rank
Computer Projects

Martin D. J. Buss

How does an organization decide which information processing project gets top priority? If it comes down to a choice between a new data communication network, a new word processing application, or a new inventory control system, which project is likely to win out? One thing is sure—information systems (IS) managers, corporate executives, and users will all have quite different perspectives on which is the most important. Attempts to resolve their conflicting views can raise everyone's blood pressure.

Differences of opinion can be particularly acute in periods of organizational change when, for example, a new vice president for finance and administration takes over responsibility for information systems, or when a newly formed computer steering committee holds its initial meetings. Likewise, a new information systems manager assuming responsibility for an existing function may feel under pressure from the boss "to come up with something" on the vexing question of priorities. Even mature, relatively tranquil, IS installations are not immune when, say, the new mover and shaker in manufacturing, fresh on the scene, asks the CEO, "How are our priorities determined? Is there a formal approach, or are we flying by the seat of our pants?"

This article first reviews the policy issues that affect the decisions on priorities and some common misconceptions about how priorities should be determined. Next, it describes an approach that takes into account the policy issues, and, last, it identifies the key factors in implementing such an approach.

Factors Affecting Priorities
Several factors influence the assignment of priorities for information processing projects, each in a different way. These are financial benefits, business objectives, intangible benefits, and technical importance. Though these considerations may seem obvious, they involve both pitfalls and misconceptions in many companies, which will be discussed in the following paragraphs.

Financial Benefits
Corporations run the risk of adopting a simplistic view when setting priorities for computer projects. Undue weight is often given to tangible financial benefits in determining

the order in which projects are funded. Thus, a project that pays for itself (either on a payback or a discounted cash flow basis) in one year will be placed higher in the queue than one taking two years.

Business Objectives

Information processing projects must further the goals of the organization. Yet translating this idea into practice often gives information systems managers a headache, since in some companies business planning itself is not well developed and there may be no formal statement of objectives. In others the quality of IS planning is inferior to that of business planning. Companies that have formal IS and business plans may lack adequate mechanisms to link the two. Furthermore, not all companies need to plan there IS activities to the same degree [1]. The characteristics of the IS plan depend on the nature of the organization. For some organizations, such as banks, where IS is a strategic weapon, fully integrated IS plans are vital. In others, where these projects have less impact on corporate performance, the need for careful planning is not so great.

Intangible Benefits

Some important benefits of an IS project cannot be readily measured (e.g., better presentation of information, improved decision support, or fulfillment of an operational need). Rather than forcing calculations to prove benefits, it seems more sensible and practical to accept the premise that information processing can sometimes benefit the corporation in important but unmeasurable ways. In fact, sometimes the intangible benefits can be more important than the tangible. This is particularly true, for example, in the case of information processing software projects such as the conversion of operating systems, the design of data networks, and the creation of databases for multiple applications.

Technical Importance

It is sometimes either essential or highly desirable to undertake one project before another, if for no other reason than the limitations imposed by the abilities of the technical staff. Also, considerations of the system's architecture may intervene. Thus the design of a new network may sensibly precede a system using data communications, and, for a bank, a new client master file may precede the introduction of a revised demand deposit system.

In organizations with a pronounced financial benefit and bottom line focus—the "support" type described by Warren McFarlan, for example—top executives may not appreciate how important technical questions, can be in setting priorities. As a result, astute information systems managers must obscure the issue by creatively combining projects into a single, salable package or by assigning resources to the technically important projects without higher managers' knowledge.

Though the four factors just described affect the priority-setting process, they may well present contradictory pictures. For instance, a project may have no financial benefits although it clearly supports business objectives (e.g., a mail campaign to support a corporate image-building program) or a project with considerable financial benefits, such as a new inventory system for product line X, may not support the business objectives of increasing market share in product line Y. A technically important project, such as the development of specialized software to improve computer security, may have few financial benefits and a questionable fit with certain business objectives. Yet it may deserve higher priority because, for example, the audit committee of the board has expressed serious concern about security.

Decision Makers

Further complicating the setting of priorities is the question of who should define information processing priorities. Consider these three common misconceptions.

Users should decide the priorities. They shouldn't; at least not alone and not when they are at a low operating level. Although they clearly are important to the priority-setting process, lower-level operating managers generally have insufficient knowledge of overall business objectives and of the technical issues to make the right decisions on their own. Senior managers are, of course, better placed to decide priorities, though even they may not always be informed about all factors. The technical importance of any project may escape them, for example.

Operating and IS managers should jointly define priorities. This view overlooks the fact that top-level executives should play an integral part in the process. This is particularly true when information systems have strategic importance and in "turn-around" situations. In such cases, closely relating the IS projects to business objectives is essential. Moreover, in any organization, only senior executives can make the final decision about the allocation of scarce resources between two equally attractive projects. They can opt for both and add resources accordingly, but leaving them out of the process preempts that decision.

A computer steering committee can decide the priorities. Sometimes that is true. However, such a committee can become involved in politics and end up focusing on financial benefits only. Moreover, a steering committee will not be a useful forum for discussion unless it includes representatives from users, IS, and senior management and has good staff support.

Without doubt, the best way to set priorities is to make them a by-product of some formal planning process at the corporate or business-unit level. Unfortunately, few organizations have planning processes so explicit and orderly that they can rely solely on them for determining information systems priorities. Furthermore, even when business-unit and IS planning is formalized, priority issues can still present serious problems.

A multibillion dollar food company recently went through a detailed planning exercise for its consumer food division. The planners and division controllers made serious efforts to translate the systems implications of the ten business-unit plans into IS projects with dollars and cents, and they suggested priorities. Yet the consolidation of the plans at the divisional level has resulted in friction and misunderstandings. The IS staff and the group head of the $2 billion division disagreed about the need for the 30% budget increase in IS expense and the proposed new systems.

Realistically, in most organizations the information systems manager must take the most active role in establishing priorities. He or she must try to reconcile conflicts regarding key criteria. Clearly, the process requires not only consideration of more than financial benefits but also the involvement of people who have a broad perspective.

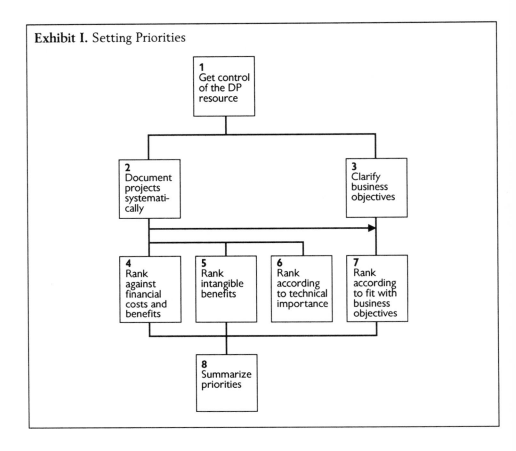

Exhibit I. Setting Priorities

How can the IS manager measure the relative importance of financial and intangible benefits, assess the fit with objectives, and express the technical importance of a range of projects in a readily understandable way?

Implementing the Approach

Exhibit I shows how to implement the process of setting priorities. Interaction along the way with senior managers is highly desirable both to get guidance—on objectives, for example—and to make them aware of the factors that affect the final decisions on project priorities.

The eight detailed steps in *Exhibit I* will probably apply to companies whose information systems are in near chaos. Companies that already have well-documented information processing activities and clear statements of business objectives should be able to focus immediately on steps 4 through 7, which describe the ranking process itself. These four steps are not sequential, and overlapping them will speed up the priority-setting process. Furthermore, an early start on step 7—assessing the fit between projects and business objectives—may shorten the list under consideration, since it should be possible to eliminate marginal projects. Also, if the objectives have a striking bottom-line focus, the analysis of intangible benefits may also be curtailed.

Finally, although the method I describe has eight discrete steps, in practice it must to some extent be iterative. This is particularly so for the examination of the financial costs and benefits of developing each project (step 4).

Setting Priorities

Step 1: get control of data processing. When a formal priority-setting process has not been adopted, a number of problems will probably already exist. One may well find individual staff members fixing priorities, a "them against us" syndrome, poor communication with users, and unilateral action by data processing managers.

Clearly, in such a situation, no approach can be effective. The newly appointed information processing manager must first gain control by taking one or more of the following actions: establishing improved mechanisms for interacting with users, reorganizing data processing and hiring new staff, creating some sort of computer steering committee, and improving the information base for the outstanding projects.

Step 2: document systematically. Part of the problem in sorting out priorities stems from inadequate documentation of project requests. There may be several deficiencies: an outdated approach, randomness in the way projects are documented, deficient authorization procedures, or poor communication about projects within the information systems department and/or between users and management. As a result, the IS manager may not have the necessary facts to evaluate and rank projects.

Since much has been written about documentation, I will not discuss this important issue in detail. In general, however, proper documentation requires establishing, in broad terms, the data required for the various classes of projects, e.g., data processing and office automation. Complete uniformity across all IS projects is likely to be impossible because organizations will be at different stages in their use of the various technologies. Managers may be obliged to estimate data for some projects (prototypes, for example), while having a more solid base for accurately calculating costs for others. Some flexibility will, therefore, always be essential.

In addition, companies should develop standard procedures by which projects are identified and submitted for approval—allowing for different classes of projects—and convert informal outstanding project requests to the new procedures and standardized formats. Planners should describe not only the tangible benefits but also the intangibles, the fit with objectives, and the technical importance of each project. Management must insist on adherence to the new procedures for all projects.

Step 3: clarify business objectives. As mentioned earlier, clarifying business objectives may prove difficult since the importance assigned to planning will differ from organization to organization. Some have formal statements of objectives, others do not. Yet companies that ignore objectives may devote scarce resources to projects with only a marginal impact. And this can be a double loss since they will also forgo the benefits that might result from deploying resources on projects that better serve their business objectives.

In an environment where formal planning is not well developed, the IS manager should take the initiative and attempt to state the business objectives personally for review by senior management. A pragmatic, broad approach is essential since no IS department can suddenly transform itself into a full-fledged corporate planning department, nor should it. The purpose of this one-time exercise is to place IS projects in their business context.

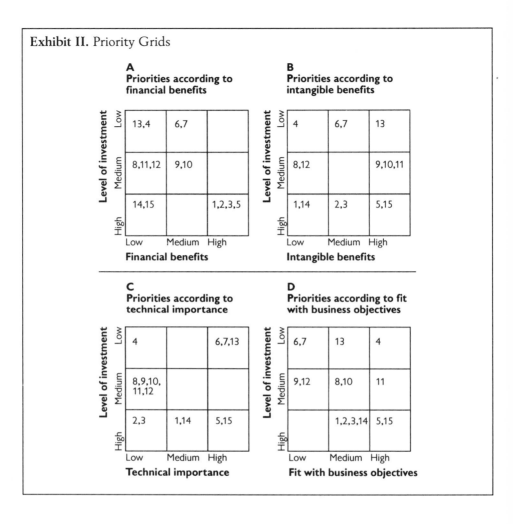

Exhibit II. Priority Grids

The IS manager is looking for guidance chiefly on two issues, namely, what the organization is trying to achieve and the nature of the key constraints. In looking at the first, he will want management views on such goals as increasing market penetration, reducing operating costs, expanding internationally, and accelerating product development. In looking into the constraints, such questions as time horizons, resources, and possible competitive responses will be important.

The best way to proceed is to combine judicious interviewing of business managers, division heads, territory managers, and others with a careful reading of internal documents and a quick review of the information processing of key competitors. The most critical element here is the interviewing of the decision makers.

Although opinions will differ among the decision makers, they will almost certainly agree on the top three or four objectives. The IS manager can build on these through discussion and review meetings with an appropriate high-level management group such as an operating committee, a policy committee, or a computer steering committee. The result will be a consensus on the list of objectives which, although not perfect, can later serve as a guide for evaluating and ranking the information processing projects in terms of their fit with company aims in step 7.

Step 4: rank against financial costs and benefits. The prerequisite for this step is the classic analysis of costs and benefits on a project-by-project basis. Since the results for each project will differ, the manager must calculate the numbers under a series of assumptions concerning in-house development, subcontract programming, purchased package, and so on. The aim must be to arrive at the optimum balance among the various means of putting applications into operation, not just the cost of carrying out the projects internally.

The necessary level of detail will depend, of course, on such factors as corporate policy, time, and availability of information. Sometimes, too, the only practical course may be to make gross estimates. Once the costs and benefits are known, the manager can show their relative priority status on a nine-square grid. *Exhibit II* illustrates the ranking of a series of computer applications for a European bank for each of the criteria discussed. The same method applies, of course, to any set of information processing projects (such as word processing, data communications, and software engineering), not just to those using the computer.

In *Exhibit II*, the low, medium, and high ratings will depend on the organization—what is high for Exxon will be low for the Pentagon! Fifteen projects, identified by number, are listed. In grid A, project 1, "current accounts," is positioned at the bottom right of the grid because it has high financial benefits and requires a high level of investment. On the other hand, project 4, "taxes," appears at the top left because it offers low financial benefits and requires a low investment.

With such an array of projects, senior managers can, at a glance, determine the relative costs and benefits of the entire portfolio of projects. They will, of course, be attracted by those that fall into the square at the top right—high financial benefits and low investment needs. Unfortunately, these are likely to be rare. Many companies, for example, that have started to tackle the problem of obsolete key applications caused by underinvestment in data processing have found that such projects are likely to be positioned at bottom left; that is, they require significant investment and yield little in the way of financial benefits. A mining company, having to quantify the benefits of redoing its 1956 payroll system, is finding that the task requires a blend of witchcraft and financial analysis. Most such analyses are highly questionable.

This same company, however, has reaped an unexpected benefit from a hard look at its information systems and at the costs, benefits, and priority issues. Senior management became convinced that it had a serious problem in the staffing of the function—it simply didn't have enough people to do anything other than the bare minimum. Given the hostile economic environment, rather than add staff, the company made an informed decision to delay projects. As a result, the IS manger could do his job without unwarranted pressure to perform the miracles he had previously been expected to produce.

Step 5: rank intangible benefits. This is a four-part process. Part 1 identifies the intangible benefits both data processing and user managers consider achievable. Part 2 determines the scoring method for the evaluation. Part 3 assigns numerical values to each project so that the benefits can be ranked in order of importance. Finally, part 4 positions the projects on a nine-square grid.

Exhibit III. Scoring Intangible Benefits

Intangible benefit	Project					
	1	**2**	**3**	**4**	**5**	**6**
Improve client service	6	3	8	9	0	0
Improve financial control	1	7	6	0	10	10
Provide management information	8	6	5	0	10	5
Standardize manual processes	3	8	7	3	10	7
Speed up decision making	4	3	0	0	10	5
Improve quality of information	3	7	6	0	7	7
Speed up information retrieval	9	6	7	5	10	7
Total	**34**	**40**	**39**	**17**	**57**	**41**
Ranking	**11**	**9**	**10**	**15**	**1**	**8**

A team made up of users, such as departmental operating managers, and of information systems professionals knowledgeable about the areas affected by the projects should carry out this process. To add impartiality to the exercise, include the head of internal audit.

Working in group sessions and independently the team members can identify the intangible benefits, with each team member bringing to the table his or her perception of what these are—quicker information retrieval, improved image, better decision making, and so on. They will probably agree quickly on some goals but need to thrash out others.

The group approach will also succeed best for part 2 of the process—the choice of scoring method. Several systems are possible. However, managers should beware of overcomplicating the process by adopting a method that is very complex or spuriously scientific. In the illustration in *Exhibit III*, for example, the team adopted a straightforward system that assigned to each intangible benefit a maximum of ten points and they decided after a short discussion not to weight or score some benefits higher than others. Weighting benefits can result in interminable arguments that serve little purpose. This is not an exact science; the objective is to arrive at a broad measure of each project's relative importance.

For part 3, the scoring of the projects against the benefits, team members should work independently and then meet as a group to iron out differences. At these meetings each person should be prepared to explain, for example, if one project scores five out of ten and another scores the maximum, what makes one twice as good as the other.

The meetings will conclude with a summary sheet similar to that in *Exhibit III*, which shows for each project the scores for every intangible benefit, the total score, and the overall ranking.

With the projects ranked in this way, part 4, positioning each on a nine-square grid, is an easy last step. All that remains is for the team to determine the range along the horizontal axis for high, medium, and low intangible benefits. Not surprisingly, the value of a project can be quite different depending on whether it is defined by its intangible or financial benefits. For instance, in grid A of *Exhibit II*, project 1, "current accounts," rates high in terms of financial benefits. Yet in grid B it rates low in intangible benefits. The opposite is the case with project 13, "communications and hardware." It is unlikely to generate cash savings but promises many intangible benefits.

Step 6: rank according to technical importance. Some projects must be completed before others. Data processing managers can show the technical importance of each of the projects in the format shown in grid C of *Exhibit II*. Here again, the vertical axis represents investment, whereas the horizontal axis shows low, medium, and high levels of technical importance. Although this represents a subjective assessment on the part of data processing managers, high-level executives can more easily see the ranking in this systematic scheme.

Step 7: access fit with objectives. Once business objectives are clarified (see step 3), users and data processing managers together can assess the quality of fit between them and the projects, using a worksheet on which projects are checked off against various objectives. It is also possible to develop a quantitative approach in which a project's contribution to an objective is indicated numerically, with a maximum score of 10, for example, for a perfect fit.

Once the degree of fit with business objectives has been established, the IS manager can then rank the projects on a similar nine-square grid format.

Step 8: summarize priorities. The exhibits will give senior management a good picture of the various ways of measuring a project's value, and, accordingly, of the complex issues involved in establishing overall priorities. To reconcile the sometimes conflicting information one can summarize the priorities on a single nine-square grid as one company did in *Exhibit II*.

The number of times any one project appears in a particular square in the nine-square matrices helps determine the final assessment. For example, project 5, "accounting," appears in the bottom right-hand corner in every case, and project 15, "master file of conditions," appears three out of four times. Evidently these two projects should have high priority.

But the final assessment depends on a company's priorities. If priorities had been assigned and measured by financial benefits in this case, the results would have been very different. Three other projects would have been placed above project 15: project 1, "current accounts," project 2, "bills of exchange," and project 3, "bonds." Yet all three "top priority" projects had only a moderately good fit with the business objectives, and two of the three had low technical importance and only some intangible benefits.

The composite grid highlights such inconsistencies and gives executives the data necessary to select priorities. Thus, in the example, top-level managers could still decide to ignore everything except financial benefits but would do so while understanding that most of the projects did not serve the business objectives effectively.

Moreover, with the knowledge of how different factors affect priorities, executives can change the degree of emphasis given to each one depending on corporate circumstances. In hard times, for example, they might decide that only tangible benefits should be considered.

Key Factors for Success

In this process of setting computer priorities, success depends on the interaction of three groups of people, namely, high-level executives, users, and information systems managers. Each has an important role to play.

Executives at the top must demonstrate a willingness to commit resources to approved high-priority projects. They should participate in setting priorities and, in particular, in determining which aspect of priority setting should be most important in any one time period. They should also help clarify the business objectives so that the whole process can be related to the underlying needs of the company. Finally, they must be willing to exercise judgment and make decisions in areas that have not traditionally involved top management.

The role of users is to commit themselves to the benefits stated in the cost and benefit analysis of each project and to involve themselves in the process so that the final decisions reflect a consensus. Particularly important here, for example, is an understanding of, and a commitment to, the intangible benefits.

IS managers must lead the project and be responsible for its progress. They must analyze the issues and develop the four priority-setting schemes for executive decision making.

Finally, a caveat: it is important to build on an existing framework for setting priorities; rarely should it be necessary or even desirable to start from scratch.

Analytical and programming resources continue to get scarcer and more costly. We have to use them effectively by allocating them to high-priority projects. Identifying these by a structured approach will help the harassed IS manager and top executives think through the issues.

Reference

1. See F. Warren McFarlen, James L McKenney, and Philip Pyburn, "The Information Archipelago—Plotting a Course," *Harvard Business Review* January–February 1983, p. 145.

Information System Project-Selection Criteria Variations Within Strategic Classes

James J. Jiang and Gary Klein

Information system (IS) project selection remains a critical task facing information systems executives [4,7]. Capital expenditures on information technology (IT) is a significant factor, perhaps accounting for as much as 50%, or more, of an organization's capital expenditures [5]. To allocate these capital resources among a multitude of diverse IS projects, IS managers need to conduct an in-depth evaluation of competing IS projects. The evaluation must consider the strategic posture of the organization to be effective [18,32].

Research into IS project selection considers a variety of measures and categories of measures [1,30]. Specific measures suggested in prior research have ranged from strictly quantitative, measurable considerations (such as net present value, return on investment, and payback period) to more qualitative, intangible factors (including project risk, organizational objectives, and user support). The significance of the political dimension in system prioritization has also been emphasized [17]. In general, IS managers must consider obvious factors of project control, external factors of the competitive environment, and internal factors of importance to the organization [6,22,26].

While the criteria of IS project selection may be varied, one theme appears repetitively in the literature: IS projects must match with organizational IS strategy [18,19]. Researchers contend that a contingency approach should be used to select the projects. At the very least, the selection criteria should vary in their importance according to an IS strategy [3,6,32]. The weights placed on criteria need to be selected based on the strategic posture of the organization or system failures are a possible consequence [32]. Under this premise, certain project-selection criteria should be considered more important than others so as to match with an organization's technology strategy. Specification of the relative importance can be crucial since a change in weights can radically alter a solution [14].

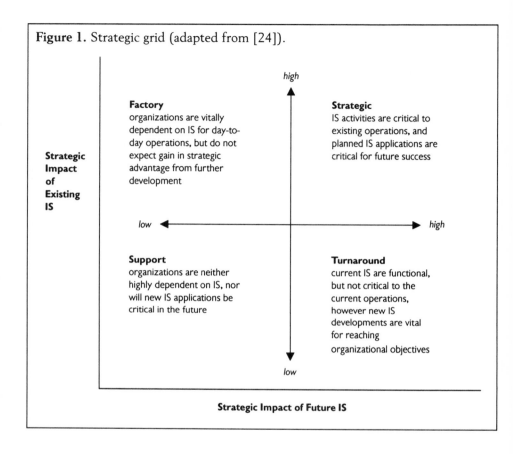

Figure 1. Strategic grid (adapted from [24]).

The purpose of this study is to explore the relative importance of each criterion perceived by IS managers within a contingency model of IS strategic relevance [20]. We believe prior research has focused too much on introducing new considerations onto the IS project-selection agenda [2]. Too little work, on the other hand, helps to understand IS project-selection criteria weights. As the IS project selection continues to remain a critical task facing IS managers [4], the understanding of IS project-selection measures has considerable practical significance.

Methodology

IS Strategic Grid

Projects are often selected based on explicit or implicit weights given to an organization's selection criteria. The weights may vary by strategic posture. Thus, a contingent use of metrics and weights on the metrics can contribute to the successful planning of IS. We choose a strategic grid model [21] as the basis of our explorations. Briefly, the model suggests that variations in IS project selection should exist based upon the levels of two dimensions: first, the importance of the existing IS to the organization's survival; and second, the importance of future IS to the organization's survival.

Table 1. Project Evaluation Criteria

1. Financial Related Criteria:
        f1: Benefit/cost ratio
        f2: Rate of return
        f3: Contribution to profitability
        f4: Growth rate
        f5: Payback period

2. Organizational Needs Related Criteria:
        o1: Contribution to organizational goals/objectives
        o2: Aid the organization in competing in the market
        o3: Internal political decisions
        o4: Importance to the organization for the future success
        o5: Importance to the functioning of the organization
        o6: Public relation effect
        o7: Importance to organization's critical success factors

3. Competing Environmental Related Criteria:
        e1: Required by regulations
        e2: Response to competition
        e3: Required by customers/suppliers
        e4: New industry standards
        e5: Lawsuit required information

4. Technical Related Criteria:
        t1: Isolated, simple, and modular project
        t2: High visibility of project
        t3: Basic subsystem to system
        t4: Basic module for operations
        t5: Availability of skilled IS personnel
        t6: Availability of needed technology

5. Risk Related Criteria:
        r1: Technical risk
        r2: Structure risk
        r3: Risk of cost overruns
        r4: Size risk

6. User's Support Related Criteria:
        m1: Political acceptance
        m2: End user understanding, cooperation, and commitment to project
        m3: Top management support
        m4: Match with users' interest/work load
        m5: Middle management support

Fig. 1 illustrates how the two time dimensions combine into four categories of interaction for descriptive and analysis purposes. The four quadrants have been defined as follows [24].

1. *Strategic:* IS activities are critical to existing operations, and planned IS applications are critical for future success.

Table 2. Sample population demographics.

Gender

Male	64
Female	24

Size of Organization (Annual gross revenues)

Under 1 million	7
1-50 million	25
51-250 million	21
251 million–1 billion	22
1-5 billion	6
Over 5 billion	7

Age

below 30	4
31-40	25
41-50	31
above 50	28

Position

Technical support staff	11
System analysts	16
Project leaders	11
IS department/ division managers	37
IS executive	12

Involvement in IS project selection

Yes	76
No	12

2. *Turnaround:* Current IS are functional, but not critical to the current operations, however new IS developments are vital for reaching organizational objectives.

3. *Factory:* Organizations are vitally dependent on IS for their day-to-day operations, but they do not expect significant gain in strategic advantage from further development.

4. *Support:* Organizations are neither highly dependent on IS, nor will new IS applications be critical in the future.

To illustrate the descriptive power of the strategic grid model, consider the process of IS planning. The activities of strategic IS planning include: 1) identify the organization's information needs; 2) find new opportunities for using information to achieve a competitive advantage; 3) define data, applications, and technology for satisfying the organization's objectives. Therefore, an IS manager in an organization which exercises a high extent of strategic IS planning activities must have a better understanding of the organization's intent on future IT developments.

From a research standpoint, the strategic grid model has several advantages. The strategic grid has an established instrument to determine membership in a strategic focus. Previous empirical research validates the premises behind the model [32]. More importantly, the two-dimensional construct allows a separation into two time frames, allowing an intuitive separation in exploring the various criteria: current IS importance and future IS importance.

Instrument

The questionnaire consists of two parts: one assesses the strategic relevance of IS in an organization; the other measures the importance of IS project-selection criteria. Established scales and items used to determine the strategic relevance of IS to an organization were utilized in this study [24]. The questionnaire of IS project-selection criteria was designed to be consistent with an extensive review of the literature. The six subcategories of IS criteria include financial, organizational/institutional, competing environmental, technical, project risk, and managerial concerns (see Table 1). These criteria cover the general expectations of project-directed criteria, internal goals, and conditions in the external environment.

To ensure understandability, the researchers had two colleagues critically review the questions. Their suggestions were incorporated into the questionnaire. Secondly, a pilot study used the questionnaire with five MBA students who were full-time managers. All ambiguous items were removed or modified. A final set of 32 items remained. All questions were on a five-point Likert-type scale (1: not important; 3: somewhat important; and 5: very important).

Subjects

The questionnaire was distributed to 300 members of the Data Processing Management Association (DPMA) in Michigan, Illinois, Pennsylvania, Ohio, Indiana, and Wisconsin. The sample population was chosen because members of DPMA represent a wide variety of organizational settings. Self-addressed return envelopes for each questionnaire were enclosed. Ninety-three questionnaires (response rate of 20.1%) were returned to the researchers. Five questionnaires were eliminated due to missing data, leaving a final sample of 88 subjects. The participants in this study held a variety of positions within the computer field reflecting considerable heterogeneity within the IS professions. Table 2 represents a summary of the demographic characteristics of the sample.

Each of the demographic variables was run in a separate MANOVA to determine any introduction of bias by the study population. The independent variables were the mean scores of the metric categories described above. Each demographic variable was treated as the dependent variable. No model found any significant relation, indicating lack of confounding on the part of the sample's demographics.

Metrics

The six categories of items used in the survey were derived from previous studies [1,3,5,8,9,11,12,20,23,26,27,28,30,31]. Although well based in the reported studies, no work exists to determine the underlying structure of these items. An exploratory analysis is appropriate to determine the best set of measures to use in the determination of possible relations since there were no a priori hypotheses about the number of scales represented by the 32 items.

Therefore, determination or verification of criteria categories is the first step conducted in order to permit examination of the differences by strategic posture. A principal-components analysis was conducted to this end. The top five eigenvalues were

Table 3. Factor loadings after varimax rotation.

Variables	Internal metrics alpha=.76	Project metrics alpha-.86	External metrics alpha=.80
f1: Benefit/cost ratio	.76	.15	.06
f2: Rate of Return	.71	.26	.04
o2: Aid in competing	.68	.15	.25
o7: Importance to critical success factors	.67	.14	.16
f5: Payback	.65	.28	.08
f3: Contribution to profit	.63	.16	.22
o1: Contribution to organizational goals	.56	.07	.14
o4: Importance to the organization's future	.56	.14	.27
o5: Importance to organization's function	.55	.12	.09
f4: Growth rate	.54	.30	.02
t4: Basic module for operations	.11	.67	.04
m5: Middle management support	.21	.65	.14
t6: Availability of technology	.33	.64	.04
t1: Isolated, simple, and modular	.03	.63	.03
t3: Basic subsystem	.00	.62	.25
t4: Availability of IS personnel	.30	.61	.08
r1: Technical	.03	.61	.08
r3: Cost overruns	.42	.56	.07
m4: Match with user interest	.30	.54	.19
m1: Political acceptance	.12	.52	.38
e3: Required by customers/suppliers	.23	.16	.67
e4: New industry standards	.35	.27	.64
e5: Lawsuit required information	.34	.13	.63
e2: Response to competition	.39	.15	.63
e1: Required by regulations	.15	.16	.58

8.35, 2.63, 2.34, 1.74, and 1.40. Three of these eigenvalues are greater than chance according to parallel analysis criteria [16]. Three factors were thus retained in a varimax rotation with loading results shown in Table 3. Item loadings greater than 0.50 with all other same item loadings less than 0.4 were assigned to the global metrics.

Examination of the items indicates the three global metrics of internal organization concerns, project management concerns, and external environment concerns hold as good descriptors. The internal metric is composed of all financial items plus five of the seven organizational needs criteria. The external environment metric contains all five competing environmental criteria. The project metric includes five of the six technical criteria, technical and cost risk, and management support issues. Reduction to three factors should not be unexpected due to the interdependency of various risk and organizational factors [1,30].

The results from the factor analysis drive the computation of three global metrics. Each of the three metrics is computed as an average of the items loaded into the factor. The homogeneity of the items within each factor was established further by computing their internal consistency reliability coefficient (coefficient alpha). The three metrics (internal, external, project) wound up with Cronbach's alphas of .76, .80, and .86, respectively.

Hypotheses

Organizations with no current emphasis on critical IS do not have the incentive to evaluate systems from a more strategic view. We, therefore, believe that IS managers in organizations with no current strategic IS posture will tend to view the criteria of financial needs and organizational concerns as the more important criteria. These expectations are due to efficiency considerations. An organization with no current strategic IS will be more concerned with the operational costs and degree to which the basic operations of an organization are supported. We thus expect the internal metric to be the most important. We expect to reject the following.

H1o) For organizations with no current strategic IS, internal metric importance will be less than or equal to project metrics.

H2o) For organizations with no current strategic IS, internal metric importance will be less than or equal to external metrics.

Organizations with systems of current strategic importance consider smooth functioning of automated systems vital to daily operations. In some cases, a 1-h interruption can cause serious harm. We predict that IS managers in this type of organization may consider external metrics less important than other criteria. We expect to reject the following.

H3o) For organizations with current strategic IS, internal metric importance will be less than or equal to external metrics.

H4o) For organizations with current strategic IS, project metric importance will be less than or equal to external metrics.

Turning to expectations of future use of IS for strategic purposes, we again examine the two dimensions. First, organizations with no expectations of future IS use for strategic gain do not consider IT critical to the survival and competitive position of the organization. This group of organizations would not require strong analysis in the selection of projects and no difference in the perceived importance of criteria is expected. However, where IS projects are vital for future business success we expect the goals of the organization and expected external environment to drive the selection of the systems. We therefore expect to reject the following.

H5o) For organizations with future strategic IS expectations, project metric importance will be greater than or equal to internal metrics.

H6o) For organizations with future strategic IS expectations, project metric importance will be greater than or equal to external metrics.

Formation of expectations into a two-dimensional grid are also appropriate. Interaction effects are possible, but dominance by the future dimension is expected since a good portion of any project portfolio will involve future projects rather than current enhancements. Therefore, we generally limit the discussion to the two time frames.

Table 4. Metric differences according to paired t-tests.

Overall means n = 88 Project metrics mean = 3.47 External metrics mean = 3.59 Internal metrics mean = 3.88			
No Current Critical Systems n = 62 Project metrics mean = 3.37 External metrics mean = 3.47 Internal metrics mean = 3.80	Project metrics vs. Internal metrics (T-value, Prob)	External metrics vs. Internal metrics	External metrics vs. Project metrics
	Test of H_1 **(4.27, 0.00)***	Test of H_2 **(3.03, 0.00)***	(0.78, 0.22)
Current Critical Systems n = 26 Project metrics mean = 3.70 External metrics mean = 3.88 Internal metrics mean = 4.06	Project metrics vs. Internal metrics (T-value, Prob)	External metrics vs. Internal metrics	External metrics vs. Project metrics
	(3.60, 0.00)*	Test of H_3 (1.17, 0.13)	Test of H_4 (1.07, 0.15)
Future Systems not Critical n = 18 Project metrics mean = 3.41 External metrics mean = 3.17 Internal metrics mean = 3.44	Project metrics vs. Internal metrics (T-value, Prob)	External metrics vs. Internal metrics	External metrics vs. Project metrics
	(.21, 0.42)	(1.21, 0.12)	(-.91, 0.19)
Future Systems Critical n = 70 Project metrics mean = 3.49 External metrics mean = 3.70 Internal metrics mean = 3.99	Project metrics vs. Internal metrics (T-value, Prob)	External metrics vs. Internal metrics	External metrics vs. Project metrics
	Test of H_5 **(6.20, 0.00)***	**(3.00, 0.00)***	Test of H_6 **(2.01, .02)***
Turnaround Quadrant n = 44 Project metrics mean = 3.36 External metrics mean = 3.60 Internal metrics mean = 3.94	Project metrics vs. Internal metrics (T-value, Prob)	External metrics vs. Internal metrics	External metrics vs. Project metrics
	(5.16, 0.00)*	**(2.84, 0.00)***	**(1.68, 0.05)***

Results

Overall and categorical means are in Table 4. Table 4 also reports the results of paired t-tests that examine each combination of the metrics for each level of time dimension.

For organizations with no current critical IS, hypotheses 1 and 2 are rejected as expected. Results indicate that IS managers in organizations in the lower quadrants of Fig. 1 place no more or less weight on project metrics than that of external environment criteria. However, internal metrics are perceived more important than either.

On the other hand, for organizations with current critical systems, hypotheses 3 and 4 are not rejected as expected. However, results indicate that internal metrics are more important than project metrics, with no significant difference existing in any other relation for those organizations in the upper quadrants of the strategic grid. This variance in expectation to actual may be due to the large number of financial items in the internal metric lowering the importance of all remaining concerns [31]. Subjects may perceive the financial aspects a good measure of current project success for a strategic focus relegating the remaining items to a lower, more equal footing. There may also be some reflection on the organizational goals of the organization as having been met (or not) by the existing system. This could be due to a recency bias of metrics used in assessing past projects in relation to strategic objectives. It is important to note that even though the internal metric is more important, both the remaining metrics are deemed as being important in an absolute sense (3.7 and 3.88 out of five for project and external metrics, respectively).

For organizations with a concern for future strategic systems (those in the right quadrants of Fig. 1) hypotheses 5 and 6 are rejected as expected. Project metrics take a back seat to both internal and external metrics. Additionally, internal metrics are found to be of more importance than the external environment. This latter result may be due to the need to incorporate the external environment into internal goals for a firm to be successful [6,28]. Also, internal goals are often more measurable than those associated with the outside world, resulting in a bias due to concreteness.

Combinations of the time dimensions into the quadrants of the strategic grid fall as expected where the data are available. Interestingly, no observation fell in the factory quadrant. Such a delineation could be expected as firms with a high dependence on current systems would be hard pressed to expect little importance of systems in the future. This lack of observation in the factory quadrant, however, means that all 26 observations with an expectation of strategic systems in the future also represent the sample population for the strategic quadrant. Likewise, all observations with no future expectations represent the support quadrant. In the factory quadrant, the requirements of future systems dominate the importance of the three metrics. This can be seen as the last entry in Table 4, which is similar to the results in the "Future System Critical" entry directly above.

Conclusion

A survey of IS professionals explored the importance of project-selection criteria for various organizations. The organizations were categorized according to strategic orientation of their IS. The strategic categories are time dimensions with each dimension considering only a presence or absence of strategic importance. Several hypotheses within the dimensions are proposed and tested.

Numerous metrics used in project selection have been reduced to three dimensions. The three dimensions fall along the lines of internal goals set by the organization, factors dictated by the external environment, and project metrics related to technical aspects, project risk, and project management. The reduction to three global metrics can be an important step in the evaluation of systems as well as the comparison of different project-selection systems. The standardization and simplification to three metrics allows our analysis of differences within strategic orientations and can serve to ease benchmarking burdens for this particular function.

One confirmed expectation is that internal efficiency metrics are most important for organizations with little strategic importance attached to current projects. Typically, firms that do not consider their current systems to have a strategic value evaluate based on efficiency and cost considerations (internal metrics). The other confirmed expectation is that organizations with a strategic emphasis on future systems consider external and internal factors more important than technical and risk considerations. Differences in organizations with current strategic emphasis on IS were found to include internal metrics being more important than all others, with no difference among the others.

The results are encouraging for IS planning and project selection. An organization can determine its weights for control purposes based on desired position within the strategic grid. IS project-selection measures may indeed match an organization's intent of the use of IS and technologies in a large number of cases. Thus, the selection of an IS project by the standards set by IS managers may be appropriate. Perhaps an equally important point, the failure to effectively follow a strategic IS plan for IS project selection can result in squandered resources and forfeited opportunities.

The results of this study can be used as a direction in selecting an appropriate technique for IS project selection. The desired position within a strategic grid can be used to set the weights in a multiple criteria selection approach. Likewise, with a multiple attribute approach, insight into how other organizations set the importance of various attributes can be useful. The levels of importance can be used as a benchmark for industry types based upon position within the strategic grid. The controls provided by a standard set of weights can alleviate many management concerns about performance and strategic posture norms. It is often difficult to evolve an organization toward a desired posture. Specific weights can be used as targets in controlling the evolution from one strategic grid posture to another.

Existing multiple criteria models for process selection often include corporate goals [29]. Instead of incorporating corporate goals directly, the results of this study suggest that corporate goals may be a predictor of weights for other criteria. Decision makers may wish to use models with more measurable criteria by considering the implications of the predicted criterion weights, or simply use the direct criteria and weights to drive a selection technique [13].

Collective decision making in project decisions is often the method used to overcome judgment errors [15]. For example, managers' project selections are often based on the political environment and past experience [28]. Committee members may often act in their own interests and avoid the organizational objectives [10]. The extent of alignment of IS projects to organizational goals is a significant factor in success and performance [25]. The results of this study show that to align project selection and strategic goals of the organization, the weights determined to be associated with the strategic grid quadrants can be used to support the process of project selection, resource allocation, and control. This places techniques for project selection, development, and control under the guidance of an underlying organizational theory, rather than the preferences of the individual stakeholders.

Still much can be done to further refine the metric weights disclosed by the study. Improved instruments need to be developed so that IS planning approaches and IS planning behaviors can be better measured. Longitudinal studies that examine the dynamics of IS planning activities are also desirable to examine the transition from one grid to another. Formal measurement techniques should be applied to individual projects within organizations to clarify the differences between systems of varying strategic importance.

References

1. R. Agarwal, L. Roberge, and M. Tanniru, "MIS planning: A methodology for systems prioritization," *Inform. Manage.*, Vol. 27, no. 5, pp. 261-274, 1994.

2. A.C. Boynton and R.W. Zmud, "Information technology planning in the 1990s: Directions for practice and research," *MIS Quart.*, vol. 11, no. 1, pp. 59-71, 1987.

3. J.I. Cash, F.W. McFarlan, J.L. McKenney, and L.M. Applegate, *Corporate Information Systems Management*, 4th ed. Homewood, IL: Irwin, 1995.

4. T.K. Clark, "Corporate systems management: An overview and research perspective," *Commun. ACM*, vol. 35, no. 2, pp. 61-75, 1992.

5. M.J. Earl, *Management Strategies for Information Technology*. Herfordshire, U.K.: Prentice-Hall, 1989.

6. P. Ein-Dor and E. Segev, "Strategic planning for management information systems," *Manage. Sci.*, vol. 24, pp. 1631-1641, Nov. 1978.

7. D.L. Goodhue, L.J. Kirsch, J.A. Quillard, and M.D. Wybo, "Strategic data planning: Lessons from the field," *MIS Quart.*, vol. 16, no. 1, pp. 11-34, 1992.

8. T. Guimaraes and I.D. McLean, "Selecting MIS projects by steering committee," *Commun. ACM*, vol 28, no. 12, pp. 1344-1352, 1985.

9. T. Guimaraes and W. E. Paxton, "Impact of financial methods project selection," *J. Syst. Manage.*, vol. 35, no. 2, pp. 18-22, Feb. 1984.

10. A.S. Huarng, "System development effectiveness: An agency theory perspective, " *Inform. Manage.*, vol. 28, no. 5, pp. 283-291, 1995.

11. J.L. King and E.L. Schrem, "Cost-benefit analysis in information systems," *Comput. Surveys*, vol 10, no. 1, pp. 20-34, 1978.

12. W.R. King, "Strategic planning for management information systems," *MIS Quart.*, vol. 1, no. 2, pp. 20-34, 1978.

13. G. Klein and P.O. Beck. "A decision aid for selecting among information system alternatives," *MIS Quart.*, vol. 11, no. 2, pp. 177-186, June 1987.

14. G. Klein, H. Moskowitz, and A. Ravindran, "Comparative evaluation of prior versus progressive articulation of preference in bicriterion optimization," *Naval Res. Logistics Quart.*, vol. 33, pp. 309-323, 1986.

15. W. Koh, "Making decisions in committees: A human fallibility approach," *J. Econ. Behavior Org.*, vol 23, no. 2, pp. 195-214, 1994.

16. G.J. Lautenschalger, "A comparison of alternatives to conducting Monte Carlo analysis for determining parallel analysis criteria," *Multivariate Behavioral Res.*, vol. 24, no. 3, pp. 365-395, July 1989.

17. A.L. Lederer and V. Sethi, "The implementation of strategic information systems planning methodologies," *MIS Quart.*, vol. 12, no. 3, pp. 444-461, Sept. 1988.

18. A.L. Lederer and V. Bardiner, "The process of strategic information planning," *Strategic Inform. Syst.*, vol. 1, no. 2, pp. 76-83, 1992.

19. J. Martin, *Strategic Information Planning Methodologies*. Englewood Cliffs, NJ: Prentice-Hall, 1989.

20. F.W. McFarlan, "Portfolio approach to information systems," *Harvard Bus. Rev.*, vol. 62, no. 3, pp. 98-103, May-June 1984.

21. F.W. McFarlan, J.L. McKenney, and R. Pyburn, "The information archipelago-plotting a course," *Harvard Bus. Rev.*, vol. 61, no. 1, pp. 145-156, 1983.

22. E.R. McLean and J. Soden, *Strategic Planning for MIS*. New York: Wiley, 1977.

23. O. Moselhi and B. Deb, "Project selection considering risk," *Construction Manage. Econ.*, vol. 11, no. 1, pp. 45-52, 1993.

24. S. Neumann, N. Ahituv, and M. Zviran, "A measure for determining the strategic relevance of IS to the organisation," *Inform. Manage.*, vol. 22, no. 5, pp. 281-299, 1992.

25. G. Premkumar and W.R. King, "The evaluation of strategic information systems planning," *Inform. Manage.*, vol. 26, no. 6, pp. 327-340, 1994.

26. A. Ragowsky, N. Ahituv, and S. Neumann, "Identifying the value and importance of an information systems application," *Inform. Manage.*, vol. 31, no. 2, pp. 89-102, 1996.

27. J.L. Riggs, M. Goodman, R. Finley, and T. Miller, "A decision support system for predicting project success," *Project Manage. J.*, vol. 23, no. 3, pp. 37-43, 1992.

28. J.M. Ruhl and L.M. Parker, "The effects of experience and the firm's environment of manager's project selection decisions," *J. Manage. Issues*, vol. 6, no. 3, pp. 331-349, Fall 1994.

29. R. Santhanam and J. Kyparisis, "A multiple criteria decision model for information system project selection," *Comput. Oper. Res.*, vol. 22, no. 8, pp. 807-818, 1995.

30. P. Shoval and R. Giladi, "Determination of an implementation order for IS projects," *Inform. Manage.*, vol. 31, no. 2, pp. 67-74, 1996.

31. D.M. Thompson and J.L. Feinstein, "Cost justifying expert systems," in *Managing Artificial Intelligence and Expert Systems*, D.A. Salvo and J. Liebowitz, Eds. Englewood Cliffs, NJ: Prentice-Hall, 1990.

32. S. Tukana and R. Weber, "An empirical test of the strategic-grid model of information systems planning," *Decision Sci.*, vol 27, no. 4, pp. 735-763, Fall 1996.

Part 3:

Tools, Techniques, and Methods

Project Portfolio Selection Techniques: A Review and a Suggested Integrated Approach

Norman P. Archer and Fereidoun Ghasemzadeh

In its broadest sense, a *project* can be defined as "a complex effort, usually less than three years in duration, made up of interrelated tasks, performed by various organizations, with a well-defined objective, schedule, and budget." A *program* is "a long-term undertaking which is usually made up of more than one project." A *task* is "a short-term effort (a few weeks to a few months) performed by one organization, which may combine with other tasks to form a project." The foregoing definitions are from Archibald (1992). A *project portfolio* is a group of projects, and/or it could also be projects in one or more programs, that are carried out under the sponsorship and/or management of an organization. Hence these projects must compete for scarce resources (people, finances, time, etc.) available from the sponsor, since it is rare that there are enough resources to carry out every project that may be proposed and which meets the organization's minimum requirements for certain criteria such as potential profitability, etc. This results in a need to select among available projects in order to meet the organization's objectives in some optimal manner, however that may be defined.

Project portfolio selection and the associated activity of managing selected projects throughout their life cycles are important activities in many organizations (Martino 1995; Cooper 1993; Meredith and Mantel 1995). There is much evidence indicating that these organizations are making serious but widely divergent efforts to estimate, evaluate, and choose project portfolios optimally (Dos Santos, 1989; Cooper, Edgett, & Kleinschmidt 1995). In fact, it has been suggested (Roussel, Saad, & Erikson 1991) that project portfolio analysis and planning will grow in the 1990s to become the powerful tool that business portfolio planning became in the 1970s and 1980s. Some of the criteria that are addressed in the process of portfolio selection include the organization's objectives and priorities, financial benefits, intangible benefits, availability of resources, and risk levels (Schniederjans and Santhanam, 1993).

In order to discuss project portfolios, we must first understand the generic properties of projects. The attributes that characterize projects include (based on Meredith & Mantel 1995):

1) **Life cycle.** From an initial beginning, a project may progress through a series of more-or-less well-defined phases through a buildup in size and resource consumption, and then begin to decline after a peak activity and finally to terminate. The generic definition of project phases includes: Concept, Definition, Design, Development/ Manufacture, Application/Installation, and Post Completion (Archibald 1992). The actual activities carried out within each phase will differ, depending upon the general class or type of project. Project classes include (Archibald 1992):

a) Commercial and government projects under contract for products or services (e.g., telecommunication equipment contracts),

b) Research, product development, engineering, and marketing (e.g., R&D for new products or services),

c) Capital facilities design and construction (e.g., major building construction),

d) Information systems (e.g., development and installation of an executive information system in a large firm),

e) Management projects (e.g., business process re-engineering projects), and

f) Major maintenance projects (e.g., renovation and expansion of a stadium).

2) **Interdependencies.** Projects often interact with other projects which may be carried out simultaneously by the organization. And there is often an interaction between the project organization (e.g., the research and development department) and other functional areas (e.g., marketing, production, finance) which have a vested interest in one way or another in the project. That is, a project may be carried out on the functional area's behalf, and/or it may consume resources which they control.

3) **Uniqueness.** Every project has some characteristics which are unique and require special attention in selecting it for inclusion in the development portfolio, or which requires some customization in the way it is managed if it is selected.

4) **Conflict.** Every project selected must compete for scarce resources and for the attention of management at every phase of its life cycle. The amount and type of resources required, and the type and intensity of management activity, including progress reviews, depends upon the phase of the project.

Among the published methodologies, there has been little progress towards achieving an integrated framework that simultaneously considers all the different criteria in determining the most suitable project portfolio. This is partly because there are many complexities in making a selection, including:

1. There are multiple and often conflicting objectives (or criteria) associated with portfolio selection.

2. Even when all the objectives have been identified, there are still problems associated with determining the trade-offs among the various criteria. In this respect, the importance of guidance from pre-determined organizational policies and budget controls cannot be over-emphasized in establishing selection guidelines. But there are still other non-tangible trade-offs; for example, are economic objectives more important than political objectives (as in the relative importance of undertaking at least one project for each department involved, as compared to an emphasis on the projects with the most overall strategic significance to the corporation). How important are these considerations, relative to overall economic considerations?

3. The evaluation of proposed individual projects is complicated by two additional factors. First, some of the criteria are qualitative, as opposed to quantitative, in

nature. The comparison of qualitative (often intangible) factors, usually based on the judgment of one or more stakeholders, is normally quite different from comparing quantitative factors, for which data or analytical models may be available to assist in the judgment process. Second, each project has risk (the probability of failure) associated with its undertaking, and there may be a large amount of uncertainty associated with both the level of this risk and the scoring of individual projects on each specific criterion. Assessing both risk and uncertainty may be difficult. There are risks associated with both the development process (technical risk) and the marketplace (commercial risk). Uncertainty in estimating project parameters tends to decline as the project moves from its early to later life cycle stages, but risk in the application of the product or service (in the marketplace or installing it in a business) can rarely be assessed until the project is complete. For example, there is normally a high risk associated with the likely technical or market success of a new product that is in an early developmental phase, and the uncertainty in the estimated risk will also be high, depending upon the organization's experience with this type of product.

4. Projects may be highly interdependent with other projects. This could be due to value contribution or resource utilization. As an example in information systems, developing and implementing an Executive Information System (EIS) might require several precursor projects (e.g., a number of Transaction Processing Systems (TPS), and so on), each of which could have benefits in its own right.

5. In addition to the difficulties associated with project objectives, often several constraints must be considered. Major constraints which are normally very important include overall project budgets, scheduling, and program considerations. Other important constraints include the market, and limitations on the workforce and its technological capabilities.

6. The number of feasible projects, especially in big organizations, is often very large, and there may be an enormous number of possible combinations of the projects to be considered for the portfolio. For example, there are potentially 2^{100} possible portfolios if there are 100 individual candidate projects. Hence, it is important to eliminate projects from consideration independently on other grounds where it is feasible to do so before the portfolio selection process begins, in order to reduce the total number of projects to be considered.

7. Selection of, or adjustments to, a project portfolio is a process which recurs at more or less regular intervals. Projects which have previously been included in the portfolio should also be re-evaluated at appropriate "milestones" or "gates" to determine whether they continue to merit further development, in competition with projects which have not previously been included. Cancellation decisions are probably the most difficult to implement, since they often involve serious behavioural and organizational consequences.

8. Finally, portfolio selection is usually not the sole responsibility of one individual. It is frequently a committee process, where objective criteria such as predicted rate of return and expected project cost are mingled with subjective criteria relating to the needs (e.g., a proposed project may be needed to support services related to an existing product) of the different organizations represented on the project selection committee.

One underlying assumption in this discussion will be that the projects being selected are from one particular class. The overall allocation of resources to each class is assumed to be an overall strategic decision arrived at by some means such as top-down planning external to the portfolio selection process. That is, in our analysis we do not expect to compare between classes such as internal information systems projects, consumer product research and development projects, and construction projects in the same portfolio selection process unless there is a direct relationship among them, such as a support association or direct competition for resources in the same organization. Otherwise it would be impossible to develop a consistent approach that fairly judges among the competing projects in making a selection decision. (For completeness, we do include several portfolio selection methods which can be used for strategic decisions concerned with allocation among classes.) It is also probable that the methodologies most useful in developing a portfolio for one class of projects may not be the best for another class (e.g., payback period may be useful for comparing long term major capital projects, but it may be irrelevant for short term consumer product development projects; development projects carried out under contract have virtually no commercial risk, while a company carrying out development for products it intends to market must consider commercial risk).

A second important assumption is that there is unlikely to be a single best way of portfolio selection. Each organization must choose, within the project class(es) being considered, the methodologies that suit its culture and that allow it to consider the project attributes it believes are the most important in making selection decisions. For this reason, although it is not feasible to consider all project portfolio or selection methodologies in this paper, we will provide a relatively broad review of a sample of project selection methodologies. This is followed by a general discussion and an approach to portfolio selection will be outlined that allows an organization to design its own decision support approach by choosing among available methodologies. Tools for *decision support*, not *decision making* tools, are emphasized in this discussion, since the thought processes in decision making should be supported and not supplanted by the tools used. This support is provided through models, data, and management of the large amounts of available information so the decision maker can make logical decisions based on what are regarded as the most important facts. In this respect, the human-computer interface plays an important role in displaying the required information in the most meaningful manner, without explicitly requiring the user to consider such distractions as known constraints or complex project interactions which can be managed automatically by the decision support system.

The objectives of this paper are: a) to evaluate the current state of the art in project portfolio selection methods and relevant computer decision support systems, and b) to suggest an integrated approach to providing decision support for portfolio selection which allows decision makers to utilize a desired subset of available methodologies in a logical manner.

In this paper, the existing literature is briefly reviewed. Some of the most popular models used for project evaluation and portfolio selection that are relevant to this work are discussed briefly, and the advantages, disadvantages, and limitations of each method are described. Then a logical approach is proposed which integrates the best aspects of these methods in a manner that allows a choice of methodologies. An integrated approach would help decision maker(s) to select a suitable balanced project portfolio based on both quantitative and qualitative objectives, subject to resource limitations and project interdependencies which could be automatically managed and displayed by a decision support system during the portfolio selection process.

LITERATURE REVIEW

There have been many published articles and books on the subject of project evaluation and selection, discussing well over one hundred different techniques (Cooper, 1993). Attempts at categorizing these techniques have been only partially successful. But it does seem possible to classify these techniques into two primary categories: *benefit measurement techniques* and *project selection/resource allocation techniques* (Baker and Freeland, 1975). Although some of the techniques we will discuss belong to both of these categories, the first category tends to deal more with the evaluation of individual projects on some basis (economic or otherwise), while the second category deals with the development of project portfolios based on known evaluations of candidate projects.

Benefit Measurement Techniques

Benefit measurement methods can be described as systematic procedures for obtaining and integrating subjective and objective benefit data. Baker and Freeland (1975) suggest the following classification of benefit measurement techniques on the basis of the thought processes that are imposed on the respondents, although it is possible for a particular benefit measurement method to belong to more than one of these classifications.

Comparative Approaches

This category includes approaches such as Q-Sort (Souder 1984), ranking (Martino 1995: pairwise comparison, and the Analytic Hierarchy Procedure or AHP), dollar metric, standard gamble, and successive comparison (Churchman & Ackoff 1954; Pessemier & Baker 1971). Of these techniques, Q-Sort is most adaptable to achieving consensus in a group situation. In these methods, first the alternatives are compared and then a set of project benefit measures is computed that is based on the stated preferences. In principle, once the projects have been arranged on a comparative scale, the decision maker(s) can proceed from the top of the list, selecting projects until available resources are exhausted. The AHP approach is discussed in more detail below. Advantages:

a) Most of these techniques are relatively easy to understand and use, and
b) they allow the integration of quantitative and qualitative attributes.

Disadvantages:

a) The large number of comparisons involved in these techniques makes them difficult to use when there are a large number of projects to compare,
b) any time a project is added or deleted from the list, the entire process must be repeated,
c) risk is not explicitly considered, and
d) they do not answer the question "Are any of these projects really good projects?"

Analytic Hierarchy Process (AHP)

The Analytic Hierarchy Process (AHP) is a comparative approach which was developed by Thomas Saaty in the 1970s (Saaty, Rogers, & Pell 1980). Since that time, it has received much attention, has been applied in a variety of areas (Golden et al. 1989), and a voluminous body of literature on it has appeared (Zahedi 1986). Its main use is in selecting one project from a list. The use of AHP in solving a decision problem involves the following steps (Johnson 1980):

Step 1. Setting up the decision hierarchy by breaking down the decision problem into a hierarchy of interrelated decision elements.

Step 2. Collecting input data by pairwise comparisons of decision elements.

Step 3. Using the "eigenvalue" method to estimate the relative weights of decision elements.

Step 4. Aggregating the relevant weights of decision elements to arrive at a set of ratings for the decision alternatives.

The AHP method has been discussed briefly (Harker 1989), and in detail (Saaty 1990). Example uses of AHP for project portfolio selection have also been described (Brenner 1994; Martino 1995). Commercial software (Expert Choice®), which is an implementation of AHP, is readily available. It also addresses some of the concerns with AHP to be discussed below.

Despite the logical and scientific foundations of AHP and its wide application, a number of criticisms of this approach have also appeared. However, the major advantages of AHP are:

a) The AHP structures the decision problem in levels that correspond to an understanding of the situation: goals, criteria, sub criteria, and alternatives. By breaking the problem into levels, the decision maker can focus on smaller sets of decisions (Harker 1989). The evidence from psychology suggests that humans can only compare about seven items at a time (Miller 1956),

b) In pairwise comparison only two factors are compared at each time. This helps analysts and decision makers to better focus, understand, and discuss issues,

c) People may often disagree on certain judgments, but these judgments usually have little or no impact on the final decisions (Harker 1989). AHP allows for performing sensitivity analysis, reducing the rhetoric in debates that can often arise in group settings (Harker 1989),

d) AHP is quite accessible and conducive to consensus building (Bard & Sousk 1990),

e) AHP handles qualitative as easily as quantitative factors.

The following disadvantages are associated with the use of the AHP method:

a) Relative ranking of alternatives may be altered by the addition of other alternatives. This issue, perhaps the most controversial aspect of AHP, has been discussed in a number of articles by both critics and proponents of AHP (Dyer 1990),

b) The bounded 9 point scale used in the AHP method inherently may give results that are outside accepted consistency standards. The problem is most severe with large numbers of alternatives, but it can exist when there are only three (Murphy 1993). Experimentation may be necessary to reach a consensus on the numerical values to be associated with the AHP semantic scale (Harker & Vargas 1987),

c) As the number of criteria and alternatives increases, the number of pairwise comparisons required of the decision maker quickly becomes burdensome (Lim

Kai & Swenseth 1993). For example, in a hierarchy with 4 levels and 6 alternatives on each level, the decision maker must make $(4*6*5)/2 = 60$ comparisons (Harker 1989). In order to reduce this problem in large scale AHP problems, Saaty and Vargas (1981) have developed a modification of the method in which fewer comparisons are performed. If this method is used, the analyst has to strike a comparison between robustness of the estimates and speed of the procedure in order to determine how many comparisons to perform (Kamenetzky 1982).

A set of techniques are available which reduce the number of pairwise comparisons in AHP that the decision maker must make during the analysis of a large hierarchy. This allows the decision maker to reduce the effort involved in the elicitation of pairwise comparisons but also allows redundancy, an important component of AHP (Harker 1987a; Harker 1987b; Harker 1989). Lim Kai and Swenseth (1993) found a point where one alternative becomes dominant to such a degree that, regardless of the effects of the remainder of the comparisons, it can not be overtaken as the preferred choice. While this *dominance point* differs for every problem, results indicate that, in this way, an average of about 50% of the comparisons can be eliminated,

d) The AHP method implicitly assumes that evaluators are inconsistent in expressing their preferences. Once some level of consistency is achieved through consistency checks, no errors should exist in the input data (Zahedi 1986). This is not actually the case in practice, since not all random errors are likely to be eliminated by consistency checks,

e) When decision makers select a project portfolio, they must often deal with some interdependency among projects. To our knowledge, this issue is not addressed in the AHP literature, and decision makers must explicitly or implicitly assume independence,

f) The AHP method does not address resource limitations in portfolio selection. We do not know whether the best portfolio of projects should only involve the projects ranked at the top of the list, and

g) The AHP method does not address the important issues of project interdependence.

Scoring Models

These approaches (Martino 1995) assume that a relatively small number of decision criteria, such as cost, work force availability, probability of technical success, etc., can be defined which will be used to specify the desirability of each alternative project. The merit of each project is determined with respect to each criterion. The scores are then combined (when different weights are used for each criterion, the technique is called "Weighted Factor Scoring," probably the most commonly used scoring model) to yield an overall benefit measure for each project.

Advantages:

a) Although the benefit measures are relative, projects can be added or deleted without affecting the benefit scores of other alternatives,

b) they allow the integration of quantitative and qualitative attributes, and

c) these techniques are relatively easy to understand and use.

Disadvantages:
  a) Risk is not explicitly considered,
  b) weights are required, which are cumbersome and difficult to evaluate,
  c) these techniques are not well suited for situations where selection of one project influences the desirability of another, and
  d) they do not answer the question "Are any of these projects really good projects?"

Benefit Contribution Models

Project benefit with these methods is measured in terms of contributions to a number of project or program objectives. The resulting measure may or may not be relative depending on the specific approach. Alternatives may be added or deleted without influencing the benefit score of other alternatives. This category includes methods such as:

i) *Economic return* (Martino 1995; Remer et al 1993): Net present value (NPV), internal rate of return (IRR), return on original investment (ROI), return on average investment (RAI), payback period (PBP), and expected value (EV). The latter allows a consideration of risk at various project stages, usually based on either IRR or NPV. The Capital asset pricing model (CAPM) can also be used (Sharpe 1964; Khan & Fiorino 1992). It has the advantage that it includes a provision for risk, but it does not appear to be suitable for discrete project comparisons. A 1991 industry survey of the use of the above techniques (not including CAPM) indicated recent movement towards the use of NPV, a moderate reduction in the use of IRR, and a significant reduction in the use of PBP (Remer et al 1993) when compared to a 1978 survey.

ii) *Benefit/Cost techniques* (Canada & White 1980). These techniques involve the calculation of a ratio of benefits to costs, where the inputs may in fact be derived from present value calculations of both benefits and costs, in order to transform them to the same time basis.

Advantages of i) and ii):
  a) Comparisons are in an easily understood language, and
  b) with certain techniques, the best projects are clearly identified by the calculated measure, depending upon the class of projects being considered.

Disadvantages of i) and ii):
  a) It is difficult to include non-tangible benefits, and
  b) detailed data are needed for estimated cash flows, etc.

iii) *Risk analysis*, including decision theory/Bayesian statistical theory/trees (Canada & White 1980; Hess 1993; Martino 1995; Riggs et al 1994), and decision theory combined with influence diagram approaches (Krumm & Rolle 1992; Rzasa, Faulkner & Sousa 1990). These approaches involve a succession of choices, where the probabilities of particular outcomes must be estimated.

Advantages:
  a) More than one stage in a project can be considered, and
  b) the expected values of outcomes at each stage can be determined.

Disadvantages:
  a) These approaches require estimates of probabilities of possible outcomes, which may be difficult to determine, and
  b) the Bayesian approach is not universally regarded by mathematicians as valid.

Market Research Approaches

There are a wide variety of market research approaches which can be used to generate data for forecasting the demand for new products or services, based on concepts or prototypes that can be presented to potential customers to gauge the potential market for the product or service. Techniques used include consumer panels, focus groups, perceptual maps, and preference mapping, among many others. Wind, Mahajan, and Cardozo (1981) give a good exposition on this topic, including related techniques for data analysis.

Advantages:

    a) The market is the driving force for any new product or service. Resources should not be wasted on developing products or services with little or no demand,

    b) projections of market demand and pricing are essential to the determination of resources that can be devoted to development projects,

Disadvantages:

    a) Market research does not consider other factors such as development, production, and distribution costs and timing,

    b) these techniques are useful only for market-driven products and services and cannot be used for internally consumed products and services, such as information systems,

    c) unless the product or service being considered is similar to one already in the market, the uncertainty in the forecasted customer acceptance rate will be extremely high.

Project Selection/Resource Allocation Techniques

Although they may be used in their own right in certain cases, project selection/resource allocation techniques may be used to represent a second stage in portfolio selection, with inputs which can be the outputs of first stage benefit measurement methods. A number of these approaches have been suggested in the literature, and several will be discussed briefly here.

Ad Hoc Approaches

i) *Profiles* (Martino 1995). This is a crude form of scoring model, where limits are set for the various attribute levels of a project, and any projects which fail to meet these limits are eliminated. The human-computer interface aspects of related approaches have been investigated by Todd & Benbasat (1993), who found that users prefer an approach which minimizes effort, and not necessarily the one which provides an optimal solution.

Advantages:

    a) It is very efficient, and

    b) it judges all projects on the same basis, given the values of particular attributes.

Disadvantages:

    a) It is very arbitrary, and requires specific limits to be set on various criteria. These may be difficult to determine.

ii) *Interactive selection* (Hall & Nauda 1990). This involves an interactive process between the managers championing projects and decision maker(s) responsible for choosing the portfolio. The key feature is that selection criteria are better articulated as the process continues.

Advantages:

    a) Project managers have an incentive to make their projects look more attractive to the decision maker (this may be a disadvantage!),

    b) it helps managers to become very familiar with all aspects of the project, and

    c) the projects are more likely to fit the strategic objectives of the decision maker(s).

Disadvantages:

    a) This may make all the projects look more alike than they really are.

Strategic Planning Tools

The strategic implications of portfolio selection are complex and varied. The best sources of related material appear in Hax & Majluf (1984) and Hax & Majluf (1996), who discuss a number of techniques for developing strategies, including the use of portfolio matrices, to be discussed below. The first two of the following relate to other tools which have been discussed in the literature.

    i) *Cognitive modeling or policy capturing* (Martino 1995; Schwartz & Vertinsky 1977). This is a method which examines global decisions to determine the components (actual decision processes) that went into them. There are two approaches: replication of decisions, and evaluation of decisions. The intent is to calibrate the decision process so future decisions can be consistent within the context of previous decisions.

Advantages:

    a) Allow the analysis of global decisions in order to understand how they were made

Disadvantages:

    a) Only past decisions can be examined, and it requires a relatively large number in order to get the maximum benefit, and

    b) these approaches are of little use in relatively new situations.

    ii) *Cluster analysis* (Mathieu & Gibson 1993). This is a method which helps in selecting projects that support the strategic positioning of the firm.

Advantages:

    a) Assists in maintaining the firm's strategic direction.

Disadvantages:

    a) Only helps in finding clusters of similar projects, but doesn't select specific projects from within the clusters.

    iii) *Portfolio Matrices.* Portfolio matrix methods can be used to prioritize and allocate resources among competing projects. The use of these methods has been promoted by several noted consulting firms during the last few years (Cooper 1993). The Strategic Decision Group (SDG) and Arthur D. Little Corp. have both developed well-known and widely used portfolio matrix methods for project portfolio selection, and their implementations are described briefly later.

Portfolio matrices are basically two-dimensionsal pictorial representations of all the projects under consideration. Figure 1 is an example of an SDG matrix model. In a portfolio matrix, usually one dimension represents the likelihood of success, and the second represents the economic value of the project. In all such matrix approaches, the position of a project within a matrix suggests the pursuit of a certain strategy. The intent is that, by using these methods, a reasonable mix of projects on the dimensions represented can be selected by decision makers.

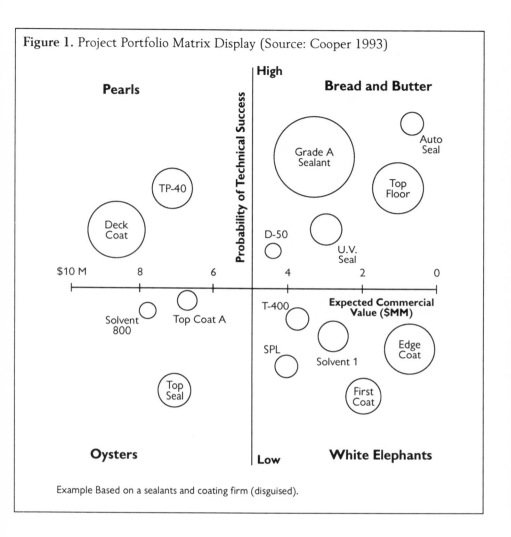

Figure 1. Project Portfolio Matrix Display (Source: Cooper 1993)

Example Based on a sealants and coating firm (disguised).

Independent of the specific type of matrix display used, the advantages of project portfolio matrices are:

a) Portfolio matrices are well organized, disciplined methodologies that facilitate the selection of a portfolio of projects,

b) Managers often neglect to use a rational economic approach. Portfolio matrices lead managers to make decisions that are more rational than if they use unaided judgment,

c) Portfolio matrix methods are judged to be successful for strategic planning by those who use them. A survey of Fortune 1000 companies showed that almost all respondents believe their use of portfolio planning methods has a positive impact (Haspelagh 1982),

d) Portfolio matrices present information to decision makers in a "user-friendly" manner. They can also be used by groups of managers in decision-making meetings,

e) Portfolio matrices give an overall perspective of all projects underway on a single map, and

f) Portfolio matrices tend to enforce a strategic discipline in decision making. They also provide a commonly understood vocabulary to facilitate idea exchange among decision makers.

The major disadvantages associated with project portfolio matrices are:

a) The scope of portfolio matrices ignores other relevant strategic issues,

b) Portfolio matrices have little theoretical or empirical support (Armstrong & Brodie 1994),

c) Use of project labels (e.g., pearl, oyster, and so on), common in this approach, are appealing and easy to use, but they may lead decision makers to overlook profit maximization (Armstrong & Brodie 1994),

d) No single empirical study has demonstrated that portfolio matrices are valuable as a decision aid (Armstrong & Brodie 1994),

e) Research showed that the BCG matrix approach interferes with profit maximizing, as may other matrix methods (Hax & Majluf 1983). As a result, some researchers have advised against using matrix methods under all circumstances, until evidence is produced that they give superior results (Armstrong & Brodie 1994),

f) Thus far, portfolio matrix techniques have seen limited success (Cooper 1993),

g) Excessive rigidity, which is inherent in these methods, could lead to a mechanistic type of thinking which would stifle rather than enhance creativity. When used by uninitiated decision makers, portfolio matrices could hinder a truly creative way of thinking (Hax & Majluf 1984), and

h) Portfolio matrices are sensitive to the operational definition of the dimensions, cut-off points, weighting scheme and the specific model used. For example, using different portfolio models in strategic planning could classify the same project as a dog, star, cash cow, or problem child (Wind, Mahajan, & Swire 1983).

Optimization Models

The objective of an optimization model is to select from the list of candidate projects a set that provides maximum benefit (e.g., maximum net present value) to the firm. Optimization models are generally based on some form of mathematical programming, which not only supports the optimization process, but takes into account project interactions such as resource dependencies, budget constraints, technical interactions, market interactions, or program considerations (Martino 1995). These models also generally support sensitivity analysis (Canada & White 1980), an important aspect of making choices when the portfolio is being fine-tuned. Optimization models based on a variety of mathematical programming techniques or combinations of these have appeared in the literature (see Martino 1995, Chapter 5, for a partial list). However, most of these models do not seem to be used extensively in practice (Souder 1973). Probable reasons for their disuse include the need to collect massive amounts of input data, the inability of most such models to include considerations of risk, and in some cases the model complexity.

There are potential uses of mathematical programming in conjunction with other approaches. For example, 0-1 integer programming could be used to apply constraints such as resource utilization and project interactions, and goal programming allows multiple objectives to be considered simultaneously (Santhanam et al 1989), while a project matrix approach is used. Applications of 0-1 integer programming are described in more detail below.

Advantages:

a) Mathematical programming approaches maximize overall portfolio objectives, and

b) they allow for interdependencies and other constraints on projects.

Disadvantages:

a) These approaches don't deal with tradeoffs between risk and return,

b) don't provide for evaluation of non-tangible benefits and costs,

c) may require data that aren't available,

d) normally cannot include risk considerations (an exception is stochastic programming),

e) with the exception of goal programming, these don't handle multiple criteria, and

f) there is danger that the results may give a false sense of accuracy, even if the input data are highly uncertain.

Zero-one Integer Programming

Zero-one (0-1) integer programming is an optimization approach to project portfolio selection. Such an optimal portfolio is a feasible one (i.e., satisfying all constraints input by the decision maker) which optimizes an overall objective function. This overall objective function could also be defined as a weighted function of various sub-objectives or criteria (i.e. a goal programming approach).

The 0-1 approach is chosen for elaboration here because, from the wide range of possible mathematical programming models, fractional solutions cannot be used in project portfolio selection, unlike the related financial portfolio problem. That is, projects are either selected or not selected. This rules out continuous techniques such as linear and nonlinear programming. Several cases are reported in the literature in which 0-1 integer programming has been used for project portfolio selection (Evans and Fairbairn 1989; Mukherjee 1994; Schniederjans and Santhanam 1993). A comprehensive discussion of 0-1 programming and a classification of different solution methods for 0-1 multiple criteria problems has been given by Rasmussen (1986).

In the following we will limit our discussion to advantages and disadvantages of the 0-1 integer linear programming (0-1 ILP) model. A more detailed discussion of 0-1 ILP applications to portfolio selection is given later.

Advantages of 0-1 ILP are:

a) Using 0-1 ILP for project portfolio selection allows implicit consideration of a multitude of different combinations of candidate projects,

b) The model structures the decision problem in a very clear and understandable manner,

c) The model allows for sensitivity analysis, creating the opportunity to analyze effects of changing the supply of one or more resources,

d) The model handles interdependence among projects, and mutually exclusive projects,

e) Mandatory and ongoing projects can be considered, and

f) The model explicitly considers resource limitations throughout the entire planning period, and also in each individual period if desired.

Table 1. A Comparison of Project Selection Methods

Method	Theoretical Basis	Project/Portfolio Characteristic									Support Characteristic					
		Multiple Objectives	Project Interdependence	Mutually Exclusive	Resource Limitations	Qualitative Attributes	Number of Projects	Project Phases	Project Risk	Parameter Estimate Uncertainty	Sensitivity Analysis	Portfolio Balancing	User-Friendly Interface	Overall Perspective	Group Support	Strategic Considerations
Comparitive																
Q-Sort					Y	Y	S–M								Y	Y
Pairwise Comparison					Y	Y	S									
Scoring		Y			Y	Y	S–L									
Analytical Hierarchy Process	Y	Y			Y	Y	S–M				Y		Y	Y	Y	
Benefit Contribution																
Economic Return	Y						S–L	Y			Y					
Risk Analysis	Y	Y					S–L	Y	Y	Y	Y					
Market Research																
Market Research		Y				Y	S									Y
Strategic Planning																
Portfolio Matrix		Y			Y	Y	S–M		Y			Y	Y	Y	Y	Y
Cognitive Modeling		Y				Y	M–L					Y		Y	Y	Y
Cluster Analysis	Y	Y				Y	M–L							Y		Y
Ad Hoc																
Profiles		Y					S–L							Y		
Optimization																
0–1 Integer LP	Y		Y	Y	Y		S–M	Y			Y					
Goal Programming	Y	Y	Y	Y	Y		S–L	Y			Y			Y		

The disadvantages of 0-1 ILP are:

   a) The model does not explicitly handle qualitative factors such as political or social issues, which are usually important and sometimes critical in portfolio selection,

   b) The model does not take risk and uncertainty factors into consideration, and

   c) The majority of solution methods developed for 0-1 programming problems thus far are not applicable to large problems (Rasmussen 1986).

Summary of Project Portfolio Selection Techniques

In this section we will summarize the characteristics of some of the portfolio selection techniques we have discussed. This discussion is relatively general, in that we do not consider special adaptations of the techniques mentioned, which may have been made to broaden and enhance the application of the technique mentioned. Column one of Table 1 shows some of the project selection techniques previously discussed, and column two indicates whether the technique has a rigorous theoretical grounding.

For each technique an indication is given of which of the set of project or portfolio characteristics shown in columns three to eleven are taken into consideration. Columns 12 to 17 are decision support characteristics which the technique may provide to decision makers. In the best of all possible worlds, a good portfolio selection technique would consider all of the project/portfolio characteristics, and provide decision support of all the types indicated. In practice this has not been the case, as shown in the table, but we will discuss this further in the next section. The following is a brief discussion of the characteristics considered and decision support supplied, in the order of the columns in the table.

Theoretical Basis of the Portfolio Selection Method: The existence of a sound theoretical basis for a portfolio selection method greatly increases the likelihood that its application will produce a result which can be trusted by decision makers. On the other hand, even if the method is theoretically strong, if it is complex to apply or requires large amounts of highly uncertain input data, decision makers will be less likely to consider using it. For example, optimization techniques are well-grounded in theory, but they are not widely used in general because of the large amount of data required, much of which may be highly uncertain. And most of these techniques do not allow the explicit consideration of uncertainty or risk.

Explicitly Supported Project/Portfolio Characteristics

Multiple Objectives: In selecting projects, more than one objective may be considered simultaneously in making portfolio selection decisions. Examples of objectives include maximize net present value, maximize profitability, maximize market share, minimize cost, etc. Objectives used will depend upon the organization, but these criteria obviously must be uniform across the entire project portfolio.

Project Interdependence: In some cases, projects may not be independent of one another. For example, one project may need to be completed before another project can begin. Other examples include situations where the success of one project may change the likelihood of success of another project (e.g. enhancing or cannibalizing sales), or there may be resource overlap where work done on one project can be used in another related project.

Mutually Exclusive Projects: A good example of mutually exclusive projects arises when several alternative approaches are proposed to solve a particular problem. Then the choice must be made among the alternatives, with only one being chosen. Optimization techniques can handle this type of constraint, even when it is considered in the context of a number of other unrelated projects.

Resource Limitations: Resource limitations are ever-present, but are not explicitly considered by methods which consider only one project at a time, such as benefit contribution and market research methods. On the other hand, constraints such as these can be handled by comparison techniques, which rank projects according to some objective(s). Then resources are typically allocated to the top ranked projects in order until they are exhausted. Some methods such as AHP address the allocation of single resources in this manner, but not multiple resources.

Qualitative Attributes: Some project attributes such as resource requirements may be expressed quantitatively. But qualitative attributes may be needed to express project characteristics such as those for which there may be considerable uncertainty or which are normally expressed as "fuzzy" values (e.g., consumer attitude towards a proposed product may be described as "lukewarm" or "enthusiastic" rather than a quantitative estimate of sales volume) or political characteristics (such as "the capability and experience of a product champion").

Number of Projects: The number of projects that can be considered during portfolio development depends upon the technique used. Smaller numbers help to reduce information overload for decision makers, making it easier to use a broader selection of selection methods. For medium to large numbers of projects, decision makers need the type of support that allows them to consider the most relevant information without being buried by it. In Table 1, the number of projects typically handled by each method is shown as S (small—less than 10), M (medium—10 to less than 30), and L (large—30 or more). There are few methods which successfully handle large numbers of projects without using relatively arbitrary selection criteria. Hence, it is important to use screening to eliminate as many projects as possible on other logical grounds not related to overall considerations (e.g., projects which have failed to pass a go-no go decision at a decision gate).

Project Phases: Most projects, unless they are very small, are broken down into phases, for ease of management control. Some of these phases represent points at which the project has reached some recognized state of completion and can be evaluated against measures of objectives achieved, such as resource consumption, perceived quality of the product or service under consideration, and degree of satisfaction with the project to that point. This allows decisions to be made on committing further resources to the next phase, putting the project on hold, or abandoning it. These decision points may be called "Gates" (Cooper 1993), or "Milestones" (Meredith & Mantel 1995). Each project which has reached a gate should be re-considered in relation to other projects, in the context of the entire project portfolio selection process. But it is also necessary at that time to consider the entire remaining life cycle in evaluating each project. This can only be done by explicitly considering the costs and benefits of all the remaining phases, which can be done with more certainty as each project phase is completed. Several of the benefit contribution and optimization techniques allow this to be done explicitly.

Project Risk: Risk should play a large role in making project selection decisions. This is very clear from the portfolio matrix approaches which frequently use risk as one of the dimensions displayed. The reason for its importance is that projects with potential for break-throughs often have a high payoff, but this is often associated with higher risk. We will define project "risk" as the probability that a project will fail. This can be estimated conditionally for each phase of the project and then combined into an overall project risk. A related measure is the "downside risk," which is the product of the amount at stake and the probability of failure. There are two important sub-categories of risk: "technical risk," which is the probability that a project will not successfully complete the development process, and "commercial risk," which is the probability that the products or services will not be successful in the marketplace, given that it has been successfully developed and manufactured. Technical risk is normally higher during the early phases of a project, declining as the project successfully progresses through its phases. Commercial risk can be estimated through market studies or by evaluation of similar products. The estimation of risk for the purpose of portfolio selection is a topic which requires further study and elaboration, and will be the topic of an additional paper.

Uncertainty: We will define uncertainty as the innaccuracy in the estimates of resource requirements, risk, and any other parameters associated with a project. Uncertainty in most parameters should also decline as the project moves through its phases, because decision makers have more accurate data upon which to base their predictions as the project moves closer to completion. Uncertainty will also depend upon the amount of past organizational experience with similar projects, technologies, and markets. How uncertainty in project parameter estimates can affect project outcome criteria such as risk, benefit/cost, cash flow, etc. may be calculated either through simulation techniques, or by considering extremes in the uncertainty ranges of the parameter estimates. Clearly, the overall estimate of gain or loss if a project is undertaken will be subject to both risk and uncertainty.

Decision Support Characteristics

Sensitivity Analysis: The value of a portfolio's objective function is an estimate of the sum of contributions from all the projects in the portfolio. Clearly, this will be dependent upon the values used for each of the independent variables or attributes of each project, such as payoffs, costs, risks, etc. Sensitivity analysis provides a means of measuring how robust the objective function is to changes in these parameters. If it is very sensitive to particular parameters, then close attention must be paid to improving the accuracy of parameter estimates. If not, then the inevitable inaccuracies in parameter estimates may not seriously impact the overall result. Sensitivity analysis also allows a determination of the impact of additional resources on the portfolio objective function. If additional resources such as financing can improve the objective significantly more than the cost of these resources, then it may be cost effective to invest more in an expanded portfolio.

Portfolio Balancing: Portfolio balance is important on certain portfolio dimensions, such as risk, size of project, and short term vs. long term projects. For example, the proportion of high risk projects should not be too high due to the fact that failures of a large number of these projects could be extremely dangerous to the future of the company. On the other hand, low risk projects may not carry the high return that is often typical of risky projects, so the expected return from the portfolio may be too low if project selection is too conservative on the risk dimension. Balance on project size is also important, because the commitment of a high proportion of resources to a few large projects can be catastrophic to the firm if more than one fails. And too many long term projects, no matter how promising they are, may cause cash flow problems.

User-Friendly Interface: Decision makers with the responsibility for making portfolio selection typically are managers who are not highly experienced computer users, but in recent years they have come to expect to use computers as decision support tools. For this reason, the computer interface must be very easy to use, should present information in a highly understandable manner (graphical, or easily read concise forms of data if at all possible) and should be based on graphical user interfaces for ease of use. A decision support system with an interface without these characteristics may not be used by managers if its use is optional.

Overall Perspective: Selecting a project portfolio is a strategic decision, and the relevant information must be presented so it allows decision makers to develop an overall view of the portfolio without overloading them with related information unless they specifically need it. An overall view is encouraged by simple plots or matrices on the general dimensions of interest to the decision makers, such as those seen in portfolio matrix plots.

Group Support: As mentioned earlier, a large proportion of portfolio selection decisions are made by groups of managers. This requires that all the managers involved in the decision should have ready access to relevant information, and that they be able to contribute their knowledge in the decision making process. This involvement can range from using simple tools that support rating the relative merits of the projects on various attributes, to more complex tools available through group decision support systems, often set up with multiple computer monitors and displays in "decision rooms," complete with human facilitator support. Characteristics of successful Group Decision Support Systems or GDSS have been determined through research studies (Buckley & Yen 1990).

Strategic Considerations: Certain methods such as Q-Sort lend themselves to overall considerations of the set of projects proposed for the portfolio, thus being qualified as strategic methods. These methods provide a means for high level classification of projects into strategic categories. Strategic planning approaches such as cognitive modeling and cluster analysis also take a broad strategic perspective (Souder 1978; Martin 1984). A more comprehensive study of concepts and tools which can be used in making relevant strategic decisions relevant to project choices is given in Hax and Majluf (1984). As discussed previously, we believe that portfolio approaches should only be applied to groups of projects which have been assigned to particular strategic categories, to avoid apple and orange comparisons.

Conclusions From The Review

The following are the conclusions we drew from our examination of existing project portfolio selection methods:

a) *Popular Use of Existing Techniques.* A review of Table 1 indicates that there are sparse areas of coverage by most of the methods examined. It also reveals why certain methods may have been proposed, because they cover project characteristics or they provide support in certain areas that other methods do not. For example, project interdependence and mutually exclusive projects are handled by optimization techniques, while project phases are explicitly handled by only some of the benefit contribution and optimization models. Parameter uncertainty is recognized as one of the more important measures in portfolio selection and management (Meredith & Mantel 1995), yet only the risk analysis technique evaluates it explicitly (see Canada & White 1980). And only risk analysis and portfolio matrix techniques explicitly consider project risk. On the other hand, a number of techniques can be applied to projects with qualitative attributes. AHP and portfolio matrices are popular among decision makers, partly because of their ability to consider a broader range of project/portfolio characteristics, and partly because they offer more decision support coverage, as can be seen in Table 1. However, AHP does not allow the consideration of multiple resource constraints. Although some of the benefit measurement techniques such as scoring, economic return, etc. are widely used because of their simplicity, they do not offer the comprehensiveness that is necessary to make appropriate choices and to achieve the required balance in complex portfolio situations.

b) *Information Overload.* Helping to reduce the amount of information that managers need to consider in making their decisions has been shown to be attractive to decision makers, since they tend to favour a least-effort approach (Todd and Benbasat 1993). On the other hand, it is important to ensure that decision makers do not forget or ignore important information during the selection process. For complicated problems which involve many projects or interrelated projects, implicit model support may be necessary if a method is to perform well. Any suggested approach to portfolio selection needs to address this issue and to provide support across the areas suggested in Table 1. That is, it should provide a user-friendly interface that is adaptable to group support, in a system that gives an overall strategic perspective and avoids information overload, but at the same time allows the decision maker to do sensitivity analysis and to balance portfolios. None of the techniques we have considered are close to filling these requirements, although the analytic hierarchy process (AHP) and portfolio matrix techniques could be considered to be the best. The following is a brief summary of the aspects of these more widely used techniques as they relate to the issues we have raised.

c) *Analytic Hierarchy Process.* AHP is well-grounded theoretically although it has its critics (see our previous discussion on AHP). It also has the advantage that it has been incorporated into a relatively usable and friendly software package called Expert Choice®, it offers support for a reasonable number of project/portfolio characteristics, and its decision support characteristics are good. Unfortunately it does not address the project risk issue which is normally an important dimension in adjusting portfolio balance, it does not consider multiple resource constraints, and AHP is time consuming to use when there is more than a small number of projects.

d) *Portfolio Matrix Techniques.* It is well-known that matrix techniques are popular for portfolio selection, but it is not so well-known that these techniques appear to be counter productive in terms of meeting stated objectives such as profit maximization (Armstrong & Brodie 1994). Table 1 shows one reason for the popularity of matrix methods—they consider a number of important project/portfolio dimensions and they provide decision support in a majority of the categories identified. Unfortunately, the lack of a solid theoretical grounding is a drawback which leads to a lack of confidence in this type of approach.

e) *Group Decision Support.* The more successful portfolio selection techniques have some provision for group support, which is essential if committee decisions are to be made. In AHP for example, pairwise comparisons of projects on several criteria can be made by several people and the results combined to provide a group result. With portfolio matrix techniques, graphical results may be viewed on a screen, providing an opportunity for input from all committee members.

f) *Project Data Bases.* Although it has not been discussed in detail in this report, the portfolio selection techniques which can be used are constrained by the availability of suitable data on current and previous projects. A comprehensive data base, that records the history of the organization's projects completed and in process, can support the estimation of parameters for current and new projects. Coupling this database to the portfolio selection system through appropriate data analysis packages would help to widen the base of portfolio selection techniques that could be considered by the organization, and would ease the data collection burden when portfolio selection is carried out. This in turn might make it possible to re-balance the portfolio at more frequent intervals (currently, most organizations do this on an annual basis), and thus decrease the time taken to get promising projects underway.

An Integrated Approach to Project Portfolio Selection

The previous discussion has covered a variety of existing portfolio selection approaches, identified a number of related problems, and given some reasons why certain techniques are more popular than others. One solution to the problems identified would be to use an integrated approach which takes advantage of the best characteristics of several existing methods. This approach would make use methods which have a good theoretical base, combined with other methods that may not be strong theoretically, but which have desirable decision support characteristics, for example. Our proposal is to use a staged approach, where the most relevant methods can be selected by the organization and used at each stage in order to build a portfolio with which decision makers could be confident. Other attempts to build decision support systems for portfolio selection have been reported (Kira et al 1990; De Maio et al 1994). However, these have been quite limited and perhaps too specific in the methods that were used, rather than providing flexible choices for the users. In the following, we consider the portfolio selection process as a three-stage process, beginning with pre-processing, and going on to processing and post-processing. This is illustrated in Figure 2. We discuss model selection and development, (the choice of techniques used in this process according to organizational needs), in part e) below. The important activities in the portfolio selection process (see Figure 2) include:

a) *Pre-Screening:* This is used to eliminate infeasible projects before the selection process begins, based on preliminary information. This helps to reduce the number which must be considered in the selection process, thereby reducing workload and information overload problems. For example, in-process projects which are at a gate or milestone could be eliminated if they are complete, to be terminated, or put on the backburner due to unsatisfactory progress. Also, large projects which do not yet have a champion or which have not yet undergone a feasibility analysis could be screened out at this stage. However, interdependence of projects, and whether or not projects were mandatory would need to be identified first.

b) *Individual Project Evaluation:* During this process, input data from individual projects are analyzed and processed into a common form which is suitable for further analysis. For example, if the method of choice were a combination of net present value combined with risk analysis, the inputs would be estimates of costs and returns at each development phase and the commercialization phase of a product or service, and the risks at each phase, or more simply the development and commercial risks. Uncertainty could also be input in the form of likely ranges for the uncertain parameters. Other inputs could include qualitative variables such as policy or political measures. Quantitative output from this stage would be (for example) each project's expected net value, risk, and resource requirements over the time frame of the project, along with calculated uncertainties in these output results, and any input qualitative variables on a common scale.

c) *Screening:* During this activity, economic calculations from the previous stage are used to eliminate any non-mandatory projects or inter-related families of projects which do not meet pre-set economic criteria such as estimated rate of return.

d) *Portfolio Selection:* This process combines the outputs of the previous stage in a manner that selects a portfolio, based on the objectives of the organization. This could involve extensive interactions with committee members in comparing potential projects on a number of objectives, or it could involve little direct intervention if an optimization technique such as 0-1 ILP were used. The output of this stage would be a preliminary ranking of the projects, based on the objective(s) specified for the portfolio, and an initial allocation of resources up to the maximum available. This would provide only a first cut at the problem, which would then proceed to the post-processing stage where final adjustments are made by decision maker(s), and re-calculations carried out as necessary to provide support during sensitivity analysis and portfolio balancing.

e) *Portfolio Balancing and Adjustment:* At this stage decision makers apply judgment to make the final adjustments to the portfolio. The decision support display would be in the form of one or more portfolio matrices, which would display graphically the critical decision variables selected by the organization for this purpose. Any interactions among the projects, such as interdependence and mutual exclusivity, have already been taken into account in previous activities and could be displayed during this stage upon request. Portfolio balancing is a judgment problem which requires feedback to the decision maker(s) on the consequences of making deletions and/or additions at this point. Data on this would come from sensitivity calculations, using the same model applied in the portfolio selection process. Hence there could be a substantial amount of iteration between the processing and the post-processing stage during the final adjustment process.

f) *Model Selection & Development:* Before beginning the portfolio selection process, the organization needs to decide which techniques it wishes to use in each stage of the process. This would probably be a one-time process (with minor and infrequent adjustments), which would depend upon the organization's culture, experience, and the availability of information needed as input. This is complicated by the fact that there is more uncertainty about projects which are proposed but not yet underway, as compared to projects which are already underway and for which there is more data available. This may require a combination of techniques to be used, depending upon uncertainty in the estimates. For example, simple checklists of must-meet criteria could be used during the early days of the project, while more sophisticated models might be used for more advanced projects (Cooper 1993). The important point is that the data provided for later stages in portfolio selection must be in a common format so appropriate comparisons can be made among projects.

Considering the selection process shown in Figure 2, pre-screening would likely be an administrative decision based on specific guidelines. Individual project evaluation could be done by a variety of benefit contribution techniques. The screening process would again probably depend on certain guidelines which might eliminate all non-mandatory projects with an internal rate of return less than 15%, for example (if this benefit contribution technique were being used). During portfolio selection, all remaining projects would be compared on some basis through one of the comparative techniques such as AHP or pairwise comparison, or by optimization. During portfolio balancing and adjustment all the projects, including those surviving the screening

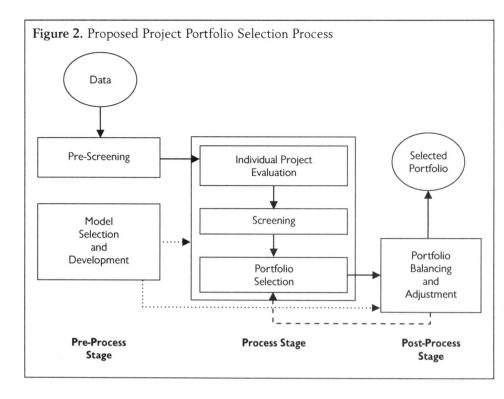

Figure 2. Proposed Project Portfolio Selection Process

process but not selected during portfolio selection, would be displayed on certain dimensions such as those used for portfolio matrices, as chosen by the organization. Information available to the users while the final balancing process is underway should include the amount of each resource consumed and the sensitivity of the objective function to changes caused by adding or deleting projects. This might require iteration back to the previous stage to refine the portfolio calculations.

Since decision makers should be directly involved with the selection process at each of its stages, support tools will be essential to implement each technique used, and the intention should be to leave the choice of specific techniques up to the decision makers. We believe that this generic approach would allow the best parts of each technique chosen to be integrated into a system which provides far better and more acceptable project portfolios than those which can be generated by any single technique we have discussed. Further studies are being done to evaluate the potential of this flexible and integrated approach, and will be reported in the near future.

APPENDIX

Strategic Decision Group (SDG) Project Portfolio Method
This discussion is an adaptation of material from a variety of sources (Cooper 1993; Hax & Majluf 1984; Matheson & Menke 1994). The SDG portfolio matrix consists of two dimensions. The first dimension represents the Expected Commercial Value

(Net Present Value or NPV) of the project given technical success. The second dimension represents the Probability of Technical Success of the project.

The two factors mentioned above are calculated for each candidate project and then all of the candidate projects are plotted in a bubble diagram. The size of the bubbles or circles denotes the amount of financial resources devoted to each project, hence serving as a third dimension, the size of the project.

Figure 1 depicts a typical SDG matrix. In this figure, each quadrant has a certain name. These names might be different depending on the country or company where the matrix is being used, but the strategy that should be followed for a project falling into that quadrant is the same since projects in the same category tend to have similar characteristics. Commonly used labels for SDG quadrants are as follows:

α) Pearl—Highly desirable projects that have both high commercial value and high probability of technical success. Identified revolutionary commercial applications and proven technological advancement projects are typical projects in this category.

β) Bread and Butter—Projects with high probability of technical success but low commercial value. Evolutionary improvements in process or product, modest extensions of existing technology or applications, and minor projects are typically in this category. These projects are often necessary because they provide the cash flow that fuels operations of the firm.

γ) Oyster—Projects with low probability of success but high commercial value are considered oysters. Revolutionary commercial applications and innovative technological advancement projects are typical of this category. Oysters must be cultivated to yield pearls to ensure the future of the firm.

δ) White Elephant—These projects have neither high probability of technical success nor high commercial value. Oysters that are found to be commercially overstated, and bread and butter projects with overstated probability of success fall into this category.

The decision rule could be to seek as many pearls as possible, invest in some oysters, try to cut back on the bread and butter ones (there are usually too many of these), and delete white elephants.

The major advantages of using the SDG portfolio matrix are:

a) It considers technological risk explicitly. This is important, especially for R&D, and

b) The model reflects the project's commercial value. In most cases this is the main reason for carrying out the project.

The most important disadvantages of the SDG method are:

a) The model does not provide any assistance as to how many oysters and/or which ones should be selected or how many bread and butters and/or which ones should be cut,

b) The model assumes that all critical resource absorption can be expressed with a single index (financial). In reality there might be other critical resources such as work force and technical resources that should also be considered,

c) The SDG method does not address the important issue of interdependence among projects. For example, what should the decision maker do if a project is a pearl but another project that gives some required inputs to that project is a white elephant?

Figure 3. Typical Elements of R&D Project Attractiveness (Source: Roussel et al. 1991)

Elements of R&D Project Attractiveness	Units in Which Attractiveness in Expressed
Fit with business or corporate strategy	• A judgment ranging from excellent to poor
Inventive merit and strategic importance to the business	• The potential power of the sought-after result to: a) improve the competitive position of the business b) be applicable to more than one business c) provide the foundation for new businesses • A judgment from high to low
Durability of the competitive advantage sought	• *Years*. If the R&D result can be quickly and easily initiated by competitors, the project is less attractive than one that provides a protected, long-term advantage
Reward	• Usually financial, but sometimes "necessity work" (e.g., satisfying regulatory bodies) or building a knowledge base that becomes the foundation for applied work
Competitive impact of technologies	• Base, key, pacing, embryonic. If a project is made up entirely of the application of base technologies, it is classified as "base"; if a project contains at least one key or pacing technology, the entire project is classified as "key" or "pacing"
Uncertainty	
Probability of technical success	• Probability units, 0.1 - 0.9. The probability that the objective will be achieved as defined
Probability of commercial success	• Probability units, 0.1 - 0.9. The probability of commercial success if the project is technically successful
Probability of overall success	• Probability units, 0.1 - 0.9. The product of technical and commercial probabilities
Exposure	
R&D costs to completion or key decision point	• Dollars
Time-to-completion or key decision point	• Time
Capital and/or marketing investment required to exploit technical success	• Dollars

d) The issue of mutually exclusive projects is not clear in the SDG model. For example, if two mutually exclusive projects fall into the pearl quadrant which one should be selected?

e) The SDG model only considers the probability of technical success. The probability of commercial success, which is an important risk factor and is sometimes more critical, is ignored,

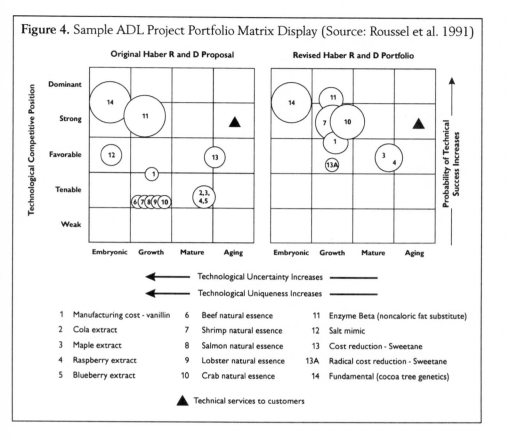

Figure 4. Sample ADL Project Portfolio Matrix Display (Source: Roussel et al. 1991)

f) Commercialization and R&D costs are not reflected in the commercial value that is represented by NPV, so some improvements are necessary in the definition of commercial value,

g) A critical limitation arises when the model is to be used as a prescriptive methodology. This limit is implicit in the difficulty of estimating a project's probability of technical success,

h) The range of uncertainty for research more than a year or two in the future is so substantial that use of NPV as a selection factor becomes not only meaningless but possibly harmful (Roussel et al., 1991),

i) The capital and marketing investment required to exploit technological success is not explicitly considered in the model.

Arthur D. Little (ADL) Project Portfolio Matrix Method

The following description of the ADL method is adapted primarily from chapter six of Roussel, Saad, & Erickson (1991). The ADL approach first examines each individual project, then places each project within portfolio structures that accommodate strategic elements most critical to the specific company and its industry. Individual projects are evaluated in terms of four key elements:

1. Competitive technological strength
2. Technology maturity
3. Competitive impact of technology
4. R&D project attractiveness

Elements of attractiveness and their importance depend on the specific company and industry. However, the most common elements of attractiveness are presented in Figure 3. The first element—fit of the project with the business or corporate strategy—is a decisive one. The remaining criteria come into consideration only if the fit is good to excellent, otherwise the project must be rejected outright.

As different attractiveness criteria have different importance, typically each criterion is weighted, say from 1 to 5, based on the type of the firm and the industry in which it competes. A simple scoring system can then be applied to give a rough ranking of the projects under consideration.

The criteria that decide project attractiveness may be used collectively or as individual components during portfolio considerations (Figure 3). These elements typically may be considered and balanced during R&D project portfolio selection.

After identifying the portfolio variables that should be balanced, these variables are plotted against each other on two-dimensional grids. Then the proposed projects are examined in these different portfolio matrices. No single display can possibly convey all the complexities of the proposed portfolio but each individual matrix raises some interesting questions. For example, is it prudent to concentrate a major part of resources in high risk projects?

Figure 4 illustrates one of several different matrices that can be applied with regard to the above mentioned criteria. Each circle in the matrix depicts a project and the recommended budget is symbolized by the area within the circle. The improved portfolio is also illustrated in the Figure beside the elementary portfolio, in the same form. Improvements are based on discussions of different issues raised when decision makers concentrate on different matrices. Typical improvements include abandoning a project, adding the resources that are taken from the rejected projects to the retained projects, improving technological competitive position, and reducing the exposure in some projects by forming an R&D partnership to reduce the costs.

Major advantages of the ADL method are:

a) ADL considers a number of qualitative characteristics of each project that make a project attractive, instead of NPV that is not suitable for R&D projects,

b) Decision makers are forced to consider R&D costs to completion explicitly, and also the capital and marketing investment required to exploit technical success,

c) The portfolio can be balanced from different points of view, and

d) The ADL model considers the probability of technical success as well as the probability of commercial success, which is another important risk factor.

The disadvantages of the ADL method are:

1. Since several matrices are used in this approach, the method can be time consuming and boring. This also leads to information overload since users have difficulty in keeping all the information in mind at one time, thus detracting from the method,

b) The model assumes that all critical resource absorption can be expressed financially. There might also be other critical resources such as work force and technical resources that should be considered during the selection process,

c) The ADL method does not address interdependence among projects,

d) The issue of mutually exclusive projects is not clear in the ADL model, which does not provide any assistance to prevent mutually exclusive projects from being selected, and

e) A critical limitation arises if the model is to be used prescriptively. This limit is implicit in the difficulty of estimating the probability of technical and commercial success.

0-1 Integer Linear Programming Optimization Method

The 0-1 ILP model includes *decision variables, an objective function,* and *constraints.* These components are described in detail below (adapted from Evans and Fairbairn, 1989).

Decision Variables

The decision variables are defined by

$$x_i = \begin{cases} 1 & \text{if project } i \text{ is included in the portfolio} \\ 0 & \text{otherwise} \end{cases}$$

for $i = 1,..., N$, where N is the total number of projects being considered.

Objective function

Project portfolio selection problems are essentially multi-objective problems involving maximization of benefits in several categories as well as minimization of cost and other resources. These objectives are conflicting in nature. For example, one might select all possible projects in order to maximize the benefits, but this solution would also result in maximization of cost.

In addition, specific projects, if undertaken, may increase benefits in some categories but also will use resources that could have been used for projects that would have increased benefits in other categories. The objective of minimization of the use of resources can be treated implicitly through the use of constraints on resources. A *value function approach* (Keeney and Raiffa, 1976) can be applied to the problem of benefit maximization in the various categories to reduce the multi-attribute problem to single-attribute (Evans and Fairbairn, 1989). This overall objective function could be a weighted function of various sub-objectives or criteria. Therefore, written in an explicit form, the objective function can be given by

$$\text{Maximize } Z = \sum_{b=1}^{B} a_b \left(\sum_{i=1}^{N} q_{ib}\, x_i \right)$$

Where Z is the value function that should be maximized; B is the number of benefit categories; a_b denotes the "importance of benefit category b" to the decision maker; and q_{ib} represents "the amount of benefit" contributed by project i to category b. One could employ the AHP method to obtain estimates of a_b and q_{ib} (Evans and Fairbairn, 1989). Within the scheme of the Expert Choice® software implementation of AHP, a_b is the global priority of benefit category b, while q_{ib} is the local priority of project i with respect to category b.

Constraints

A project portfolio selection problem usually has several constraints. For example, the availability of resources which are necessary for performing the projects such as cost, facility, workforce, and so on, and also the rate of their consumption during the execution period of the projects, e.g., the cash flow of the projects, may all impose constraints.

If the total cost to completion of the selected projects (c_i) should not exceed a certain amount (C), then the following constraint should be set

$$\sum_{i=1}^{N} c_i x_i \leq C$$

If the planning period is divided into T planning periods, denoted by $t = 1,...,T$, and maximum allowed cost for project i during period t (c_{it}) should not exceed a certain amount in each period t (C_t), then the constraint set would be

$$\sum_{i=1}^{N} c_{it} x_i \leq C_t \quad for \; t = 1,...,T.$$

The same type of constraints could be established for each of the other limited resources such as workforce (e.g., computer staff software development time) and machine time (e.g., computer time). It should be noted that the cost and other resources that have already been spent on the projects are considered sunk, and would not be considered explicitly in the model. They are implicitly reflected in the total amount of resources that are necessary for the completion of the projects.

If there are K sets of mutually exclusive projects, and S_k is the set of k mutually exclusive projects for $k = 1,..., K$, then the set of constraints is given by

$$\sum_{i \in S_k} x_i \leq 1 \quad for \; k = 1...K$$

Constraints of this type could be used to consider different schedules for a specific project.

Mandatory and ongoing projects which should not be eliminated may also exist in the portfolio. These projects must remain in the model and can be added to the portfolio once it is selected, because they consume resources that should be considered explicitly. The following set of constraints guarantees the inclusion of these types of projects in the selected portfolio.

$$x_{i \in S_m} = 1$$

where S_m is the set of mandatory projects, and

$$x_{i \in S_o} = 1$$

Here, S_o is the set of ongoing projects that should be continued.

Projects which must be discontinued can be eliminated by the following constraint

$$x_{i \in S_d} = 0$$

where S_d is the set of ongoing projects that should be eliminated from consideration. This constraint could also be useful in sensitivity analysis.

Interdependent projects can also be considered in the model. Let P_l be the set of precursor projects for a particular project l, where $l = 1,..., L$. In other words if project l is to be selected, then all of the projects in set P_l must be selected. This is controlled by the following set of constraints.

$$\sum_{i \in P_l} x_i \geq N(P_l) * x_l \quad for \ l = 1...L$$

where $N(P_l)$ is the number of projects contained in the set P_l.

If only one project from a set of projects, R_m, must be chosen before project m can be selected, this can be managed by

$$\sum_{i \in R_m} x_i \geq x_m \quad for \ m = 1,...,M.$$

Many other types of constraints could be defined for this model, depending on the situation. For example, one could specify required relationships for different types of projects (e.g., the number of projects in a certain category must be at least twice the number of projects in another category). Enlarging the constraint set does facilitate obtaining an optimal solution (Evans and Fairbairn, 1989).

References

Archibald, Russell D. (1992). *Managing High-Technology Programs and Projects* (Second Edition), New York, NY: Wiley.

Armstrong, J.Scott, & Brodie, Roderick J. (1994). Effects of portfolio planning methods on decision making: Experimental results, *International Journal of Research in Marketing*, 11, 73-84.

Baker, N. R., & Freeland, J. (1975). Recent advances in R&D benefit measurement and project selection methods. *Management Science*, 21, 1164-1175.

Bard, Jonathan F., & Sousk, Stephen F. (1990). A tradeoff analysis for rough terrain cargo handlers using the AHP: An example of group decision making, *IEEE Transactions on Engineering Management*, 37(3), 222-227.

Brenner, Merrill S. (1994). Practical R&D project prioritization, *Reasearch Technology Management*, 37(5), 38-42.

Buckley, S.R., & Yen, D. (1990). Group decision support systems: Concerns for success, *The Information Society*, 7, 109-123.

Canada, John R., & White, John A. (1980). *Capital Investment Decision Analysis for Management and Engineering*, Englewood Cliffs, N.J.: Prentice-Hall.

Churchman, C.W., & Ackoff, R.L. (1954). An approximate measure of value, *Operations Research*, 2.

Cooper, Robert G. (1993). *Winning At New Products* (Second Ed.), Reading, MA: Addison-Wesley.

Cooper, R., Edgett, S., & Kleinschmidt, E. (1995). Private Communication.

De Maio, Adriano, Verganti, Roberto, & Corso, Mariano (1994). A multi-project management framework for new product development, *European Journal of Operational Research*, 78, 178-191.

Dos Santos, B.L. (1989). Selecting information system projects: Problems, solutions and challenges, *Proceedings of the Hawaii Conference on System Sciences*, 1131-1140.

Dyer, James S. (1990). Remarks on the Analytic Hierarchy Process, *Management Science*, 36(3), 249-258.

Evans, Gerald W., & Fairbairn, Robert (1989). Selection and scheduling of advanced missions for NASA using 0-1 integer linear programming, *Journal of the Operational Research Society*, 40(11), 971-981.

Golden, Bruce L., Wasil, Edward A., & Levy, Doug E. (1989). Applications of the Analytic Hierarchy Process: A Categorized, Annotated Bibliography. *The Analytic Hierarchy Process: Applications and Studies* (Golden, Bruce L., Wasil, Edward A., & Harker, Patrick T., Eds).

Hall, D.L., & Nauda, A. (1990). An interactive approach for selecting IR & D projects, *IEEE Transactions on Engineering Management*, 37(2), 126-133.

Harker, Patrick T. (1987a). Alternative modes of questioning in the Analytic Hierarchy Process. *Mathematical Modelling*, 9, 353-360.

Harker, Patrick T. (1987b). Incomplete pairwise comparisons in the Analytic Hierarchy Process, *Mathematical Modelling*, 9, 837-848.

Harker, Patrick T., & Vargas, Luis G. (1987). The theory of ratio scale estimation: Saaty's Analytic Hierarchy Process, *Management Science*, 33, 1383-1403.

Harker, Patrick T. (1989). The art and science of decision making: The Analytic Hierarchy Process. In *Analytic Hierarchy Process: Applications And Studies* (Golden, Bruce L., Wasil, Edward A., & Harker Patrick T., Eds.).

Haspelagh, P. (1982). Portfolio planning: Uses and limits, *Harvard Business Review*, 60(1), 58-73.

Hax, Arnoldo C., & Majluf, Nicolas S. (1984). *Strategic Management: An Integrative Perspective*, Englewood Cliffs, N.J.: Prentice-Hall.

Hax, Arnoldo C., & Majluf, Nicolas S. (1996). *The Strategy Concept and Process: A Pragmatic Approach* (Second Ed.), Upper Saddle River, N.J.: Prentice-Hall.

Hess, Sidney W. (1993). Swinging on the branch of a tree: Project selection applications, *Interfaces* 23(6), 5-12.

Johnson, C.R. (1980). Constructive critique of a hierarchical prioritization scheme employing paired comparisons, *Proceedings of the International Conference of Cybernetics and Society*, New York, NY: IEEE.

Kamenetzky, Ricardo D. (1982). The relationship between the Analytic Hierarchy Process and the additive value function, *Decision Sciences*, 13, 702-712.

Keeney, R.L., & Raiffa, H. (1976). *Decisions With Multiple Objectives: Preference And Value Tradeoffs*, New York: Wiley.

Khan, Arshad M., & Fiorino, Donald P. (1992). The capital asset pricing model in project selection: A case study, *The Engineering Economist*, 37(2), 145-159.

Kira, Dennis S., Kusy, Martin I., Murray, David H., & Goranson, Barbara J. (1990). A specific decision support system (SDSS) to develop an optimal project portfolio mix under uncertainty, *IEEE Trans. Engineering Management*, 37(3), 213-221.

Krumm, F.V., & Rolle, C.F. (1992). Management and application of decision and risk analysis in Du Pont, *Interfaces*, 22(6), 84-93.

Lim Kai, H., & Swenseth, Scott R. (1993). An iterative procedure for reducing problem size in large scale AHP problems, *European Journal of Operational Research*, 67, 64-67.

Martino, Joseph P. (1995). *R&D Project Selection*, New York, NY: Wiley.

Matheson, James E., & Menke, Michael M. (1994). Using decision quality principles to balance your R&D portfolio, *Research Technology Management*, (May-June), 38-43.

Matthieu, R.G., & Gibson, J.E. (1993). A methodology for large-scale R&D planning based on cluster analysis, *IEEE Transactions on Engineering Management*, 40(3), 283-292.

Meredith, Jack R., & Mantel, Samuel J., Jr. (1995). *Project Management: A Managerial Approach* (Third Ed.), New York, NY: Wiley.

Miller, G.A. (1956). The magical number seven, plus or minus two: Some limitations on our capacity for processing information, *Psychology Review* 63, 81-97.

Morison, A., & Wensley, R. (1991). Boxing up or boxed in? A short history of the Boston Consulting Group share/growth matrix, *Journal of Marketing Management*, 7, 105-129.

Mukherjee, Kampan (1994). Application of an interactive method for MOLIP in project selection decision: A case from Indian coal mining industry, *International Journal of Production Economics*, 36, 203-211.

Murphy, Catherine Kuenz (1993). Limits on the analytic hierarchy process from its consistency index, *European Journal of Operational Research*, 65, 138-139.

Pessemier, E.A., & Baker, N.R. (1971). Project and program decisions in research and development, *R & D Management*, 2(1).

Rasmussen, L.M. (1986). Zero-one programming with multiple criteria, *European Journal of Operational Research*, 26, 83-95.

Remer, Donald S., Stokdyk, Scott B., & Van Driel, Mike (1993). Survey of project evaluation techniques currently used in industry. *International Journal of Production Economics* 32, 103-115.

Riggs, Jeffrey L., Brown, Sheila B., & Trueblood, Robert P. (1994). Integration of technical, cost, and schedule risks in project management, *Computers & Operations Research*, 21(5), 521-533.

Roussel, P., Saad, K., & Erickson, T. (1991). *Third Generation R&D: Managing the Link to Corporate Strategy*, Cambridge, MA: Harvard Business School Press and Arthur D. Little Inc.

Rzasa, Philip V., Faulkner, Terrence W., & Sousa, Nancy L. (1990). Analyzing R&D portfolios at Eastman Kodak, *Research Technology Management*, (Jan.-Feb.) 27-32.

Santhanam, R., Muralidhar, K., & Schniederjans, M. (1989). A zero-one goal programming approach for information system project selection, *OMEGA*, 17(6), 583-593.

Saaty, Thomas L. (1990). An exposition of the AHP in reply to the paper "Remarks on the analytical hierarchy process," *Management Science*, 36(3), 259-268.

Saaty, Thomas L., Rogers, Paul C., & Pell, Ricardo. (1980). Portfolio selection through hierarchies, *The Journal of Portfolio Management*, 6(3), 16-21.

Schniederjans, Mark J., & Santhanam, Radhika (1993). A multi-objective constrained resource information system project selection method. *European Journal of Operational Research*, 70, 244-253. .

Schwartz, S.L., & Vertinsky, I. (1977). Multi-attribute investment decisions: A study of R&D project selection, *Management Science*, 24, 285-301.

Sharpe, W.F. (1964). Capital asset prices: A theory of market equilibrium under conditions of risk, *Journal of Finance*, 425-442.

Souder, W.E. (1973). Analytical effectiveness of mathematical models for R&D project selection, *Management Science* 19(8), 907-923.

Souder, William E. (1975). Achieving organizational consensus with respect to R & D project selection criteria. *Management Science* 21(6), 669-681.

Souder, W.E. (1978). A system for using R&D project evaluation methods, *Research Management*, 20(5), 29-37.

Souder, William E. (1984). *Project Selection and Economic Appraisal*, New York, NY: Van Nostrand Reinhold.

Todd, Peter, & Benbasat, Izak (1993). An experimental investigation of the relationship between decision makers, decision aids, and decision making effort, *INFOR*, 31(2), 80-100.

Wensely, R. (1981). Strategic marketing: Betas, boxes, or basics? *Journal of Marketing*, 45, 173-181.

Wind, Y., & Mahajan, V. (1981). Designing product and business portfolios, *Harvard Business Review*, 59, 155-165.

Wind, Yoram, Mahajan, Vijay, & Cardozo, Richard N. (1981). *New Product Forecasting*, Lexington, MA: Lexington Books.

Wind, Y., Mahajan, V., & Swire, D.J. (1983). An empirical comparison of standardized portfolio models, *Journal of Marketing*, 47, 89-99.

Zahedi, Fatemeh (1986). The Analytic Hierarchy Process—A survey of the method and its applications, *Interfaces*, 16(4), 96-108.

A Practical R&D Project-Selection Scoring Tool

Anne DePiante Henriksen and Ann Jensen Traynor

Assessing the potential value to the organization of a proposed research and development (R&D) project is a challenge faced by every decision maker who must allocate limited resources to a plethora of candidate projects. This decision is complicated by the fact that at the outset, the probability a project will be successful in its technical objectives is usually difficult to know [10,55]. Furthermore, even if we could predict with 100% certainty that a proposed R&D project will achieve its technical objectives and produce results, the ultimate impact of those results within the scientific and technological community is never totally apparent in advance. These factors make the successful selection of R&D projects a twofold challenge: first, to select projects that will be technically successful, have significant impact, and bring the organization great rewards, and second, to not overlook such a project when it is one of the choices.

Methods and techniques for selecting projects have appeared in the literature for at least 40 years and there have been hundreds of published studies. Approaches tend to be either quantitative and qualitative, ranging from rigorous operations research methods to social-science-based interactive techniques. Overviews on the topic of R&D project selection are presented by Baker and Pound [2], Baker and Freeland [3], Booker and Bryson [8,9], Steele [66], Hall and Nauda [25], Danila [17], Sanchez [57], Gaynor [22], and Schmidt and Freeland [59]. A current overview of the R&D project selection literature is presented in Table 1.

R&D project selection methods can usually be placed into one of the following categories:
* unstructured peer review;
* scoring;
* mathematical programming, including integer programming (IP), linear programming (LP), nonlinear programming (NLP), goal programming (GP), and dynamic programming (DP);
* economic models, such as internal rate of return (IRR), net present value (NPV), return on investment (ROI), cost-benefit analysis, and option pricing theory;
* decision analysis, including multiattribute utility theory (MAUT), decision trees, risk analysis, and the analytic hierarchy process (AHP);

239

Table 1. R&D Project Selection Literature Summary Table

Reference and Evaluation Approach

Averch, H. (1993)
Discussion of importance of portfolio considerations in project selection; advocated scoring against weighted criteria with peer review for basic research; emphasizes importance of *ex ante* and *ex post* analysis of portfolio "success"

Baker, N. and J. Freeland (1975)
Review of quantitative methods of R&D project selection; emphasizes understanding both the behavioral aspects of the decision process and the effects of benefit interactions

Bard, J. F., R. Balachandra, and P. E. Kaufmann (1988)
Interactive decision support system (DSS) for screening existing projects and evaluating new ones; portfolio optimization using mixed nonlinear integer programming (NLIP) to maximize expected (economic) return

Bard, J. F. (1990)
Multiple criteria utility function formulated as a goal programming problem and solved with a heuristic algorithm

Bedell, R. J. (1983)
Generalized decision model for R&D selection/termination that incorporates firm strategy in decision process

Behanec, M., V. Rajkovic, B. Semolic, and A. Pogacnik (1995)
Portfolio planning with an expert system consisting of a decision tree and qualitative *if-then* rules

Booker, J. M. and M. C. Bryson (1985)
Comprehensive literature survey of decision methods for project selection with discussion of each kind of method

Brenner, M. S. (1994)
Uses analytic hierarchy process (AHP) for selecting and weighting criteria; uses informal rating of projects by project champions against criteria

Cardus, D., M. J. Fuhrer, A. W. Martin, and R. M. Thrall (1982)
Cost-benefit analysis combined with scoring; discussion of additive vs. multiplicative scoring algorithms

Chun, Y. H. (1994)
Uses expected net present value (NPV) of an R&D project, conditional upon its (calculated projected) success or failure, to derive optimal project ordering parameters

Cook, W. D. and Y. Roll (1988)
Relates R&D capital investment decisions to both the level of productivity and optimal use of existing capacity—measured using engineering (economic) approach

Costello, D. (1983)
Scoring approach with zero-sum point allocation procedure; incorporates nonquantitative assessment by senior management of budget request into selection decision

Czajkowski, A. F. and S. Jones (1986)
Integer programming (IP) formulation with explicit consideration of benefit and technical interactions

Danila, N. (1989)
Review of the main families of R&D project selection in relation to the different categories of firm strategy

Dean, B. V. and M. J. Nishry (1965)
Scoring model incorporating economic profitability estimates in the scoring algorithm

Dias Junior, O. P. (1988)
Multicriteria decision problem in which criteria are linguistic fuzzy sets; the resulting ILP problem results in fuzzy set of nondominated alternatives

Fox, G. E., N. R. Baker, and J. L. Bryant (1984)
Present value of project interactions is modeled and optimal portfolio obtained using mixed ILP

Gaynor, G. E. (1990)
Provides checklist of important questions to ask and criteria to consider in selecting projects

Golabi, K. (1987)
Uses multiattribute utility theory (MAUT) to construct value functions; maximizes total value of portfolio of projects using ILP

Goldstein, P. M. and H. M. Singer (1986)
Discusses computational errors in Fox, et al. (1984) that invalidate their illustrative example; however, correction supplied by authors supports the Fox, et al. central premise

Hall, D. L. and A. Nauda (1988)
Emphasizes formalized interactive process to integrate R&D selection with business strategy; no particular methodology stressed, but taxonomy of selection methods is presented

Hess, S. W. (1993)
Decision trees for screening new projects that incorporates qualitative criteria into a single expression of expected NPV

Iyigun, M. G. (1993)
Delphi for project screening and an interactive DSS for resource allocation (See Kocaoglu and Iyigun (1994))

Jin, X. Y., A. L. Porter, F. A. Rossini, and E. D. Anderson (1987)
Interactive, spreadsheet-based scoring model

Khorramshahgol, R. and Y. Gousty (1986)
Delphi method in combination with goal programming (DGP) to solve multiobjective cost-benefit analysis portfolio optimization problem

Kocaoglu, D. F. and M. G. Iyigun (1994)
An integrated DSS consisting of scoring for project screening, AHP for criterion weights, Delphi for collecting information on requirements, ILP with heuristics for resource allocation, and NPV for analysis of benefit interactions

Kostoff, R. N. (1983)
Cost-benefit analysis using ratio of present worth of benefits to present worth of costs

Kostoff, R. N. (1988)
Scoring method that incorporates peer review

Krawiec, F. (1984)
Scoring combined with probabilistic risk assessment (PRA)

Kuwahara, Y. and T. Yasutsugu (1988)
Cost-effectiveness analysis

Libertore, M. J. (1988a)
An Expert Support System (ESS) based on AHP that is explicitly linked to strategic planning; a spreadsheet model is used for rating projects, and benefit-cost analysis with ILP is used for resource allocation

Liberatore, M. J. (1988b)
See Libertore (1988a)

Liberatore, M. J. (1989)
See Libertore (1988a)

Lockett, G., et al. (1986)
AHP as a tool for portfolio planning

Lockett, G. and M. Stratford (1987)
Comparison of AHP with MAUT in R&D project selection problem

Mandakovic, T. F. and W. E. Souder (1990)
Integrated organizational process model consisting of an interactive behavioral decision aid (BDA) Q-sort combined with decentralized hierarchical modeling (DHM)

Mehrez, A. (1988)
MAUT for comparing the expected discounted present worth (DPW) to the expected utility of the DPW of the portfolio; DPW obtained using Capital Asset Pricing Model

Moore, Jr., J. R. and N. R. Baker (1969a)
Multiple criteria scoring model that uses additive algorithm

Moore, Jr., J. R. and N. R. Baker (1969b)
Multiple criteria scoring model that uses normal distribution intervals to assign points; comparison of rank-order consistency of scoring to both profitability index and LP selection models

Newton, D. P. and A. W. Pearson (1994)
Option pricing theory economic model

Oral, M., O. Kettani, and P. Lang (1991)
Project evaluation by scoring using simplified Delphi process; pairwise comparisons (modified AHP) to generate a concordance matrix; ILP constrained by availability used to obtain a kernel of nondominated projects

Ringuest, J. L. and S. B. Graves (1989)
Multiobjective LP to maximize profit and market share; produces a set of nondominated solutions (vs. single answer) for further consideration

Ringuest, J. L. and S. B. Graves (1990)
Multiobjective LP that treats cash flows over time in a more general way than NPV and produces a set of nondominated solutions

Roussel, P. A., K. N. Saad and T. J. Erickson (1991)
Integrated R&D portfolio planning linked to organizational strategy and mission

Rzasa, P. V., T. W. Faulkner, and N. L. Sousa (1990)
Rigorous portfolio planning based on expected NPV; use of influence diagrams for criteria identification and decision trees for risk analysis

Schmidt, R. L. (1993)
NLIP formulation that explicitly considers benefit, outcome, and resource interactions

Schmidt, R. L. and J. R. Freeland (1992)
Review of systems approach literature for R&D project selection process stressing the process itself and insight gained rather than a specific answer

Silvennionen, P. (1994)
Qualitative portfolio planning with emphasis on technical needs analysis

Souder, W. E. (1978)
Reviews eight types of R&D project selection models; suggests appropriate organizational use of different methods; for project ranking advocates a Q-sort/NIK psychometric approach with nominal, controlled interaction (modified Delphi process)

Souder, W. E. and T. Mandakovic (1986)
BDA and DHM psychometric approaches for facilitating maximal organizational involvement in the R&D selection process

Stadje, W. (1993)
Bayesian adaptive dynamic programming

Steele, L. W. (1988)
Historical overview of R&D project selection and project selection methods

Stewart, T. J. (1991)
Interactive DSS to solve a non-linear multicriteria optimization problem in portfolio planning; resulting NLP solved using heuristic algorithm

Uenohara, M. (1991)
Strategic portfolio planning emphasizing core technologies in the context of the R&D time horizon (today vs. tomorrow vs. day after tomorrow); uses the Boston Consulting Group matrix

Venkatraman, R. and S. Venkatraman (1995)
Ties R&D project selection and scheduling to the product life cycle; selections made using heuristic approach

- interactive methods, such as Delphi, Q-sort, behavioral decision aids (BDA), and decentralized hierarchical modeling (DHM);
- artificial intelligence (AI), including expert systems and fuzzy sets;
- portfolio optimization.

In the portfolio optimization approach to R&D project selection, one considers the proposed project package as an aggregate in the context of the organization's mission and strategic goals [54]. Any logical combination of the indicated techniques can be used to construct an organization's "optimal" R&D portfolio. For example, Delphi may be used to obtain and weight relevant criteria, scoring to carry out preliminary screening, IP to construct the portfolio, and NPV to allocate resources. The most recent trend has been to combine the different approaches into an integrated, interactive, manager-friendly, computer-based decision support system (DSS). The computer DSS can then be used directly by decision makers to analyze "what if" scenarios for different parameter sets and portfolio compositions [31,39,51].

The proponents of many R&D project-selection methods have not appeared too concerned about the level of complexity of their particular technique. Some approaches presented in the literature are so mathematically elaborate that they necessitate the assistance of an expert decision analyst in order to be usable by more real-world managers. As a consequence, very little use has been made by managers of many of these approaches [27,37,38,44,57]. Concern over this fact has led to suitability studies and method-use recommendations [62,63]. Fahrni and Spätig [20] even attempted to organize the various approaches into an application-oriented guide for determining the most appropriate technique for a particular situation.

The purpose of this paper is to present a flexible R&D project-selection method that can be used by real-world managers to rank R&D project alternatives. This method is flexible because the organization can customize it to the specific R&D objectives desired, and because it can be used both to assess new projects and to evaluate continued funding for existing projects. The method presented here is a significant improvement over past ones for the following reasons:
- it represents a rigorous treatment of the general approach most often used by practicing managers;
- it relies on researcher-accepted peer review in the form of a user-friendly questionnaire;
- it handles tradeoffs among criteria in the most rigorously correct manner;
- it takes into account the fact that the value of a project is a function of both merit and cost;
- it can be used for all the progressive states of R&D;
- it can incorporate qualitative judgments.

In this R&D project-selection tool, projects that have identical but differently distributed evaluation responses will be ranked differently. This occurs not solely as a consequence of the criteria weights, but as an inherent consequence of the construction of this scoring algorithm. This capability is an important characteristic of a scoring project-selection tool when tradable criteria are involved. The algorithm more correctly "selects" the optimal portfolio consistent with the institution's R&D emphasis because it is constructed to express the fundamental mathematical relationship between tradable criteria.

The model presented in this paper was applied at a federal research laboratory that engages in both basic and applied R&D. In this federal laboratory, decisions must be made annually to fund both new and ongoing research projects from competing proposals. The selection criteria important to this institution are the same for all categories of R&D (basic versus applied versus incremental). What varies between the different categories of R&D is the relative importance of the selection criteria, that is, their relative weights. The selection model proposed is ideally suited to handle this variable-weight, multicriteria decision problem.

The necessity to select R&D projects from a group of candidates arises for two reasons: first, resources are usually in shorter supply than the number of potential projects and second, it is incumbent on the institution to proactively guide research efforts in a directions consistent with its mission and R&D strategy. Often, however, decisions to fund or continue funding research projects are not made in the context of either the organization's global strategic objectives or its desired balance between R&D types. The project-selection tool used should be capable of generating an R&D portfolio consistent with the desired balance of risk, return, and other factors specific to the different kinds of R&D the organization wishes to support.

For basic research, where the objectives are exploration and knowledge, the criteria are difficult to quantify and the outcome is highly uncertain, R&D selection models that permit qualitative judgment tend to be more accepted by managers. Furthermore, it is a fact that selection models incorporating peer review are the ones most readily accepted by researchers themselves [35,60,69]. These factors are important to take into account when an R&D project-selection process is developed, because without the buy-in of management and of the researchers, implementation will be difficult and the results will most likely be viewed as suspect. In addition, the evaluation process chosen should be a clear vehicle for focusing proposed R&D projects on those characteristics that the organization wishes to emphasize and that it will be most likely to reward.

Project Selection Using Scoring

Scoring as a technique for project selection has appeared in various forms in the literature since the 1950s [1,12,15,18,25,29,34,48,49]. A brief review of the cited papers appears in Table 1. Scoring is appropriate when there is a low degree of interdependence between projects, that is, when the activities and results of one project do not depend on the activities and results of a different project. The most common approach is to rate potential projects against a set of criteria and then to obtain a figure of merit for each proposal by combining the results of the ratings using some type of algorithm. The criteria can be weighted in the algorithm to emphasize the importance of some criteria over others. The most common algorithms used to date have been either purely additive or purely multiplicative. The alternatives are then ranked using the results of the algorithm to facilitate decisions regarding resources.

Scoring has distinct advantages over other methods of project selection. It is quantitative enough to possess a certain degree of rigor, yet not so complex as to mystify and hence discourage potential users. Scoring can accommodate nonquantitative criteria into the selection process by relating question responses to a constructed, ordinal scale.[1] Scoring can incorporate peer review into the selection process if the evaluators chosen are peers of the proposing researchers. Scoring does not require detailed economic data, some of which may not readily be available. Furthermore, scoring tools can be customized by an organization to articulate the characteristics it wishes to emphasize.

Four key unresolved issues are associated with scoring as an R&D project-selection method, which we intend to address in this paper. First, the figure of merit produced by scoring is not a sufficient measure of the value of a project; it is not even a measure of relative value. Second, purely multiplicative or purely additive algorithms for calculating scores cannot correctly reflect the tradeoffs inherent in the traditional set of R&D project-selection criteria. Third, project selection is often treated as a one-time exercise to be performed and then forgotten, and this attitude can be encouraged by inadequate scoring techniques. Last, the concept of generating a "score" for an R&D project can be a great source of researcher animosity toward the project-selection process.

The score produced as a result of the algorithm is not, in general, a measure of relative value in the same sense that it is a measure of relative merit. That is because the resulting figure of merit does not usually include an explicit consideration of relative project cost. Value is a function of both merit and expenditure of resources. Therefore, value assessment for selecting an R&D project should take into account the relative cost of the alternatives. If the figure of merit is in some way combined with a relative measure of cost, a measure of relative value for the alternatives can be obtained. The ranking model proposed here incorporates explicitly both merit and relative cost.

The additive and multiplicative algorithms that have been presented to date in the literature have been either purely one or the other. While both additive and multiplicative algorithms have their place, neither one alone can effectively deal with that fact that R&D project selection is a multicriteria decision problem.[2] In a multicriteria decision problem, tradeoffs among the various criteria are the norm, and so the decision-support method utilized should be able to explicitly account for those tradeoffs. An approach to quantifying the aggregate effectiveness of technologies possessing performance characteristics that can be traded against one another during the design process is discussed in detail by Martino [46]. That approach has been adopted in this study for ranking alternative R&D projects with tradable criteria.

Often, the project-selection process is regarded as an isolated event without any integral connection to the outcomes of the projects that it selected. The most important long-term benefit that accrues to the organization from undertaking such a methodical evaluation of the value of proposed R&D projects is that the outcomes of the projects form a basis for future assessment of the evaluation process itself. In other words, the outcome of projects can be used to assess retrospectively how well the evaluation process did in rating and ranking the proposed projects. (Unfortunately, however, this does not provide any information regarding projects that were not selected.) Through this process of comparing preproject speculation to postproject accomplishments, important new criteria or new information regarding existing criteria may emerge. This information can be used to improve and refine the R&D project-selection process for future use.

The "number" generated as a result of the evaluation process is only useful for comparing and ranking alternatives with that set. However, the process of generating such a number often produces the feeling, especially among researchers, that their project is being "graded."[3] It is important to emphasize here (and in the real world) that there is no significance to the numerical result of the algorithm other than for the purpose of ranking. Furthermore, it is not a meaningful exercise to compare numerical results across independently ranked sets of projects or to compare scores across different research of funding categories. Clear communication on this point is essential for the acceptance of a selection process that uses scoring.

Ranking Project Alternatives

Criteria Determination and Weighting

The first step in setting up a peer-review scoring process for R&D project selection is to decide on the criteria against which the proposed projects will be evaluated. This can be done using an informal inquiry process such as a questionnaire or stakeholder meeting, or a more formal method such as Delphi or analytic hierarchy process. The advantage of a formal process over an informal one is that rigor brings with it a certain amount of credibility; however, it also takes more time and resources. Formal or informal, the most important points are to be sure that the appropriate stakeholders provide the necessary input and that the criteria set is complete but not redundant.

Four main criteria were determined to be of importance to the federal research facility where this study was conducted. These criteria were termed the four R's for relevance, risk, reasonableness, and return. *Relevance* addresses the degree to which the proposed project supports the organization's mission and strategic objectives and is a pursuit the organization would benefit from undertaking. *Risk* addresses the level of scientific and/or technical uncertainty associated with the project, and to match the response scale of the other criteria, it is evaluated by assessing the probability of success. *Reasonableness* addresses whether or not the level of resources proposed will permit successful completion of the project objectives on time and within budget. *Return* addresses the perceived level of impact that the proposed work would have in the scientific and technical community and to the organization, *if the project were successful.* Return has three separate components: basic or fundamental research return; programmatic or applied research return; and business return.[4] The relative weights of these different kinds of return will depend on the category of R&D being considered, a point discussed further on.

How were these criteria selected and how can we be sure they comprise the most "correct" set? As stated previously, there are formal and informal ways to obtain criteria. These criteria were obtained informally through meetings with scientists and engineers, managers, and funding decision makers. The most correct set of criteria is the one the majority of stakeholders feel most accurately and fully captures the essence of the institution's R&D objectives, yet is not redundant. In this case, the institution is a federal R&D laboratory where basic and programmatic research return are highly valued, but a business component related to two issues is also of interest: first, the federal government's role in U.S. industry, and second, the ability of the proposed project to strengthen the institution's core competences. Mission relevance, a level of risk appropriate to the R&D category, and efficient use of resources are also important criteria. In this particular case, market-related variables and financial criteria are of little significance.

Once the criteria have been determined, they must be weighted to reflect the preferred emphasis of the organization and the particular category of R&D. For example, the amount of risk associated with a basic science research project can be higher than would be tolerable for an applied research project. Consequently, the relative weight on the risk question (i.e., probability of success) would be lower for basic research than for applied research. On the other hand, the weight on scientific return should be higher in the basic research funding category, and the weight on applied research return should be higher in the applied research funding category.

The purpose of weighting is not only to emphasize the most appropriate criteria, but also to facilitate self-selection of the optimal R&D portfolio. In other words, the weight distribution can be used to generate a balanced portfolio made up of the best and most appropriate projects in each R&D category that exhibit the desired characteristics.

Actual numerical values for the weights can be obtained, like the criteria themselves, either formally or informally. One approach consists of rating the lowest priority criterion with a value of one and then scaling the other criteria relative to that criterion.

Peer-Review Evaluation Questionnaire

Evaluation of the proposed projects is carried out using a questionnaire consisting of six questions based on the four R's: one question each for relevance, risk, and reasonableness and one each for the three kinds of return. A slight variation of the question structure is

---

Figure 1. Example questionnaire for use by peer review teams for assessing merit of proposed projects during R&D project-selection process.

Project Selection Questionnaire
(For each question, please circle or check one answer)

1. **Relevance:** What is the degree to which this proposed project supports this organization's mission and objectives?
   A. Very high   D. Low
   B. High   E. Very low
   C. Average

2. **Risk:** What do you believe the probability is that this proposal/project could successfully achieve its stated scientific/technical objectives?
   A. Very high   D. Low
   B. High   E. Very low
   C. Average

3. **Reasonableness:** What do you believe the probability is that this proposal/project could successfully achieve its stated scientific technical objectives on time and on budget with the requested level of resources?
   A. Very high   D. Low
   B. High   E. Very low
   C. Average

4. **Basic Research Return:** Rate the scientific/technical impact of this proposed project, if successful.
   A. Very high   D. Low
   B. High   E. Very low
   C. Average

5. **Programmatic Research Return:** Rate the programmatic impact of this proposed project, if successful.
   A. Very high   D. Low
   B. High   E. Very low
   C. Average

6. **Business Return:** Rate the business impact of this proposed project, if successful.
   A. Very high   D. Low
   B. High   E. Very low
   C. Average

---

necessary for interim review of ongoing projects. The questionnaires are shown in Figures 1 and 2. A copy of the appropriate questionnaire (new project versus interim review) is then provided with each proposal to the members of the peer-review teams, along with a more detailed explanation of the meaning of each question. Question responses range from "very low" to "very high." The responses are mapped, using a Likert-type scale, to the values of one to five, with "very low" corresponding to one and "very high" to five. The one-to-five scale was used (versus zero-to-four) to preclude mathematical difficulties that would arise if zero appeared as a denominator and to avoid zeroing out the total figure of merit should one of the multiplied questions receive the lowest possible response.

Figure 2. Example questionnaire for use by peer review teams for assessing merit of continuing projects during R&D project-evaluation process.

Interim Project Evaluation Questionnaire
(For each question, please circle or check one answer)

1. Relevance: What is the degree to which this project supports this organization's mission and objectives?
A. Very high   D. Low
B. High   E. Very low
C. Average

2. Risk: What is the degree to which this project is achieving its initially stated scientific/technical objectives?
A. Very high   D. Low
B. High   E. Very low
C. Average

3. Reasonableness: What is the degree to which this project is making satisfactory progress on time and on budget within the allocated level of resources?
A. Very high   D. Low
B. High   E. Very low
C. Average

4. Basic Research Return: Rate the scientific/technical impact of this proposed project, if successful.
A. Very high   D. Low
B. High   E. Very low
C. Average

5. Programmatic Research Return: Rate the programmatic impact of this proposed project, if successful.
A. Very high   D. Low
B. High   E. Very low
C. Average

6. Business Return: Rate the business impact of this proposed project, if successful.
A. Very high   D. Low
B. High   E. Very low
C. Average

The advantage of using a questionnaire is that it can be easily customized for a particular organization. For a private sector firm, for example, issues such as potential economic return and marketability would be of importance, and questions pertaining to those topics could be included in the questionnaire.

Constructing an Algorithm to Obtain a Figure of Merit
After a questionnaire is filled out by every peer-review team for each proposed project, the results must be compiled into a figure of merit using some kind of algorithm. Weighted additive algorithms and weighted multiplicative algorithms have been used

in the past, but they have certain limitations that have not been adequately resolved by previous scoring approaches.

One of the major limitations of purely additive or purely multiplicative algorithms concerns criteria that are tradable. For example, the probability that a proposed project will successfully accomplish its scientific/technical objectives is, in general, inversely related to its potential return, that is, when one is high, the other tends to be low and vice versa. Risk (in terms of probability of success) and return are therefore tradable criteria in this model.

At times, it is desirable to encourage a high return at the expense of incurring a higher level of risk (or lower probability of success). Purely multiplicative algorithms cannot produce figures of merit that correctly express this preference because multiplication will always produce the highest figure of merit when the two tradable responses are both in the midrange of the response scale. To rectify this, tradable quantities should be added together so that it is the sum of the question responses that contributes to the overall figure of merit. A simple example can help show which approach more correctly expresses the institution's attitude toward high-risk projects with huge potential payoffs. For a proposal with the highest possible rating for return (5) and the lowest rating for probability of success (1), adding together return and probability of success produces the same score ($5 + 1 = 6$) as a proposal with a midrange rating in each ($3 + 3 = 6$). Contrast this with the results of multiplication of those same question responses which produces the highest score when the responses are both in the middle of the response scale ($5 \times 1 = 5$ versus $3 \times 3 = 9$).

For criteria that are not tradable and that contribute independently to the quality of a proposed project, it is more appropriate to multiply the question responses in the algorithm. Unlike adding tradable criteria, multiplying independent criteria (or independent groupings of tradable criteria) emphasizes the importance of each one individually and minimizes the potential selection of proposals that are extremely poor performers in any one independent category. On a scale of one to five, for example, a low score of one for an important criterion would result in that criterion contributing nothing to the proposal's figure of merit.

To weight the criteria so that they reflect the desired emphasis of the organization for a specific kind of R&D (basic versus applied versus incremental), tradable question responses in the same added grouping are each multiplied by a weighting factor to reflect their relative level of importance. Multiplied question responses in the same grouping are each raised to an exponent to reflect their relative level of importance [46]. Weights in the same added group or multiplied group are then independently normalized.

As an example, if question response $A(Q_A)$ and question response $B(Q_B)$ are determined to be tradable, then they would constitute a group. Response Q_A would be multiplied by weight w_{11} and response Q_B would be multiplied by weight w_{12}. The group would appear in the algorithm as $(w_{11}Q_A + w_{12}Q_B)$. If question response $C(Q_C)$ was determined not to be tradable with the group $(w_{11}Q_A + w_{12}Q_B)$, and if increases in both QC and group $(w_{11}Q_A + w_{12}Q_B)$ were each positively correlated with the project's level of desirability, then Q_C and group $(w_{11}Q_A + w_{12}Q_B)$ would be multiplied together in the numerator. Each of those "groups" would be weighted exponentially according to its relative level of importance, and the result would appear as:

$$Q_C^{w_{21}}(w_{11}Q_A + w_{12}Q_B)^{w_{22}}.$$

Weights w_{11} and w_{12} would be normalized and weights w_{21} and w_{22} would be normalized. Increases in question responses that correlate negatively with a project's level of desirability would appear in the denominator of the algorithm.

Applying the above logic to the six question responses in the questionnaire (Figures 1 or 2), the following algorithm can be constructed:

$$S_c = \frac{1}{4}\left\{ q_1^{w_{11}} q_3^{w_{12}} \left[w_{21}q_{22} \left(w_{31}q_4^{w} + w_{32}q_6^{41} \right) \right] w_{13} - 1 \right\} \tag{1}$$

where q_i is the peer evaluator Likert-scale response for the ith question and w_{jk} is the kth weight in the jth multiplicative or additive group. In this algorithm, scientific return is treated as tradable with programmatic/business return, and all return is considered tradable with probability of success. The probability of success/return group is then multiplied by both the relevance response and the reasonableness response. The quantity one is subtracted to shift the range from zero to four, and then the entire expression is divided by four to scale it between zero and one.

The fact that this approach explicitly accounts for tradeoffs represents an improvement over previous models because it more readily selects projects that possess the desired set of characteristics. A meaningful case to examine is the one where six proposals receive identical question responses of five fours and a single one, but where those marks are distributed differently. Would the rankings in that case that result properly reflect management's priorities? We will revisit this question later.

Scaling the Funds Request

The concept of value analysis in project selection implies that due consideration has been given to the relative cost of the competing projects. Because value is a function of both merit and cost, the figure-of-merit expression must be expanded to incorporate the level of resources needed to achieve the project's stated technical objectives.

The amount of the funding requested for a project is usually orders of magnitude greater than the maximum possible value for the figure of merit. To include both merit and cost in the same value assessment equation and have the results mean anything, it is necessary to scale the magnitude of the funds request. Assuming the funds requests constitute a distribution, the funds requests can be scaled so that the dollar amount is the same order of magnitude as the figure of merit.

To scale the funds requests from one to five, the following equation is used:

$$f = 1 + \frac{\text{req - min}}{(\text{max-min})/4} \tag{2}$$

where f is the scaled funds request, min is the minimum funding request in the proposal group, max is the maximum funding request in the proposal group, and req is the actual amount of funding requested. Using this equation, the midrange funding request would receive a scaled funds request of three, the lowest a scaled funds request of one, and the highest a scaled funds request of five. This is, of course, a linear mapping of the funds request; however, it is not necessary that the mapping be linear; a different equation can be used that would result in a nonlinear mapping. This scaled funds request that is combined with the figure of merit to obtain a value index for the proposed projects.

Ranking Project Alternatives Based on Value Index

The figure of merit and the scaled funds request are combined into a value index using the following equation:

$$V = aS_c + \frac{b}{4.8}\left(\frac{4S_c + 1}{f} - .02\right) \tag{3}$$

where a and b are normalized weights reflecting the relative importance of the figure of merit term versus the funds scaling term, S_c is the figure of merit, f is the scaled funds request, and the mathematical manipulations are necessary as before to shift and scale the numerical result to between zero and one.

This particular form for the value index equation has some very desirable properties. Note that the value index does not decrease linearly with increased funding. This non-linearity is important because it is not desirable that the value index be inversely proportional, or more than inversely proportional, to the funding request. Also, as the ratio of a over b increases (decreases), the value index increases (decreases) slightly for the identical figure of merit and scaled funds request. Increasing the ratio of a over b corresponds to placing a stronger emphasis on the figure term (versus the funds scaling term).

How can we determine if the distribution of funding that results from this ranking process represents the highest total utility possible to the decision makers with the available funds? Should we be concerned that there may be some other distribution of funds among the proposed projects in which awards different from the requests will result in a higher total utility?

The answers to these questions are best understood by recalling that this process ranks proposed projects with clearly defined technical objectives to be accomplished at a clearly stated cost. A different amount of funding for any given proposal necessarily corresponds to a different set of objectives. While it is certainly possible to award funding that differs from the researcher's requested amount, it may not be appropriate for the decision makers to engage in this kind of activity. As an alternative, the proposing scientists could be asked to submit several funding scenarios for consideration with an outline of associated tasks. However, it is important to bear in mind that a certain critical mass of funding is necessary to accomplish something of consequence, and that one-half of the funding does not necessarily equate to one-half of the stated results. The objective of this exercise is to maximize total utility (which presumably it does) for the proposed set of projects at the proposed levels of effort.

Let us now return to the question of six proposals receiving identical question responses of five fours and a single one, but where these marks are distributed differently across the six questions. How do the six proposals rank relative to each other?

Table 2. Results of Using Combined Additive/Multiplicative Algorithm to Discriminate Between Six Different R&D Projects with Differently Distributed but Identical Question Response Levels.

Relevance q_1	Risk[1] q_2	Reasonableness q_3	Scientific Return q_4	Programmatic Return q_5	Business Return q_6	Merit/Value Index[2]
1	4	4	4	4	4	0.38/0.26
4	1	4	4	4	4	0.60/0.40
4	4	1	4	4	4	0.38/0.26
4	4	4	1	4	4	0.68/0.45
4	4	4	4	1	4	0.71/0.47
4	4	4	4	4	1	0.71/0.47

(1) The level of risk is assessed by evaluating the probability of success, because this results in a response scale that matches the others (i.e., 1 being the lowest and 5 the highest).

(2) All weights of a grouping are equal for purposes of this calculation and normalized. For example, if there are three components of a multiplied group, then each is weighted 1/3. A funds scaling factor of 3 was used for the value index calculation.

For a purely additive or purely multiplicative algorithm with equal criteria weights, all scores would be identical. The same is not true for this combined algorithm

Table 2 shows the figure of merit and value index obtained using (1) and (3) for six such proposals. Relevance, reasonableness, and the risk/return grouping are equally important and are each weighted one-third (w_{11}, w_{12}, and w_{13}). Weights within all other two-member groups are also set equal.

When either relevance or reasonableness has a question response of one, the overall figure of merit and value index are appropriately low. When risk receives the question response of one, however, the figure of merit and value index rise significantly. This is because the algorithm inherently recognizes the risk/return tradeoff and "knows" that the penalty should be moderated for low probability of success (response of 1) when it is accompanied by a high potential return (all fours). When the question response of one appears in either programmatic or business return, the figure of merit is the same for each and the value index is the same for each. When the one appears in the scientific return category, the result is lower than when it appears in either programmatic or business return. This is viewed as a positive feature at the federal research facility where this method was developed, because the institution places a high premium on scientific return. An algorithm that produces a figure of merit identical for a value of one in any of the three return categories could be generated by adjusting the relative weights in the algorithm. It is worth noting that for this case, the final rankings are the same for both the figure of merit and the value index calculations.

We conducted computer experiments to test whether the combined figure of merit algorithm with tradeoffs produces statistically different rankings than either the purely multiplicative or additive ones. Systematically varied proposal question responses were calculated into a figure of merit using a purely additive, a purely multiplicative, and this combined algorithm. Spearman rank correlation coefficients were obtained for the additive versus multiplicative algorithms and for the additive versus combined and the multiplicative versus combined algorithms. Similar steps were taken to obtain value indices for the three pairs. While all three comparisons resulted in coefficients that fell well within the range for rejecting the null hypothesis, the coefficient for the additive versus multiplicative comparison was 0.96, but the coefficients for the additive versus combined and the multiplicative versus combined algorithm were lower at 0.81.

Software Decision Support Tool

A software DSS was developed using Microsoft Excel®. The software is a custom application programmed with Excel® macros that gives decision makers user-friendly access to the model. The software acts as a database for the proposal responses and calculates figures of merit and value index results. The DSS ranks proposed R&D projects with respect to both figure of merit and value index and indicates the funding cutoff point for each, consistent with available amount of funding. With the DSS, decision makers can carry out "what if" scenario analyses by varying weights, algorithms, and funding levels. The software can also be used to produce output for presentation.

Implementation

This technique of project selection, based on both merit and value, was developed for the internal R&D projects funding office of a federal national laboratory. The emphasis of this laboratory is primarily defense; however, recently there has been a move to undertake research of interest to the private sector, particularly if that research can be shown to have "dual use." Initially, this method was implemented concurrently with the usual, more informal evaluation and ranking processes. We will describe the results of the concurrent use of this method for new project proposals in the basic science research category.

One questionnaire was handed out to the peer evaluation teams with each new project proposal. These proposal evaluation teams consisted of peers entirely from within the institution. Each team returned one questionnaire per proposal, which was the consensus of team discussion. There were 207 proposed new projects with funding requests in excess of $43 million. Only $5.6 million worth of those proposed new projects could actually be funded, with no restrictions on how many projects could constitute that $5.6 million.

In order to rank the proposed projects using (1) and (3), appropriate weights had to be chosen. Since this particular case involved basic science research, the weights in Table 3 were used for (1), which are consistent with previous discussion.

In addition, the values of a and b used for (3) were three and one; that is, 75% of the weight was given to the merit term and 25% to the funding term. This ratio was found empirically to incorporate the concept of value while simultaneously not biasing the portfolio in favor of lots of tiny projects.

Scores and value indexes were calculated for all 207 basic research new initiatives using (1) and (3) with the weights indicated above. A total of 30 proposals were ranked high enough by score to make the $5.6 million funding cutoff. This compares

Table 3. Relative and Normalized Weights Used with (1) to Obtain Relative Ranking of Basic Science R&D Projects at a Federal National Laboratory

Criterion	Weight	Relative Value	Normalized Value
Relevance	w_{11}	1	1/5
Reasonableness	w_{12}	2	2/5
Risk/Return	w_{13}	2	2/5
Risk	w_{21}	1	1/4
Return	w_{22}	3	3/4
Scientific	w_{31}	5	5/6
Prog/Business	w_{32}	1	1/6
Programmatic	w_{41}	2	2/3
Business	w_{42}	1	1/3

to 32 proposals actually funded by the institution. Of the 30 proposals selected for funding by score, only 16 were among the 32 actually funded by the institution. A total of 37 proposals were ranked high enough by value index to make the funding cutoff. Of the 37 proposals selected for funding by value index, only 15 were among the 32 actually funded by the institution. Of those proposals in agreement with the actual funding case, two of the proposals selected by score were not selected by value, and one proposal selected by value was not selected by score. The low percentage of overlap between proposals selected by this method and ones actually funded by the institution (17 out of 32) warranted further investigation.

After discussions with members of the project funding office, it was discovered that the new proposals were not treated as a single group but were actually subdivided into nine different basic science subcategories, for example, materials, bioscience, earth science, chemistry, and computation. Each subcategory had its own peer-review evaluation team and each team was autonomous in decision making regarding its own funding allotment. This meant that a score awarded in one category may be lower (or even much lower) than a score awarded in a different category, yet both proposals could be successful in obtaining funding.

We looked at each of the nine basic science subcategories individually. In four of the nine subcategories, the proposals ranked the highest by this method were also the ones actually funded by the institution. In four other subcategories, the majority of the proposals ranked highest by this method were the ones funded by the institution. In two of these cases, however, one proposal funded by the institution scored significantly lower than four higher ranked proposals, and in the other two cases, two proposals funded by the institution scored significantly lower than two higher ranked proposals. In the remaining basic science subcategory, the five proposals ranked highest by this method were not funded by the institution. While the figures of merit of the highest ranked and the funded proposals in this category were not different enough to be statistically significant, this could suggest further investigation. Overall, however, agreement between proposals ranked high by this method and actually funded by the institution (22 out of 32) was much greater when considering the subcategories than the aggregate group. Serious inconsistencies existed in only one subcategory.

This result underscores the idea that proposal scores and value indexes cannot be legitimately compared across independent categories. However, it also calls into question the much larger issue concerning how proposals in one subgroup can receive lower scores in the aggregate ranking than proposals in another subgroup, yet still be funded. One explanation is that the decision to allocate funding to autonomous subcategories may permit substandard proposals in one subcategory to be funded at the expense of higher quality proposals in a different subcategory that just happens to have an abundance of high-quality proposals. Another explanation is that proposals across different subcategories actually are of commensurate quality, but that peer review teams express that quality on different response scales. There is also the possibility that other criteria not articulated by this questionnaire were operating in the selection process; that is, for peer-review teams in which there was not good agreement between rank by this method and actual funding, some other implicit criteria were being considered by the teams.

Only the institution can adequately resolve these issues and determine if the best proposed projects are, in fact, the ones receiving the funding. It might be important in cases where peer-review teams function independently to include some of the same individuals on every team in order to interject some degree of uniformity in the response scales.

Summary and Conclusion

The purpose of this project was to present a method for performing R&D project selection based on the relative value to the organization of the proposed research. A comprehensive overview of the most recent R&D project-selection literature was also provided.

An improved scoring technique for R&D project evaluation and ranking was presented that explicitly incorporates tradeoffs among evaluation criteria. The resulting figure of merit was then combined with a scaled funds request to obtain a value index for each proposed project. The value index algorithm produced a measure of project value that accounted for value as a function of both merit and cost. We showed that the combined additive/multiplicative algorithm correctly discriminates for the desired characteristics and that it ranks proposals consistent with the institution's intended emphasis.

As an initial activity, questionnaires were filled out parallel to the institution's customary selection process. A preliminary analysis of the results illuminated some issues suggesting further investigation. More detailed analysis of the results of those questionnaires is planned. We hope eventually to include interim project evaluation, as well as retrospective productivity assessments and postproject impact analysis. We are actively seeking new situations in which to apply this model.

It is important to keep in mind that the purpose of value-based project selection is not to encourage a portfolio of many small projects, but instead to promote cost effectiveness and maximum utility in R&D activities. It is incumbent on management to structure a selection process that stresses the appropriate criteria so as to encourage the desired characteristics in proposed projects, that is, to promote proposals with characteristics the institution prefers to reward. Effective, successful implementation of a comprehensive R&D project-selection process and follow-up impact assessment require a dedicated commitment from management, the researchers, and the peer-review teams. An important caveat on the use of any formal decision support tool is that it should never be a substitute for management judgment and leadership.

Acknowledgment

The authors gratefully acknowledge T. Helm for many enlightening discussions during the course of this project. They would like to thank Dr. S. Schmidt, Dr. S. Gerstl, and S. Cross of the Los Alamos National Laboratory Directed Research and Development (LDRD) Program Office for their assistance and support. They also thank several anonymous reviewers for their very helpful remarks.

References

1. H. Averch, "Criteria for evaluating research projects and portfolios," in *Assessing R&D Impacts: Methods and Practice*, B. Bozeman and J. Melkers, Eds. Norwell, MA: Kluwer, 1993, pp. 264-277.

2. N. R. Baker and W. H. Pound, "R&D project selection: Where we stand," *IEEE Trans. Eng. Manag.*, vol. EM-11, pp. 124-134. Dec. 1964.

3. N. Baker and J. Freeland, "Recent advances in R&D benefit measurement and project selection methods," *Manage. Sci.*, vol. 21, no. 10, pp. 1164-1175, 1975.

4. J. F. Bard, R. Balachandra, and P. E. Kaufmann, "An interactive approach to R&D project selection and termination," *IEEE Trans. Eng. Manag.*, vol. 35, pp. 139-146, Aug. 1988.

5. J. F. Bard, "Using multicriteria methods in the early stages of new product development," *J. Oper. Res. Soc.*, vol. 41, no. 8, pp. 755-766, 1990.

6. R. J. Bedell, "Terminating R&D projects prematurely," *Res. Manage.*, vol. 26, no. 4, pp. 32-35, 1983.

7. M. Behanec, V. Rajkovic, B. Semolic, and A. Pogacnik, "Knowledge-based portfolio analysis for project evaluation," *Inform. Manage.*, vol. 28, no. 5, pp. 293-302, 1995.

8. J. M. Booker and M. C. Bryson, "Annotated bibliography on decision analysis with applications to project management," Los Alamos National Laboratory, Los Alamos, NM, Tech. Rep. LA-10027-MS, 1984.

9. J. M. Booker and M. C. Bryson, "Decision analysis in project management: An overview," *IEEE Trans. Eng. Manag.*, vol. EM-32, pp. 3-9, Feb. 1985.

10. R. A. A. Boschi, H. U. Balthasar, and M. M. Menke, "Quantifying and forecasting exploratory research success," *Res. Manage.*, vol. 22, no. 5, pp. 14-21, 1979.

11. M. S. Brenner, "Practical R&D project prioritization," *Res. Technol. Manage.*, vol. 37, no. 5, pp. 38-42, 1994.

12. D. M. Cardus, J. Fuhrrer, A. W. Martin, and R. M. Thrall, "Use of benefit-cost analysis in the peer review of proposed research," *Manage. Sci.*, vol. 28, no. 4, pp. 439-445, 1982.

13. Y. H. Chun, "Sequential decisions under uncertainty in the R&D project selection problem," *IEEE Trans. Eng. Manag.*, vol. 40, pp. 404-413, Nov. 1994.

14. W. D. Cook and Y. Roll, R&D project selection: Productivity considerations," *R&D Manage.*, vol. 18, no. 3, pp. 251-256, 1988.

15. D. Costello, "A practical approach to R&D selection," *Technol. Forecasting and Social Change*, vol. 23, pp. 353-368, 1983.

16. A. F. Czajkowski and S. Jones, "Selecting interrelated R&D projects in space planning technology," *IEEE Trans. Eng. Manag.*, vol. 33, pp. 17-24, Feb. 1986.

17. N. Danila, "Strategic evaluation and selection of R&D projects," *R&D Manage.*, vol. 19, no. 1, pp. 47-62, 1989.

18. B. V. Dean and M. J. Nishry, "Scoring and profitability models for evaluating and selecting engineering projects," *Oper. Res.*, vol. 13, no. 4, pp. 550-569, 1965.

19. O. P. Dias, Jr., "The R&D project selection problem with fuzzy coefficients," *Fuzzy Sets and Syst.*, vol. 26, no. 3, pp. 299-316, 1988.

20. P. Fahrni and M. Spätig, "An application-oriented guide to R&D project selection and evaluation methods," *R&D Manage.*, vol. 20, no. 2, pp. 155-171, 1990.

21. E. Fox, N. R. Baker, and J. L. Bryant, "Economic models for R&D project selection in the presence of project interactions," *Manage. Sci.*, vol. 30, no. 7, pp. 890-902, 1984.

22. H. Gaynor, "Selecting projects," *Res. Technol. Manage.*, vol. 33, no. 4, pp. 43-45, 1990.

23. K. Golabi, "Selecting a group of dissimilar projects for funding," *IEEE Trans. Eng. Manag.*, vol. 34, pp. 138-145, Aug. 1987.

24. P. M. Goldstein and H. M. Singer, "A note on economic models for R&D project selection in the presence of project interactions," *Manage. Sci.*, vol. 32, no. 10, pp. 1356-1360, 1986.

25. D. L. Hall and A. Nauda, "A strategic methodology for IR&D project selection," in *Proc. 1988 IEEE Engineering Management Conf.*, 1988, pp. 59-66.

26. S. W. Hess, "Swinging on the branch of a tree: Project selection applications. *Interfaces*, vol. 23, no. 6, pp. 5-12, 1993.

27. J. C. Higgins and K. M. Watts, "Some perspectives on the use of management science techniques in R&D management," *R&D Manage.*, vol. 16, no. 4, pp. 291-296, 1986.

28. M. G. Iyigun, "A decision support system for R&D project selection and resource allocation under uncertainty," *Project Manage. J.*, vol. 24, no. 4, pp. 5-13, 1993.

29. X. Y. Jin, A. L. Porter, F. A. Rossini, and E. D. Anderson, "R&D project selection and evaluation: A microcomputer-based approach," *R&D Manage.*, vol. 17, no. 4, pp. 277-288, 1987.

30. R. Khorramshahgol and Y. Gousty, "Delphic goal programming (DGP): A multi-objective cost/benefit approach to R&D portfolio analysis, *IEEE Trans. Eng. Manag.*, vol. 33, pp. 172-175, Aug. 1986.

31. D. F. Kocaoglu and M. G. Iyigun, "Strategic R&D project selection and resource allocation with a decision support system application," in *Proc. 1994 IEEE Int. Engineering Management Conf.*, pp. 225-232.

32. R. N. Kostoff, "A cost/benefit analysis of commercial fusion-fission reactor development," *J. Fusion Energy*, vol. 3, no. 2, pp. 81-93, 1983.

33. —, "Evaluation of proposed and existing accelerated research programs by the office of naval research," *IEEE Trans. Eng. Manag.*, vol. 35, pp. 271-279, Nov. 1988.

34. F. Krawiec, "Evaluating and selecting research projects by scoring," *Res. Manage.*, vol. 27, no. 2, pp. 22-26, 1984.

35. C. E. Kruytbosch, "The role and effectiveness of peer review," in *The Evaluation of Scientific Research*, D. Evered and S. Harnett, Eds. Chichester, UK: Wiley, 1989, pp. 69-85.

36. Y. Kuwahara and T. Yasutsugu, "An empirical view of a managerial evaluation of overall R&D cost-effectiveness,," in *Proc. 1988 IEEE Engineering Management Conf.*, 1988, pp. 67-71.

37. J. Lee, S. Lee, and Z. T. Bae, "R&D project selection: Behavior and practice in a newly industrializing country," *IEEE Trans. Eng. Manag.*, vol. 33, pp. 141-147, Aug. 1986.

38. M. J. Liberatore and G. J. Titus, "The practice of management science in R&D project management," *Manage. Sci.*, vol. 29, no. 8, pp. 962-975, 1983.

39. J. J. Liberatore, "A decision support system linking research and development project selection with business strategy," *Project Manage. J.*, vol. 19, no. 5, pp. 14-21, 1988a.

40. —, "An expert system for R&D project selection," *Math. Comput. Modeling*, vol. 11, pp. 260-265, 1988b.

41. M. J. Liberatore, "An extension of the analytic hierarchy process for industrial R&D project selection and resource allocation," *IEEE Trans. Eng. Manag.*, vol. 34, pp. 12-18, Feb. 1989.

42. G. Lockett, B. Hetherington, P. Yallup, M. Stratford, and B. Cox, "Modeling a research portfolio using AHP: A group decision process," *R&D Manage.*, vol. 16, no. 2, pp. 151-160, 1986.

43. G. Lockett and M. Stratford, "Ranking of research projects: Experiments with two methods," *OMEGA*, vol. 15, no. 5, pp. 395-400, 1987.

44. P. M. Maher and A. H. Rubenstein, "Factors affecting adoption of a quantitative method for R&D project selection," *Manage. Sci.*, vol. 21, no. 2, pp. 119-129, 1974.

45. T. F. Mandakovic and W. E. Souder, "Experiments with microcomputers to facilitate the use of project selection models," *J. Eng. Technol. Manage.*, vol. 7, no. 1, pp. 1-16, 1990.

46. J. P. Martino, *Technological Forecasting for Decision Making*, 3rd ed. New York, NY: McGraw-Hill, 1993, pp. 96-105.

47. A. Mehrez, "Selecting R&D projects: A case study of the expected utility approach," *Technovation*, vol. 8, pp. 299-311, 1988.

48. J. R. Moore, Jr. and N. R. Baker, "An analytical approach to scoring model design—Application to research and development project selection," *IEEE Trans. Eng. Manag.*, vol. EM-16, pp. 90-98, Aug. 1969a.

49. —, "Computational analysis of scoring models for R and D project selection," *Manage. Sci.*, vol. 16, no. 4, pp. B-212-B-232, 1969b.

50. D. P. Newton and A. W. Pearson, "Application of option pricing theory to R&D," *R&D Manage.*, vol. 24, no. 1, pp. 83-89, 1994.

51. M. Oral, O. Kettani, and P. Lang, "A methodology for collective evaluation and selection of industrial R&D projects," *Manage. Sci.*, vol. 37, no. 7, pp. 871-885, 1991.

52. J. L. Ringuest and S. B. Graves, "The linear multi-objective R&D project selection problem," *IEEE Trans. Eng. Manag.*, vol. 36, no. 1, pp. 54-57, 1989.

53. —, "The linear R&D project selection problem: An alternative to net present value," *IEEE Trans. Eng. Manag.*, vol. 37, pp. 143-146, May 1990.

54. P. A. Roussel, K. N. Saad, and T. J. Erickson, *Third Generation R&D: Managing the Link to Corporate Strategy.* Boston, MA: Harvard Business School Press, 1991.

55. A. H. Rubenstein and H. H. Schröder, "Managerial differences in assessing probabilities of technical success for R&D projects," *Manage. Sci.*, vol. 24, no. 2, pp. 137-148, 1977.

56. P. V. Rzasa, T. W. Faulkner, and N. L. Sousa, "Analyzing R&D portfolios at Eastman Kodak," *Res. Technol. Manage.*, vol. 33, no. 1, pp. 27-32, 1990.

57. A. M. Sanchez, "R&D project selection strategy: An empirical study in Spain," R&D *Manage., vol. 19, no. 1, pp. 63-68, 1989.*

58. R. L. Schmidt, "A model for R&D project selection with combined benefit, outcome and resource interactions," *IEEE Trans. Eng. Manag.*, vol. 40, pp. 403-410, Nov. 1993.

59. R. L. Schmidt and J. R. Freeland, "Recent progress in modeling R&D project-selection processes," *IEEE Trans. Eng. Manag.*, vol. 39, pp. 189-201, May 1992.

60. "Peer review reforms get good review," *Science*, vol. 265, p. 467, July 22, 1994.

61. P. Silvennoinen, "R&D project selection for promoting the efficiency of energy use," *R&D Manage.*, vol. 24, no. 4, pp. 317-324, 1994.

62. W. Souder, "A scoring methodology for assessing the suitability of management science models," *Manage. Sci.*, vol. 18, no. 10, pp. B-526-B-543, 1972.

63. W. E. Souder, "A system for using R&D project evaluation methods," *Res. Manage.*, vol. 21, no. 5, pp. 29-37, 1978.

64. W. E. Souder and T. Mandakovic, "R&D project selection models," *Res. Manage.*, vol. 29, no. 4, pp. 36-42, 1986.

65. W. Stadje, "Optimal selection of R&D projects," *Appl. Math. Optimization*, vol. 28, no. 2, pp. 149-160, 1993.

66. L. W. Steele, "What we've learned: Selecting R&D programs and objectives," *Res. Technol. Manage.*, vol. 31, no. 2, pp. 17-36, 1988.

67. T. J. Steward, "A multi-criteria decision support system for R&D project selection," *J. Oper. Res. Soc.*, vol. 42, no. 1, pp. 17-26, 1991.

68. M. Uenohara, "A management view of Japanese corporate R&D," *Res. Technol. Manage.*, vol. 34, no. 6, pp. 17-23, 1991.

69. U.S. General Accounting Office, *Peer Review: Reforms Needed to Ensure Fairness in Federal Agency Grant Selection: Report to the Chairman, Committee on Governmental Affairs.* Washington, DC: U.S. Senate/US-GAO, 1994.

70. R. Venkatraman and S. Venkatraman, "R&D project selection and scheduling for organizations facing product obsolescence," *R&D Manage.*, vol. 25, no. 1, pp. 57-70, 1995.

Endnotes

1. The constructed scale, however, may be related to a natural scale such as a statistical distribution. See [48].

2. An excellent discussion of the characteristics and merits of additive versus multiplicative scoring algorithms is contained in [49].

3. This does not pertain to the issue of researchers whose proposals are ranked poorly within the set. It relates to the fact that even top-ranked proposers still view the scoring process as a grading exercise rather than a ranking exercise.

4. Business return consists of activities that facilitate interactions of the federal laboratory with the private sector, for example, work that could generate a Cooperative Research and Development Agreement (CRADA).

Action-Oriented
Portfolio Management

C. Thomas Spradlin and David M. Kutoloski

There are a number of industries in which R&D places great sums of money at risk in facing an uncertain future; examples include pharmaceuticals, oil and gas exploration, and motion picture production. In pharmaceuticals, significant scientific complexity, regulatory risks and market uncertainties magnify the need for insightful decision making. Among approaches to the management of an R&D portfolio, decision analysis (DA) continues to prove its applicability and effectiveness as a methodology equipped to tackle such underlying issues and to increase shareholder value. In this article, we present a method for structuring the conversations around portfolio decision making and for reaching a conclusion in a timely manner deserving of consensus.

Evaluation vs. Management

Matheson has written that the two primary constituents of the effective management of R&D activity are "... the economic evaluation of potential R&D results and the development of alternative R&D programs" (1). In our experience, pharmaceutical portfolio managers work tirelessly and incessantly on the former while devoting little attention to the latter. The word "manage" means to handle or direct with a degree of skill, or to alter by manipulation; it implies action. By this definition, the management of a portfolio involves the act of changing it, or of intentionally leaving it alone rather than changing it.

Much of what is written and spoken about portfolio management actually has to do with portfolio evaluation, which involves no explicit notion of action. We take the position that the act of evaluating the portfolio has minimal value. Portfolio management is valuable because of the value-enhancing actions that are taken as a consequence of the analysis. As this article is concerned more with the decision process than with the pharmaceutical industry, we assume the reader's familiarity with both basic DA and the industry's drug development process. Additional discussion of DA can be found in (2) and (3). The drug development process is discussed in (4) and (5).

Drawbacks to Prioritization

Business units need to allocate resources to a collection of opportunities, but they do not have sufficient resources to fund all of them at the currently required level. Alternately,

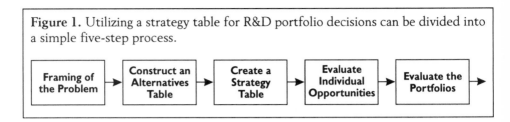

Figure 1. Utilizing a strategy table for R&D portfolio decisions can be divided into a simple five-step process.

they wish to reconsider their portfolio of investments to find a more attractive allocation of resources. In the past, they have used various methods to evaluate each of the opportunities and then to prioritize them. The prioritization provides a rank-ordered list of the projects, ordered generally by importance to the company, but this is not always clearly the case.

We feel that this approach suffers from several drawbacks. It offers only a little guidance to those who must make resource allocation decisions. Why not just allocate all the resources to the most important project? It focuses attention on the individual opportunities, rather than on the portfolio of opportunities. It does not capture and describe the inevitable relationships among the opportunities. Prioritization of the projects does not encourage consideration of alternative courses of action, either for each opportunity by itself or for the portfolio collectively. Finally, prioritization is not efficient, in that it may involve evaluation of courses of action that the business unit would not consider viable choices anyway.

We encourage instead the use of a tool known among decision analysts as a strategy table. The strategy table helps to avoid such shortcomings by explicitly comparing alternative strategies, or, in this case, portfolios. Columns in the table correspond to decisions, or areas where the business unit must make resource allocations at some level. Listed in the columns are individual alternatives, or candidate courses of action for each decision. Because a strategy implies a collection of decisions, a strategy table is complete only when specific, actionable alternatives for the various decisions are grouped together into a portfolio. It is these portfolios that are evaluated, and one of them is chosen for implementation.

The remainder of this article discusses process steps for building and evaluating R&D portfolios utilizing a strategy table. We will dissect the process into five components, as schematically represented in Figure 1.

1. Framing the Problem

The first step in undertaking a strategy-table approach to R&D portfolio management is to agree on which opportunities are to be considered. To identify these opportunities, a project team of experts from various functional areas is assigned responsibility to participate in the exercise with the decision analysts (in this case, the authors). For each opportunity we have an account of the current activity and a list of the resources already allocated to it. Note that if the business unit is willing to borrow resources to augment its budget, then the borrowed amount becomes an integral part of the budget. Indeed, borrowing is an opportunity that needs to be considered in the analysis.

Also associated with each opportunity is a description of the activities that should proceed in the future in order to bring the opportunity to market. For example, if phase 2 clinical trials are underway, then the future plans involve the phase 3 studies. Presumably, some portion of the resources needed for the future need to be allocated now, within the current budget period.

The next step is painful but critically important. The decision maker, or owner of the resources to be allocated in the decision, must consider the opportunities and classify them into three categories: the doomed projects, the equivocal projects, and the favorite projects.

The first, the doomed projects, includes those opportunities for which the decision maker, for whatever reason, knows that he will be unwilling to allocate future resources. From our experience in the pharmaceutical industry, only in rare instances would there ever be a doomed project. The second category includes the equivocal projects, where the decision maker is honestly undecided about future allocations; he is willing to consider alternatives. Finally, the third category might be called the favorites. It almost always has one or more projects, and those are the ones in which the decision maker intends to proceed with the plan of current and future activities, regardless of the results of any analysis.

The process of dividing into three categories is important because it clarifies for all participants which projects are available for decision making. It is clear that doomed projects will not be funded in the future, and that the favorites are sure to be funded at the currently planned level. Therefore, the only decisions to be made involve the equivocal projects. In keeping with our philosophy of concentrating on decisions (potential actions), rather than on portfolio evaluation, we are now finished with the doomed and the favorites, except that the resources allocated to them have to be subtracted from the business unit budget. The remainder is the amount available to be allocated to the equivocal projects. The process has, at this juncture, already helped to focus the problem.

2. Building an Alternatives Table

In conjunction with the project team, the analysts hold a meeting involving extended business-unit research management, project managers, and others, such as marketing personnel, who understand the issues facing each of the equivocal projects. We brainstorm alternative courses of action for each of these opportunities. By definition, there must be at least two alternatives for each, otherwise there is no decision. Thus, at a minimum, we investigate the momentum and the null alternatives.

The momentum alternative is defined as pursuing the current development plan identified in the initial conversation with the project personnel. The null alternative involves ceasing all activities following those currently underway. Beyond these two alternatives, we encourage creative thought in proposing other candidate courses of action for each project. For reasons to be explained below, we also collect rough estimates—for each alternative for each project—of the resources required from the upcoming budget period.

We find that these brainstorming sessions generate interesting candidate courses of action for the projects, as demonstrated in Figure 2. Once the participants understand that to offer an alternative is not tantamount to advocating it, ideas flow freely. Our

Figure 2. An alternatives table is used to brainstorm various alternatives for each equivocal project. Brief written descriptions of each alternative provide guidance for emphasizing the specific recommended action.

	Project A	Project B	Project C	Project D
	Momentum	Momentum	Momentum	Momentum
	Stop (null)	Stop (null)	Stop (null)	Stop (null)
	Delay 6 months	Delay 3 months	License out	
	25% more money	Double resources		

insistence on alternatives helps to dislodge expert thinking from the momentum alternative, and alternatives are offered that have not been considered, at least in public, before this meeting. Unfettered discussion of the proposed alternatives helps to disclose relationships among the projects. For example, two products might share development resources, so that the cost of developing both might be less than the sum of the individual project costs. Also, people responsible for one project feel particularly free to suggest alternatives for other projects, since they are not anchored to momentum. All of the alternatives generated can be collected into an alternatives table, like the one in Figure 2.

3. Creating a Strategy Table

A subsequent meeting of a smaller group is held to create strategies, or alternative portfolios, from the alternatives table. For each such portfolio, a single alternative is chosen from each column of the alternatives table. Such a combination of alternatives—one for each project—comprises a portfolio.

First, we define the momentum strategy as the combination of all the momentum alternatives. We do this to ensure that all participants are aware of current plans. This step also helps the participants understand how to use the alternatives table to generate portfolios. The idea of the exercise is to create a strategic theme that might describe the business of the future, and then to choose combinations of alternatives consistent with that theme. Nevertheless, practice is required for a group accustomed to the individual project paradigm to be able readily to form reasonable portfolios.

Examples of strategic themes that could guide the selection of a portfolio are: domination of a niche market; maintaining business in already-established therapeutic areas; or maintenance of a balanced portfolio. In the first, management might identify a niche market in which one could gain a significant leadership position by concentrating research in that area. In the second, management might consider it important to continue research in a number of therapeutic areas in order to maintain the company's presence in those areas, and because of expectations of future discovery research. In seeking a balanced portfolio, one might wish to ensure that the company has a steady progression of new product launches.

The discussion of the strategic themes suggests coherent combinations of alternatives for the various projects. Notably, no matter how thorough the brainstorming of alternatives for the individual projects, the consideration of strategic themes suggests

Figure 3. A strategy table depicts rival portfolios for consideration in an analysis. Each portfolio is constructed by selecting a theme and then mapping out courses of action from the alternatives table that match the portfolio's theme.

	Project A	Project B	Project C	Project D	Funding Options
Portfolio 1	Momentum	Momentum	Momentum	Momentum	0
Portfolio 2	Momentum	Delay	Stop	Momentum	Borrow $100
Portfolio 3	Momentum	2x resources	License out	Stop	0
Portfolio 4	Delay	2x resources	Momentum	Momentum	Sell plant for $50

yet more alternatives, particularly as people think about how the various projects might be jointly managed.

After the alternative portfolios are generated, each is subjected to a simple test of acceptability. For each candidate, we ask, "Could we, and would we, pursue this portfolio?" In order to answer the first question, we use the rough estimates of costs collected during the generation of the alternatives for each project. If these costs sum to more than the budget, then the portfolio fails that test and is not considered further, unless there is an explicit statement of how the deficit is to be overcome. Investigating funding options beyond the current R&D budget becomes yet another column in the table. Because candidate portfolios are strictly comparable only if they have the same cost, it might be necessary to add columns for borrowing to cover deficits or additional investments to provide for resources that are in excess for a given portfolio.

We compare candidate portfolios with respect to expected net present value, although selection of a portfolio is not limited to this criterion. For example, others may wish to compare candidate portfolios with respect to a productivity index. Whatever measure(s) is (are) selected for the current analysis, we believe it is essential for the project team to agree to the appropriateness of the measures on which rival portfolios are to be compared before subjecting any opportunity to evaluation. For this example, the project team wished to maximize net present value. In order to ensure that any differences among portfolios are not attributable to differences in cost, we borrow or invest funds on the side in order that they all have the same cost.

For the second question, a member of the group at the time of portfolio formation writes a brief rationale describing why that strategy might be an attractive one, and that description, along with the candidate portfolio, is presented to management for consideration. A positive answer to the question of whether we would pursue the portfolio says that management feels the portfolio is reasonable and worth implementing if it should prove most attractive in the subsequent analysis.

A completed strategy table might look like Figure 3.

4. Evaluating Individual Projects

In order to evaluate the candidate portfolios, we divide the strategy table into a number of noninterdependent columns, as in Figure 3. For each column, we hold a meeting of people with expertise in that particular area. For example, we talk with project

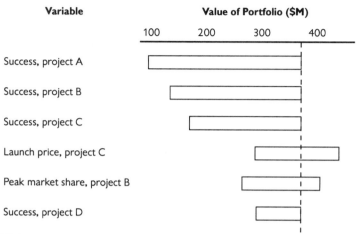

Figure 4. A sensitivity analysis highlights the impact of critical variables on the portfolio. In this case, the failure of Project A would decrease the portfolio's value by approximately $289 million.

management, various R&D, and marketing personnel. We use the methods of DA to elicit information on the determinants of value for each of the different alternatives for each project. Importantly, we do not attempt to evaluate any alternative from the alternatives table, which was not included in a candidate portfolio since it is not explicitly considered in any actionable portfolio. Similarly, if only one alternative appears in the strategy table for a given project, it is not necessary to evaluate that alternative, since no decision is to be made if there is only one alternative.

The value of R&D projects depends on the likelihood and expense of reaching the market, and the profits after marketing. We use a number of tools for estimating these quantities. For the probability of reaching market, we use a standard probability wheel as part of a standard gamble, a conventional DA approach to eliciting the probability of a chance event. If the project faces more than one milestone before market, we elicit the probability of achieving each, conditioned on success on the previous ones.

Only rarely can people estimate post-launch profits without decomposing those profits into component parts and thinking about the components individually. For instance, they think of sales and costs separately, and they usually think of sales in terms of price, market share, and market size. We allow each group to decompose post-launch profits into the components that allow them to define each clearly and to think about the possible outcomes, given that the project comes to market. We ask for low (but realistic) base case, and high (but realistic) values for each of these components. Standard DA methods permit estimating probability distributions on these uncertainties, using these low, base, and high values (6,7).

Some alternatives have features more complex than might initially be imagined. For example, launch of project A might result in cannibalization of sales of existing products. While it is our intent to capture only that value of a portfolio that is incremental to existing business, it might be necessary to accommodate such features explicitly in modeling in order to capture significant portfolio effects.

5. Evaluating the Portfolios

All of the assessed quantities are entered into a spreadsheet for estimating the cash flows that might result under each alternative selected in any of the portfolios. Switches in the spreadsheet allow the various alternatives to be turned off and on, depending on the portfolio and its choice of alternatives. When the portfolio is assembled, cash flows are aggregated.

The spreadsheet is used to analyze the sensitivity of the value of a given portfolio to the uncertain inputs it contains. This analysis is presented by means of a tornado diagram for each portfolio. The low, base case, and high values for each uncertainty are used to compute the cash flows or other measure of interest, varying these values for only one uncertainty at a time, while the other uncertainties maintain their base case. For example, a tornado diagram for one portfolio might look like Figure 4.

Because the tornado diagram presents a base-case value of each of the portfolios, it is possible that this stage of the evaluation provides a clear picture of which is the best portfolio. In particular, it allows the decision maker to juxtapose the tornado diagrams for two portfolios and examine whether any uncertainty common to both might swing the decision. For example, even though the success or failure of project A may be the greatest single determinant of value for two rival portfolios, its success or failure would not depend on which other projects are chosen, and uncertainty about its fate should not make it difficult for us to select a portfolio.

If the choice of portfolios is not clear from the above analysis, identification of the key determinants of value within a portfolio is used to guide the collection of additional information. For example, if the analysis indicates that portfolios 1 and 2 are the leading candidates, and that the choice between them is not clear, one might wish to undertake additional research on the key determinants of value in those two portfolios. This might take the form of market research, for example, or of a study of the regulatory history of a class of drugs under consideration.

Ultimately, the objective of the analysis is to present to the decision makers a summary of the risk and reward associated with each candidate portfolio so that they might begin implementing the best one. This risk and reward is described by probability distributions for the value of each of the candidate portfolios. These can be computed, using standard DA techniques, from the values assessed for the various uncertainties for each of the alternatives. In fact, the spreadsheet containing all the information can be interrogated for an "optimum" combination of the alternatives, in case such an optimum might not have been chosen as one of the candidate portfolios.

In addition to graphic presentations of risk and reward, it is possible to use the assessed quantities to prepare simple tables that provide the same information. Such a table is depicted in Figure 5.

All of the illustrations to this point have assumed that we wish to choose the portfolio with the greatest expected NPV. As previously mentioned, decision makers might be interested in other measures as well, such as the pattern of new product launches associated with each possible choice. Conceptually, a table like the probability table can be constructed for each such measure. Armed with a table of this sort

Figure 5. Results of an analysis are summarized for decision-making purposes. Here, a simple representation of the risks and rewards of the competing portfolios is supplied to the project team.

	Probability of a loss	Probability of 0 < value < 100	Probability of a value > 100
Portfolio 1	21%	47%	32%
Portfolio 2	15%	41%	44%
Portfolio 3	41%	22%	37%
Portfolio 4	25%	50%	25%

Figure 6. The strategy table for the business unit depicts relationships among projects for a common portfolio theme. Notice that the alternatives for Projects F and G are equivalent for each portfolio, capitalizing on the projects' synergies.

Portfolio	Project A	Project B	External Opportunity	Project C	Project D	Project E	Project F	Project G
Current Momentum	Stop	License Out	Nothing	Develop slow	Develop for one indication	Develop	Develop	Develop
Similar Products	Develop current product	Develop product	License in product X	Develop fast	Develop for two indications	Stop	Stop	Stop
Corporate Strategy	Develop current product	License Out	License in product X	Develop fast	Nothing	Stop	Develop	Develop
Single Market Focus	Develop current product	Stop	Nothing	Nothing	Develop for one indication	Stop	Develop	Develop
New	Develop new product	Develop product	License in product X	Develop fast	Develop for one indication	Develop	Develop	Develop

for each measure of interest, the decision maker has at his disposal the raw materials needed for the decision, and action.

Helping a Business Unit

We recently employed the use of the strategy table for a business unit within Lilly. For brevity, we will provide a brief overview of the effort and will exert more emphasis on the outcomes and lessons learned. The names and numbers of the projects have been disguised for proprietary reasons.

A business unit requested our help to solve a dilemma in which the projected spending for its portfolio exceeded the current budget. Several meetings allowed the business unit team to quickly proceed through the first two steps: 1) framing the problem to identify the seven equivocal projects, and 2) creating the alternatives table. In the discussions of alternatives for one project, a team member identified an external opportunity that,

Figure 7. The results of the portfolio analysis highlight the positive value of both the Current Momentum and New portfolios. It also demonstrates the unattractiveness of the Single Market Focus portfolio.

	Probability of a loss (value < $0)	Probability of 0 < value < $50M	Probability of a value > $50M	Expected NPV ($M)
Current Momentum	6%	28%	66%	73.0
Corporate Stategy	15%	43%	42%	44.7
Similar Products	15%	37%	48%	47.5
Single Market Focus	75%	18%	7%	-24.5
New	3%	17%	80%	100.0

coupled with the current project, could leverage this existing asset for the business unit, focusing on a specific Disease X. Thus, another column for the External Opportunity was added to our table. Following our suggested process, step 3 provided the completed strategy table, depicted in Figure 6.

The team created five portfolios for evaluation, including the current plan. By electing to guide the team through the candidate portfolio selection process, significant insights were uncovered. Discussions revealed that certain information and clinical tasks could be shared by two projects. Thus, it made sense to leverage this synergy by following a similar course of action for each. Notice that the alternative in the Project F and G columns is replicated for each project, although not for each portfolio. Other discussions revealed that Project D could infringe on sales of one of the favorite projects. The model explicitly calculated this cannibalization factor.

The decision makers of this business unit were interested in measuring expected net present value incremental to the value of the existing business unit portfolio (the favorite projects). As such, we arrived at the quantitative results shown in Figure 7. The Current Momentum portfolio compared well relative to the rival portfolios, with the exception of the New portfolio. Both the Momentum and New portfolios appear to have very beneficial effects compared to the existing portfolio of favorite projects (Single Market Focus). In subsequent conversations with the decision makers, budget constraints that were once thought to be imposed were reconciled. This allowed the team to fund and take action on all equivocal projects to any designated level.

The team commented on the effectiveness of the process, deeming it valuable in the conversations and insights generated and its focus on actions. We look forward to applying the technique to other portfolio opportunities.

References

Matheson, James E. "Overview of R&D Decision Analysis," in *Readings on the Principles and Applications of Decision Analysis*, ed. Ron Howard and James Matheson. Strategic Decisions Group: Palo Alto, 1984, pp. 329-330.

Keeney, Ralph L. and Howard Raiffa. *Decisions with Multiple Objectives: Preferences and Value Tradeoffs*. Cambridge University Press: New York, 1993.

Howard, Ronald A. "Decision Analysis: Practice and Promise." *Management Science*, Vol. 34, No. 6, June 1988, pp. 679-695.

Troetel, William M. "How New Drugs Win FDA Approval." *U.S. Pharmacist*, No. 11, Nov. 1986, pp. 54-65.

Jacknowitz, Arthur I. "Development of New Drugs." *U.S. Pharmacist*, No. 12, Oct. 1987, pp. 38, 41-42.

Keefer, Donald L. and Samual E. Bodily. "Three-Point Approximations for Continuous Random Variables." *Management Science*. Vol. 29, No. 5, 1983, pp. 595-609.

Clemen, Robert. *Making Hard Decisions: An Introduction to Decision Analysis*. 2nd edition, Duxbury Press, 1996.

Practical R&D Project Prioritization

Merrill S. Brenner

How do you allocate limited R&D funds to an unlimited set of potential new projects? How do you select funding for projects that cover a broad range of industries, perhaps ranging from high-profitability, low-volume specialty materials to high-volume, low-margin commodities? How do you compare small, technology-based, high-growth markets with large, established, low-growth markets? How do you consolidate the information you need into a common set of terminology and parameters so that you can evaluate projects and allocate resources?

One solution developed at Air Products is a project selection process that permits us to optimally allocate limited R&D resources among the many proposals made every year for new projects. The process identifies the key issues for success, builds consensus among the decision-makers, and requires the project champions to state their project proposals in the framework most useful to the decision-makers. The techniques also help to focus efforts on the most critical aspects of a project to maximize the potential for winners.

Our process is to:

1. Identify and select criteria, and aggregate them into a logical framework.

2. Weight the criteria and build consensus about their relative importance.

3. Evaluate the project proposals using the weighted criteria. Projects are profiled to focus on solving weaknesses and can be revised and re-evaluated.

4. Allocate resources to maximize project progress.

5. Exercise judgement—there are always issues to consider that are outside of the framework, and sensibility checks must take place for a successful process.

This process is built around a technique called the analytic hierarchy process developed by Professor Thomas L. Saaty of the University of Pittsburgh (1). In our use of this process, the emphasis has been to facilitate the exchange of information about critical issues and to develop consensus via a structured and documented process. The decision model that results from this process can be represented by the structure in Figure 1.

The goal for R&D prioritization is simply to select winning new projects. Such projects will have a combination of characteristics that are expected to lead to considerable benefits and a high probability of success. The criteria represent the factors that

---

Figure 1. The R&D prioritization process brings professionalism and objectivity to the selection of winning new projects.

Key Features

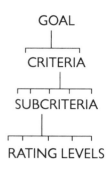

GOAL

CRITERIA

SUBCRITERIA

RATING LEVELS

• The technique structures the decision by logical levels. The criteria are the factors that make sense to the decision-makers.
• The technique employs pairwise comparisons, which help people to think more clearly and succinctly about each factor. Each parameter is weighted against every other one and a conscious decision made about their relative importance. Dealing with only two items at a time allows for better understanding and discussion; the analytic hierarchy process provides the arithmetic to combine the pairwise comparisons into an overall ranking of factors.
• The technique includes a consistency check. This reflects that if A is greater than B and B is greater than C, then A must also be greater than C to be consistent.
• The rating levels extend an order of magnitude from best to worst to facilitate meaningful differentiation of projects.
• Management determines the criteria important to their decision. The project experts determine how well the project meets the criteria.
• The process requires an objective and unbiased facilitator.
• The technique can handle qualitative factors as easily as quantitative ones.
• The procedure defines and documents the criteria for a decision, leading to a paper trail of the choices and the reasons they were made.
• The process defines and documents the status of a program at the time it is proposed, permitting a later assessment of actual progress or re-evaluation based on new information.

---

establish whether or not the goal has been reached. The subcriteria are more specific factors within the broader categories. The lowest section of the model contains the actual rating levels. These contain both qualitative and quantitative parameters, such as "$10 MM of sales per year" or "high flexibility of design," by which a project can be characterized.

The people who decide funding and resource allocations are the ideal group to develop this model. By doing so, they will reveal their thought processes about selecting successful projects. This has a high benefit in communicating to the rest of the organization what kinds of projects should be proposed.

The project champions must propose their projects principally in the terminology of the criteria determined by the decision-makers. Our process is analogous to an entrepreneur proposing a business idea to a venture capitalist for funding, or a business manager proposing a significant investment to the board of directors. This procedure brings a professionalism and objectivity to the funding process. There are four steps:

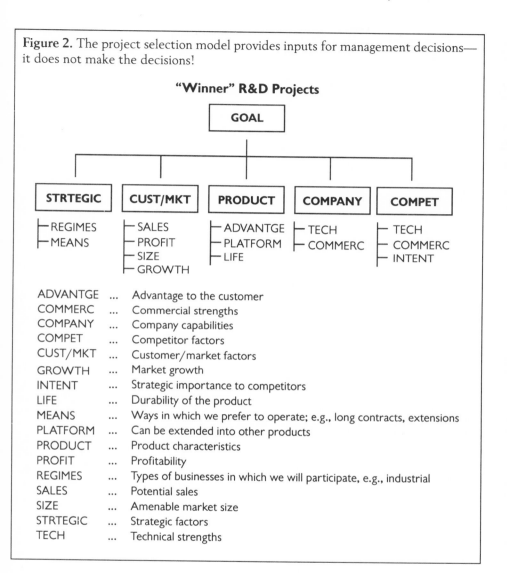

Figure 2. The project selection model provides inputs for management decisions—it does not make the decisions!

"Winner" R&D Projects

ADVANTGE	...	Advantage to the customer
COMMERC	...	Commercial strengths
COMPANY	...	Company capabilities
COMPET	...	Competitor factors
CUST/MKT	...	Customer/market factors
GROWTH	...	Market growth
INTENT	...	Strategic importance to competitors
LIFE	...	Durability of the product
MEANS	...	Ways in which we prefer to operate; e.g., long contracts, extensions
PLATFORM	...	Can be extended into other products
PRODUCT	...	Product characteristics
PROFIT	...	Profitability
REGIMES	...	Types of businesses in which we will participate, e.g., industrial
SALES	...	Potential sales
SIZE	...	Amenable market size
STRTEGIC	...	Strategic factors
TECH	...	Technical strengths

1. Criteria Selection

Criteria are generated in group sessions using questions to activate and energize input. Open-ended questions can help to identify the criteria for selecting winning new projects:

- What are the factors that have made your projects successful?
- What are the characteristics of the projects that have helped your career?
- What criteria do you use when choosing a project?
- What makes a project good?
- What do you try to avoid in a project?
- When you think about a project, what characteristics do you consider?
- Where does your organization tend to be successful?

Also, posing the questions in somewhat personal terms helps to elicit practical, rather than theoretical or hypothetical, responses.

These sessions tend to be lively and enlightening brainstorming exercises. Many criteria are proposed, but as the overlaps are eliminated, the criteria aggregated, and the definitions refined, a relatively small set of 20-30 criteria emerge that are repeatedly used. A typical model would look like Figure 2, but would also show the details of weights and rating levels.

The model provides input for management decisions—it does not make the decisions. Many factors need to be considered outside of the model, including:

• Portfolio Issues: How many high-risk versus low-risk projects? How many large versus small projects? How many short-term versus long-term projects?

• Implementation Factors: We assume that after selecting the best projects, they will be managed well. This is, of course, essential to fulfilling their winner potential, but implementation factors are not useful for selection of projects. All project champions will promise exceptional implementation, so this factor does not differentiate among project proposals.

• Political Issues: If one of the champions is a senior corporate executive likely to have additional information, it might be prudent to select the project.

• Personnel Issues: Perhaps there is a particular individual who would experience significant personal development by participating in a lower-rated project, or a technical expert who might leave the group without the work of a project that would not normally make the cut.

• Frequently Changing Factors: Anything that is going to change from year to year is not an appropriate selection factor. The fact that a regional plant needs to be loaded this year will not help in selecting projects next year. These kinds of factors restrict the capability of performing year-to-year project comparisons.

• Cost: One of the most volatile of the frequently changing factors is the cost of the project. This is best handled outside of the model for three reasons:

1. In a bad budget year, cost can become an overwhelming issue; in a good budget year, it might be given a lower weight.

2. Cost is very hard to estimate, especially at an early stage of a project.

3. The project cost should be appropriate for the project benefits. The objective should be to allocate the necessary resources for the best projects and to spend the appropriate amount for the expected benefit. In other words, cost is not a selection criterion, but is used to determine how many of the best projects can be afforded.

• Probability of Success: To a large extent, this is the overall answer of the model, that is, the probability of "winning."

2. Criteria Weighting

Once the criteria are identified and aggregated into a structure, pairwise comparisons are used to develop weights for them. All of the comparisons will look like Figure 3, which is from the Expert Choice software routinely used in this process (2). This might be read as "the advantage to the customer is moderately more important than the durability of the product when considering the product factors related to this project being successful." If the group consensus was that the advantage to the customer should be more important, the arrow would be cursored up and the words

---

Figure 3. Pairwise comparisons are used to weight the criteria.

GOAL: "WINNER" R&D PROJECTS

With respect to
PRODUCT < GOAL

ADVANTAGE: Advantage to the customer
is MODERATELY more IMPORTANT than
LIFE: Durability of the product

```
EXTREME  ----------
VERY STRONG ------
STRONG ------------
MODERATE --------- <---
EQUAL ------------
```

---

would change. For example, if the arrow were moved to "strong," the statement would be that "advantage to the customer is strongly more important than the durability of the product." This format gives the decision-makers both a graphical and a verbal idea of the decision that they are making. The display can be numerical as well.

The pairwise comparisons are performed for all of the upper levels of criteria and sub-criteria. At the rating level, which often reflects decisions between such quantitative questions as, "How much more important is $10 MM/year of sales versus $5 MM/year of sales," we typically forgo the pairwise comparisons and use linearly scaled weights. A sensibility check with the decision-makers is always performed to test whether these assumptions make sense.

The Expert Choice software then combines the pairwise comparisons and creates weights for each factor; these sum up to 100 percent of the project decision. At this point, a series of sensibility checks is employed. Bar graphs are shown for visualization of the weighted factors. The top ten criteria usually represent most of the decision, and these are tested against the decision-makers' perceptions of the top factors they consider when selecting a project. The highest rating for each of the top ten factors is also discussed to determine if those ratings really describe an ideal project. Occasionally, a few comparisons will be performed again to adjust one or two factors that are (usually) too highly weighted.

3. Project Evaluation and Profiling
Only consistent sets of projects are put through this process. Most of our work has been with development projects. Projects might primarily emphasize technology development or market development (market demand being expanded via new offerings), but in both cases they represent development projects for which funding is usually discretionary. With these bounds, excluded projects include:
• Capital Support: If the capital has been approved, the facility will be built—the project is not discretionary.
• Customer Service and Support: If a customer has a problem, it must be fixed.

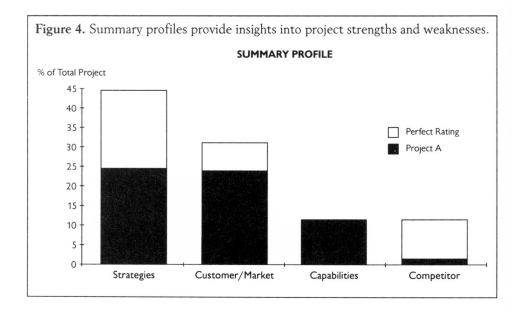

Figure 4. Summary profiles provide insights into project strengths and weaknesses.

- Maintenance: Again, if the equipment or plant has a problem, we are going to fix it.
- Exploratory Research: These programs cannot be assessed against the same criteria that are used for development projects.

While this paper focuses on development projects, we have used similar models, with considerably different criteria, to evaluate exploratory programs. Furthermore, if a model was needed for determining levels of maintenance or technical services versus other categories of expenditures, a different decision support model could be developed.

At this point, the project champions use worksheets to describe and rate their projects against the established criteria. The project ratings will then be discussed by teams. This works best with a group composed of the project champion, two or three people who are going to attend all of the project proposal sessions, and one or two of the project champions from other areas for balance and cross-checking. This approach will keep the definitions from wandering over time and also moderate over-selling by the champions.

After these discussions, each project is profiled (Figures 4 and 5). Profiling provides extremely valuable information by looking at each criterion and category to see how the particular project measures up versus the highest rating that it could get. In a summary representation of a high-volume gas applications development example (Figure 4), profiling four typical categories of criteria, the project has a modest fit with the strategies (the most important criteria here), a very good fit with the customer and market criteria (so it is the right kind of market), and is ideal in terms of the company capabilities (So the organization had appropriate and strong skills and resources). However, the project has a significant problem since the competitors are also very good in this technology and market. Perhaps the nature of the product offering needs to be redefined to be more differentiated from the competition; e.g., by providing more performance or service instead of a commodity product.

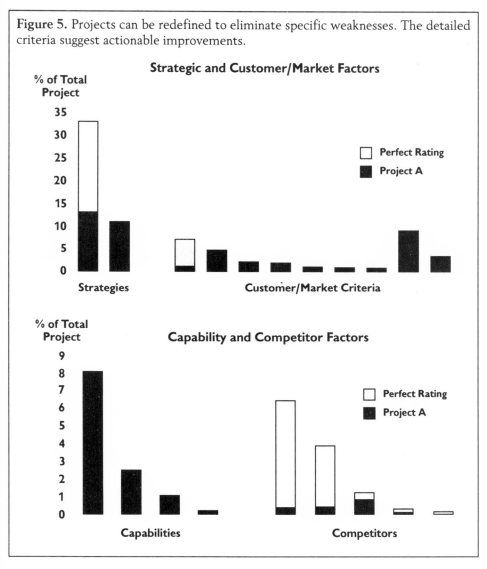

Figure 5. Projects can be redefined to eliminate specific weaknesses. The detailed criteria suggest actionable improvements.

The specific subcriteria profiles (Figure 5) illustrate that this project is weak in only a few of the strategic and customer/market factors, but it is weak across the board versus the competitors' capabilities. These profiles provide far more information than just the total score; they help identify ways that the focus of the project can be adjusted to achieve higher performance.

For this project, the weak strategic criterion is the nature of the offering. This is basically a commodity sale, without proprietary technology or unique capabilities. The weakest customer/market factor is profitability, which likely reflects that the product is being sold by low pricing and that the competition is strong and provides similar

Figure 6. Project funding can be optimized to maximize progress.

Final Project Ratings

Project	Rating	Total Staffing	Total Cost	Priority
A	90	5	750	
B	87	4	600	Clearly
C	84	4	600	"A"
D	81	2	500	Fully
E	80	4	600	Funded
F	78	3	450	
G	75	5	750	
H	64	5	600	
I	62	4	500	
J	60	4	500	"B"
K	57	2	250	Re-Define
L	55	4	450	and Focus
M	53	3	350	
N	51	5	400	
O	48	3	350	
P	37	3	400	
Q	35	2	250	Clearly
R	33	3	500	"C"
S	31	4	350	Not Funded
T	30	3	250	

offerings. This project should be modified to add unique technology or services to differentiate the company from the competition, permitting premium pricing. If that is not possible, perhaps the development work should stop or the product should be handled by the sales force.

Each proposed project is profiled, and then the champions can submit any revisions. The profiles can also be used to check the status and progress of the project a year later.

4. Resource Allocation

After the revisions and final profiling, the total score for the project is tabulated with the projected staffing and cost (Figure 6). This listing typically produces clear "A priority" or winner projects and these should be fully funded to completion. There also generally is a set of clear "C priority" projects, which should not be funded at all. The difficult ones are the "B priority" projects. The funding and resources for these should be focused on alleviating their weaknesses and attempting to raise them into the "A" category. If they cannot be salvaged, they should be eliminated. Finally, the priority list of projects is reviewed for portfolio factors, to ensure a reasonable mix of risk, timing, and size. This is when the non-model factors are considered.

Through this prioritization process, we are able to stretch our funds farther and to complete more projects. This process has been successfully applied in a number of organizations at Air Products, resulting in multiple examples of projects being turned into winners by identifying and eliminating key weaknesses. Without this process, we might have to deal with resource allocation limits by drawing a single dividing line and dropping all of the projects below the line or by cutting every project by a fixed percentage to keep everything alive, but not adequately funded. This prioritization process provides a superior approach to dealing with limited resources, permitting more of the best projects to be completed.

Acknowledgements

The use of Expert Choice for R&D project prioritization resulted from the vision and persistence of Mike Kazarnowica and Jim Sykes. Kay David was helpful in producing the outputs from these exercises, including this paper.

Notes

See for example, *The Analytic Hierarchy Process* (McGraw-Hill, NY, 1980 and *Decision-Making for Leaders* (Lifetime Learning Publications, Belmont, CA 1982).

Expert Choice, Inc., 4922 Ellsworth Avenue., Pittsburgh, PA 15213.

Benefit-Cost Ratio: Selection Tool or Trap?

Stephen Smith and Joh Barker

In an attempt to manage the complexity of the project selection decision, some IT consultancies are applying a powerful tool from the finance discipline: the Benefit-Cost Ratio (BCR). However, a number of concerns have risen regarding BCR as a measure of both project acceptability and project selection. (While many project managers may find this a useful shortcut for project robustness, the financial literature suggests that extreme care should be exercised where this is used as a basis for project selection.) BCR is derived from the mathematics of Net Present Value (NPV) and is subject to the assumptions of the discounting model. These assumptions are not always valid for technology projects. Likewise, for project selection, technology is often an enabler rather than a measure of direct revenue gain or attributable cost savings. For such projects, degree of alignment with business strategy is the more important criterion.

BCR and Project Acceptability

The BCR, or profitability index, divides the NPV of the cash inflows by the NPV of the cash outflows, such that:

$$BCR = \frac{NPV \; Costs}{NPV \; Revenues}$$

$$\text{where } NPV = \frac{Cashflow_{year \; 0}}{(1+k)^0} + \frac{Cashflow_{year \; 1}}{(1+k)^1} + \frac{Cashflow_{year \; 2}}{(1+k)^2} + \ldots + \frac{Cashflow_{year \; n}}{(1+k)^n}$$

and k is the required rate of return.

Projects with a BCR of 1 or more are potentially acceptable.

Projects with a BCR of less than 1 should be rejected [1].

The discounting of cash flows is used to account for the time value of money [2]. This provides a built-in estimate for the opportunity cost of those inflows that require borrowing or investing throughout the life of the project. As indicated above, the usual acceptance criterion for the BCR method is that any project returning a ratio of 1 or more is potentially acceptable, although at least one text recommends setting a hurdle ratio of 1.33. Regardless of whether the hurdle ratio is set at 1 or something higher, BCRs that exceed the hurdle ratio are of net benefit to the sponsor. Anything less than the hurdle ratio should be rejected.

Problems With BCR

Powerful as the BCR is, financial analysts generally don't use it in isolation. Why not?

Problem 1: BCR is a Relative Measure.

First, the BCR indicates only the relative profitability of a project, but when comparing different projects, the absolute contribution to shareholder wealth must also be considered. Any project with a BCR of 1 or more is profitable at the minimum acceptable rate of return, but the calculation doesn't show the size of returns. A $10 project could show a BCR of 10, while a $10-million project might only show a BCR of 1. Clearly, the absolute size of the project matters.

Given that absolute size matters, and projects with a BCR of 1 or more meet the minimum required rate of return, profitable projects should be ranked by absolute size. To do otherwise could mean rejecting the projects providing the greatest increase in wealth in favor of those that seem to have the greatest rate of return. Most business managers and shareholders would not regard such a practice as good business decision-making.

Interestingly, however, some of the literature supporting BCR seems to recommend exactly that. At least one text suggests that projects with a BCR of less than 1.33 should be rejected. It is not entirely clear to us why the hurdle ratio has been set at 1.33. Yet, to reject any project with a BCR of 1 or more is to reject profitable business opportunities. Common sense indicates that projects with the highest rates of return are often the riskiest. Rejecting all but the most profitable projects therefore exposes the business to more risk than is necessary, as well as limiting growth. In order to force a worthwhile project to cross the extra hurdle, project managers might also need to sacrifice quality for short-term gains (for example, by using cheaper, lower-quality equipment) and possibly even inadvertently engineer a situation where the project becomes a financial burden in the long run.

Problem 2: BCR is Subject to the Assumptions of the Net Present Value Formula.

The second problem with BCR is that it is derived from the NPV formula. The NPV was designed to model an environment where there is a substantial up-front investment followed by an ongoing revenue stream; cost and revenues are easily traced to the investment decision; and the size of the investment and the size of the revenue stream are known with some degree of certainty.

Typically this is not the situation confronting IT project managers. Usually IT projects are of short duration and have complex interdependencies and high uncertainties. Market forces continue to pressure IT projects into delivery timetables of less than 12 months. Frequently, stage gates are introduced as a basis for risk containment and project evaluation. These stage gates identify milestones throughout a project's life where the decision is to continue, change direction or cease the assignment. Stage gates are also useful in containment or at least explicit identification of scope changes.

Scope changes are often more keenly experienced in IT where market and technology pressures mean the final project delivery may vary significantly from the initial charter. All these pressures add uncertainty to the measurement of cost streams, the identification of revenue streams, and the relevance of *time value* for investment.

The short timetables for IT projects also cause the project manager to become a negotiator for resources—rather than an owner, as in a functional organization. This results in short-term teams, which are built to achieve a task and then returned to their functional home base—be it the IT department, the customer, or the process environments. Cost allocation for short-term, often part-time, shared resources is a highly complex and inexact area of management accounting. The fixed-cost nature of much of the resource cost means that the project charges often reflect an organization's allocation policies rather than a true measure of resource consumption or opportunity cost.

Uncertainty in the project management world is managed through risk identification, risk quantification, and risk response development. The latter is concerned with avoidance, mitigation and/or acceptance of the risk consequences. With all responses, a contingency value should be estimated and included in the planned cash outflows. Given that the risk responses are identified, and valued in the cash flows, care must be exercised to ensure that the discount factor reflects interest forgone rather than the business risk already included in the cash flow estimates.

A more technical explanation of risk is covered by the term, *cost of capital*. Companies often establish a preferred discount factor based on their corporate cost of capital. This cost of capital is equivalent to the return that financiers require for investment in the business. It includes three factors: a return for deferred consumption, an allowance for inflation, and a return for the systematic risk or variability inherent with the proposal [3]. Where BCR uses the company cost of capital as the relevant discount factor, and has included contingencies in the cash outflows, then the financial penalties of risk are overstated.

The BCR and Project Risk Management

The above discussion on the selection of an appropriate discount factor indicates that approving and funding projects is a very inexact science. Therefore, if those providing the funds seem overly cautious, it is probably because they have good reason to be prudent: funds providers rely heavily on the performance of the project and so, by providing finance, they expose themselves to some risk. As a result, project financing is more expensive than conventional financing because of the time managers and technical experts spend evaluating and monitoring the project, the charges made by lenders for assuming additional risks, and insurance coverage.

A common method financiers use to manage their exposure to project risk is to fund a project portfolio. Ideally, the projects in the portfolio should be independent. If they are dependent on each other, risk increases, because when one fails, the others are at more risk of failure. If they are independent, risk is reduced, because not only do failures not have flow-on effects, it is likely that some—hopefully most—projects will succeed and compensate for the failures. Of course, projects often incorporate dependencies (for example, ERP system implementations), so it might be possible to diversify away only a small amount of the risk.

A Leap of Faith: British Airways

In 1994, British Airways (BA) discovered that approximately one-third of its customers were in some way dissatisfied with their flights, but less than 10 percent of these unhappy customers made contact with customer relations. The benefits of keeping customers happy had been established: Research indicated that a delay in responding to complaints led to a 30–45 percent decline in the possible intent to reuse BA.[1] However, the effect of this decline in possible intent on actual behavior was not clear.

Nevertheless, BA's strategic focus at the time, under the direction of CEO Colin Marshall, was to "put the customer first" (which, of course, meant more than simply taking off and landing on time). As a result, BA invested £4.5 million (approximately US$9 million) in a system that enables customers to register complaints faster [1,2]. It must be stressed that the financial benefits were not known, so a cost-benefit ratio analysis would not have produced meaningful results. However, the intangible aspects of the project—fit with business strategy and improved customer information—meant that even if the project generated no additional income itself, it provided the foundation for further projects to win back the estimated £400 million of potentially lost revenue dissatisfied customers represented [3]. That is, in this instance, strategic consideration of the project was far more important than short-term emphasis on revenues and costs.

References

1. Weiser, Charles R. July 1994. "Best Practice in Customer Relations." *Consumer Policy Review*, 130–137.

2. Cash, James I. Jr. 1 May 1995. "British Air Gets on Course." *Informationweek*, p. 140.

3. Gooding, C. 24 Feb. 1994. "Technology: A Caress for the Customer." *Financial Times*, p. 19.

The BCR and Portfolio Selection

So how should we select projects for a portfolio? Resource constraints mean that only some technically feasible and economically attractive projects can be selected. At the same time, managers want to ensure that as much as possible of the available resources are used profitably. In a quantitative sense, the real project selection decision, therefore, is not whether to accept or reject a given project, but how to maximize return and resources used, while minimizing risk. The subjective nature of these constraints has led one author to liken the project selection process to choosing a Miss World—highly subjective and, at best, able to provide a reasonable (probably not exactly correct) result.

Until the late 1960s, some influential finance authors argued that the BCR is ideal for identifying the most efficient projects (those with the highest ratios). However, more recent finance texts state that unless a complex modification is made to the formula, the BCR is inaccurate when used with interdependent or mutually exclusive projects. Furthermore, it cannot aggregate several small projects to displace one large project so as to achieve a better risk, return, and resource usage profile [4]. To make matters worse, there is no foolproof substitute procedure for ranking investments either. The problem is that ranking implies the use of a cutoff rate above the cost of money and a rejection of investments that would be acceptable except for the rationing situation. Also, the opportunity cost of future time periods may well be different from that of the present, as capital becomes either scarcer or more freely available.

A Final Word on Project Selection

The main issue for project selection is, "Should we do this?" Overreliance on BCR or, indeed, any financial measure emphasizes the tangible over the intangible. This can inhibit a *leap of faith* that is often critical for information technology projects.

The rate of change and uncertainty in the systems development process means that many technology projects are leading-edge. Leading-edge projects fail to provide the repeatability that reduces risk and guides cost and revenue predictions. Moreover, these projects require an appreciation of as yet unseen and only dimly perceived changes to fundamental processes. This requires a leap of faith. The British Airways case, in the sidebar, illustrates the need for a leap of faith rather than an emphasis on BCR.

An indiscriminate focus on BCR will ignore global, less easily quantifiable, issues such as business strategy, business structure, and technical infrastructure. For project selection this requires a move from highest BCR to a longer-term customer focus and a more broadly based evaluation of current and strategic infrastructure issues. The later requires analysis of how the business process is supported by technology today and tomorrow.

BCR: One Measure Amongst Many

The foregoing arguments are meant to induce caution and to guide the reader against an overemphasis on BCR. While financial considerations play a significant role throughout the life of projects, information technology is usually too uncertain to be captured by a single measure. Probabilistic financial metrics, with reference and constant realignment to specified objectives, are preferable.

By recognizing the inherent measurement difficulties with BCR, the project manager can be directed toward a more formal acceptance of the range of outcomes and predicted impact. Such measurement needs to be aligned with the business objectives. Constant focus on the business objectives with adequate appreciation for the range of outcomes will enable the project manager to focus on what the business values. And what the business values is not always the highest BCR.

Some Definitions

1. BCR as defined in standard Finance texts:

$$BCR = \frac{\left[\dfrac{Cashflow^1}{1+k^1} + \dfrac{Cashflow^2}{1+k^2} + ... + \dfrac{Cashflow^n}{1+k^n}\right]}{Initial\ Cash\ Outlay}$$

where k is the required rate of return.

2. In addition to the effect of potential interest forgone on the value of money, inflation expectations have a substantial influence on value via their influence on interest rates overall. It is generally agreed that the nominal, or observed, interest rate on any security includes a premium for inflation. The higher the anticipated inflation, the higher this premium needs to be set. Known as the "Fisher" effect, the nominal interest rate (i) required to generate a real (inflation adjusted) increase in wealth at a given rate (r) regardless of expected inflation (p) can be calculated as $I = r + \pi + r\pi$.

In most applications, analysts ignore the term $r\pi$ and write $i = r + \pi$.

3. There are two methods for estimating the cost of capital. The first, Capital Asset Pricing Model, calculates a beta through time series analysis of prior results. The second, Weighted Average approach, calculates the market values from both debt and equity sources.

4. This is actually a weakness of the Net Present Value formula from which the BCR is derived. The NVP does not tell us how much capital had to be committed to the investment. Because of the risk, return, and resource usage considerations outlined above, two or more small investments may well be better than one large investment, even though the large investment has a larger NPV (or BCR) than any one of the small investments.

This article is reprinted from the May 1999 *PM Network* with permission of the Project Management Institute Headquarters, Four Campus Boulevard, Newtown Square, PA 19073-3299 USA, Phone: (610) 356-4600 Fax: (610) 356-4647. Project Management Institute (PMI) is the world's leading project management association with over 40,000 members worldwide. For further information contact PMI Headquarters at (610) 356-4600 or visit the web site at www.pmi.org.

A Capital Budgeting Model Based on the Project Portfolio Approach: Avoiding Cash Flows Per Project

G. Chris Moolman and Wolter J. Fabrycky

Capital budgeting is primarily concerned with the potential performance of individual projects. Performance is usually a function of cash outflows and cash inflows on a per-project basis, where the net present value, the internal rate of return, and other selection criteria are common performance measures found in the literature. For example see, Brigham and Gapenski [1], Park and Sharp-Bette [8], and Thuesen and Fabrycky [10].

Of specific interest in this paper is the pioneering work of Weingartner [12] concerning deterministic capital budgeting, as well as works that extend Weingartner's contribution. The issue of interrelated projects has received considerable attention. See Weingartner [11], Srinivasan and Kim [9], and Kumar and Lu [5]. Correlated cash flows in risk analysis has also been addressed by several authors. For example, see Giaccotto [3] and Hillier [4].

This paper is concerned with deterministic modelling in capital budgeting when projects consume common resources. The concept of a cash flow per project is critically reviewed and some serious weaknesses are identified when resources are shared. These weaknesses are addressed in the next section. In the third section, a generic capital budgeting model is formulated that overcomes these weaknesses. The fourth section gives some arguments to justify the proposed model. In the fifth section a detailed example is provided. Finally, the paper is summarized, conclusions are stated, advantages and disadvantages of the proposed model are outlined, and future research opportunities are suggested.

Throughout this paper, it is assumed that resources are shared among different projects. Also, the terms project and product are used interchangeably. The main reason for this is that all costs are considered to be incurred only in the acquisition and utilization of resources; both projects and products consume resources.

Weaknesses of Cash Flow Per Project

Typically in capital budgeting, a cash flow is associated with each project, whether or not the cash flow is correlated with other cash flows, or whether the correlation coefficient is known or not. To derive the cash flow per project, cash inflows and cash outflows for the project must be known or are assumed known.

Cash inflows do not usually pose a problem, especially when revenues from different projects are not correlated (also an assumption for the purposes of this paper). However, cash outflows do pose a problem, especially when different projects consume common resources. To accurately determine the cash outflow for a project, all relevant costs, including fixed cost, must be allocated to that project. An accurate allocation of fixed cost, based on proportional usage or consumption, can be determined from

$$C^{p'} = \frac{k_{p'}}{\sum\limits_{p=1}^{P} k_p} = \frac{\bar{k}_{p'} X_{p'} C}{\sum\limits_{p=1}^{P} \bar{k}_p X_p} \tag{1}$$

$C^{p'}$ in (1) is the cost of the resource to be allocated to project p'. C is the cost of the resource that must be allocated to projects, typically the depreciable cost or, in some cases, the acquisition cost of the specific resource. The pth project (of which there are P in total) demands a capacity of k_p the resource, while k_p denotes the capacity demanded by project p' ($p' \in P$). This capacity may be any relevant unit, for example duration or number of units produced. As a simple example, assume two projects (P_1 and P_2), and only these two projects, demand 100 and 30 hours, respectively, per period from a specific resource over the life of the resource. Furthermore, assume that the capacity of the resource is 160 hours per period and that the resource costs $1,000. The fairest cost to be allocated to P_1 is $(100/(100+300))^*1,000 = \$769$.

An argument can be made that the denominator in (1) should be the total capacity of the resource (160 in this case). However, this will result in some costs not being allocated to projects if the capacity of the resource is not fully (100 oercent) utilized. Non-optimal project selection may result from this approach.

In (1), X_p is the number of units produced, while $\bar{k}_p$ is capacity demanded of a resource per unit of production such that $k_{p'} = \bar{k}_{p'} X_{p'}$ and $k_{p'} = \bar{k}_{p'} X_{p'}$. If the demand for any product, say p^* ($p^* \neq p'$) changes from $X^1_{p^*}$ to $X^2_{p^*}$ ($X^1_{p^*} \neq X^2_{p^*}$), it follows from (1) that the costs to be allocated to p' change as a result of the change in production quantity in p^*. Therefore, to allocate the cost of a resource to the different products utilizing the resource in such a way that the costs fairly represent the respective demands on the resource, the following must be known: 1) all projects comprising the project portfolio, and 2) the production quantity of each product in the portfolio. This can be seen from the relationship between $C^{p'}$, p, P, and X_p in (1). However, this is exactly what is to be determined: which projects to undertake (or which products to produce), as well as the production quantity of each product. Thus, when resources are shared among different projects the actual cash flow per project, the project selection, and the production quantity (if applicable) are all interrelated. This interrelationship is largely left unaddressed in the literature. An example of the inherent flows in the cost allocation approach is given in the section, "An Illustration," where a choice must be made about which of the four products, P_1, P_2, P_3, or P_4 must be produced. With classical techniques it is suggested that P_1, P_2 and P_3 be produced with a profit of $370,790. On closer scrutiny it is found that the maximum profit from these products is $147,600. However, if P_4 is partially introduced, a profit of $171,800 can be obtained. See the sub-section, "Analyzing Results from Weingartner's Model" for a detailed analysis of this discrepancy.

Another potential problem with classical deterministic capital budgeting models is that the project selection decision variable is usually continuous between zero (the project is not accepted at all) and one (the project is fully accepted). What does it mean if a project is fractionally accepted? What specifically does the fractional acceptance refer to: output, revenue, income before taxes, net income from continuing operations, etc.? An underlying assumption of a continuous decision variable is that there exists a linear relationship between the project selection variable and the cash flow of the project. More specifically, the underlying assumption is that resources come in continuous amounts. In most cases, this is not a valid assumption. Park and Sharp-Bette [8, pp. 282], summarize the problem as follows: "... generally, though, it is not possible to accept fractional projects without changing the nature of their cash flows." A project is either accepted or it is not accepted. The output, revenue, and cost should be separate decision variables.

Capital Budgeting Model Development

In this section a capital budgeting model is developed that will determine which projects to select, as well as the output quantity of each project in each period, such that the aforementioned problems are overcome. The concepts of cash flows per project and fractional project acceptance will not be utilized. Instead, exact output quantities and associated costs and revenues will be specified. Also, resource acquisition and utilization requirements will be modelled explicitly. Linear mixed integer programming will be used. The principles on which the model is based are explained first. Then the objective function and constraints are developed.

Principles Behind the Model

There are three basic principles behind this model. The first is that all costs are incurred in the acquisition and utilization of resources. These costs are not allocated to projects. Thus, a project, per se, does not incur any cost for the purposes of capital budgeting. Hence, the concept of a cash flow per project is avoided. The second principle behind the model is that all costs are considered variable at some level. Some of the principles of Activity-Based Costing are used to consider the variability of costs at different levels. All costs are linearly variable with either unit, batch, product sustaining, and facility sustaining activities. The third principle is that a project portfolio approach is used to determine the specific portfolio (consisting of the relevant projects with associated production quantities, if applicable) that will yield the greatest profit. This is in direct contrast with the classical approach where individual projects which yield the most profit are selected. Product portfolio, as used here, means the selection of products or projects that will yield the highest profit, where each product or project is associated with a specific output quantity. As used herein, the term product portfolio has nothing to do with the classical notion of diversification of risk. The modelling is deterministic.

The objective of obtaining the project portfolio that yields the greatest profit is made possible by separating all relevant monetary amounts from the demand on resources. This separation is achieved by including in the objective function, and only in the objective function, the definition of profit, along with a set of constraints that determine the demand on each resource. However, some constraints may contain elements of the objective function.

Elements of the Objective Function

The objective is to maximize the net present value of profit. Profit is defined, for simplicity, as the difference between all cash inflows and cash outflows on a before tax basis. The objective function consists of three elements. The first indicates the revenues and costs associated with the activities representing the four levels of variability. The second element embraces the resource acquisition and disposal costs. The third reflects the costs associated with borrowing and lending.

The first element (costs associated with the four levels of variability) is addressed first. The only source of cash inflow from the levels of variability is sales. The unit variable contribution margin for a single time period is given by

$$\sum_{p-1}^{P} \left\{ S_{pt} - \sum_{r=1}^{R}\sum_{a=1}^{A} D_{ptra}C_{ptra}^{x} - MC_{pt}^{x} \right\} X_{pt}. \tag{2}$$

The only decision variable in (2) is X_{pt}, the number of units to product a product p in period t. S_{pt} and MC_{pt} indicate the sales price and direct material cost, respectively, per unit of product p in period t. The parameters r and a represent the applicable resource and activity, respectively. D_{ptra} and C_{ptra} indicate the amount of resource consumption and the associated cost per unit of resource, respectively, per activity for each resource in each period for all projects.

As a simple example of (2), assume that two hours of direct labor (D) are required at a cost (C) of \$20 per hour to convert raw material at a cost (MC) of \$50 into a final product that sells for \$200 per unit. The unit variable contribution is $(200 - 2*20 - 50) X_{pt} = 110 X_{pt}$. The so-called overhead costs (all costs that do not vary in direct proportion with the number of units produced) are incorporated in the other three levels of variability, and are given for a single time period by

$$\sum_{1-b,y,z}\sum_{p=1}^{P}\sum_{r=1}^{R}\sum_{a=1}^{A} D_{ptra}^{l}C_{ptra}^{l} \{B_{ptra} + Y_{pt} + Z\}. \tag{3}$$

The decision variables in (3) are B_{ptra} (the number of batches to produce a product p using resource r in activity a in period t), Y_{pt} (the product sustaining indicator), and Z (the facility sustaining indicator). Both Y_{pt} and Z are 0-1 integer variables. If Y_{pt} is zero the company should not be in business at all, but if it takes on the value of one it should be in business at least for some periods. If Y_{pt} takes on the value of one, the magnitude of output, X_{pt}, as contained in (2), must also be determined. However, if the deliverable is a product sustaining entity (e.g., the design of an aircraft engine), the number of units produced is irrelevant ($X_{pt} = 0$) and all costs and resource consumption are directly related to Y_{pt}. D^l_{ptra} and C^x_{ptra} are similar to D_{ptra} and C^x_{ptra} in the unit variable contribution margins, except that it is associated with different levels of activity ($l = b$ = batch; $l = y$ = product sustaining; and $l = z$ = facility sustaining).

It should be noted that the batch level decision variable, B_{ptra} (the number of batches to produce) will normally take on the smallest possible value. This occurs because the objective function is the maximization of cost and B_{ptra} indicates cost. Unrealistically big batch sizes may occur. Therefore, B_{ptra} will only have purposeful meaning if the actual number of batches are limited (a space limit) to either the number of units that a batch can consist of, or if a quality defect cost is also incorporated. A qualify defect cost will result in a trade-off between the cost of additional batches versus the cost of rework. It should also be noted that any indirect material cost must be incorporated in the parameter C^l_{ptra}.

The second element of the objective function is the resource acquisition and disposal requirements and is given for a single period by

$$\sum_{r=1}^{R} \{C^+_{tr}M^+_{tr} - C^-_{tr}M^-_{tr}\} \tag{4}$$

M^+_{tr} and M^-_{tr} in (4) are decision variables establishing the number of units of resource r to acquire and dispose of, respectively, in period t. when the acquisition or disposal of resources occur in discrete units, the values of M^+_{tr} and M^-_{tr} must be limited to integers. Alternatively, if the acquisition and disposal of resources are continuous, M^+_{tr} and M^-_{tr} would be continuous. C^+_{tr} and C^-_{tr} are the unit costs associated with M^+_{tr} and M^-_{tr}, respectively. If there is a cash outflow as a result of the disposal of resources, the value of C^-_{tr} will be negative.

The last element in the objective function is the effect of borrowing and lending. The direct cost of borrowing and the benefit from lending are represented by the interest rates applicable to borrowing and lending given by I_w and I_v, respectively. The amount to be borrowed and the amount to be lent in period t are given by W_t and V_t, respectively. Accordingly, the cost for borrowing and the benefit from lending are given by

$$I_v V_t - I_w W_t \tag{5}$$

The expressions in (2) through (5) can now be combined into a single objective function. However, each is given for a single period. To get the net present value for profit, (2) through (5) must be expanded to be time-sensitive and discounted to the present. A single objective function comprising the time-sensitive expansions of (2) through (5), with a discount rate I, is given by

$$MAX \sum_{p=1}^{P} \sum_{r=1}^{T} (1+I)^{-t} \left\{ S_{pt} - \sum_{r=1}^{R} \sum_{a=1}^{A} D_{ptra} C_{ptra}^{x} - MC_{pt}^{x} \right\} X_{pt}$$

$$- \sum_{r=1}^{T} \sum_{r=1}^{R} (1+I)^{-t} \{ C_{tr}^{+} M_{tr}^{+} - C_{tr}^{-} M_{tr}^{-} \}$$

$$- \sum_{l=b,y,z} \sum_{p=1}^{P} \sum_{t=1}^{T} \sum_{r=1}^{R} \sum_{a=1}^{A} (1+I)^{-1} D_{ptra}^{l} C_{ptra}^{l} \{ B_{ptra} + Y_{pt} + Z \}$$

$$+ \sum_{t=I}^{T} (1+I)^{-1} \{ I_{v} V_{t} - I_{w} W_{t} \}. \tag{6}$$

It would be appropriate to separate the cash inflow from the cash outflow in (6), because the total cash outflow in each period is required for continuity in financial status over time (this is accomplished with the set of $[\Pi]$ constraints—to be discussed later), and budgetary constraints may be imposed on the total cash outflow (in the set of $[\beta]$ constraints). Thus, if multiple time periods are used or if budgetary constraints are imposed and (6) is not simplified, numerous terms will be duplicated in the problem formulation.

To consider the opportunity costs and to simplify the formulation, the total cash outflow can be set equal to the total amount to be borrowed, W_{t}. The total cash outflow in each period (excluding interest on borrowed funds in (5)) is given by

$$W_{t} = \sum_{l=x,b,y,z} \sum_{p=1}^{P} \sum_{r=1}^{R} \sum_{a=1}^{A} (D_{ptra}^{l} C_{ptra}^{l} + MC_{pt}^{x})$$

$$\times \{ X_{pt} + B_{ptra} + Y_{pt} + Z \} + \sum_{r=1}^{R} \{ C_{tr}^{+} M_{tr}^{+} \}. \tag{7}$$

Also, the total cash inflow in each period (excluding interest on invested funds) is given by

$$V_{t} = \sum_{p=1}^{P} S_{pt} X_{pt} + \sum_{r=1}^{R} C_{tr}^{-} M_{tr}^{-}. \tag{8}$$

The assumption is made in (7) and (8) that the disposal of resources results in a positive cash inflow. If this is not the case, the last term in (7) must contain the disposal cost, as given in (4), and the last term in (8) must be removed. Interest on excess funds must be incorporated. Since W_{t} and V_{t} now denote the cash outflows and cash inflows, respectively, two new variables are used to determine the net profit/debt in each period. These variables are $PROF_{t}$ and DT_{t}, indicating the profit and debt, respectively, in period t. The relationship between the net profit/debt in each period, the cash inflow/outflow in each period, and the applicable interest rates are given by

$$PROF_{t} + DT_{t} = (1+I_{v})PROF_{t-1} - (1+I_{w})DT_{t-1} + V_{t} - W_{t}. \tag{9}$$

The relationship in (9) indicates that the financial situation in the current period is the financial situation in the previous period, prorated at the applicable interest rates, plus the net cash flow in the current period. The reason that two different variables are given for the financial situation in a period is due to the fact that many linear programming packages restrict decision variables to non-negative values. If the net financial position is positive in a period, $PROF_t$ will have a positive value, and if the net financial situation is negative, DT_t will have a positive value. Thus, at most one of the variables $PROF_t$ and DT_t can have a non-zero value in each period. The objective function in (6) can now be restated, subject to (7), (8), and (9) as constraints, as

$$MAX \sum_{t=0}^{T} (1+I)^{-t} \{PROF_t - DT_t\}. \tag{10}$$

Constraints and Constraint Sets

There are ten different constraints, or sets of constraints, to be denoted by the Greek letters in square brackets in front of each constraint set. A constraint is referred to as a set of constraints if the constraint is recurring with respect to some parameter. As an example, the set of $[\rho_{tr}]$ constraints are recurring with respect to all relevant resources and with respect to all relevant time periods (which are denoted by $\forall r$, $\forall t$ towards the end of the constraint). Constraints will subsequently be referred to be the associated Greek letters, but, without the subscripts. The constraints are structured in such a way that the decision variables are all on the left hand side of the equation and the constants on the right hand side.

The set of $[\rho]$ constraints is very important. They are used to trade off the cost of acquiring additional resources (or the benefit/cost of disposing of excess resources) against the benefit of changed output, as given by (2). The first term of these constraints accumulates the total demand over all levels of variability for each resource in each period. This total demand should be less than, or equal to, the existing capacity for the resource, plus the additional capacity that will be disposed of. K_{tr}^o is the total capacity available for resource r in period t. On the other hand, K_{tr}^+ and K_{tr}^- indicate the capacity per unit of resource considered for acquisition and disposal, respectively. The set of $[\eta]$ constraints are required to ensure that the product sustaining costs are, in fact, incurred if production does take place. The $[\psi]$ constraint is required to ensure that the facility sustaining costs are incurred if anything is products. BM_{pt}^y and BM^z are the "Big-M" values and are constraints just bigger than the probable values of the first terms in the sets of the $[\eta]$ and $[\psi]$ constraints, respectively. The set of $[\delta]$ constraints places a ceiling on the production quantity of each product in each period equal to the market demand. If inventory is considered the set of $[\delta]$ constraints would be too stringent. However, inventory is omitted herein for the sake of simplicity. Total cash inflows are given in the set of $[\xi]$ constraints and are defined in (8) while the total cash outflows are given by the set of $[\alpha]$ constraints and are defined in (7). The set of $[\beta]$ constraints are used to impose budget limitations on cash outflows in each period, if applicable. The set of $[\pi]$ constraints, as defined in (9), gives the relationship between the financial status in any period and cash flows. The set of $[\kappa]$ constraints is required to ensure continuity in resource capacity over time. Finally, the $[\chi]$ constraints is given to initialize the value of profit or debt at time zero when the modelling begins. Next the model is given, followed by a complete glossary of all decision variables, parameters, subscripts and superscripts.

$$Max \sum_{t=1}^{T} (1+I)^{-t} \{PROF_t - DT_t\}$$

subject to

$$[\rho_{tr}] \quad \sum_{l=x,b,y,z} \sum_{p=1}^{P} \sum_{a=1}^{A} D^l_{ptra} \{X_{pt} + B_{ptra} + Y_{pt} + Z\} - K^+_{tr}M^+_{tr} + K^-_{tr}M^-_{tr} - K^o_{tr} \le 0 \quad \forall r,$$

$$[\eta_{pt}] \quad X_{pt} - BM^y_{pt}Y_{pt} \le 0 \quad \forall t, \forall p$$

$$[\psi] \quad \sum_{p=1}^{P} \sum_{t=1}^{T} X_{pt} - BM^z Z \le 0$$

$$[\delta_{pt}] \quad X_{pt} \le MD_{pt} \quad \forall t, \forall p$$

$$[\xi] \quad V_t - \sum_{p=1}^{P} S_{pt}X_{pt} - \sum_{r=1}^{R} C^-_{tr}M^-_{tr} = 0 \quad \forall t$$

$$[\alpha_t] \quad W_t - \sum_{l=x,b,y,z} \sum_{p=1}^{P} \sum_{r=1}^{R} \sum_{a=1}^{A} (D^l_{ptra}C^l_{ptra} + mC^x_{pt})$$

$$\{X_{pt} + B_{ptra} + Y_{pt} + Z\} - \sum_{r-1}^{R} \{C^+_{tr}M^+_{tr}\} = 0$$

$$[\beta_t] \quad W_t < W_t^{\cdot} \forall t$$

$$[\pi_t] \quad PROF_t - DT_t - (1+I_v)PROF_{t-l} + (1+I_w)DT_{t-l} - V_t + W_t = 0 \quad \forall t$$

$$[\kappa_{tr}] \quad K^0_{tr} - K^0_{t-l,r} - K^+_{t-l,r}M^+_{t-l,r} + K^-_{t-l,r}M^-_{t-l,r} = 0 \quad \forall r, \forall t$$

$$[x] \quad PROF_o - DT_o = PROF^o$$

Decision Variables

B_{ptra}	=	Batch size for activity using resource r for product p in period t
DT_t	=	Net debt in period t
K^0_{tr}	=	Total capacity of resource r available in the beginning of period t
M_{tr}	=	Number of units of resource r to acquire in period t (0-1 integer if discrete)
M^+_{tr}	=	Number of units of resource r to dispose of in period t (0-1 integer if discrete)
$PROF_t$	=	Net profit in period t
V_t	=	Total cash inflow in period t
W_t	=	Total cash outflow in period t
X_{pt}	=	Production quantity of product p in period t
Y_{pt}	=	Product sustaining indicator for product p in period t (0-1 integer)
Z	=	Facility sustaining indicator (0-1 integer)

Parameters

BM^y_{pt}	=	A number bigger than the probable production quantity of product p in period t

BM^z = A number just bigger than the total probable production quantity

C_{tr}^+ = Acquisition cost per unit of M_{tr}

C_{tr}^- = Net cash inflow expected from the disposal of a unit of M_{tr}

C_{ptra}^l = Cost per unit consumption D_{ptra}

D_{ptra}^l = Amount of resource r consumed by activity a in period t for product p

I = Discount factor

I_v = Interest rate applicable for investment of excess funds

I_w = Interest rate applicable for borrowed funds

K_{tr}^- = Capacity per unit of resource r considered for disposal in period t

MC_{pt}^x = Direct material cost per unit of product p in period t

MD_{pt} = Market demand for product p in period t

$PROF^o$ = Initial wealth (positive or negative)

S_{pt} = Sales price per unit of product p in period t

W_t^* = Total budget limit in period t

Subscripts and Superscripts

a = Activity, with a maximum of A

b = Batch level activity

l = Level of variability ($l = x,b,y,z$)

p = Product or project, with a maximum of P

r = Resource, with a maximum of R

t = Time period, with a maximum of T

x = Unit level activity

y = Product sustaining activity

z = Facility sustaining activity

Model Justification

The purpose of this section is to justify the proposed model on a general basis, as contrasted to the specific example provided in the subsequent section. The basic approach is to determine the amount of cash flows and number of problem formulations required by using Weingartner's Horizon Model (when resources are shared among different projects) to ensure that answers will be obtained that are at least as good as those obtained from the model proposed in this paper. "Good answers" are measured relative to the highest realistically achievable profit. (See the section, "Analyzing Results From Weingartner's Model," in the subsequent section.)

To determine the number of cash flows and problem formulations required the following necessary (but not sufficient) conditions must be met for optimality using Weingartner's approach:

1. Each project's cash flow must be correct and truly representative of the proposed project.

2. Resources acquired and utilized must be considered discrete, when appropriate.

These conditions are not independent. It was shown in (1) that the cost to be allocated to a project (based on proportional usage), in order to obtain a cash flow per project, is determined by the project portfolio as well as the production quantity of each project in the portfolio.

Also, to meet the second requirement for optimality and usefulness, the denominator in (1), the total demand on each resource, must be known to determine the total resource requirement. There are (2^{P^*}) combinations of all projects (including the do-nothing alternative), where P^* is the maximum number of projects sharing some resources (not necessarily the same). If one resource unit is added to any of the resources shared by different projects, the denominator in (1) changes. This change in capacity will result in a change in the cost to be allocated to a project, which may lead to a different cash flow per project, and eventually a different project selection. There are ΠQ_{r^*} such changes over all shared resources in each project portfolio, where Q_{r^*} is the maximum number of resource units considered for resource r^*. Therefore, in order to fulfill the stated requirements for optimality and usefulness, at least (2^{P^*}) ΠQ_{r^*} cash flows are required. However, this amount assumes that all project selection decision variables are 0-1 integer values and that, for each potential project portfolio, the decision-maker knows exactly which combination of projects and resources yield the best solution. If one, and only one, additional problem formulation is required for each of these two very restrictive assumptions, the total number of cash flows and problem formulations required to ensure that answers will be obtained by Weingartner that are at least as good as those obtainable by the proposed odel, is given by

$$3(2^{P^*})\sum_{r^*=1}^{R^*}Q_{r^*}. \tag{11}$$

P^* in (11) indicates the number of products sharing some or all of R^* resources, each of which has a maximum of Q_{r^*} units. As an example of (11), if four products are under consideration (see the example in the section, "An Illustration"), and if two resources are required with maximum numbers of units of four and ten, respectively (machines and laborers), then the total number of cash flows and problem formulations required is $3(2^4)(4)(10)=1,920$.

An Illustration

Most numerical examples on capital budgeting in the literature assume some cash flow per project as input. Since the concept of a cash flow per project is specifically avoided when resources are shared among different projects (see discussion around (1)), these examples are of little use. Robin Cooper [2] illustrates how Activity-Based Costing (ABC) can lead to product costs that are drastically different from what he terms the "conventional costing system."

The proposed model is illustrated with a simple example. The raw data from Cooper's article are used with a few additional items added in the last column of Table 3 and Table 4. Tables 1, 2, and 3 contain the data used by Cooper. The only difference is that the quantities are 100 times greater than the quantities he used. The pioneering model of Weingartner [12] and the proposed model are then both exercised with the same set of data. Different answers are obtained, analyzed, and compared.

Table 1. Demand on resources per product.

Product	Quantity per Year	Material $ per Unit	Direct Labor Hrs per Unit	Machine Hrs per Unit
P_1	1,000	6	0.5	0.5
P_2	10,000	6	0.5	0.5
P_3	1,000	18	1.5	1.5
P_4	10,000	18	1.5	1.5

Table 2. Annual resource consumption rates and costs.

Product	Material $ per Unit	Direct Labor Hours	Machine Hours	No. of Set-ups	No. Of Orders	No. of Times Handled	Product Sustaining Cost
P_1	6,000	500	500	100	100	100	1
P_2	60,000	5,000	5,000	300	300	300	1
P_3	18,000	1,500	1,500	100	100	100	1
P_4	180,000	15,000	15,000	300	300	300	1
Consumption	264,000	22,000	22,000	800	800	800	4
Unit Costs	10%	$10	$15	$120	$125	$25	$50,000
Dollar Value	$25,400	$220,000	$330,000	$96,000	$100,000	$20,000	$200,000
TOTAL		**$992,400**					

Table 3. Product costs.

Product	Conventional Accounting	Activity-Based Costing	Product Price
P1	$22.55	$90.10	$110
P2	$22.55	$26.20	$60
P3	$67.66	$116.30	$120
P4	$67.66	$52.40	$80

Table 4. Resource data.

Resource	Acquisition Cost	Unit Capacity Hrs per Year
Laborer	$1,000	2,000
Machine	$100,000	5,000

Input Data

Four products are considered for production: P_1, P_2, P_3, and P_4. All of these consume the same resources in similar processes. The resources are one type of labor and one type of machine. Table 1 gives the market demand per product and the demand that a unit of each product places on the different resources.

Products P_1 and P_2 are relatively small, while P_3 and P_4 are relatively large and consume (on a unit basis) more resources than P_1 and P_2. On the other hand, smaller quantities are demanded of P_1 and P_3 than of P_2 and P_4. The total demand that each product places on each of the resources, based on the market demand, is given in Table 2.

Direct labor cost is \$10 per hour, and machine operating cost is \$15 per hour. (Note that Cooper considers only "overhead costs," which are all the costs given in Table 2, except material cost.) The "overhead" on material cost is considered to be 10 percent of the actual material cost. The columns "Material," "Direct Labor Hours," and "Machine Hours" all contain values that vary in direct proportion to the number of units produced. The next three columns indicate batch activities, while the last column indicates product sustaining activities and costs. The product costs for the data are presented in Table 3.

Two categories of cost are given in Table 3: 1) as calculated by the conventional costing system, and 2) as calculated with the use of activity-based costing. The product unit costs, as presented in Table 3, are those obtained by Cooper. The last column in Table 3 contains the market prices for these products (not provided by Cooper). Table 4 contains the resource data.

Using Weingartner's Approach

To apply classical capital budgeting techniques, cash flows must now be developed for each project. The cash flows consist of the revenues per product (the unit price of each product in Table 3 multiplied by the market demand in Table 1), the product costing data (Table 3), and the resource acquisition cost (Table 4). The resource acquisition cost, or investment cost, must still be allocated to the respective products in order to determine the full cash flow per product. The acquisition cost of the resource is allocated to each product in direct proportion to the amount of resource time consumed by that product (labor hours and machine hours are the cost drivers, regardless of the accounting system used).

The machine investment cost for P_1 is calculated from (1) as $\{(500/5,000) * \$100,000\} = \$10,000$ (from Tables 2 and 4). The labor investment cost is calculated similarly as $\{(500/2,000) * 1,000\} = \$250$. Therefore, the total investment cost to be allocated to P_1 is \$10,259, regardless of the accounting system used. The non-investment cash flow for P_1 using conventional costing is calculated as $(110 - 22.55) * 1,000 = \$87,450$ (from Tables 5, 3, and 1, respectively). Assuming the investments are made in Year 0, and the other cash flows in Year 1, the total cash flows per product (using conventional costing and activity-based costing) are given in Tables 5 and 6, respectively.

Weingartner's basic Horizon Model (see [12] for the general formulation) can be used to solve the problem. (Note that the solution is actually obvious only because of the simplicity of the problem.) The input and output from the software package Lindo

Table 5. Cash flows using conventional costing.

Year	P_1	P_2	P_3	P_4
Yr. 0	$-10,250	$-102,500	$-30,750	$-307,500
Yr. 1	$87,450	$74,500	$52,340	$123,400
Net Cash Flow	$77,200	$272,000	$21,590	$-184,100

Table 6. Cash flows using activity-based costing.

Year	P_1	P_2	P_3	P_4
Yr. 0	$-10,250	$-102,500	$-30,750	$-307,500
Yr. 1	$19,900	$338,000	$3,700	$276,000
Net Cash Flow	$9,650	$235,500	$-27,050	$-31,500

for Weingartner's Horizon Model, using the data in Table 6 are given in Model 2. The input for the model is the section up to and including the statement "End." The remainder is the output. No restrictions are placed in Model 2 on the amount of money that can be borrowed, WO, other than that all money required is considered borrowed.

MAX 87450 P1 + 374500 P2 + 52340 P3 + 123400 P4 - WO

SUBJECT TO

2) 10250 P1 + 102500 P2 + 30750 P3 + 307500 P4 - WO = 0
3) P1 <=   1
4) P2 <=   1
5) P3 <=   1
6) P4 <=   1
END

OBJECTIVE FUNCTION VALUE
1) 370790.00

VARIABLE	VALUE	REDUCED COST
P1	1.000000	.000000
P2	1.000000	.000000
P3	1.000000	.000000
P4	.000000	184100.000000
WO	143500.000000	.000000

The values in the column "VALUE" indicate that projects P_1, P_2, and P_3 are fully accepted while project P_4 is not accepted. The horizon is chosen to be Year 0. The same results are obtained if the horizon is chosen to be Year 1. In contrast to Model 2, Model 3 provides Weingartner's Horizon Model for the case where the cash flows are calculated using ABC.

$$\text{MAX} \quad 19900 \text{ P1} + 338000 \text{ P2} + 3700 \text{ P3} + 276000 \text{ P4} - \text{WO}$$

SUBJECT TO
2) 10250 P1 + 102500 P2 + 30750 P3 + 307500 P4 - WO = 0
3) P1 <=   1
4) P2 <=   1
5) P3 <=   1
6) P4 <=   1
END

OBJECTIVE FUNCTION VALUE
   1) 245150.00

VARIABLE	VALUE	REDUCED COST
P1	1.000000	.000000
P2	1.000000	.000000
P3	.000000	7050.000000
P4	.000000	31500.000000
WO	112750.000000	.000000

In Model 3, only projects P_1 and P_2 are accepted, with a total profit of $245,150. The conventional costing method (which leads to the selection of three projects) has 51 percent ($125,640) more profit than with ABC, while the investment cost for the conventional costing system is only 27 percent ($30,750) more than what is required for the ABC model.

Analysing Results from Weingartner's Model
The results obtained from Weingartner's model are now evaluated to determine how accurate they are. This evaluation consists of taking the results from Weingartner's Model and working backwards to determine what profit results from the actual revenues and costs. The conventional costing results are analyzed first. Model 2 (as well as Table 6) suggest that projects P_1, P_2, and P_3 be undertaken, and that project P_4 be dropped. From Table 2 the total amount of direct labor hours and machines hours required are both 7,000. It is evident from Table 4 that four laborers and two machines are required. All batch-related activities are executed 500 times, and only three product sustaining costs are incurred. The total revenue to be generated is calculated from Tables 1 and 5 as

Revenues = (110*1,000) + (60*10,000) + (120*1,000) = $830,000

It is assumed that labor can be provided only in whole units, while machine operating cost is incurred in direct proportion to usage. The total expenses are the material

Table 7. Summary of results.

	WEINGARTNER Conventional Cost		WEINGARTNER Activity-Based Cost		PROPOSED MODEL	
	Profit	PP	Profit	PP	Profit	PP
Original	$370,790	(1, 2, 3)	$245,150	(1, 2)	$225,000	(2)
Actual	$147,600	(1, 2, 3)	$149,900	(1, 2)	$225,000	(2)
Processed	$171,800	(1, 2, 3, 4)	$149,900	(1, 2)	(None Required)	

cost (once again, at 10 percent to be consistent with Cooper's results) labor acquisition cost, labor cost, machine acquisition and operation cost, batch costs, and product sustaining costs. For simplicity, fixed batch sizes are assumed regardless of production quantity. This means that batch costs can be considered proportional to production quantity. The total expenses (primarily from Table 4) and profit are then calculated as

$$\text{Expenses} = (84,000*0.1) + (4*1,000) + (8,000/2,00)*2,000*10$$
$$+ (2*100,000) + (7,000*15) + 500*(120 + 125 + 25)+ (3*50,000)$$
$$= \$682,400$$
$$\text{Profit} = 830,000 - 682,400 = \$147,600$$

The actual profit amount for producing only P_1 , P_2, and P_3 ($147,600) is significantly less than the $370,790 estimated by Weingartner's Model in Model 2. The primary reason for this discrepancy is that resource capacity comes in discrete amounts and must be considered accordingly. Further analysis reveals that 3,000 (10,000 - 7,000) hours of available machine capacity and 1,000 (8,000 - 7,000) hours of labor capacity is idle, although already paid for. It can now be determined if it is profitable to "fill up" the capacity with production of units of P_4. Presumably, the best strategy would be to first fill up the least available capacity (the 1,000 hours of labor is "free"—having already been paid for). If this strategy proves to be insufficient, additional capacity can be made available to the resource that has no excess capacity in the least discrete amounts, or multiples thereof. If the available labor capacity of 8,000 hours is fully utilized by also producing P_4, the profit decreases by $18,420, mainly because of the additional product sustaining cost of $50,000. However, if an additional laborer is added (for total capacity of 10,000 hours for both labor and machines) the profit increases to a total of $171,800 (see Moolman [6] for calculations).

Similar discrepancies occur in the results from using ABC. From Model 3 and Table 7 it is evident that projects P_1 and P_2, and only these two projects, must be fully pursued for an eventual profit of $245,150. However, the actual profit from undertaking these two projects is $149,900 (which is obtained in a manner similar to the conventional costing system). This profit differs by a significant amount ($95,250) or 39 percent, from the profit indicated by Weingartner's Model. Again there is unused capacity. However, based on product profitability, none of this excess capacity can be used profitably (see Moolman [6] for calculations). This means that the best results, based on Weingartner and further processing, yield a profit of $149,900.

Using the Proposed Model

Model 4, a simplified version of Model 1, is now used to solve the problem. Since only a single period is under consideration and because there are no direct budget limitations, (6) is used as the objective function instead of (10), subject to (7) through (9) as

$$MAX \ \sum_{p=1}^{4} \left\{ S_p - \sum_{a=1}^{2} D_{pa} C_{pa}^x - MC_p^x \right\} X_p - \sum_{p=1}^{4} C_p^y Y_p - \sum_{r=1}^{2} C_r^+ M_r^+$$

subject to

$$[\rho_r] \ \sum_{p=1}^{4} \sum_{a=1}^{2} D_{pra} X_p - K_r^+ \leq K_r^o \ \forall r$$

$$[\delta_p] \ X_p \leq MD_p \ \forall p$$

$$[\eta_p] \ X_p - BM_p Y_p \leq 0 \ \forall p$$

There are two main groups of activities for which cost is incurred on a unit basis. These are the machine operational cost ($0.5 \times 15 = 7.5$ from Tables 1 and 2, respectively), and the batch costs (($120 + 125 + 25) \times 100 / 1,000 = 27$ from Tables 2 and 1). The last element of the first term of the objective function is the material cost, MC ($6 \times 0.1 = 0.6$ from Tables 2 and 1). The parameter value associated with X1 in the objective function is the unit variable contribution margin and is calculated as the revenue ($110) – machine operating costs ($7.50) – batch costs ($27) – material cost ($0.60) = $74.90. The second term in the objective function represents all the product sustaining costs, which amount to $50,000 for each product. The variables M and L represent the number of machines and laborers, respectively, to acquire. Constraints 2 and 3 in Model 5 are the resource capacity constraints and comprise the set of [ρ] constraints in the general model formulation of Model 4. The coefficients of X_i ($i = 1,..., 4$) are the respective demands that each product places on each resource. These are given in Table 1. Constraints 4 through 7 in Model 5 comprise the set of [δ] constraints in Model 4 and indicate that each production quantity, X_i, should not exceed its respective market demand in Table 1. Constraints 8 through 11 in Model 5 are comprised of [η] constraints in Model 4. The notation "GIN" and "INTE" after the end of the problem formulation indicate general integer and 0-1 integer values.

MAX 74.9 X1 + 43.8 X2 + 68.7 X3 + 47.6 X4 - 50000 Y1 - 50000 Y2 - 50000 Y3 - 50000 Y4 - 21000L - 100000M

SUBJECT TO

2) 0.5 X1 + 0.5 X2 + 1.5 X3 + 1.5 X4 - 2000L $\Leftarrow$ 0
3) 0.5X1 + 0.5 X2 + 1.5 X3 + 1.5 X4 - 5000M $\Leftarrow$ 0
4) X1 $\Leftarrow$ 1000
5) X2 $\Leftarrow$ 10000
6) X3 $\Leftarrow$ 1000
7) X4 $\Leftarrow$ 10000

8) X1-1001 Y1 $\Leftarrow$ 0
9) X2 - 10001 Y2 $\Leftarrow$ 0
10) X3 - 1001 Y3 $\Leftarrow$ 0
11) X4 - 10001 Y4 $\Leftarrow$ 0 END; GIN L, M; INTE X1, X2, X3, X4

OBJECTIVE FUNCTION VALUE
  1) 225000.00

VARIABLE	VALUE	REDUCED COST
L	3.000000	21000.000000
M	1.000000	100000.000000
Y1	.000000	-24974.900000
Y2	1.000000	50000.000000
Y3	.000000	-18768.700000
Y4	.000000	-426047.600000
X1	.000000	.000000
X2	10000.000000	.000000
X3	.000000	.000000
X4	.000000	.000000

Summary of Results

The results from the example are summarized in Table 7 with three categories in columnar form. These categories are the results based on Weingartner's Model using the data from both the conventional costing ("Conventional Cost") and activity-based costing ("Activity-Based"), as well as the results from the proposed model ("Proposed Model"). Each of these categories is divided into profit ("Profit") and project portfolio ("PP"). The results in the conventional costing and activity-based costing categories in Table 7 are obtained from the concept of a cash flow per project, using Weingartner's basic Horizon Model [12]. The results in the last category in Table 7 are obtained from the proposed model where the project portfolio approach is used and where costs are not allocated to projects (concept of cash flow per project is avoided).

The first row in Table 7 gives the values obtained from the respective modeling techniques: Weingartner's basic Horizon Model, using conventional costing and activity-based costing, and the proposed model. The second row gives the profit that would actually result if the projects, as suggested by the different methods, are pursued as suggested. The third row indicates the possible improved values from the "Actual" row if the "Actual" values are post processed in an attempt to profitably utilize excess capacity, or to acquire additional capacity.

It was illustrated in the section, "Analyzing Results from Weingartner's Model," that the original claim of a profit of $370,790 using conventional costing is incorrect, due mainly to resources being mostly discrete in nature. When the discrete nature of resources is considered and the actual processing is done by hand, adding P_4, the profit will increase to $171,800. The same holds for the activity-based costing approach. It is evident from Table 7 that the proposed model not only performs better (see the "Actual" row), but the original and actual values are the same, and post-processing is not required.

Summary and Conclusions

This paper exposed the problems associated with the concept of using cash flow per project for capital budgeting purposes when resources are shared among different projects. An alternative method was developed and illustrated in the section, "An Illustration." The proposed model is based on a project portfolio approach in which relationships are established between variable resource acquisition and consumption and the resultant benefit from production. Cost is not allocated to projects and the concept of a cash flow per project is avoided. All costs are incurred in the acquisition and consumption of resources and the consumption of resources is variable at any one of the following levels: unit, batch product sustaining, or facility sustaining. The objective is to select the project portfolio (comprised of projects and production quantities) that maximizes profit.

The main conclusion from this paper is that better capital budgeting decisions can be made if costs are not allocated to projects or products; that is if the concept of cash flow per project is avoided when resources are shared among projects. The so-called cost of a product (except for raw materials) becomes irrelevant for the purposes of capital budgeting when resources are shared. This is illustrated in the section, "An Illustration," the results of which are summarized in Table 7.

It is illustrated from (11) that the decision about which of four products to produce in a single period (each product consumes the same two resources and the resources are limited to four and ten units, respectively) would require approximately 1,920 problem formulations for a solution, based on the concept of cash flow per project, to ensure answers at least as good as those from the proposed model. The proposed model provides the final answers from a single run.

The main advantages of the proposed model are the following: 1) It provides answers that are at least as good as those obtained by the classical notion of cash flows per project, and probably better (especially when resources are shared); 2) Specific output quantities are modeled (a project cannot be accepted fractionally); 3) Specific resource requirements are modeled; 4) New constraints can be added to the proposed model without changing the other constraints (e.g., when more products are considered), as long as the constraints are not contradictory. With the notion of cash flow per project, the actual cash flow per project must be changed each time a product or a resource is added.

The main disadvantages of the proposed model are the following: 1) It is more complex and requires more computing power; 2) Taxes are not included; 3) The debt-equity structure is not addressed.

Research opportunities exist in the following areas: 1) The main disadvantages outlined in the previous paragraph might be overcome; 2) Variable market supply and demand functions could be incorporated, 3) Other objectives can be incorporated in the objective function (e.g., maximizing the rate of return, the market share, and minimizing the cost of excess capacity).

References

Brigham, E.F. and L.C. Gapenski, *Financial Management: Theory and Practice*, The Dryden Press, 1991.

Cooper, R., "The Rise of Activity-Based and Costing—Part One: What is an Activity-Based Cost System?" *Journal of Cost Management*, Summer 1988, pp. 45-54.

Giacotto, C., "A Simplified Approach to Risk Analysis in Capital Budgeting With Serially Correlated Cash Flows," *The Engineering Economics*, Vol. 29, No. 4, 1984, pp. 273-286.

Hillier, F.S., "A Basic Approach to the Evaluation of Risky Interrelated Investment," in Byrne R. F., A. Charnes, W. W. Cooper, O.A. Davis, and D. Gilford, *Studies in Budgeting*, North-Holland Publishing Company, 1971, pp. 3-47.

Kumar, P.C. and T. Lu, "Capital Budgeting Decisions in Large Scale, Integrated Projects: Case Study of a Mathematical Programming Application," *The Engineering Economist*, Vol. 36, No. 2, Winter 1991, pp. 127-150.

Moolman, G.C., *An Aggregate Capital Budgeting Model using a Product Portfolio Approach*, Unpublished Ph.D. Dissertation, Virginia Polytechnic Institute and State University, 1994.

Ostrenga, M.R., T.R. Ozan, R.D. Mcilhatten, and M.D. Harwood, *The Ernst and Young Guide to Total Cost Management*, John Wiley & Sons, 1992.

Park, C.S. And G.P. Sharp-Bette, *Advanced Engineering Economics*, John Wiley & Sons, 1991.

Srinivasan, V. and Y.H. Kim, "Evaluating Interrelated Capital Projects: An alternative Framework," *The Engineering Economist*, Vol, 33, No. 1, Fall 1987, pp. 13-30.

Thuesen, G.J. and W. J. Fabrycky, *Engineering Economy*, Eighth Edition, Prentice Hall, 1993.

Weingartner, H.M., "Capital Budgeting of Interrelated Projects: Survey and Synthesis," *Management Science*, Vol. 12, No. 7, 1966, pp. 485-616.

Weingartner, H.M., *Mathematical Programming and the Analysis of Capital Budgeting Problems*, Prentice Hall, 1963.

Reprinted with the permission of the Institute of Industrial Engineers, 25 Technology Park, Norcross, GA 30092, 770-449-0461. Copyright © 1997.

Part 4:

Best Practices and Applications

Best Practices for Managing R&D Portfolios

Robert G. Cooper, Scott J. Edgett and Elko J. Kleinschmidt

Effective new product development is emerging as the major corporate strategic initiative of the decades ahead. Those corporations that succeed at new product development will be the future Mercks, HPs, 3Ms, and Microsofts; those that fail will invariably disappear or be gobbled up by the winners.

A vital question in this new products warfare is: "How should the business most effectively invest its R&D and new product resources (1)?" Many people see portfolio management as the solution. Portfolio management addresses such questions as: "Which new product or development projects should you undertake? What is the right balance and mix of projects? How should you allocate your resources across various development projects?"

Portfolio management is a critical topic because it integrates a number of key decision areas, all of which are problematic (2): project selection and prioritization, resource allocation across projects, and implementation of the business's strategy (3,4).

The underlying goal of the current investigation is to provide insights into how businesses manage their R&D and new product portfolios, what the top performers do differently, and the lessons that companies can put into practice in order to achieve more effective portfolio management. An exploratory study, already undertaken, focused on a limited sample of leading firms, and described and categorized their portfolio management approaches (see 5, 6, 7). The current study broadens the base, and seeks insights into which portfolio management approaches are the most popular, the strengths and weaknesses of each method, and which methods yield the best performance results (see "How the Research Was Done").

Businesses in the survey sample cover a wide variety of industries, with the chemicals and advanced materials industry representing the largest group. Almost half the businesses in the sample have annual revenues in the $100 million to $1 billion range, with 37.9 percent exceeding $1 billion annual revenue.

Portfolio Management Performance
How well is portfolio management working? This is both a fundamental and a vital question. We outline portfolio management performance results in the first section of this article, since the answer underlies so many of the results reported later.

The Latest Study

Two previous *Research Technology Management* articles have reported on case studies dealing with portfolio management (6, 7). This article is based upon a new survey of 205 businesses conducted in cooperation with the Industrial Research Institute. In this latest study, the authors found that some companies are indeed achieving better portfolio-related results than others. The leaders reported greater success in developing portfolios that reflected strategic alignment, good value, faster cycle time, and a reasonable balance among projects. The strengths, weaknesses and levels of business satisfaction with different aspects of portfolio management are also assessed and reported on in this article.

Portfolio performance is a multifaceted concept; consequently, six metrics were constructed to capture how well the business's portfolio is performing. These metrics include decision effectiveness and efficiency, and having the right balance of projects, high-value projects, and a strategically aligned portfolio—see Table, Figure 1. All are metrics that emerged as goals in our exploratory study (5).

Portfolio management appears to be working in a moderately satisfactory fashion, on average, in our sample of businesses. Mean scores across the six performance metrics are typically mid-range—not stellar, but not disastrous either—although there are some differences across metrics (see Figure 1, in which the black bars show mean values). The results:

• Businesses, on average, obtain *reasonable alignment* between their portfolio of projects and the business's strategy.

• Portfolios contain *moderately-high-value projects*, on average.

• Spending breakdowns (across projects) *reflect the business's strategy fairly well*, on average.

But portfolio performance is markedly lower, on average, in the area of the *right number of projects* and *project balance*, namely:

• Project gridlock exists in the portfolio pipeline, on average, with *projects not being done on time!*

• Businesses tend to *lack a balanced portfolio* of projects (balance in terms of short term versus long term, high risk versus low risk, and so on).

• Businesses have *too many projects* underway, given the resources available (which might in turn explain the gridlock and timeliness problem above). Performance on this metric is the weakest of the six.

The distribution of performance results between businesses is very broad, with some firms achieving excellent performance and others reporting dismal scores (see Table, Figure 1). Therefore, mean or average performance ratings shown as bar charts in Figure 1 should be used with caution, simply because only a minority of businesses are average.

These substantial differences in portfolio performance across businesses, together with the moderate-to-low mean performance scores on some metrics, are provocative. They suggest that many businesses are performing in a substandard fashion, and that much improvement is needed in the way many enterprises' portfolios are managed.

How the Research Was Done

A detailed survey questionnaire was developed in concert with the IRI's Research on Research Committee. The questionnaire dealt with a number of topics, including:

- Importance of portfolio management and reasons why.
- General nature of the portfolio management method used by the business.
- Details of the portfolio methods used.
- Dominant method used.
- Criteria used for selecting and ranking projects.
- Satisfaction with method(s) used.
- Performance of the business's portfolio management method.
- General demographics (industry, business size, etc.).

Most of the questions were close-ended (i.e., required the respondent to check a box or circle a number), although some open-ended questions were included to solicit verbal comment. Many of the questions required ratings on 1-5 scales.

The questionnaire itself was carefully structured, exhaustively reviewed by a committee of industry experts from the IRI, and pre-tested on eight businesses via personal interviews.

A list of businesses known to be active in product development in North America was prepared, including the IRI membership list (largely CTOs of larger firms in the U.S.) as well as other private lists compiled by the authors. Although not the total population of all firms undertaking R&D and product development in the U.S., the list is a fairly representative one.

The eventual response rate was a respectable 205 businesses (25.8 percent), and there are no noticeable biases in the responding businesses versus those in the original mailing (i.e., the responses reflect the population). Additionally, there are no differences in the response patterns between IRI and non-IRI members or between major industry groups; consequently, the two samples are combined and results are presented together.

The breakdown of respondents by industry is:

High technology 17.6%
Processed materials 8.3%
Industrial products 8.3%
Chemicals & advanced materials 28.3%
Consumer products 12.2%
Health care products 6.3%
Other 19.0%

—R.C., S.E., E.K.

This large performance spread begs the question: What is it that the better performers are doing differently than the poor performers? To answer this question, a single portfolio performance gauge was developed, based on the six metrics in Figure 1 (8, 9). The top 20 percent of businesses, measured by their portfolio performance on this gauge, were singled out, and their results and practices were contrasted to the

Figure 1. Portfolio Performance Results on Six Key Metrics.

Respondent Distribution on Performance Metrics

Metric	Percent of Businesses Indicating	
	No or Poor[*]	Yes or Good
Projects are aligned with the business's objectives.	8.7	74.4
Portfolio contains very-high-value projects.	9.7	55.1
Spending reflects the business's strategy.	15.9	57.4
Projects are done on time—no gridlock.	30.2	29.7
Portfolio has good balance of projects.	35.9	30.8
Portfolio has right number of projects.	43.5	24.1

* No or Poor score = 1 or 2 on the 5-point scale; Yes or Good score = 4 or 5.

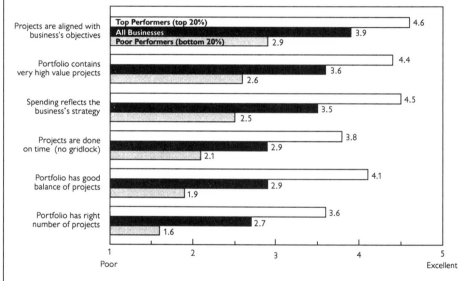

- All differences between Top and Poor Performers are significant at the 0.001 level.
- Performance metrics are rank-ordered according to mean scores (best at top of exhibit).

bottom 20 percent. Thus, the term "top 20 percent" means the 20 percent of businesses whose portfolios perform the best in terms of the six metrics in Figure 1.

As might be expected, the top 20 percent achieve dramatically stronger portfolio performance results across all six performance metrics (Figure 1, the pairs of shaded bars). However, the two areas in which the top 20 percent really excel are:

- Portfolio balance—achieving the right balance of projects.
- The right number of projects for the resources available.

Both are areas in which the average business performs fairly weakly.

Importance of Portfolio Management

Portfolio management is a critical task in the business—vitally important to success—according to at least some senior managements. Figure 2 provides the mean importance

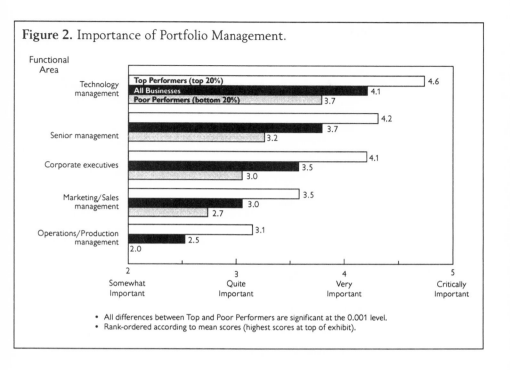

Figure 2. Importance of Portfolio Management.

- All differences between Top and Poor Performers are significant at the 0.001 level.
- Rank-ordered according to mean scores (highest scores at top of exhibit).

scores, broken down by executive function. Not surprisingly, senior management in technology (CTOs, VPs of R&D, etc.) attach the most importance to portfolio management; they are followed by senior management overall, and then by corporate executives (all three management groups score in excess of 4 out of 5, where 5 = critically important).

The fact that Marketing/Sales managements score only a mid-range 3.5 out of 5 is a concern. Clearly, there is a view that the heads of one of the most important partners in product development—the people who interface with the customer—do not place the same importance on the role of portfolio management. The fact that Marketing/Sales senior management has not vigorously bought into the concept and importance of portfolio management represents a serious deficiency in the widespread acceptance and implementation of portfolio management.

Additionally, and perhaps less of a surprise, Operations/Production managements view portfolio management as the least important of all the functional management groups.

The top 20 percent of businesses place much more importance on portfolio management than do the bottom 20 percent—consistently and significantly (see Figure 2, the pairs of shaded bars). This is true regardless of functional area. Thus, there is a direct link between whether a business recognizes portfolio management to be important, and the portfolio results it achieves. Once again, however, technology managers score by far the highest here, with senior technology management in the top 20 percent rating portfolio management a very high 4.6 out of 5 in importance. Marketing/Sales and Operations/Production managements continue to see portfolio management as less vital, even among the top-performing businesses.

Figure 3. Satisfaction with Portfolio Management Method.

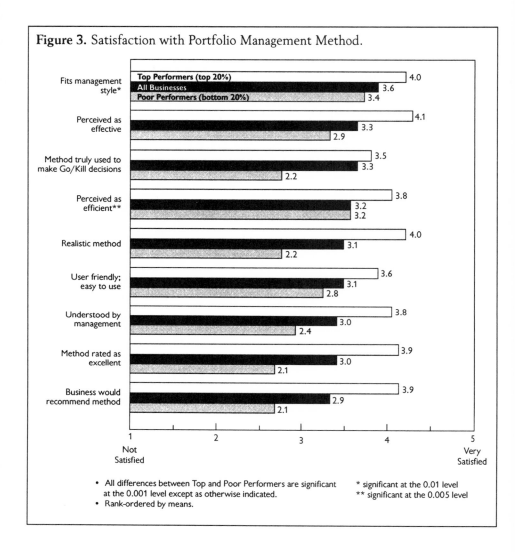

Satisfaction with Portfolio Methods

How do managements view their portfolio management methods in terms of key parameters such as effectiveness, efficiency, realism, and ease-of-use? And would they recommend their approach to other businesses?

Managements are *not particularly satisfied* with their portfolio management approach (see Figure 3). Note the mid-range, middle-of-the-road scores achieved here. The most positive facets of the process (and both are important) include:

• The portfolio management process used fits the business's management style.
• The method is perceived as being effective (i.e., makes the right decisions).

These elements are the best, but still the mean scores achieved here point to much room for improvement. The remainder of Figure 3 reveals much more disturbing results. On average:

- The portfolio method is used—somewhat.
- It is not particularly efficient (somewhat laborious and wastes time).
- It is not especially realistic in capturing key facets of the portfolio problem.
- The method is not particularly user-friendly or easy to use.
- It is not understood well by senior management.

The two lowest-scoring items in Figure 3 are noteworthy. On average, businesses do not rate their method as excellent (rather, a mid-range, fairly mediocre rating is given); nor do they strongly recommend their portfolio approach or method to others.

Once again, there is a large spread in responses between businesses. This underscores the substantial differences in performance and satisfaction—that about 10 percent or fewer businesses and their managements are indeed very pleased with their portfolio management approach, but that the great majority are not. For example, almost one-third of businesses surveyed rate their portfolio management approach as anything but excellent; and more than one-third would clearly not recommend their approach to others! Repairs are clearly needed in the case of most businesses.

As might be expected, managements in the top 20 percent of the businesses are much more satisfied with their portfolio management methods than are managements in the poorer performers. Consider the differences between the top 20 percent performers and the bottom 20 percent in Figure 3.

The three strongest discriminators between top and poor performers in Figure 3 are:
- The top 20 percent boast *more realistic portfolio methods*, that capture key facets of the portfolio problem.
- They rate *their method as excellent*.
- The top 20 percent would *highly recommend their methods* to others.

Additionally, the portfolio methods used by the top 20 percent tend to be understood well by senior management, are perceived to be effective, and are indeed used to make Go/Kill decisions.

Nature of Portfolio Methods

Is portfolio management really carried out with an explicit, well-defined method, following clear procedures and encompassing all projects, as some recent books suggest it should be (2,5)? Or is portfolio management more an unconscious or informal decision process, with no defined method or rules of the game? Even more important, does it really matter? Should businesses be relying on more systematic portfolio methods? Or are the pundits all wrong? The formality and explicitness of the portfolio management methods used are explored now, along with their impact on performance.

The typical business fares in a fairly mediocre fashion when it comes to the explicitness of the portfolio management process (see Figure 4). For example, on average:
- Businesses use a somewhat established, somewhat explicit method for portfolio management and project selection (a mid-range score here).
- Management buys into the portfolio management somewhat—their actions support its use.
- The rules and procedures for portfolio management are somewhat defined.

But, portfolio management methods score lower in terms of:
- Treating all projects as a portfolio (considering all projects together and comparing them against each other).

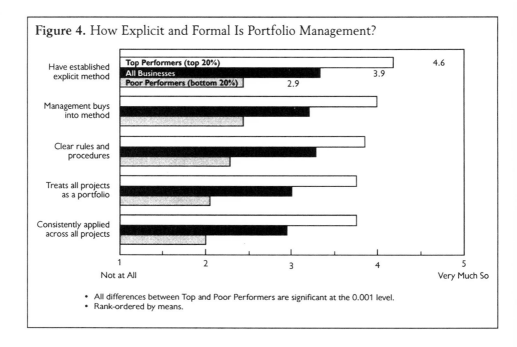

Figure 4. How Explicit and Formal Is Portfolio Management?

- All differences between Top and Poor Performers are significant at the 0.001 level.
- Rank-ordered by means.

• Consistently applying the method—across all appropriate projects.

Note that the range and spread of practices and scores is quite high in Figure 4 (10), suggesting major differences in practices across the sample of businesses.

Having a consistently applied, explicit portfolio management process impacts strongly on performance. Consider the major and significant differences between the top 20 percent and poorer performers in Figure 4.

The top 20 percent, when compared to poorer performers:

• Have an explicit, established method for portfolio management.

• Management buys into the method, and supports it through their actions.

• The method has clear rules and procedures.

• Treat projects as a portfolio (consider all projects together and treat them as one portfolio).

• Apply the method consistently across all appropriate projects.

These differences between top and poor performers are major, and all differences are highly statistically significant. Moreover, all differences are about equal; no one element has a greater impact on performance than another. The conclusion is that businesses that achieve positive portfolio results—a balanced, strategically aligned, high-value portfolio, with the right numbers of projects and good times-to-market (no gridlock)—boast a clearly defined, explicit, all-project, consistently applied portfolio management process that management endorses. Poor performers lack this!

The majority of businesses claim to be using a *formal system* for portfolio management (56.5 percent of businesses, top of Figure 5). The rest use an informal system or no system at all. The top 20 percent of businesses clearly have a preference, however, for a formal system. Note that the great majority of the top businesses (77.5

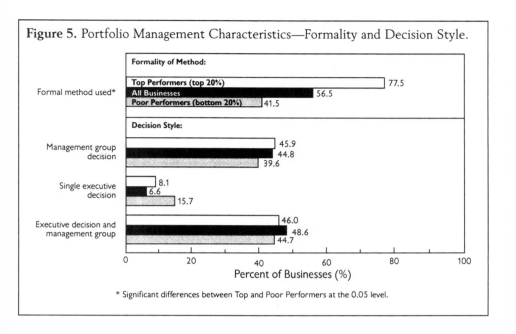

Figure 5. Portfolio Management Characteristics—Formality and Decision Style.

Formality of Method:

Formal method used*
- Top Performers (top 20%) — 77.5
- All Businesses — 56.5
- Poor Performers (bottom 20%) — 41.5

Decision Style:

Management group decision
- 45.9
- 44.8
- 39.6

Single executive decision
- 8.1
- 6.6
- 15.7

Executive decision and management group
- 46.0
- 48.6
- 44.7

Percent of Businesses (%)

* Significant differences between Top and Poor Performers at the 0.05 level.

percent) use a formal portfolio management system. By contrast, only 41.5 percent of poor performers have elected to use a formal portfolio management system.

Group decision-making appears to dominate in portfolio management: 44.8 percent of businesses handle Go/Kill and investment decisions on projects at meetings in which managers discuss projects as a group, use their best judgment and make decisions (see bottom of Figure 5).

In another 6.6 percent of businesses, a senior manager or executive makes the portfolio or Go/Kill decisions. Finally, both decision processes apply in 48.6 percent of businesses.

The group decision approach appears to work best; at least, it is the choice of the top-performing businesses. The top 20 percent emphasize the management group approach more (45.9 percent of businesses versus 39.6 percent for poor performers), whereas poor performers rely more heavily on a senior executive to make the decision (15.7 percent of poor performers versus only 8.1 percent of the top 20, see Figure 5). These differences are tendencies only, and not statistically significant.

Almost half the businesses use portfolio management only at the business unit or SBU level; that is, funds or resources are somehow allocated to the business unit (for example, via a corporate planning and allocation process), and then the business unit operates and manages its own portfolio of projects. A total of 48.4 percent of businesses indicate that this is their mode of operation (see Figure 6).

A small minority undertake portfolio management at the corporate level only (6.9 percent of respondents); that is, all projects from all businesses are considered together and centrally; projects are prioritized and/or selected, and resources are allocated across the business to undertake these projects. In effect, the project portfolio model becomes part of (or supersedes) the corporate planning and resource allocation method.

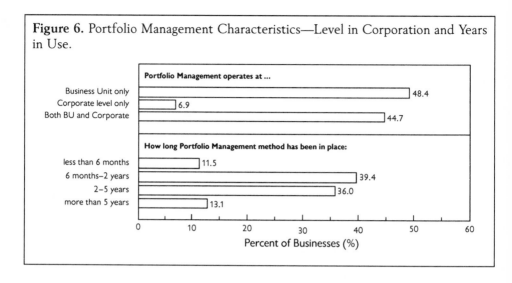

Figure 6. Portfolio Management Characteristics—Level in Corporation and Years in Use.

A significant number of businesses do both; that is, they operate portfolio management within the business unit, and they also have a centralized or corporate portfolio management method (44.7 percent of respondents).

Despite its importance, portfolio management is quite new to most businesses. About half the businesses have been using their current method of portfolio management for two years or less, and only a small minority (13.1 percent) have used their current portfolio method for five years or more (see Figure 6).

The top 20 percent have the edge when it comes to longevity of the portfolio method. A total of 69.2 percent of top performers have used their method for more than two years, compared to only 40 percent of the poor performers (recall that about half of the businesses have used their current method for two years or more).

The Most Popular Methods

Which portfolio methods are the most popular? And which methods dominate the portfolio decision process? Here, we explore the frequency of use of the various methods, and whether or not each method is the dominant decision tool. Note, however, that just because a method proves popular is no reason to assume it is the *correct* method, or even that it yields better performance. As we see later, quite the reverse is true—the most popular method yields the worst results!

Financial methods dominate portfolio management and project selection approaches. These methods include various profitability and return metrics, such as NPV, RONA, ROI, or payback period. A total of 77.3 percent of businesses use such an approach in portfolio management and project selection (see Figure 7). Most often, a financial method is used to rank projects against each other; that is, a project's expected financial results or economic value is determined, and that value is used to rank-order projects against each other in order to decide the portfolio of projects (38.1 percent of all businesses employ this ranking approach).

Figure 7. Popularity of Portfolio Methods Employed.

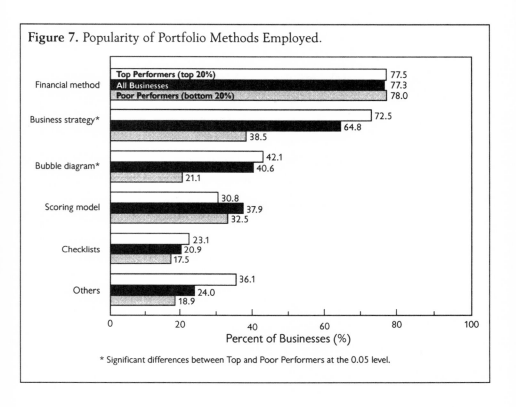

* Significant differences between Top and Poor Performers at the 0.05 level.

A slightly less popular method is to compare a financial measure against a hurdle rate in order to make Go/Kill decisions on individual projects (which, in turn, determines the list of active projects, and hence the portfolio; 28.4 percent of businesses). Some businesses do both: The project's financial value is used to rank projects against each other, and is also compared to a hurdle to make Go/Kill decisions (10.2 percent of businesses).

Many businesses use multiple methods, so that the percentages in Figure 7 add up to well over 100 percent. Thus, we queried respondents about which method is the dominant one—the method that dominates the decision process. Figure 8 shows the breakdown of dominant methods used (adds to 100 percent). Once again, financial methods prove the most popular, with 40.4 percent of businesses citing this as their dominant method of portfolio management and project selection.

Other methods are also popular, and in descending frequency of use, include (see Figures 7 and 8):

• The *business's strategy* as the basis for allocating money across different types of projects; for instance, having decided the business's strategy, money is allocated across different types of projects and into different envelopes or buckets. Projects are then ranked or rated within buckets (5, 7). A total of 64.8 percent of businesses use this approach; for 26.6 percent of businesses, this is the dominant method. The dimensions of these buckets vary greatly by business, but the most popular splits or buckets, according to the study, are by:

• Market.

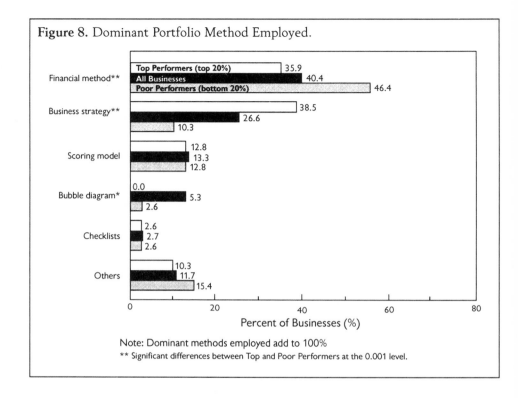

Figure 8. Dominant Portfolio Method Employed.

Note: Dominant methods employed add to 100%
** Significant differences between Top and Poor Performers at the 0.001 level.

• Development type (maintenance, exploratory, systems, frontier research, line extensions, and so on).
• Product line.
• Project magnitude (major or minor).
• Technology area.
• Technology platform types.
• Area of strategic thrust.
• Competitive need.
• *Bubble diagrams or portfolio maps*, in which projects are plotted on an X-Y plot, much like bubbles or balloons. Projects are categorized according to the zone or quadrant they are in (e.g., pearls, oysters, white elephants, and bread-and-butter projects) (2,5,6). A total of 40.6 percent of businesses use portfolio maps; only 8.3 percent of businesses use this as their dominant method.

Myriad bubble diagram plots are possible; Figure 9 shows the more popular plots identified in the current study, with the common risk/reward plots at the top of the list, and by a considerable margin.
• *Scoring models*, whereby projects are rated or scored on a number of criteria (for example, low-medium-high, or 1-5 or 0-10 scales). The ratings on each scale are then added to yield a *Total or Project Score*, which becomes the criterion for project selection and/or ranking decisions. A total of 37.9 percent of businesses use scoring models; in 18.3 percent, this is the dominant decision method.

Figure 9. Popular Bubble Diagram Plots.

Rank	Type of Chart	Axis		Axis	%
1	Risk vs. Reward	Reward: NPV, IRR, benefits after years of launch, market value	BY	Probability of success (technical, commercial)	44.4
2	Newness	Technical newness	BY	Market Newness	11.1
3	Ease vs. Attractiveness	Technical feasibility	BY	Market attractiveness (growth potential, consumer appeal, general, attractiveness, life cycle)	11.1
4	Strengths vs. Attractiveness	Competitive position (strengths)	BY	Attractiveness (market growth technical maturity, years to implementation)	11.1
5	Cost vs. Timing	Cost to implement	BY	Time to impact	9.7
6	Strategic vs. Benefit	Strategic focus or fit	BY	Business intent, NPV, financial fit, attractiveness	8.9
7	Cost vs. Benefit	Cumulative reward	BY	Cumulative development costs	5.6

Rank ordered, in descending order of popularity; last column shows percentage breakdown of buble diagram usage (as a percent of businesses using bubble diagrams)

• *Check lists,* in which projects are evaluated on a set of Yes/No questions. Each project must achieve either all or a certain number of Yes answers to proceed. The number of Yes's is used to make Go/Kill and/or prioritization (ranking) decisions. Only 17.5 percent of businesses use check lists, and in only 2.7 percent is this the dominant method.
• *Other:* Twenty-four percent of businesses indicate that they use some other method than the ones described above. A closer scrutiny of these "other" methods reveals that most are variants or hybrids of the above models and methods, for example:
• Many respondents describe a strategically driven process, much like the strategic method outlined above.
• A number use multiple criteria—profitability, strategic, customer appeal—but not necessarily in a formal scoring model format.
• Some businesses use probabilities of commercial and technical success, either multiplied together or multiplied by various financial numbers (EBIT, NPV)—a variant of the financial methods above.

What the Top 20 Percent Do
Businesses whose portfolios perform the best have decided preferences for which portfolio model or method dominates their decision process (see Figure 8).
• Top performing businesses *rely much less on financial models* and methods as the dominant portfolio tool than does the average business. By contrast, poor performers place much more emphasis on financial tools. For example, only 35.9 percent of the

Figure 10. Strengths/Weaknesses for Each Portfolio Method (based on Performance metrics).

Performance Metric	Financial Methods	Strategic Methods	Scoring Model	Bubble Diagrams	Significant Differences between methods (ANOVA)	Methods that are better*
Projects are aligned with business's objectives	3.76 X	4.08	3.95	4.11 ★	NS	–
Portfolio contains very high value projects	3.37 X	3.77	3.82 ★	3.70	.05	Scoring & Strategic > Financial
Spending reflects the business's strategy	3.50	3.72 ★	3.59	3.00 X	NS	–
Projects are done on time – no gridlock	2.79 X	3.22 ★	3.13	2.90	0.10	Strategic > Financial
Portfolio has good balance of projects	2.80 X	3.08	3.20 ★	3.20 ★	NS	–
Portfolio has right number of projects	2.50	2.93 ★	2.70	2.25	NS	Strategic > Financial

★ = Best method on each performance criterion

X = Worst method on each criterion

Ratings are 1–5 mean scores for each method, when used as dominant portfolio method. Here 1 = Poor and 5 = Excellent
* = Duncan's Multiple Range Test

top 20 percent rely on financial models as their dominant method, whereas 56.4 percent of poor performers use this as their dominant portfolio method.

• The top 20 percent let the business strategy allocate resources and decide the portfolio much more so than do poor performers. Only 10.3 percent of poor performers use the business's strategy as the dominant method, compared to 38.5 percent of the top 20 percent. Indeed, business strategy methods are the *number-one method* for the top 20 percent of businesses, used even more than popular financial approaches as the dominant decision tool here (see Figure 8).

The use of other methods—scoring models, check lists, bubble diagrams—as the dominant approach is too infrequent to allow meaningful comparison of top and poor performers (Figure 8). Similarly, whether or not various methods—financial, scoring models, etc—are used at all does not correlate with performance, simply because there is such overlap of methods used; the typical business uses 2.4 different portfolio methods or tools (Figure 7), hence it is difficult to correlate mere usage with performance.

Strengths and Weaknesses

Managements are not particularly satisfied with their portfolio approaches across a broad array of satisfaction measures (Figure 3), while portfolio methods used generally achieve only moderate-to-mediocre performance results (Figure 1). Here, we

Figure 11. Strengths/Weaknesses for Project Selection Methods (based on Satisfaction metrics).

Performance Metric	Financial Methods	Strategic Methods	Scoring Model	Bubble Diagrams
Method truly used to make Go/Kill decisions	2.87 X	2.87 X	2.95	3.00 ★
Fits management style	3.52	3.72	3.73	3.40 X
Understood by management	2.83 X	3.25 ★	3.13	3.00
User friendly easy to use	3.10	3.14	3.04 X	3.40 ★
Realistic method	3.06 X	3.16	3.13	3.30 ★
Perceived as efficient	3.09	3.23	3.47 ★	2.90 X
Perceived as effective	3.08 X	3.29	3.47 ★	3.70 ★
Method rated as excellent	2.91 X	3.06	3.04	3.20
Business would recommend method	2.80 X	3.06	2.82	3.50 ★

★ = Best method on each performance criterion

X = Worst method on each criterion

Ratings are 1–5 mean scores for each method, when used as dominant portfolio method. Here 1 = Poor and 5 = Excellent
* = Duncan's Multiple Range Test

look again at the satisfaction and performance scores, but this time for each specific portfolio method. In so doing, the strengths and weaknesses of each method are pinpointed.

Only four portfolio models are dominant in enough businesses that conclusions about their key strengths and weaknesses can he made. These are: strategic approaches, financial methods, scoring models, and bubble diagrams.

1. *Strategic Approaches*—Overall, portfolio management based on strategic approaches fares well in terms of most performance metrics and many of the satisfaction measures (11) (see Figures 10 and 11):

• Strategic approaches yield a portfolio of projects that is aligned with the business's strategic direction; not surprisingly, this is the Number 1 method on this metric (tied with bubble diagrams).

• The resulting portfolio of projects contains excellent value projects; this is the Number 2 method here—only scoring models do better.

• The resulting spending breakdown of projects in the portfolio reflects the business's strategic priorities—the best method on this metric.

Thus, strategic approaches, not surprisingly, have particular strengths in the areas of strategic alignment and strategic priorities, but also yield a portfolio of excellent value projects.

Additionally, strategic approaches are viewed positively in terms of the following:
• They fit management's style of decision making—the Number 1 method here, along with scoring models.
• The method is well understood by senior management—Number 1 on this metric.
• It is a very realistic method and captures many facets of the decision situation—the Number 2 method here, next to bubble diagrams.
• The method is user-friendly and easy to use—the Number 2 method, again second to bubble diagrams.

Additionally, strategic approaches are thought to be about average in terms of both effective and efficient decision methods for portfolio management, yielding the right decisions in a timely manner. Their only weakness is that they are not really used to make Go/Kill decisions on projects (although all methods suffer here as well; but strategic approaches fare worse than average), and the method does not yield the best balance of projects in the portfolio (again, all methods suffer here).

2. *Financial Methods*—Despite their popularity, financial methods are rated as having *many more weaknesses than strengths:*
• Financial methods fail to match the right number of projects in the portfolio for the resources available; all methods are weak here, but financial methods yield the worst results.
• They fail to yield a properly balanced portfolio (balance between high risk and low risk, between long and short term, etc). Financial methods are the weakest of all methods here, producing the most unbalanced portfolios.
• They fail to deal with the portfolio gridlock issue (many projects are late to market); again, these are the weakest of all methods.
• Financial methods and their results are not totally understood by management—the weakest of all methods.
• They are not really used to make Go/Kill decisions (although all methods are weak here).
• They are not particularly realistic methods, failing to capture key elements of the situation and decision; again, they are the worst of all methods.
• Financial methods are not effective decision tools: that is, they yield the wrong decisions, and are the worst of all methods here.
• Finally, they are not particularly time-efficient—the second worst, with bubble diagrams faring worst.

No particular distinctive strengths are evident for financial methods.

3. *Scoring Models*—Although used only by a minority of businesses as their dominant portfolio method, scoring models appear to have a number of redeeming features, particularly with respect to selecting high-value projects and being suited to management's decision-making style. Surprisingly, scoring models also fare well in strategic terms:
• Scoring models yield portfolios that are aligned with the business's strategic direction—a strong rating, and Number 3 on this metric, close behind strategic methods and bubble diagrams.
• They yield portfolios with *high-value projects*—the best of any method.
• They fit management's decision-making style—the best of all methods.

• They also yield a portfolio whose spending breakdown reflects the business's strategic priorities—Number 2 next to strategic methods.
• Scoring models are time-efficient—Number 1 on this metric.
• They are also effective, yielding the right decisions—Number 2 here, next to bubble diagrams.
• Scoring models result in well-balanced portfolios (tied with bubble diagrams for Number 1).
• Of all the methods, scoring models are the most used for truly making Go/Kill decisions, but bear in mind that all methods are deficient here.

Scoring models tend to be weaker in terms of user-friendliness (not as easy to use as some methods), and also when it comes to having the right number of projects in the portfolio for the resources available.

4. *Bubble Diagrams*—These see less frequent use as the dominant method, and therefore, the strengths/weaknesses accorded them are based on a greatly limited sample size. Particular strengths are:
• Bubble diagrams are the best method for yielding a portfolio of projects aligned with the business's strategic direction (tied with strategic methods).
• They are effective models, yielding the right decisions—the Number 1 method here.
• They are user-friendly and easy to use—Number 1 of all methods.
• They are a realistic method, capturing many facets of the decision situation—Number 1 on this metric as well.
• They also yield a high-value portfolio of projects (second to scoring models here).

Bubble diagrams do have a few weaknesses, however:
• They do not deal well with the issue of number of projects in the portfolio for the resources available (they yield too many projects, and are tied for worst method here).
• They are not particularly time-efficient models, and are rated the most laborious of all methods.
• They are weakest when it comes to yielding a portfolio whose spending breakdown reflects the strategic priorities of the business.

Specific Selection Criteria

Figure 12 reveals the proportion of businesses using different criteria for selecting and prioritizing projects against each other. Note that because multiple criteria are used, these percentages add up to well over 100 percent. Not surprisingly, the top two criteria parallel the portfolio methods used, noted in Figure 7 and 8. They are:
• Strategic fit and ability to leverage core competencies.
• Payoff (financial and reward).

Approximately 90 percent of businesses use each criterion to select and compare projects, with the strategic criterion used slightly more often (see Figure 12). Other vital criteria, although used somewhat less frequently, include:
• Project risk and probability of success.
• Timing.
• Technological capability of the business to undertake the project.

Commercialization capability, protectability of the venture (e.g., ability to achieve sustainable competitive advantage via patents or proprietary knowledge) and synergy

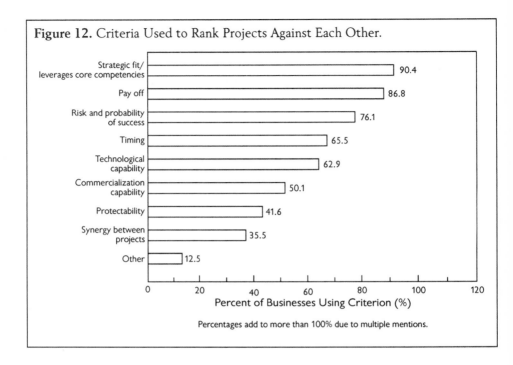

Figure 12. Criteria Used to Rank Projects Against Each Other.

Percentages add to more than 100% due to multiple mentions.

between projects are relied on much less as important selection and prioritization criteria (see Figure 12).

Note that most businesses use multiple criteria for project selection and prioritization. For example, the percentages in Figure 12 add to 523 percent, the conclusion being that the average business uses about 5.2 criteria each to select projects. This result is reassuring, because much anecdotal evidence suggests that some firms are too quick to rely on a single criterion—namely, financial—to select projects, and in so doing, are making naive selection decisions. Moreover, using *more* criteria seems to be connected to better performers; the top performers, on average, rely on 6.2 criteria for project selection, whereas the poor performers use only 4.4 criteria, on average.

A hierarchical approach to project selection is proposed as one method of using selection and ranking criteria for project selection. A hierarchical approach uses rounds during which projects are rated and ranked, and the best are selected. The first round may use several criteria, such as "strategic fit" and "payoff," to weed out the poorer projects; the second round uses other criteria, such as "timing" and "risk/probability of success," and narrows the field of projects. The result after several rounds is a short list of the top-ranked projects.

This method is a familiar one, and likely captures what many people do, whether intuitively or formally, when selecting projects. It is similar to a scoring model in that a list of criteria is used, but instead of weights to give certain criteria more importance (as in scoring models), rounds are used, with the more important criteria applied in the earlier rounds. The use of "must meet" criteria followed by "should meet" criteria is an example (5,8).

Figure 13. Selection Criteria in First and Second Round Tradeoffs (percentage of business citing).

Criteria	Important in First Round	Important in Second Round
Strategic fit/leverages core competencies	78.3%	22.2% [8]
Pay-off	69.5%	36.9% [5]
Risk & probability of success	54.7%	39.4% [4]
Technological capability	48.3%	31.0% [6]
Timing	34.0%	42.9% [1]
Commercialization capability	33.5%	40.9% [2]
Synergy between projects	15.3%	26.6% [7]
Protectability	14.2%	39.9% [3]
Other	40.3%	–

First round criteria are rank-order (by usage).
Second round rankings are shown in parenthesis.

The specific criteria used in each selection round are shown in Figure 13. Not surprisingly, the same list of criteria, with approximately the same rank-order, appears (compare Figures 13 and 12). For the first-round decision, the two most important criteria are, once again:
• Strategic fit and ability to leverage core competencies.
• Payoff (financial and reward).

The rest of the first-round criteria are much as they are in Figure 12: risk, technological capability and timing. Once again, note that most businesses use multiple criteria for the first round, with the average business relying on 3.9 criteria each.

What is interesting is to observe the *second-round* criteria: that is, given that the project meets the payoff or strategic fit criteria, what separates the "good projects" from the "poor" in the next round? The most important is timing, followed by commercialization capability and protectability (see Figure 13). The distribution of responses for the second round is much more diverse than for the first; however, the top three criteria are mentioned only somewhat more frequently than the next three (risk and probability of success, payoff and technological capability).

Moving Forward

Overcoming the challenge of developing an effective portfolio approach is no small task. Our investigation confirms that there are no magic solutions. A number of companies, however, are developing, implementing and achieving better results from their portfolio management approach. As this study has indicated, the best businesses, in terms of portfolio performance, are indeed doing many things differently than the poorer-performing organizations, and can serve as a model for your own business.

The overall conclusion is that none of the portfolio methods has a monopoly on the strengths, and some, including the most popular and the most hyped methods, definitely have their weaknesses. This conclusion strongly suggests that no one method provides a universal solution, and points to the need for a hybrid or combined approach—using several portfolio methods concurrently—as the preferred solution. Additionally, one might wish to de-emphasize the use of financial methods as the single or dominant approach.

Acknowledgements

The authors would like to thank the Industrial Research Institute for its help and support in the design and execution of this study. Equally, we thank Esso Chemical Canada Ltd (Exxon Chemical in Canada), and the Innovation Research Center at McMaster University for providing the financial support to undertake the study.

References and Notes

1. Some firms restrict "portfolio management" to new and improved products, and platform projects with new product potential. Other firms include virtually any development project, such as process improvements, cost reductions, minor product improvements, customer projects, and so on. Thus, terms such as "new product portfolio" or "R&D portfolio" are used interchangeably in this article.

2. Roussel, P., Saad, K.N. and Erickson, T.J. *Third Generation R&D, Managing the Link to Corporate Strategy.* Harvard Business School Press and Arthur D. Little Inc, 1991. Cooper, R.G. and Kleinschmidt, E.J. "Winning businesses in Product Development: Critical Success Factors." *Research Technology Management* 39, 4 (July-Aug 1996): pp. 18-29.

3. Cooper, R.G. and Kleinschmidt, E.J. "Winning Businesses in Product Development: Critical Success Factors." *Research Technology Management* 39, 4, (July-Aug 1995): pp. 18-29.

4. Cooper, R.G. and Kleinschmidt, E.J. "An Investigation into the New Product Process: Steps, Deficiencies and Impact." *Journal of Product Innovation Management* 3, 2, (1986): pp. 71-85.

5. Cooper, R.G., Edgett, S.J. and Kleinschmidt, E.J. *Portfolio Management for New Products.* Reading, MA: Addison-Wesley, 1998.

6. Cooper, R.G., Edgett, S.J. and Kleinschmidt, E.J. "Portfolio Management in New Product Development: Lessons from the Leaders—I." *Research Technology Management* 40, 5, (Sept.-Oct 1997) pp. 16-28.

7. Cooper, R.G., Edgett, S.J. and Kleinschmidt, E.J. "Portfolio Management in New Product Development: Lessons from the Leaders—II." *Research Technology Management* 40, 6, (Nov.-Dec. 1997).

8. Cooper, R.G. *Winning at New Products: Accelerating the Process from Idea to Launch.* Reading, MA: Addison-Wesley, 1993.

9. Factor analysis was undertaken on the six performance metrics in Figure 1 (SPSS-X routine, Varimax rotation, principal components analysis). The results: only a single factor was uncovered, suggesting that the six performance metrics could be combined into a single scale (simple unweighted addition of the six metrics)—a composite score. This single performance scale or gauge is a very robust one, with a high internal consistency (Cronbach coefficient alpha = 0.812).

10. Not all projects should be included in the portfolio (for example, very minor projects or maintenance type projects); thus, "appropriate" projects are specified here.

11. Some of these differences in performances and satisfaction are statistically significant; others are not (see Figures 10 and 11), but nonetheless show definite trends and tendencies.

How SmithKline Beecham Makes Better Resource-Allocation Decisions

Paul Sharpe and Tom Keelin

In 1993, SmithKline Beecham was spending more than half a billion dollars per year on R&D, the lifeblood of any pharmaceuticals company. Ever since the 1989 merger that created the company, however, SB believed that it had been spending too much time arguing about how to value its R&D projects—and not enough time figuring out how to make them more valuable.

With more projects successfully reaching late-stage development, where the resource requirements are greatest, the demands for funding were growing. SB's executives felt an acute need to rationalize their portfolio of development projects. The patent on its blockbuster drug Tagamet was about to expire, and the company was preparing for the impending squeeze: it had to meet current earnings targets and at the same time support the R&D that would create the company's future revenue streams. The result was a "constrained-budget mentality" and a widely shared belief that SB's problem was one of prioritizing development projects.

Major resource-allocation decisions are never easy. For a company like SB, the problem is this: How do you make good decisions in a high-risk, technically complex business when the information you need to make those decisions comes largely from the project champions who are competing against one another for resources? A critical company process can become politicized when strong-willed, charismatic project leaders beat out their less competitive colleagues for resources. That in turn leads to the cynical view that your project is as good as the performance you can put on at funding time.

What was the solution? Some within the company thought that SB needed a directive, top-down approach. But our experience told us that no single executive could possibly know enough about the dozens of highly complex projects being developed on three continents to call the shots effectively. In the past, SB had tried a variety of approaches. One involved long, intensive sessions of interrogating project champions and, in the end, setting priorities by a show of hands. Later that process evolved into a more sophisticated scoring system based on a project's multiple attributes, such as commercial potential, technical risk, and investment requirements. Although the approach looked good on the surface, many people involved in it felt in the end that the company was following a kind of pseudoscience that lent an air of sophistication to fundamentally flawed data assessments and logic.

The company had also been disappointed by a number of more quantitative approaches. It used a variety of valuation techniques, including projections of peak-year sales and five-year net present values. But even when all the project teams agreed to use the same approach—allowing SB to arrive at a numerical prioritization of projects—those of us involved in the process were uncomfortable. There was no transparency to the valuation process, no way of knowing whether the quality of thinking behind the valuations was at all consistent. "Figures don't lie," said one cynical participant, "but liars can figure." At the end of the day, we couldn't escape the perception that decisions were driven by the advocacy skills of project champions—or made behind closed doors in a way that left many stakeholders in the process unpersuaded that the right road had been taken.

As we set out in 1993 to design a better decision-making process, we knew we needed a good technical solution—that is, a valuation methodology that reflected the complexity and risk of our investments. At the same time, we needed a solution that would be credible to the organization. If we solved the technical problem alone, we might find the right direction, but we would fail to get anyone to follow. That is typically what happens as a result of good backroom analysis, however well intentioned and well executed it is. But solving the organizational problem alone is just as bad. Open discussion may lead to agreement, enabling a company to move forward. But without a technically sound compass, will it be moving in the right direction?

The easy part of our task was agreeing on the ultimate goal. In our case, it was to increase shareholder value. The hard part was devising a process that would be credible to all of the interested parties, including top management, dozens of project teams, the heads of SB's four major therapy areas, and executives from key functions such as strategic marketing, finance, and business development—all spread across Europe, the United States, and Japan. In particular, the traditional advocates in the process—the project teams and their therapy area heads—would have to believe that any new process accurately characterized their projects, including their technical and commercial risks. Those who were more distant—leaders of other project teams and therapy areas, regional and functional executives, and top management—would require transparency and consistency. How else could they make any meaningful contribution to the teams' thinking, or compare projects to one another, or understand how projects might affect one another?

Most organizations think of decision making as an event, not a process. They attach great importance to key decision meetings. But in most cases, and SB is no exception, the real problems occur before those meetings ever take place. And so the process that SB designed—a three phase dialogue between the project teams and the company's decision makers—focused on the inputs to the resource-allocation decisions and the role of the organization in preparing those inputs.

Phase I: Generating Alternatives
One of the major weaknesses of most resource-allocation processes is that project advocates tend to take an all-or-nothing approach to budget requests. At SB, that

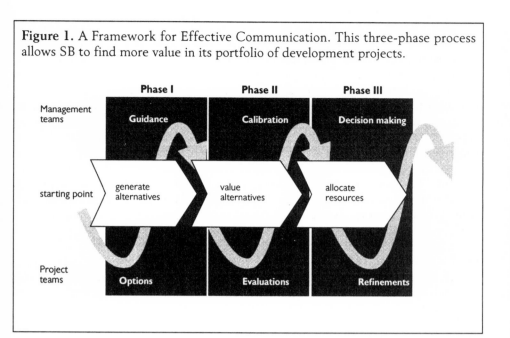

Figure 1. A Framework for Effective Communication. This three-phase process allows SB to find more value in its portfolio of development projects.

meant that project leaders would develop a single plan of action and present it as the only viable approach. Project teams rarely took the time to consider meaningful alternatives—especially if they suspected that doing so might mean a cutback in funding.

And so we insisted that each team develop at least four alternatives: *the current plan* (the team would follow the existing plan of activity), a *"buy-up" option* (the team would be given more to spend on the project), a *"buy-down" option* (the teams would be given less money to spend on the project), and a *minimal plan* (the team would abandon the project while preserving as much of the value earned to date as possible). Working with a facilitator, a team would begin by describing a project's objective, which usually was to develop a particular chemical entity targeted at one or more diseases. Then it would brainstorm about what it would do under each of the four funding alternatives.

Consider a compound under development in SB's cancer area. The current plan was to develop the drug in two formulations, intravenous and oral, for the treatment of two tumor types, A and B, by investing $10 million beyond what had already been invested. (The numbers in this example are not actual figures.) When the team working on the project was asked to develop alternatives to the current plan, they balked. Their project has always been regarded as a star and had received a lot of attention from management. They believe they already had the best plan for the compound's development. They agreed, however, to look at the other alternatives during a brainstorming session.

Several new ideas emerged. Under the buy-down alternative, the company would drop one of the product forms (oral) in one of the markets (tumor type B), saving $2 million. Under the buy-up alternative, the company would increase its investment by $5 million in order to treat a third tumor type (C) with the intravenous form. When the value of those alternatives was later quantified, a new insight emerged. Although the buy-up option increased costs considerably, it also increased value by 30%. Suddenly it occurred to one team member that by selecting only the most valuable combinations of products and markets, they might both increase value significantly and reduce costs in comparison with the current plan. That insight led the team to a new and even more valuable alternative than any they had previously considered: target all three markets while cutting back to just one product form in each market. (See the exhibit "Developing Project Alternatives.") This solution was so powerful that it quickly won project team support and management endorsement as an improvement over the current plan. Although such results are not an inevitable result of insisting alternatives, they are unlikely to occur without it.

Considering alternatives for projects had other benefits. First, ideas that came out of brainstorming sessions on one project could sometimes be applied to others. Second, projects that would have been eliminated under the previous all-or-nothing approach had a chance to survive if one of the new development plans showed an improved return on investment. Third, after walking through preliminary back-of-the-envelope financial projections, the teams had a better picture of the elements of their development plans— time to market, for example, or claims made on the drug's label—had the greatest impact on the drug's expected value. The team could then focus its development work accordingly.

Near the end of this phase, the project alternatives were presented to a peer review board for guidance before any significant evaluation of the alternatives had been performed. Members of the review board, who were managers from key functions and major product groups within the pharmaceuticals organization, tested the fundamental assumptions of each alternative by asking probing questions: In the buy-down alternative, which trial should we eliminate? Should a once-a-day formulation be part of our buy-up alternative? Couldn't we do better by including Japan earlier in the current plan? The discussion session improved the overall quality of the project alternatives and helped build consensus about their feasibility and completeness.

The project teams then revised their alternatives where appropriate and submitted them again for review, this time to the group of senior managers who would, at a later point in the process, make the final investment decisions on all the projects. The group included the chairman of the U.S., European, and international drug divisions; and other senior managers from major corporate functions.

In SB's process, alternatives are created and presented to the senior management group for discussion before any significant evaluation of project alternatives is performed. In many organizations, investment alternatives are presented together with an evaluation; in others, the alternatives are evaluated as soon as they are put forth, before they are fully fleshed out. Instant evaluations often focus on what's wrong with an idea or the data supporting it; they offer insufficient attention to what's right about an idea or how can it be improved.

Although it takes discipline to keep from debating which of the project alternatives are best, it is critical to avoid doing so at this early stage in the process. Premature evaluation kills creativity and the potential to improve decision making along with it.

At SB, we wanted to be sure that we had developed a full range of project alternatives before starting to judge their value. To accomplish that end, the role of the project teams would be to develop the initial alternatives, and the role of management

Figure 2. Developing Project Alternatives. When a project team in SB's cancer area began to consider alternatives for a compound in development, it found that it could create more value for less money.

1 Current plan			2 Buy-down plan			3 Buy-up plan			4 New buy-down plan		
tumor	intravenous	oral	tumor	intravenous	oral	tumor	intravenous	oral	tumor	intravenous	oral
A	✓	✓	A	✓	✓	A	✓	✓	A	✓	
B	✓	✓	B	✓		B	✓	✓	B	✓	
						C	✓		C	✓	

What is the current development plan for this compound?	What if the project's costs had to be reduced?	What if more money were available?	What if we drop the oral form for A and B in order to pursue C?
Develop it for two tumor types in both intravenous and oral formulations.	We would drop the oral program for tumor type B.	We would expand the program to include a third tumor type.	This provides higher expected shareholder value *for less investment* than the current plan.
For an additional investment of $10 million, the expected value of the product is $400 million.	Compared with the current plan, this plan saves $2 million in costs and gives up $20 million in value.	Compared with the current plan, this plan adds $130 million in expected value for an extra $5 million in investment.	Compared with the current plan, this plan adds $100 million in expected value and saves $2 million in costs.
The current plan results in a 40:1 return on investment.	The buy-down plan results in a 48:1 return on investment.	The buy-up plan results in a 35:1 return on investment.	This results in the highest return on investment–63:1.

would be to improve the quality of the alternatives by challenging their feasibility, expanding or extending them, or suggesting additional possibilities.

Phase II: Valuing Alternatives

Once we had engineered the process that took us through phase I, we needed a consistent methodology to value each one of the project alternatives. We chose to use decision analysis because of its transparency and its ability to capture the technical uncertainties and commercial risks of drug development. For each alternative, we constructed a decision tree, using the most knowledgeable experts to help structure the tree and assess the major uncertainties facing each project. (See the insert "How SB Overhauled Its Investment Process.")

We developed six requirements for achieving credibility and buy-in to the valuation of each alternative:

How SB Overhauled Its Investment Process

It was no small task for SB to introduce a new resource-allocation process into a pharmaceutical development area that included 20 major projects, dozens of managers, and more than half a billion dollars of investment. How was a large, complex organization going to overhaul its investment process? The answer was: gradually.

Before the new process was introduced to the entire 20-project portfolio, it went through two pilot tests—first, on a single development project for migraines and, second, on a subsection of the portfolio that included 10 projects. The company's head of development, Paul Nicholson, believed that the people who would be using the new process, such as his staff in the development area and leaders of SB's functional areas, should have significant involvement in the process's design and gradual implementation.

It was important to address the anxiety people felt at the prospect of such a major change. Would the new process, project team members wondered, mean a cutback in their funding? Would it mean termination of their projects? In an industry like pharmaceuticals, where a project leader may work on as few as five or six projects in an entire career, such anxieties could not be taken lightly.

To manage the issue, Nicholson made a commitment to the teams that during the initial pilot no investment decisions would be made. The only objective would be to develop the new approach and gauge its viability.

During the pilot test, we worked to build a valuation methodology that would win the confidence of its future users. The core of the methodology that prevailed was decision analysis. That approach includes problem framing, the creation of alternatives, the use of decision trees to represent risk, options analysis, sensitivity analysis (to represent different viewpoints and focus attention on value drivers), and key output measures of risk-adjusted return. Although such tools are in widespread use, they cannot be applied in cookie-cutter fashion. SB spent considerable effort tailoring the tools to its specific applications.

The pilot phase served to develop consensus about all dimensions of the new process, from its general philosophy to the specific templates and formats that were designed. The project teams and therapy areas were satisfied that the new process could accurately represent their projects, even in complex areas such as the risk associated with product development and commercialization. Regional and functional management as well as decision makers could see that transparency and consistency were built into the process. The pilot was followed by a full-scale rollout of the new process in 1995.

The acid test of whether a valuation methodology has won credibility is this: it is credible if it no longer attracts attention to itself. When that happens—as it did at SB by late 1995—the attention of the organization shifts from How should we measure value? to How can we create more value?

- First, the same information set must be provided for every project. We developed templates that are consistent in scope but flexible enough to represent the differences among the projects and their alternatives.

Figure 3. Creating a High-Value Portfolio

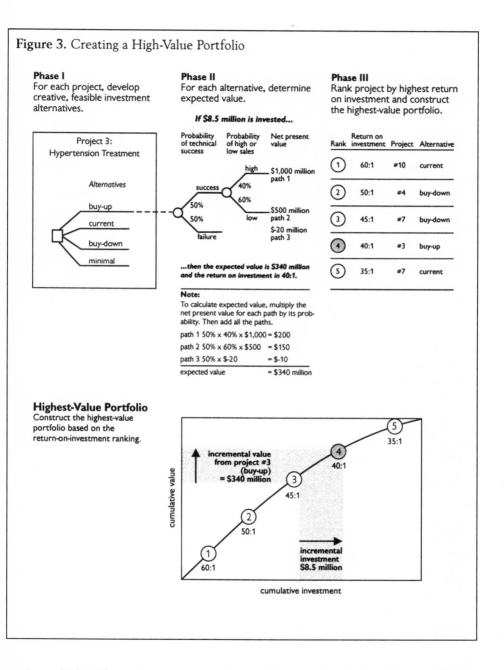

Phase I
For each project, develop creative, feasible investment alternatives.

Project 3:
Hypertension Treatment

Alternatives

buy-up

current

buy-down

minimal

Phase II
For each alternative, determine expected value.

If $8.5 million is invested...

Probability of technical success	Probability of high or low sales	Net present value
	high	$1,000 million path 1
success	40%	
50%	60%	
50%	low	$500 million path 2
failure		$-20 million path 3

...then the expected value is $340 million and the return on investment in 40:1.

Note:
To calculate expected value, multiply the net present value for each path by its probability. Then add all the paths.

path 1 50% x 40% x $1,000 = $200
path 2 50% x 60% x $500 = $150
path 3 50% x $-20   = $-10
expected value   = $340 million

Phase III
Rank project by highest return on investment and construct the highest-value portfolio.

Rank	Return on investment	Project	Alternative
1	60:1	#10	current
2	50:1	#4	buy-down
3	45:1	#7	buy-down
4	40:1	#3	buy-up
5	35:1	#7	current

Highest-Value Portfolio
Construct the highest-value portfolio based on the return-on-investment ranking.

incremental value from project #3 (buy-up) = $340 million

incremental investment $8.5 million

cumulative value

cumulative investment

• Second, the information must come from reliable sources. Experts from inside and outside the company must be selected before anyone knows what their specific inputs will be regarding the major uncertainties the development team faces.
• Third, the sources of information must be clearly documented. The date and place of each interview with an expert must be recorded along with the key assumptions

that were made and any important insights that came up in the conversation. Thus management can dig as deep as it likes into the assessment's "pedigree" to test its quality.

• Fourth, the assessments must undergo peer review by experienced managers across functions and therapeutic areas. Those managers can then make comparisons across all projects and gauge, for example, if the project teams are being consistent in assessing similar uncertainties. They can determine, for instance, if the teams are using similar assumptions when assessing the probability of passing key development milestones.

• Fifth, the valuations must be compared with those done by external industry observers and market analysts to establish that the numbers are realistic.

• Sixth, the impact of each variable on the project's expected value must be identified. Doing so gives management and the project teams a clear understanding of the key value drivers so that they can focus decision making and implementation in ways that add the most value.

We agreed early on that the project teams would use ranges rather than single-point forecasts to describe future possibilities. Using ranges enhances credibility by avoiding false precision. In previous development cycles, nothing derailed us faster than having a strategic marketing expert stand in front of a room full of scientists while trying to defend a statement like, "The worldwide market for Alzheimer's disease treatments in 2010 will be $21.2 billion." The use of ranges—with thorough explanations of the high and low ends—has become standard practice at SB for forecasting all uncertainties, from product profile to market share to prices achieved.

We increased transparency and consistency in yet another way by having a specially designated group of analysts process the valuation information and draw preliminary insights. Having this work done by a neutral group was a relief to many project team members, who were rarely satisfied with the previous approaches to valuation, as well as to the top management group, who were tired of trying to make sense of widely disparate types of analysis. As the company's CFO for pharmaceuticals put it, "Inconsistent valuations are worse than none."

Once the alternatives had been valued, a second peer-review meeting was held to make sure that all the participants had a chance to question and understand the results. The step was designed to ensure that no surprises would emerge when the decisions were being made. And again, the peer review was followed by a senior management review that provided an opportunity to challenge, modify, and agree on the underlying assumptions driving the valuations. During the meeting, however, the senior managers were explicitly asked not to begin discussing which alternatives to invest in; instead, they were asked only to confirm that they understood and believed the valuations. And if they didn't, why not? What seemed out of line?

In this give-and-take, senior managers and project team members were able to learn from one another. For example, senior executives wanted to be sure that all the cross-project effects had been taken into account. Was marketing success in one project dependent on establishing a franchise with an earlier product? Would a new product cannibalize an existing product, and if so, would the result be a higher or a lower total value? Was the technical approach in two projects the same, so that success in one would mean success in the other? Did SB have the staff in its technical departments—or the ability to contract out—in order to accelerate three projects simultaneously?

Such conversations improved the quality of the valuations and led to additional learning about technical commercial synergy.

Once everyone had reviewed the valuation of the project alternatives and agreed that the inputs and logic were valid, the stage was set for successful decision making in the next phase. Suppose an agreement had been reached that a certain drug had only a 10% probability of obtaining approval in oral form. Suppose it turned out after a roll-up of all the project alternatives that the 10% probability killed the project because its expected value was too low. Under SB's new approach, no one could come back and arbitrarily challenge the probability assessment. Instead, someone would need an argument that would overturn the project's pedigree—the basis of the 10% assessment in the first place. Given the thorough nature of the process, the creation of such an argument would be extremely difficult unless significant new information had come to light.

For example, in one case a senior manager remarked that a project team had given an estimate of a product's likely registration with the FDA that was too high. The response from the project team was, "What probability would be more appropriate, if this one is too high?" The facilitator probed the manager's thinking: "Do you think it's too high relative to other projects? Or that it's too high based on other considerations?" he asked. Following another exchange of views with the expert who had offered the original probability assessment, the judgment stood. In the end, the likelihood of FDA registration turned out to be a key driver of value. The manager who had challenged the estimate was satisfied that the company was using the best information available and did not question the ultimate funding decision.

That exchange illustrates an important dimension of SB's decision-making process. If challenges such as "too high" or "too low" are accepted without requiring the skeptics to put forth alternative estimates or clear rationales, then snap judgments by senior managers can carry the same weight as carefully researched plans. When that happens, project team members become cynical. They come to expect that management will badger them into providing estimates that yield the answers they want.

Phase III: Creating a Portfolio and Allocating Resources

The goal of this phase was to create the highest-value portfolio based on all the project alternatives that had been developed. This was no easy task: with 20 major projects—each of which had four well-conceived alternatives—the number of possible configurations was enormous. We appointed a neutral analytic team, rather than the project advocates, to carry out a systematic approach to identifying the highest-value portfolio based on return on investment.

The portfolio could then be examined along a number of strategic dimensions, including stability under different scenarios, balance across therapeutic areas and stages in the development pipeline, and feasibility of success given SB's technical and commercial resources. Because the senior managers had already agreed—and vigorously debated—the underlying project descriptions (phase I) and valuations (phase II) for each alternative, they now focused their complete attention on the portfolio decisions.

It turned out that the portfolio with the highest expected return on investment represented a significant departure from the status quo. Only four projects would receive their expected funding, ten would get increased funding, and six would cut back. The senior management group was able to discuss the new portfolio without wasting time and energy questioning the numbers and assumptions.

The first 14 project decisions, which involved increasing or maintaining funding levels, were made without controversy. However, when it came time to discuss the first project whose funding would be cut, the manager of the relevant therapeutic area challenged the decision. The meeting's chairman listened to his case for maintaining the current funding and then asked whether that case was reflected in the project valuations. The manager agreed that it was, but repeated the argument that SB would loose value by terminating the project. The chairman agreed that value would be lost but pointed out that the funds originally scheduled for the project would create more value when applied elsewhere. That ended a potentially explosive discussion.

The new process not only reduced the controversy in the resource-allocation process, it also led the company to change its investment strategy. Although top management had set out to cut back on the company's development budget, they now saw their investment decision in a new light: they believed the new portfolio to be 30% more valuable than the old one—without any additional investment. Furthermore, the marginal return on additional investment had tripled from 5:1 to 15:1. To exploit this opportunity, the company ultimately decided to increase development spending by more than 50%.

The three-phase process—generating alternatives, valuing them, and creating a portfolio—has led to shared understanding among decision makers and development staff about the best investment options for the company. The process the company adopted is based on experience that no single value metric, facilitation technique, peer review meeting, or external validations approach on its own can solve the complex resource-allocation problem faced by many companies like SB. In the end, we learned that by tackling the soft issues around resource allocation, such as information quality credibility, and trust, we had also addressed the hard ones: How much should we invest and where should we invest it?

Integrating the Fuzzy Front End of New Product Development

Anil Khurana and Stephen R. Rosenthal

Many companies formulate product strategies, routinely choose among new product concepts, and plan new product development projects. Yet, when asked where the greatest weakness in product innovation is, the managers at these companies indicate the fuzzy front end (1). They recite some familiar symptoms of front-end failure:
• New products are abruptly canceled in midstream because they don't "match the company strategy."
• "Top priority" new product projects suffer because key people are "too busy" to spend the required time on them.
• New products are frequently introduced later than announced because the product concept has become a moving target.

Times have changed since 1983 when Donald Schön described product development as a "game" in which "general managers distance themselves from the uncertainties inherent in product development and ... technical personnel protect themselves against the loss of corporate containment"(2). Since then, new product development has become a core business activity that needs to be closely tied to the business strategy and a process that must be managed through analysis and decision making (3). Now, general managers cannot distance themselves from the uncertainties of product development, nor can technical personnel protect themselves against corporate commitment.

As enhanced capabilities for concurrent engineering, rapid prototyping, and smoothly functioning supplier partnerships have helped reduce product design and development times, management attention has begun to shift to cross-functional-front-end strategic, conceptual, and planning activities that typically precede the detailed design and development of a new product (4). Here, new product ideas gain the shape, justification, plans, and support leading to their approval and subsequent execution. Yet, despite widespread recognition of the front end's importance, there has been limited systematic examination directed at improving its effectiveness.

Our exploratory study of front-end activity in eleven companies highlights best practice based on our assessment of seven critical activities. We begin by taking a systems view of the front-end process based on existing academic and practitioner literature.

After discussing how companies should manage the front end as part of a normative model of the process, we use data from case studies to identify challenges and solutions (5). Next, we describe an approach for creating a successful process and present a checklist and diagnostic for front-end practice.

What Is the "Front End"?

Prior research has focused on the success factors for new product development (NPD). While many of these factors relate to design execution and project management issues, some pertain to the front end (6). Consistent with Roberts's model, we classified the front-end-related success factors identified in prior research into foundation and project-specific elements (7). The distinction is important because the two require different skills and levels of effort. Also, without adequate foundation elements, product and project success becomes a matter of luck. Project-specific activities focus on the individual project and require the project team's effort to ensure a useful product definition and project plan. These include a product concept statement and evaluation, product definition, and project planning. Foundation elements, on the other hand, cut across projects and form the basis for project-specific activities. Thus they typically require enterprise-wide support, senior management participation, and a cross-functional effort.

Foundation Elements

Without a clear product strategy, a well-planned portfolio of new products, and an organization structure that facilitates product development via ongoing communications and cross-functional sharing of responsibilities, front-end decisions become ineffective (8). Achieving these preconditions provide a foundation for streams of successful new products.

Key product strategy elements include the formulation and communication of a strategic vision, a product-platform strategy, and a product-line strategy to support the go/no-go decision for a new product (9). Previous research suggests that familiarity with the product strategy enables appropriate decisions on NPD timing and target markets and also an assessment of the fit between the product and the core competence of the business unit (10).

In addition to a product vision, business units need to plan their portfolio of new product development activities, which goes beyond the traditional marketing view of having a product for every segment, market, and price point. Portfolio planning should map all new product initiatives across the business to balance risk and potential return, short and long time horizons, or mature and emerging markets. At the same time, the portfolio plan should ensure consistency with the product and business strategy (11). If well done, it facilitates the allocation of scarce resources to new product development projects.

An essential precondition is establishing the organization structure for new product development. Decisions on structure, communication networks, and roles are made at a business-unit level. Research has highlighted several requirements for the product development organization and its functioning (12), such as using a matrix or project form, organizing NPD around core business/product teams rather than traditional functions, using design and communication tools including information systems, and establishing controls and incentives as rewards (13).

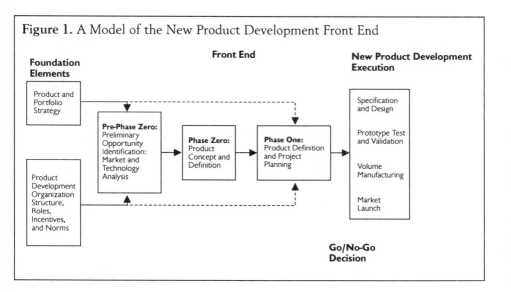

Figure 1. A Model of the New Product Development Front End

Project-Specific Elements

Product-specific front-end activities help clarify the product concept, define product and market requirements, and develop plans, schedules, and estimates of the project's resource requirements. However, they stop far short of creating detailed designs and specifications for the product and its components.

The product concept is a preliminary identification of customer needs, market segments, competitive situations, business prospects, and alignment with existing business and technology plans. Research suggests that the product concept should be clear so that managers can sense whether the newly defined opportunity seems worth exploring (14). Managers need to understand customer needs and identify the potential technologies and applications to satisfy them (15). For tangible products, the product concept is usually illustrated with a sketch or three-dimensional model. Because such concepts are relatively inexpensive to produce, managers often create several before selecting one to fully design and develop. Early targets—measured in product cost, product performance, project cost, and time to market—set the stage for generating various product concepts.

The product definition, an elaboration of the product concept (16), incorporates judgments about the target market, competitive offerings, and the time and resources for bringing the new product to market. The definition activity includes identification of customer and user needs, technologies, and regulatory requirements. These lead to a choice of product features and functions, target market segments, and design priorities. Research on the implementation of the front end indicates that an explicit, stable product definition and an understanding of the trade-offs among customer requirements, technology, and resource/cost constraints are important factors for success (17).

Project planning includes project priorities and tasks, a master schedule, projected resource requirements, and other supporting information. Here, it is critical to communicate the project priorities, provide adequate resources, and anticipate contingencies. And, despite progress in new product development practices, typical systems do not adequately address these critical issues (18).

The Front-End Process

We take a process view of the front end because earlier studies and our preliminary research suggested that the individual activities, while logically interrelated, often are treated independently (19). Accordingly, we present a systems view of the front end (See Figure 1). This process description is consistent with growing empirical evidence of the need to simultaneously consider overall product strategy (foundation elements) with project-relevant input such as product ideas, market analysis, and technology options (20). *Thus understanding the interrelationships between the activities is as important as the activities themselves.*

Product strategy and portfolio plans should drive the complete new product development effort, in conjunction with the capabilities and competencies of the product development organization, with its inherent assumptions about roles, communications, and culture. These elements are thus preconditions or foundations for the explicit activities in new product development. Many companies implement a formal phase-review management system to define and guide the explicit project-specific activities: this review process involves the process itself, roles that make it work, and primary deliverables (21).

• *Phases of the Front-End Process.* Companies generally begin work on new product opportunities (often called "pre-phase zero") when they first recognize, in a semiformal way, an opportunity (22). If the newly defined opportunity is worth exploring, the company assigns a small group, sometimes including suppliers, to work together on the product concept and definition (phase zero).

In phase one, the company assesses the business and technical feasibility of the new product, confirms the product definition, and plans the NPD project. Thus the development team identifies the new product, its development, and the business rationale for proceeding. The front end is complete at the end of this phase when the team presents the business case and the business unit either commits to funding, staffing, and launch of the project or kills the project.

• *Front-End Roles.* A core team (including the project leader) and an executive review committee of senior functional managers responsible for making the go/no-go decision typically conducts the process we've described. During phase one, if not sooner, companies assign individuals from all functional areas as members of the core team for the product development project. Normally, if a company approves the project at the end of phase one, a full complement of people to design, develop, test, manufacture, and launch the new product supplements the core team. Previous studies have indicated that team structure varies in composition, size, and leadership (23). Often, the core team includes selected suppliers as partners; their knowledge of technology, costs, and design and manufacturing lead times can contribute to product definition and project planning.

• *Primary Front-End Deliverables.* The front-end activities result in the product concept (clear and aligned with customer needs), the product definition (explicit and stable), and the project plan (priorities, resource plans, and project schedules) (24).

Table 1. Front-End Activities

	Typical Practices	Degree of Implementation		
		High	**Medium**	**Low**
Foundation Elements	Product strategy formulation and articulation	Clear and well communicated by a responsible individual or group	Partly exists, but no individual or group is consistently responsible	Unclear or nonexistent
	Product portfolio planning	Explicit and thorough	Implicit at best	Not done or considered
	Product development organization structure	Clear and well communicated	Clear in theory but not always in practice	Ambiguous
Project-Specific Elements	Product concept	Detailed customer and technology choices and features with clear priorities	Detailed customer and technology choices and features, unclear priorities	Haphazardly done
	Product definition	Complete and generally unchanging	Complete but unstable	Incomplete at go/no-go decision
	Value chain considerations in product definition	Upstream and downstream issues considered; part of routine core team responsibilities	Many issues considered; project manager responsible for ensuring all such issues are covered	Product development means product only; supply chain issues rarely brought up
	Front-end project definition and planning	Explicit and thorough	Done but not rigorous	Casual

Continued

Front-End Challenges and Solutions

To understand the front-end processes and practices at fifteen business units in eleven U.S., Japanese, and European companies, we interviewed more than seventy-five managers (for our research approach, see the Appendix). Our study focused on incremental innovations—the majority of NPD efforts. Accordingly, our findings deal with improving the performance of existing products or extending them to new applications, rather than with developing radically new products.

We have grouped the typical practices that characterize the foundation elements and project-specific activities into three implementation clusters—high, medium, and low (See Table 1). This analysis of our data also supports our earlier literature-based classification of the three foundation elements and the three project-specific activities. Our analysis does recognize an additional activity: adding value-chain considerations to the front-end process.

We found significant gaps in how the case study companies implemented the seven front-end elements, even for those companies that claimed to have the front-end product generation processes we described earlier (See Table 1). Even the companies that prepared their own detailed process descriptions generally didn't avoid problems

		Degrees of Implementation in Companies Studied		
	Implementation	**High**	**Medium**	**Low**
Foundation Elements	Product strategy 　Product vision 　Technology planning	D,F,G,J	B,E,H,I,K	A,C
	Product portfolio planning 　Evaluation of risk and diversification 　Cross-project understanding 　Link to resource planning	F,J	A,D,E,G,K	B,C,H,I
	Product development organizational structure 　Cross-functional project organization 　Clear roles 　Established communication structures 　Leadership by executive reviews	F,G,J	A,C,D,H,I,K	B,E
Project-Specific Elements	Product concept 　Clear concept 　Understand management vision for product 　Identify customer needs	C,D,F,G	A,B,I,J	E,H,K
	Product definition 　Complete and explicit definition 　Stable; avoid unnecessary change 　Anticipate market and technology evolution	C,F	A,D,G,I,J	B,H,K
	Value chain considerations 　Early supplier involvement 　Downstream issues—logistics, service 　Service and logistics representative on team	A,F,J	C,D,G,H	B,E,I,K
	Front-end project definition and planning 　Clear project priorities 　Aggregate NPD project planning 　Contingency planning	F,J	A,C,D,G,H,K	B,E,I

Table 1. Front-End Activities *(Continued)*

Note: Letters refer to the eleven companies in the research.

that they could have resolved at the front end. In fact, only companies F and, possibly, G and J could claim to have most of the capabilities for an effective front end.

Foundation Elements at the Case Study Companies

Next we discuss in detail how the case study sites managed the foundation elements in order to provide insights for companies trying to improve their NPD efforts.

• *Product strategy.* Our research suggests that despite their intentions, very few companies have clear product strategies to guide their decisions on new product opportunities. In our sample of eleven companies, we rated only two as outstanding (F and G) and two as satisfactory (D and J), while the remaining seven were seriously lacking. We identified several deficiencies in formulating and articulating a product strategy and the connections between product strategy and the core NPD activities (See Figure 1):

- There were product development teams and product managers, but no one was in charge of formulating a product strategy, even at the senior management level.
- Several of the companies made new product development decisions based on project-specific criteria rather than considerations of strategic fit.
- Business strategy was not specific to markets and products.
- R&D, largely insulated from the product development group, funded projects based on superior technology rather than on their potential to satisfy particular product requirements.

The outstanding companies in our sample had countered these deficiencies. The power of a clear product strategy was evident at company F, where we studied the fourth in a series of eight planned sequential product launches based on a common platform (25). The company had designed this platform to meet explicit customer, market and technology guidelines, with which each successive release was consistent. The vision of the business, product, project, and technology enabled successive product development teams for this platform to consistently deliver a product that met every target.

- *Product Portfolio Planning*. More than a third of the companies studied did not plan a product development portfolio. Even when they did, planning at all but two of the research sited, F and J, was sporadic and incomplete. This neglect can be traced to a combination of vague product strategy, measurement difficulties in establishing risk/return profiles, and ambiguous overall responsibility.

While company H traditionally lacked a clear product strategy, senior managers had begun to realize that they were in a mature, threatened business. In response, they made their function managers aware of basic portfolio planning, with encouraging results. Their portfolio now includes a combination of different products with both established and new technologies, instead of traditional projects with incremental improvements to the familiar product line. The company also enhanced the role of the executive review committee, known as the product approval committee, to include assessment of the match between a new product concept and the existing product portfolio in risk, time horizons, and markets.

In contrast, company F—which is very successful in its business—constantly monitored the parameters of its product development portfolio, such as time horizon, risk, expected returns, required investments, and needed capabilities. Senior managers and project and product managers continually discussed the nature of the development portfolio and additions to make.

Regardless of the methods a company uses for new product portfolio planning, it needs to be part of an integrated front-end process. Our research suggests that there is often a discontinuity between portfolio planning and the front end of the traditional process. For example, if a project is killed at the front end because of technological infeasibility, the resulting gap in the development portfolio will become apparent only if front-end activities and portfolio planning are linked.

- *Product Development Organization Structure*. We focus here on three roles at the front end—the project leader, the core team, and the executive review group—and on related communication structures (26). At the companies that measured best along this dimension (F, G, and J), the project leader was responsible for promoting the interests of the project and the core team right from the start. This role included lobbying for support and resources (being an "ambassador") and coordinating technical or design issues (27). These project leaders initiated such communication early during the product/project definition and planning stages. At company F, project managers established communication channels, role definitions, and cross-functional mechanisms for the development team, as part of the product and project definition.

All the companies in our sample, except for companies B and E, had a cross-functional core team do the analytic work of product definition and project planning. However, the role of the team varied among the companies and development products. Company A's first autonomous product development team was successful because four ambitious, creative team members communicated well. However, subsequent teams were not as successful because the core team members were unclear about their responsibility increasing the product concept and definition. In contrast, teams at company F operated more systematically and successfully. A small core team including the idea champion, a senior manager, and a potential project leader met early on and negotiated key roles and responsibilities. This nucleus group then recruited the full team and ensured that all members agreed on the definition of roles and responsibilities. This structure of team roles and responsibilities was part of the product concept statement and was formally acknowledged in the product definition and project planning documents. Establishing the core team early, clearly defining roles and responsibilities for the team, and facilitating supporting communications played a major role in company F's success both in new product development process and the market itself.

Product success appears to be strongly associated with establishment of a cross-functional executive review committee. Only companies F and J had such a review. Company A's review committee focused on technical issues, with the result that executives failed to have a holistic perspective. In contrast, the committee at company F used each phase review to develop strategic and operational skills and establish norms for communications and consensus building. It also guided the core team while making critical choices and trade-offs or making decisions that might have an impact on the business unit's strategy beyond that particular product. At both companies F and J, the executive group worked like a business team rather than functional representatives, consistently developed product strategy and engaged in new product portfolio planning, and formulated explicit project priorities (time, cost, and quality).

For an effective front-end process, the roles of the project leader, the core team, and the executive review committee must complement each other. Explicitly defining these roles by answering the following questions will make the front end less "fuzzy":
• Should the core team resolve product definition and project planning issues or refer them to an executive committee?
• Who is responsible for ensuring that product definition and concept testing are balanced between thoroughness and speed?
• Who should ensure that resources are allocated to a project, as specified in the project plan?
• Who should identify emerging technologies for inclusion in future product platforms?

- Who has the authority to ensure that products developed by several business units or a unit and one or more "partners" are aligned along product/component interfaces, development schedules, market focus, and technology commitments?

Project-Specific Activities at Case Study Companies.

Now we concentrate on project-specific activities at the front end: clarifying the product concept, stabilizing the product definition, considering the value chain in the product definition, and defining and planning the front-end project.

- *Product Concept.* Our research revealed that clarifying the product concept at the front end was surprisingly difficult. Only four companies (C, D, F, and G) had succeeded in consistently developing clear, explicit, and precise descriptions of the product concept. At several companies, the concept was unclear because senior managers did not communicate their expectation of the product's core benefits, choice of market segments, and pricing to the development team.

One company resolved this gap between management's vision of the product concept and the team's understanding of it by setting specific criteria for the features appropriate to the product. It created a database for new product features—based on various inputs from field service, special customers, R&D, marketing, and customer feedback. It then assessed these inputs in phases zero and one, based on senior management's vision of the product, engineering feasibility, marketing needs, resource requirements, price targets, and schedule—and classified them into "red," "green," and "yellow" items. The company would never pursue red items in the current program (but could consider them for the next-generation product). Green items were necessary of the current product; the company chose them based on need, feasibility, and other constraints. Yellow items needed more evaluation, so the company postponed them for subsequent release.

At several case study sites, the product concept was unclear because the companies H and K, products lack what Clark and Fujimoto call "external integrity" (28). To make customer expectations and product features more consistent, sophisticated companies (such as companies C and F) try to look beyond the customer's "voice" to "action," by using techniques such as videotapes of customers' use of existing products.

- *Product Definition.* All the companies in our study realized the pivotal importance of the early product definition. Yet most had failed to generate clear, stable definitions. While rapid shifts in technology and markets make it impossible for some companies to freeze the product definition, most of the companies studied acknowledged the difficulties this caused in the execution stages of product development projects and the high associated costs. In fact, only managers at companies C and F felt that they had developed approaches for dealing with instability and change.

For technology-driven companies (especially company H), delays in product definition entailed the risk of an unstable, expanding definition in which design engineers continued to add unneeded complexity. Managers at companies C and F made a concerted effort to freeze the product definition early on. For them, the challenge was to balance the requisite flexibility with the avoidable uncertainty.

Company F discovered a creative solution for keeping up with and capturing market information while minimizing changes in the product definition—what we call the "missed elevator" approach. The program manager realized that technological or feature enhancements for any product would never end. He required the product definition to include new features and feasible solutions to customer needs, as long as they could definitely be achieved by the planned milestone for that product release. If a customer need or technology-driven feature "missed the elevator," it would go into the next product release or "elevator." This approach to managing product development by having multi-release platform planning may become the next form of product development and management. Not only does it help achieve the balance between stability and flexibility, but it also leverages technological strengths and organizational resources (29). Thus more companies now include, in their front-end deliberations, the definition of multiple-release products in which each release intentionally involved only a moderate level of new technology development

• *Value Chain Considerations.* While NPD research has highlighted the supplier's role in new product development, we found that some companies have a broader value chain perspective at the product concept and definition stages (30). This becomes necessary as product designs and market delivery systems are more competitive and complex. And customers do not buy only the tangible product by a package that includes the product itself, the company, the brand image, the sales interaction, the delivery process, the after-sales service, and the follow-up relationship. The development team should envision and plan for this package at the front end; otherwise it may ignore downstream requirements and not design products for ease of distribution, installation, or repairs.

We found that these practices, while familiar at the execution stage, are less aggressively and creatively pursued at the front end. Of the eleven companies in the study, only four (A, D, F, and J) were adequate along this dimension. We observed several failures and some creative solutions. Company A, a special industrial products manufacturer, faced new maintenance problems and poor telecommunications support in providing field service. As a result, field service engineers became regular members of the core development team at the front end. At company D, the new product development team consulted with so-called "customer supply specialists."

As another example, Hewlett-Packard's printer division had thousands of stock-keeping units (SKUs) for its products being shipped to different parts of the world. HP resolved this problem of excess variety with "design for postponement"; it redesigned the product so that only the core printer SKU was stocked in regional distribution warehouses. It stocked attachments such as power packs, power cables, connectors, and even instruction manuals in different languages at the distribution points and assembled the final package for shipment only after it received a firm shipment order. In fact, it designed the packaging itself so that it could easily insert and assemble all the attachments. The result was enhanced flexibility and reduced inventory costs, along with the needed product variety (31). For all subsequent product development efforts, HP has routinely included downstream considerations at the front end.

• *Front-End Product Definition and Planning.* At this part of the front end, we observed confusion about project priorities, incomplete resource planning, and inadequate contingency planning. Our discussions with core team members and project leaders led us to believe that fuzzy project priorities were the single most important reason for NPD delays, product over-engineering, and product-strategy mismatches. For example, company A initiated its mid-range product as a cheap-technology, low-performance version of its high-end product. Yet management had always visualized a cheap-technology, high-performance product. Finally, when the product came on the market several months behind schedule, it exceed its performance targets but no longer met its unit-cost goals. At another company, managers solved this common problem by comparing—at the front end—three kinds of project priorities for any new product development project: scope (product functionality), schedule (timing), and resources (cost). Senior management, the core team, and the (as yet unappointed) project leader at the pre-phase zero stage decided the relative ranking of the three priorities for the project's duration and communicated it to all project participants.

Companies must anticipate resource requirements, train people to acquire the necessary capabilities, and then ensure needs-availability matching based on project priorities. Executives repeatedly told us that they had too few people to staff their many NPD projects. At company J, managers used a capacity matrix to assess and assign staff. Senior managers selected the best projects, set goals, and reserved resources. Company F, which also used a form of capacity matrix, faced a complicated challenge of resource planning. Like every organization, it had a core group of irreplaceable people who were in great demand for every project. When planning a next-generation product, the managers realized that the team member they wanted was heading a current project. To avoid such problems in the future, management resolved to both train more people for such assignments and also plan early for staffing and skills requirements.

Companies can manage the risks of new product development with thorough contingency planning—generating multiple product concepts, developing alternative technologies in parallel and, in some instances, even creating competing designs for products and subsystems (32). Yet, surprisingly, we found that most companies (including company F) focused contingency plans most on regulatory issues such as safety or environmental requirements. Apparently, project planners assumed that they would find technology solutions without considering cost and quality. When the timing of a new product introduction is important, reasonable back-up plans are needed to avoid delayed market launch. One approach is to build in contingent product features in case the planned ones do not work. Taking risk management seriously and linking product definition activities with project planning can lead to appropriate contingency plans.

Recognizing Interrelationships

New we discuss several critical interrelationships among individual success factors and approaches for managing them (33). Our examples are from company F, which had the most effective front end of the cases studied.

Companies should consider product strategy and the product development portfolio at the start of the project-specific front end. Company F held a kickoff meeting even before it had refined the concept and assembled the full core team. Attendees included senior managers, the idea champion, and some core team members. While much discussion focused on the basic product concept, it also included how the concept filled a gap in the business strategy and how it related to and compared with other products and on-going projects. As a result, subsequent problems of mismatches between the product and the product strategy or shortage of project staffing were rare.

Companies should have a clear product strategy to enable a stable product definition. Everyone at company F accepted the notion that product strategy should guide technology choices and selected product features. Thus the company used its multi-release product strategy to simplify the definition: its adoption of the "missed elevator" approach simultaneously encouraged stable technology and feature choices that were governed by a long-term vision over several product releases, while facilitating new releases on time.

Companies should integrate portfolio planning and NPD project planning. Company F had established two distinct but formally linked planning processes. The strategic planning process involved managers from various functions and considered product strategy, product development portfolios, and overall resources. Thus portfolio planning yielded long-term commitments that the managers could invoke when planning staff requirements and project priorities for a specific new product concept. They implemented two important practices when planning individual projects: establishment of schedules and allocation of staff and budgets, and specification of inputs such as technology from other business groups. First, they made the strategic business plan available to all core team members and considered the product definition in the context of the strategic business plan. Second, senior managers oversaw the core team's decisions and actions. For example, the project manager may be part of the strategic business planning process or may report to someone who is.

A Well-Engineered Front-End Process

How can a company improve its front-end practices to achieve success in new product development? It is enough to improve the activities we have described? We suggest that best practice in new product development goes beyond simply adopting these activities. Success depends on how companies integrate dimensions and elements of product development (34).

Our research highlighted certain challenges in integration of the front end beyond the obvious need for cross-functional effort. First because project-specific activities build on foundation activities, companies should ensure that the foundation elements are aligned with the product development process and project-specific activities. Second, they should ensure consistency between strategic and operational activities. The challenge is to make strategy explicit enough to guide day-to-day choices for new product development. We found integration of these two factors was rare but extremely potent. At the companies studied, we observed several kinds of integration problems:

• Senior managers sometimes delegated the formulation of a product strategy to product and R&D managers.

• The product development staff often made decisions that affected other products and business unit strategy. (While the core team faces technical uncertainty about the product and manufacturing and distribution processes, resolving cross-project issues or providing guidelines should be senior management responsibilities.)

• Managers in various functions and organizational levels rarely ensured consistency and links among R&D activities, product strategy, and current product development. (Huge R&D investments can be wasted by pursuing superior technology capability unnecessary to the organization's espoused business strategy.)

• Managers frequently took on product development projects without committing adequate resources. (Often there is a misconception that project development staff working on multiple projects improved efficiency. The result is long delays in product launch and lost revenues. With ongoing downsizing in many companies, this kind

Table 2. Checklist for Diagnosing the Front End

Formality of Front-End Process	Integration of Activities
☐ 1. Customer and market information is used early on to set scope for product (target markets, customer segments, features, price).	☐ 1. There is a clear vision of product lines and platforms for specific markets.
☐ 2. Core team jointly reviews product concept and senior management formally approves.	☐ 2. R&D and NPD have matching agendas and plans.
☐ 3. Early concept and other feasibility prototypes are planned, tested, and completed at front end so that there are no surprises later.	☐ 3. Balance is sought and achieved among multiple NPD projects belonging to different platforms/product lines (e.g., risks, novelty).
☐ 4. Product definition is explicitly developed and documented.	☐ 4. Project priorities are consistent with product strategy, portfolio plans, and resource availability.
☐ 5. Major supplier and tooling considerations are explicit at front end.	☐ 5. Resource allocations consider multiple project requirements and their relative priorities and pre-existing project commitments.
☐ 6. Manufacturing, distribution, and logistics requirements are planned; product concept is modified to reflect process and logistics constraints.	☐ 6. Early identification of technical and organizational interfaces is done for systems products so that development can proceed smoothly.
☐ 7. Need for new technology for products is clearly stated.	☐ 7. Core front-end team includes representatives from manufacturing, logistics, and after-sales service, apart from engineering and marketing.
☐ 8. Project targets (time, cost, quality) and relative priorities are clear.	☐ 8. Staffing policies and project-specific staffing are consistent with the product strategy.
☐ 9. Resource requirements are formally defined.	☐ 9. Need for new innovations is anticipated so that extensive innovation is not required during the product development process.
☐ 10. Roles and responsibilities for tasks and communications for core team are clear and well executed.	☐ 10. If there is uncertainty on any dimensions—e.g., technology or markets—organization had carefully planned alternative approach.
☐ 11. Roles for executive review team are clear and well executed (review criteria, decision responsibility, ongoing interaction with core team).	

of neglect is becoming chronic (35). Senior managers need to help product and R&D managers understand a project's relative importance.)
• Senior managers did little to measure and reward cross-functional teamwork. (Front-end participants need to know that management values this contributions.)

Balancing Front-End Explicitness and Flexibility
Management of the front end also requires a balance between getting things right and being flexible during NPD execution. Other front-end elements and activities should also be balanced. There is a natural tension between planning to reduce risk

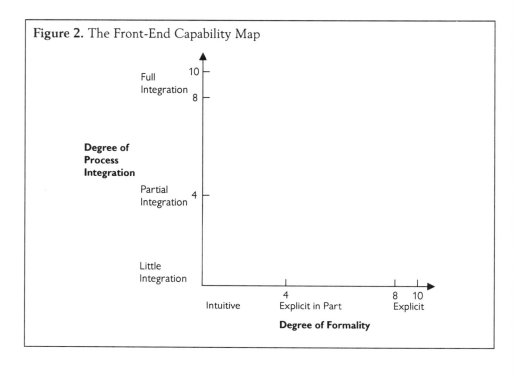

Figure 2. The Front-End Capability Map

and responding to inherent uncertainties. For example, we suggest that product strategy and portfolio planning be explicit, yet we recognize that some subsequent shifts in the product definition are inevitable, forcing contingent actions. Furthermore, postponing the final decisions at the front end by continuing the development of parallel concepts or solutions may reduce uncertainty (36). While our research did not focus on this issue, we believe that there must be a balance between front-end planned activities and ongoing iteration during the NPD project, between making "final" decisions early and intentionally keeping open parallel alternatives, and between establishing product development targets through analysis and working by instinct alone (37).

Diagnosing Front-End Activities

Based on our study findings, we propose that companies evaluate their front end on degree of formality and the integration of activities. The dimensions—formality and process integration—can measured on a checklist (See Table 2). The items are derived from previous research and our case study findings on the need for formality and integration at the front end. The diagnostic statements evaluate the explicitness and formality of front-end practices. The statements on integration document how well these and other front-end activities are integrated.

A senior business unit manager such as the vice president of R&D, chief technology officer, or director of new product development should assess business practices and then calculate the score of the business unit, counting a check for any item as one point. The sum of the scores on the formality statements gives the formality score;

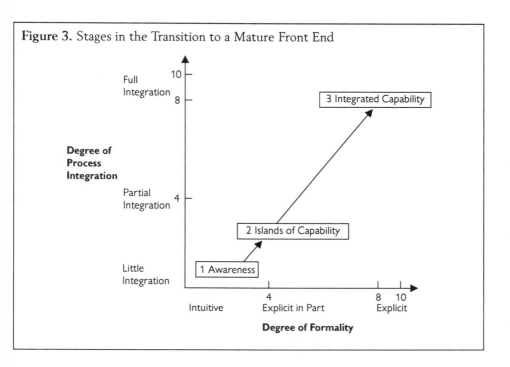

Figure 3. Stages in the Transition to a Mature Front End

the sum of the integration statements, the integration score. The manager can then map the score on each dimension on the front-end capability map (See Figure 2).

The mapping indicates how well (or poorly) a business unit is doing along the two dimensions of formality and integration. Our research indicates that world-class companies score eight or more on both dimensions. Companies that score three or less on either dimension have a deficient front end and are likely to have major problems with their product development efforts. Senior management needs to find ways to improve these efforts; the checklist is a first step to understanding where and what to improve. What is more difficult is to understand how. In the next section, we discuss how companies and business units can plan a transition to a better-managed front end.

Managing the Transition
All the companies we studied were moving toward a more explicit, integrated front end. They were trying to build complementary capabilities to support the critical go/no-go decisions and development plans for new product concepts. Yet each was taking a different path at a different rate.

Stages of Evolution
We see three stages in the product development front end, not including the stage in which a company has no formal front end—the pre-emergent stage (38). The next stages are "awareness," "islands of capability," and "integrated capability" (See Figure 3). The triggers to reach the awareness stage from the pre-emergent stage are typically growth, additional product line complexity, or competitive pressures for either

more product innovation or lower product development costs. In any case, at the awareness stage, companies recognize the significance of the front end but have little capability associated with it. They score poorly on both the formality and integration dimensions, as did companies B, E, and H in our sample.

• *Islands of Capability* (Stage Two). Our study suggests that most leading product innovators are at the islands of capability stage, including companies A, C, D, I, J, and K. These companies realize the potential of having a well-managed front end and have some of the required capabilities, but inconsistently. Missing are many elements of front-end process integration. Companies find it easier to improve the formality of this process than to address the subtle gaps in integration.

How can companies evolve from "awareness" to "islands of capability"? That depends on what the business unit has already achieved and what capabilities it needs, given its industry and company. We identified two broad approaches to achieving stage two. First, those companies that have barely begun to understand the importance of the front-end—for example, company H—should recognize that product development is a senior management responsibility. Managers should carry out several structured activities, such as the diagnostic test. Second, those companies that recognize the importance of the front end—such as companies B and E—should formally and systematically conduct various front-end activities. Those activities include having an explicit product definition, estimating technology requirements early, and planning resources.

• *Integrated Capability* (Stage Three). Front-end product development integrations, the hallmark of stage three, is quite rare. We believe that most companies don't understand that this stage is significant in terms of required capabilities, and achieving it takes concerted effort. At the few companies with this degree of process integration—analysis and decisions have been both explicit and rigorous, and all front-end activities are managed as a single process. Stage three companies execute NPD projects better and faster than their competitors and are more likely to introduce a winning product. One can honestly say of these companies that "well begun is more than half done."

How can companies make a transition from "islands of capability" to "integrated capability"? Some stage two companies have much of the required formality but not necessarily the degree of integration to yield substantial benefits. Most stage two companies should focus on understanding the various dimensions of integration. Among our sample, we identified three clusters of companies that required somewhat different approaches to get to stage three. These three clusters represent generic front-end states and problems that many companies face.

While companies in the first cluster, A and K, have passed stage one, they still have a long way to go. They need to focus closely on senior management involvement in creating a product vision. Improvements in front-end formality and integration, while not easy, will be easier if the product development group can understand its purpose better.

Companies C and D make up the second cluster. These companies will realize improvements from refinements in the front-end process. They need to make their front-end activities more explicit and, in particular, understand how to better manage their technology and resource requirements. Once they progress on these dimensions, they can focus more on cross-functional and integration problems.

The third cluster of companies, I and J, were the most advanced among the stage two companies. Front-end explicitness is not their main problem. Instead, their challenge is to work on cross-product issues and technological uncertainties. By having close ties among strategic planners and project personnel, they will understand the links among projects and anticipate matches or mismatches between future market needs and current technology and product plans. They need to establish closer connections between their R&D and product development groups so that they can anticipate overall technological progress and product-specific technological uncertainty.

• *Sustaining Stage Three.* Clearly, reaching stage three is not easy; even those companies that have achieved it continue to require improvements. Changes in competition, technologies, tools, and organizational structures and relationships may need changes in at least some front-end practices (39).

How can companies F and G improve? We found that these companies had minor deficiencies at their front ends (by using the diagnostic test in Table 2). Yet, the companies have potential for improvement. For example, knowing what to finalize and approve in product concept and definition, and what to keep flexible and open to change is important. Achieving a proper balance calls for more than just personal intuition and tacit understanding. Making explicit the connections between product requirements and internal technology development remains an elusive capability. And maintaining continuous link among business-unit vision, product strategy, technology, and new products is an ongoing challenge. Managers at stage three companies need to evaluate and apply innovations such as developing carefully planned product architectures and platforms or adapting a front-end process—such as Cooper's—to deal with the dynamics of current technological, market, and organizational realities (40).

Conclusion

Most companies have unnecessarily fuzzy front-end systems. The best way to integrate the front-end process is to use an overall systems perspective and thoroughly assess the current state of the front end. Fixing what appears to be broken requires the ability to see the interrelatedness of issues and the development of a coherent agenda.

We caution against oversimplification: not all companies should adopt the same front-end solution, and most will need to adopt more than one. For example, we found that companies used executive reviews in different ways and with mixed success; some case study companies changed the role of the executive review group for different products. In general, company size, decision-making style, operating culture, frequency of new product introduction are some factors that are critical to a preferred front-end solution. We discourage companies from importing a particular process or procedure that has worked well for others unless their contexts are clearly similar (41).

Managing to become less fuzzy means integrating seemingly disparate but related strategic and operational activities, typically crossing functional boundaries. The solution must be balanced with the emerging realities of business and the environment. With proper diagnosis, consensus, and commitment, companies can enhance product development performance over the long term.

Appendix

We conducted our research between April 1994 and April 1995 (a). Of the sixteen companies invited to participate, eleven accepted. We chose companies based on whether they had a product-generation process and if they had NPD processes for one to eight years. Our final sample includes seven U.S. and four Japanese companies (all Fortune 500 companies or their equivalent in Japan) in various industries ranging from consumer packaged goods to electronics to industrial products (See Table A for more information on specific industries). There are seven U.S., six Japanese, and two European business units (we interviewed managers at multiple business units at two companies). Business-unit size ranged from $300 million to $2.5 billion in annual sales, and 600 to 20,000 employees; company sizes ranged from $2 billion to $55 billion, and 20,000 to 300,000 employees. Further, we classified the companies as "active" or "neutral"; the active sites participated very closely in research, and we had open access to them. At the neutral sites (companies B, E, G, and K), we had only one opportunity to get the data directly, i.e., only one visit or series of interviews. Naturally, the data from these companies are less detailed, although we obtained the essential information.

We adopted an exploratory and "action-oriented" approach because we iterated among data collection, analysis, and feedback. We conducted our research at three to four company sites, analyzed data, presented partial results to a group of participants at "dissemination" workshops, wrote reports for their review, revised our knowledge base and conceptual models, and went on to the next case sites. Thus, implicitly and by design, we adopted the grounded theory approach (b).

We spent more than 200 hours interviewing more than seventy-five managers. On average, for each active site, we spent between eight and forty hours interviewing from three to twenty-five managers; for each neutral site, we spent eight to fifteen hours interviewing up to eight managers. We held four days of dissemination workshops with more than twenty-five different managers from several research companies. We interviewed managers (ranging from functional managers to company president) from marketing, R&D, software development, engineering, manufacturing, field service, finance, accounting, strategic planning, product management, NPD process owners, and corporate/business-unit general management.

For most of the case sites, we used secondary data collection in an effort to understand the industry and company background. We then adapted our basic research and interview questions to match the company profile. Thus most of the interviews were largely unstructured to support our exploration of the relatively undefined nature of the front end of product development.

The basic unit of analysis for our cases was the process of the front end of new product development. However, due to access, confidentiality, time and contrasts, we used several approaches to understand and evaluate the process. As Table A shows, our interviews took two different forms: (1) a study of individual NPD projects (multiple projects at each company) and (2) an in-depth study of business unit practices with regard to the process adopted for the front end of new product development. (We included multiple business units at two companies because these business units were in widely different markets or technologies, or because they were perceived to have distinctive front-end NPD practices.)

Notes

a. In addition to the eleven cases directly involved in this research, we also draw on and cite examples from prior knowledge of several cases of new product development projects that the second author researched in 1989 to 1991. See:

Table A. Description of Sample Companies

Business Unit Code	Ownership	Core Businesses	Level of Analysis (Multiple products and/or NPD process)
A	United States	Equipment for publishing industry	NPD Process and two specific product projects
B	Japan	OEM for system devices (e.g., printers, PCs, software drivers) and major electronic components	NPD Process
C	United States, Germany	Specialized health-care equipment	NPD Process
D	United States	Consumer packaged goods	NPD Process
E	United States	Pharmaceuticals	NPD Process
F	United States	Medical products	NPD Process and two specific product projects
G	Japan	Super, mainframe, and mid-range computers	NPD Process
H	United States	Office equipment	NPD Process and four specific product projects
I	Japan	Variety of electronics products from micro devices to printers to notebook computers	NPD Process at corporate level and in three separate business units and one specific product project
J	United States, Europe	Durable white goods, such as washers and cooking products	NPD Process in two separate business units and three specific product projects
K	Japan	Production technologies and equipment business unit of major electronics company	NPD Process

S.R. Rosenthal, *Effective Product Design and Development* (Homewood, Illinois: business One Irwin, 1992).

b. B. Glaser and A. Strauss, *The Discovery of Grounded Theory: Strategies for Qualitative Research* (Chicago: Aldine Publishers, 1967); and

K.M. Eisenhardt, "Building Theory from Case Research," *Academy of Management Review*, volume 14, number 4, 1989, pp. 532-550.

References

This research was sponsored and supported by the Boston University Manufacturing Roundtable, School of Management, and a research grant from Seiko Epson Corporation, Japan. The authors acknowledge the cooperation of the U.S., Japanese, and European companies that participated. They also thank Professors Jinichiro Nakane and Hiroshi Katayama of Waseda University, Japan, and acknowledge the help of Paul Callaghan, doctoral student at Boston University, in data collection.

1. The notion of the fuzzy front end and its importance was first introduced in :
P.G. Smith and D.G. Reinertsen, *Developing Products in Half the Time* (New York: Van Nostrand Reinhold, 1991).

See also:

A. Khurana and S.R. Rosenthal, "Discovering the Shortcomings in the 'Front-End' of New Product Development: Findings from Cross-Industry Case Studies" (Boston: Boston University School of Management, Manufacturing Roundtable working paper, 1996);

K.B. Clark and S.C. Wheelwright, *Leading Product Development* (New York: Free Press, 1995);

S.R. Rosenthal, *Effective Product Design and Development* (Homewood, Illinois: Business One Irwin, 1992);

A.K. Gupta and D.L. Wilemon, "Accelerating the Development of Technology-Based New Products," *California Management Review*, volume 32, Winter 1990, pp. 24-44; and

R.G. Cooper and E.J. Kleinschmidt, "New Products: What Separates Winners from Losers?", *Journal of Product Innovation Management*, volume 4, September 1987, pp. 169-184.

2. See D.A. Schön, *The Reflective Practitioner: How Professionals Think in Action* (New York: Basic Books, 1983), p. 266.

3. H.K. Bowen, K.B. Clark, C.A. Holloway, and S.C. Wheelwright, "Development Projects: The Engine of Renewal," *Harvard Business Review*, volume 72, September–October 1994, pp. 110-120.

For a business process view, see:

T. Davenport, *Process Innovation: Reengineering Work through Information* (Boston: Harvard Business School Press, 1983), chapter 11.

4. See Cooper and Kleinschmidt (1987);
Gupta and Wilemon (1990);
Smith and Reinertsen (1991);
Rosenthal (1992); and
Clark and Wheelwright (1995).

For a study of factors explaining "good" product definition, see:

G. Bacon, S. Beckman, D. Mowery, and E. Wilson, "Managing Product Definition in High-Technology Industries: A Pilot Study," *California Management Review*, volume 36, Sprint 1994, pp. 32-56.

Of the key factors for NPD success identified by Bacon et al. and other researchers, several pertain to front-end issues: product-core competence fit, senior manager responsibility for NPD planning, clear understanding of user needs, explicit description of product concept and definition, careful planning, specifying contingency plans, and resource planning. For purposes of description and understanding, we divide Bacon et al.'s interpretation of product definition into product strategy, product definition, and project definition, primarily because these activities involve different analytical and implementation approaches. See, also:

W.E. Souder, *Managing New Product Innovations* (Lexington, Massachusetts: Lexington Books, 1987);

Booz Allen & Hamilton, "New Product Development in the 1980s" (New York: Booz Allen & Hamilton, 1982); and

R. Rothwell, C. Freeman, A. Horsley, V.T.P. Jervis, A.B. Robertson, and J. Townsend, "Sappho Updated—Project Sappho Phase II," *Research Policy*, volume 3, number 3, 1974, pp. 258-291.

5. We first identified a series of operational problems encountered in new product development and linked them to activities and practices at the front end. For that analysis, see:
Khurana and Rosenthal (1996).

6. Bacon et al. (1994); and
Gupta and Wilemon (1990).

While there has been limited research on the front end, researchers who study new product development often include some NPD success factors that pertain to the front end. See, for example:

Smith and Reinertsen (1991);

Rothwell et al. (1974); and

R.G. Cooper and E.J. Kleinschmidt, "Determinants of Timeliness in Product Development," *Journal of Production Innovation Management*, volume 11, November 1994, pp. 381-396.

7. Roberts and Fusfeld call a set of foundation-type activities "critical functions for enhanced innovation." They portray project-specific activities as a six-stage process starting with pre-project activities. See:

E.B. Roberts and A.R. Fusfeld, "Staffing the Innovative Technology-Based Organization," *Sloan Management Review*, volume 22, Spring 1981, pp. 19-34.

8. M. McGrath, *Product Strategy for High-Technology Companies* (Burr Ridge, Illinois: Irwin, 1995).

9. These are the top three levels of the strategic hierarchy presented by McGrath (1995). McGrath describes product strategy in a four-level hierarchy starting with strategic vision and then proceeding to product-platform strategy, product-line strategy, and, finally, individual projects.

10. Bacon et al. (1994).

11. McGrath (1995); and

R.G. Cooper and E.J. Kleinschmidt, "New Product Performance: Keys to Success, Profitability, and Cycle Time Reduction," *Journal of Marketing Management*, volume 11, September 1995, pp. 315-337.

12. McGrath (1995);

D.G. Ancona and D.F. Caldwell, "Beyond Boundary Spanning: Managing External Dependence in Product Development Teams," *Journal of High-Technology Management Research*, volume 1, number 1, 1990, pp. 119-135; and

D.G. Ancona and D.F. Caldwell, "Bridging the Boundary: External Process and Performance in Organizational Teams," *Administrative Science Quarterly*, volume 37, December 1992, pp. 634-665.

13. Selected research on these issues includes:

K.B. Clark and T. Fujimoto, *Product Development Performance* (Boston: Harvard Business School Press, 1991); and

K. Imai, I. Nonaka, and H. Takeuchi, "Managing the New Product Development Process: How Japanese Companies Learn and Unlearn," in R. Hayes, K. Clark, and P. Lorenz, eds., *The Uneasy Alliance: Managing the Productivity-Technology Dilemma* (Boston: Harvard Business School Press, 1985), pp. 337-375;

L. Dwyer and R. Mellor, "Organizational Environment, New Product Process Activities, and Project Outcomes," *Journal of Product Innovation Management*, volume 8, March 1991, pp. 39-48; and

D. Dougherty, "Interpretive Barriers to Successful Product Innovations in Large Firms," *Organization Science*, volume 3, May 1992, pp. 179-202.

14. Cooper and Kleinschmidt (1995).

15. The creation of product concepts is discussed in:

C.M. Crawford, *New Products Management*, 3rd edition (Homewood, Illinois: Irwin, 1991).

Customer requirements should drive all product design and development, including the creation of product concepts. There is a growing body of information on how such requirements ought to be obtained and translated into product requirements. One familiar technique for translating customer requirements into product attributes is quality function deployment (QFD). See:

J.R. Hauser, and D. Clausing (1988), "The House of Quality," *Harvard Business Review*, volume 66, May-June 1988, pp. 63-73; and

G.L. Urgan and J.R. Hauser, *Design and Marketing of New Products*, 2nd edition (Englewood Cliffs, New Jersey: Prentice-Hall; 1993).

16. Bacon et al. (1994).

17. Bacon et al. (1994); and

K.M. Eisenhardt and B. Tabrizi, "Accelerating Adaptive Processes: Product Innovation in the Global Computer Industry," *Administrative Science Quarterly*, volume 40, March 1995, pp. 84-110.

18. R.H. Hayes, S.C. Wheelrwright, and K.B. Clark, *Dynamic Manufacturing* (New York: Free Press, 1988);

Dwyer and Mellor (1991); and

R. Cooper, "Third-Generation New Product Processes," *Journal of Product Innovation Management*, volume 11, January 1994, pp. 3-14.

19. See Rosenthal (1992);

Smith and Reinertsen (1991);

Cooper (1994); and

R.G. Cooper, "Stage-Gate Systems: A New Tool for Managing New Products," *Business Horizons*, volume 33, May-June 1990, pp. 44-54.

20. Bacon et al. (1994); and

Cooper and Kleinschmidt (1995).

21. For a description of phase review systems, see:

Cooper (1990); and

Rosenthal (1992), chapter 2. See also:

M.E. McGrath, M.T. Anthony, and A.R. Shapiro, *Product Development Success through Product and Cycle-Time Excellence* (Boston: Butterworth-Heinemann, 1992).

22. An alternative approach that is emerging in the best companies is based on platform planning and emphasizes that product opportunities are related to the development of product platforms. See:

McGrath (1995); and

M.H. Meyer, P. Tetzakain, and J.M. Utterback, "Metrics for Managing Research and Development" (Cambridge: MIT Sloan School of Management, working paper 3817, 1995).

23. S.C. Wheelwright and K.B. Clark, *Revolutionizing Product Development* (New York: Free Press, 1992).

Several product development researchers have raised the issue of roles, e.g. project managers (Wheelwright and Clark, 1992), and core team and executive reviews (McGrath et al., 1992). However, our interest is in looking at how these roles influence the front end of new product development and what challenges arise as a result of the interactions among these roles.

24. In some companies that do platform planning in a serious way, one can visualize the development of a platform concept or architecture also as a front-end deliverable.

25. Meyer et al. (1995).

26. Wheelwright and Clark (1992).

27. Ancona and Caldwell (1990): and

Ancona and Caldwell (1992).

28. Clark and Fujimoto suggest that in such cases, there is often "little or no attention to integrating a clear sense of customer expectations into the work of the product development organization as a whole." See:
K.B. Clark, and T. Fujimoto, "The Power of Product Integrity," *Harvard Business Review*, volume 68, November-December 1990, pp. 107-118.

29. Though not all platforms or product lines can plan for multiple releases at frequent intervals, proactive planning of product releases a few years ahead is desirable. For example, Sony does not necessarily plan multiple releases but achieves the same objective by freezing the product design early on. It then begins work on the next product model concurrently to incorporate changes in customer needs or technology. See:
Meyer et al. (1995);
McGrath (1995); and
S. Sander-Walsh and M. Uzumeri, "Managing Product Families: The Case of the Sony Walkman," *Research Policy*, volume 24, September 1995, pp. 761-782; and
P.R. Nayak and J.P. Deschamps, *Product Juggernauts* (Boston: Harvard Business School Press, 1995).

30. See, for example:
R.R. Kamath, and J.K. Liker, "A Second Look at Japanese Product Development," *Harvard Business Review*, volume 72, November-December 1994, pp. 154-170.

31. K.A. Howard, "Postponement of Packaging and Product Differentiation Lowers Logistics Costs," IN A.K. Chakravarty, ed., *Globalization of Technology, Manufacturing, and Service Operations* (New Orleans: Tulane University, Goldring Institute, A.B. Freeman School of Business, Proceedings of Symposium, 7-8 January 1994).

32. Apparently, such redundancy is at the heart of Toyota's development success. See:
A. Ward, J.K. Liker, J.J. Cristiano, and D.K. Sobek II, "The Second Toyota Paradox: How Delaying Decisions can Make Better Cars Faster," *Sloan Management Review*,, volume 36, Spring 1995, pp. 43-61. In the context of design, simultaneously working on multiple subsystem/component alternatives generally leads to a faster product development cycle. We suggest that the same is true for planned and anticipated redundancy in the fact of technological or other risks.

33. Other interrelationships that have been mentioned in previous research, e.g., Bacon et al. (1994), and used at several case study sites include: the need for strategic alignment between product development efforts and overall business strategy, the direct links between product definition and project planning, the close association of project planning and staffing policies, and the need to modify the roles and responsibilities of key organizational members as a function of project complexity and size.

34. P. Lawrence and J. Lorsch, *Organizations and Environments* (Homewood, Illinois: Irwin, 1969); and
Clark and Fujimoto (1991).

35. D. Dougherty and E.H. Bowman, "The Effects of Organizational Downsizing on Product Innovation," *California Management Review*, volume 37, Summer 1995, pp. 28-44.

36. Ward et al. (1995); and
M. Iansiti, "Shooting the Rapids," *California Management Review*, volume 38, Fall 1995, pp. 1-22.

37. This notion of balance also reflects our agreement with an article on balancing instinctive and fully analytical decision making. See:
A. Langley, "Between 'Paralysis by Analysis' and 'Extinction by Instinct'," *Sloan Management Review*, volume 36, Spring 1995, pp. 63-76.

38. In the "pre-emergent" stage, a company had no formal front end, nor does it perceive the need for one; none of the companies we studied fell into this category. This situation is common either in start-up companies in which a few principals make product development decisions informally, or in business units where structured product innovation is not yet the basis for competition. NPD activities for such organizations are tightly integrated, but often a few senior managers do this tacitly.

39. See, for example:
S.K. Goldman, R.N. Nagel, and K. Preiss, *Agile Competitors and Virtual Organizations: Strategies for Enriching the Customer*, (New York: Van Nostrand Reinhold, 1995).

40. See Meyer et al. (1995);
McGrath (1995); and
Sanderson-Walsh and Uzumeri (1995).
For a proposed new model of the stage-gate system, see:
Cooper (1994).

41. A full description of why a company should adopt more than one front-end solution, and what these solutions might look like, is beyond our scope. While we do not yet have a full map of "compatible contexts," some of the contingencies we have discovered are: radicalness of product, maturity of industry, experience of the business unit with formal front-end processes, small or large firm, and entrepreneurial or conservative firm. We are currently writing a paper that more fully develops this perspective.

Project Prioritization in a Large Functional Organization

Margaret W. Combe

In large functional organizations, projects frequently arise in the depths of the company's "stovepipes," where the needs for operational improvements are felt. How do such functional organizations effectively focus project activity and resources on cross-functional, strategic projects and on the operational improvements that are best aligned with company strategy?

In a functional setting, the tendency is to aim projects at what the Total Quality Management advocates would refer to as "continuous improvement." Because projects are defined within functional units, they are necessarily targeted at changes limited to the purview of that functional area, rarely going beyond the boundaries of the work that touches that organizational unit.

This functional view of projects causes four problems for a company:

- First, *breakthrough projects are rarely identified* because breakthroughs tend to implicate an entire process, which is infrequently in one organizational unit.
- Second, when large cross-functional projects are commissioned by management, they *create conflicts with functional priorities* and confusion over resourcing.
- Third, *company strategy may be inadequately coordinated* as functional areas independently identify and implement projects aimed at those strategies.
- Finally, it is *difficult to prioritize competing functional continuous improvement* projects against one another on the basis of their alignment with company strategy.

In short, functional organizations have a difficult time getting the most effective bang for their project bucks.

The dilemma is not an easy one to resolve because both continuous improvement and breakthrough projects are important for the success of any large organization. Without breakthrough projects, there is no growth, but without continuous improvement, there is no increasing efficiency to fund the growth. The objective, therefore, is not to ignore functional continuous improvement efforts, but rather to:

- select those that best align with overall company strategy
- ensure that such efforts are leveraged in the organization, benefiting it most broadly.

The challenge for large functional organizations is to drive strategy, both growth strategy and continuous improvement strategy, through the organization. Project prioritization is not a function of senior management or of the Project Office lining up the portfolio and assigning weights or rankings. Instead, priorities must derive from the company's strategy. The strategy must be clear enough that it allows internalization of the prioritization criteria down to the level of project sponsors and managers.

The Challenge for One Functionally Organized Company

Northwestern Mutual Life Insurance Company is recognized as the most admired life insurance company by *Fortune* magazine. Its solid hold on that prestigious position has been a function of its attention to product quality, high returns for policy owners and control of costs. Project activity in the company was directed to fine tuning a smoothly functioning machine to ensure continued superiority in these areas.

In recent years, emerging nontraditional competition in the financial services industry has forced a new look at the game. Product options available to customers are expanding, and the company is responding by breaking into new product lines and markets. Competition in distribution and new product startup costs are challenging the company's cost superiority. Breakthrough projects are required to leapfrog the competition and roll out new product lines, but continuous improvement, on an accelerated scale, is required to maintain competitive cost structures.

The company quickly found that its traditional bottom-up identification of projects was inadequate to ensure selection of the most important things on which to spend our resources.

We have initiated five key devices at Northwestern Mutual for driving both breakthrough and continuous improvement strategy and for selecting projects that leverage those strategies.

Device 1—Strategy-Defining Projects

For a company in transition, it is crucial to get everyone marching to the same beat. This means redefining the company's vision and ensuring that it is well communicated in terms that everyone can understand and use in decision-making. In some companies, a forceful CEO defines and drives this vision. We found that the CEO's vision was a good start, but huge, unanswered questions remained about how that vision might actually work in practice. So we set out to explore strategy at a more operational level.

A portion of the CEO's vision was that the company would sell a broader range of financial services products and that salespeople would obtain referrals through alliances with other types of financial services institutions.

We initiated strategy-defining projects to answer the question: How would this strategy operate, and what would be the implications throughout the organization? One of the first strategy-defining projects was to define how the "agent of the future" would operate: What would he do as part of his day; what would be his challenges; with whom would he be interfacing; what technology, information, etc., would he have to access to do his job?

A team worked for approximately three months and defined the new work world of the NML salesperson, explaining what products he would require to meet the needs of the new referrals, what services he would perform for his customers, etc.

The new work structure of the agent identified implications for how business was conducted in other areas of the company. For instance, there were implications for how agents would be trained and how customer service would be provided. This spawned additional strategy-defining projects to explore how these pieces of the business would work.

These strategy-defining projects identify gaps in our current operations that must be filled to advance to the envisioned future and a critical path of key work efforts needed. Continuous improvement projects have been nominated for the project portfolio as a result.

The results of these efforts are published on the company's intranet so that, as internal divisional improvement efforts are initiated, they can align themselves with the vision.

Device 2—Strategic Plan Segmentation and Focus

The purpose of a strategic plan is to point the way. If it points the way only to major change, it misses the opportunity to align the organization's continuous improvement with that change.

We have chosen to segment the strategic plan into two main thrusts:
- strengthen the foundation
- build on the foundation.

In the section on strengthening the foundation, priorities are set for improvement efforts. The plan does not specify the work efforts; rather, it outlines key areas for improvement and establishes measures and targets. For instance, we identify as a strategy improving the productivity of agents and describe the target as a percentage improvement in the insurance premium they generate per year.

In the section on building the foundation, major growth strategies are defined, again with measures and targets. Such things as new markets, new product lines, new geographic reach, and new businesses are fleshed out in this section, and their tie to the company's foundation is enunciated.

The strategic plan items are then prioritized, not in terms of a ranking, but in terms of desired application of resources. The plan items and their associated goals are rated by senior management on three scales:
- period in which significant movement toward goals is required (short-term to long-term)
- degree of key peoples' time to be committed
- investment of money to be made.

The resulting prioritization of goals identifies urgency and size of efforts directed toward achieving them. The plan and its priorities also reside on the intranet.

Device 3—Resource Targets

In the past, Information Technology resources were apportioned to functional units based mostly on history of project activity. The functional units used this staffing to resource their continuous improvement efforts. All IT resources were allocated to functional units.

We have stripped off a large share of pooled resources to be used for strategic, breakthrough projects. The dollar amount is set as an investment budget before each year's planning cycle. Each division retains a smaller continuous improvement budget, represented by a small pool of division-discretionary IT resources. A target is also set for this budget during the planning cycle.

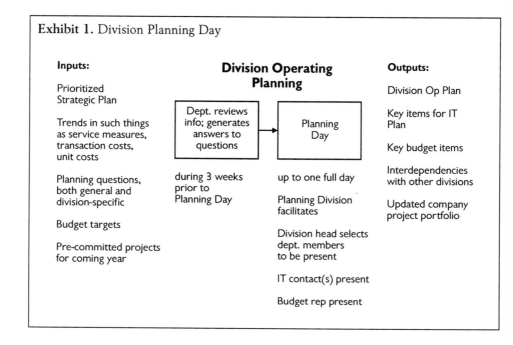

Exhibit 1. Division Planning Day

Inputs:

Prioritized Strategic Plan

Trends in such things as service measures, transaction costs, unit costs.

Planning questions, both general and division-specific

Budget targets

Pre-committed projects for coming year

Division Operating Planning

Dept. reviews info; generates answers to questions → Planning Day

during 3 weeks prior to Planning Day

up to one full day

Planning Division facilitates

Division head selects dept. members to be present

IT contact(s) present

Budget rep present

Outputs:

Division Op Plan

Key items for IT Plan

Key budget items

Interdependencies with other divisions

Updated company project portfolio

Device 4—Alignment of Functional Plans

Functional planning had been independently done in the past and submitted for synthesis of the various division plans. Without the benefit of a clear strategic plan or interpretation of that plan on an operational level, there was a great deal of mismatch. Divisional plans did not advance key strategies; one division's plan incurred costs and required significant work from another (and no corresponding items were found in those plans); multiple technology platforms were proliferated.

The alignment of functional plans requires a great deal of intervention and iteration. We found that the best way to accomplish it was in face-to-face planning sessions, where issues could be raised and misalignments brought to light and resolved before budgets and resources had been committed.

We are now conducting a facilitated planning day with each division. As seen in Exhibit 1, the sessions are facilitated by the Planning Division, and both a one-year and a three-year plan are produced. IT planners and budget staff participate in the process to ensure that budget targets and IT resource allocations are respected and negotiated as priorities are set. The beginning point for the Planning Day is the focused and prioritized strategic plan. The Planning Division identifies questions for the operating division so that it is forced to consider how it will carry out strategies that affect it. Outputs from the Planning Day include a divisional operating plan, preliminary budget, preliminary IT resource requirements, additions to the company project portfolio, and identified interdependencies.

The facilitator challenges the divisions with questions in advance and during the Planning Day to ensure alignment with company strategies, stretch the level of improvements, and ensure that interdependencies are resourced.

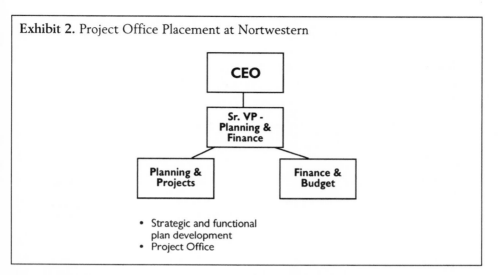

Exhibit 2. Project Office Placement at Nortwestern

CEO

Sr. VP - Planning & Finance

Planning & Projects

Finance & Budget

- Strategic and functional plan development
- Project Office

Device 5—Disciplined Project Initiation and Tracking

Many organizations do a credible job of chartering projects and tracking the technical completion of projects, ensuring that budget and specifications are met. But we have found that the emphasis of these activities needs to move from the *completion of projects* and toward the *accomplishment of strategic goals*. Key changes we have made in project initiation are as follows.

• Responsibility for defining a) the tie to strategy and b) interdependencies rests in the hands of the project sponsor and project manager. This accountability invests everyone in the organization in achievement of company goals and alignment of functional plans. If attempts are made to centrally adjudicate the ties to strategy, functional competition for resources prevails over the broad view.

• Deliverables are described in terms of benefits to be harvested for the organization. Thus, for instance, delivery of a new technology is not a deliverable, but the measurable productivity to be gained from it is a deliverable. This focus allows clear ties to strategy and allows self-management of the project toward the desired end.

With deliverables defined as benefits to be harvested, *project tracking* should be focused on deviation from delivery of those benefits. For instance, a project that we tracked was the development of a technology platform that promised to improve agent productivity by prefilling forms with up-to-date client information. Current data-capture methods limited the ability to consolidate information by client. The project was technically able to deliver the platform on time and within budget but with a severely reduced benefit in agent productivity. We were thus able to focus management decision-making on either slowing down the platform project's costs in favor of other priorities or increasing the investment in data-capture methods to deliver the originally forecast benefits.

The Role of the Project Office in Functional Prioritization

We have found that the placement of the Project Office in conjunction with the corporate Planning function is key to successful alignment of strategy with project priorities. It is also helpful to align the function with the financial and budget offices (see Exhibit 2).

The Project Office at Northwestern Mutual Life plays the following roles in driving strategy through projects.

• Lead strategy-defining projects—Key project managers from the Project Office lead many of the company's strategy-defining projects, working with senior management of functional areas to set direction and vision.

• Maintain the company's project portfolio—An accounting of the projects supporting the strategy is maintained with budgets and people allocated. These projects are brought to the senior management's executive committee for initiation and tracked from the Project Office to determine any deviations from planned benefits achievement.

• Help project sponsors and managers to maintain alignment—The Project Office works closely with project groups to help them articulate their projects' goals, deliverables, cost-benefits, and interdependencies.

• Identify implications of project portfolio—The Project Office monitors the portfolio of projects and helps to ensure that schedule changes, scope revisions, etc., are communicated and properly accounted for in the activities of interdependent efforts. For instance, if changes in plans cause multiple introductions to agents at the same time, the Project Office facilitates a review and disposition of the conflict.

• Support good project management—The Project Office continually identifies best practices and pitfalls in project management and communicates to all project managers. The Office consults with project managers on a regular basis.

Summary

No fail-safe process exists for ensuring that strategy is driven into careful project prioritization in a large functional organization. There are continuing dangers of suboptimization, misalignment, competing priorities, and bottom-up strategy development. However, ongoing interventions to bridge the functional gaps are effective in preventing egregious problems in spending for the wrong projects.

In applying interventions or "devices" such as those described, a number of overriding considerations should be foremost in management's thought process.

• Make the strategy clear and tangible. The more that can be done to define the strategy in operational terms, the easier it will be to execute it. The clearer the sense of urgency and the more measurable the goal to be achieved, the more precise will be the targets of projects aimed at these strategies.

• Make everyone responsible for achievement of strategy. No central staff organization should be the keeper of the priorities. The staff organization can be helpful in interpreting strategy issues and interdependencies, but it should be operating management that is accountable for ensuring the alignment of its work with company goals.

• Measure achievement of target benefits, not completion of projects. Keep management and project managers focused on the contribution to plan goals, not on the technical completion of project specifications.

This article is reprinted from *1998 Proceedings of the Annual Project Management Institute Seminars & Symposium* with permission of the Project Management Institute Headquarters, Four Campus Boulevard,

Newtown Square, PA 19073-3299 USA, Phone: (610) 356-4600 Fax: (610) 356-4647, Project Management Institute (PMI) is the world's leading project management association with over 40,000 members worldwide. For further information contact PMI Headquarters at (610) 356-4600 or visit the web site at www.pmi.org.

Creating Project Plans to Focus Product Development

Steven C. Wheelwright and Kim B. Clark

The long-term competitiveness of any manufacturing company depends ultimately on the success of its product development capabilities. New product development holds hope for improving market position and financial performance, creating new industry standards and new niche markets, and even renewing the organization. Yet few development projects fully deliver on their early promises. The fact is, much can and does go wrong during development. In some instances, poor leadership or the absence of essential skills is to blame. But often problems arise from the way companies approach the development process. They lack what we call an "aggregate project plan."

Consider the case of a large scientific instruments company we will call PreQuip. In mid-1989, senior management became alarmed about a rash of late product development projects. For some months, the development budget had been rising even as the number of completed projects declined. And many of the projects in the development pipeline no longer seemed to reflect the needs of the market. Management was especially troubled because it had believed its annual business plan provided the guidance that the marketing and engineering departments needed to generate and schedule projects.

To get to the root of the problem, the chief executive first asked senior managers to compile a list of all the current development projects. They discovered that 30 projects were under way—far more than anticipated, and, they suspected, far more than the organization could support. Further analysis revealed that the company had two to three times more development work than it was capable of completing over its three-year development planning horizon. (See the chart "PreQuip's Development Predicament: Overcommitted Resources.")

With such a strain on resources, delays were inevitable. When a project ran into trouble, engineers from other projects were reassigned, or more commonly, asked to add the crisis project to their already long list of active projects. The more projects they added, the more their productivity dropped. The reshuffling caused delays in other projects, and the effects cascaded. Furthermore, as deadlines slipped and development costs rose, project managers faced pressure to cut corners and compromise quality just to keep their projects moving forward.

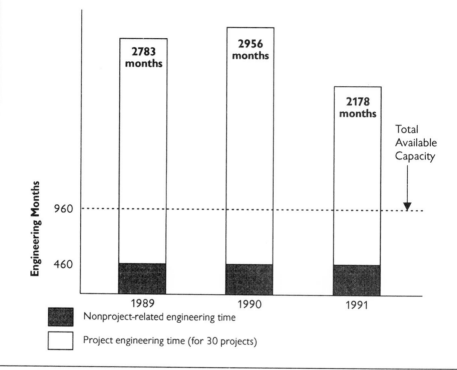

Figure 1. PreQuip's Development Predicament: Overcommitted Resources. Pre-Quip had 960 engineering months each year to allocate to development work. But combining the time it would take to keep its current 30 projects on schedule with the time engineers spent doing nonproject development work, the company found it had overcommitted its development resources for the next three years by a factor of three.

The senior management team also discovered that the majority of PreQuip's development resources—primarily engineers and support staff—was not focused on the projects most critical to the business. When questioned, project leaders admitted that the strategic objectives outlined in the annual business plan had little bearing on project selection. Instead, they chose projects because engineers found the technical problems challenging or because customers or the marketing department requested them. Pre-Quip had no formal process for choosing among development projects. As long as there was money in the budget or the person making the request had sufficient clout, the head of the development department had no option but to accept additional project requests.

Many engineers were not only working on non-critical projects but also spending as much as 50% of their time on nonproject-related work. They responded to requests from manufacturing for help with problems on previous products, from field sales for help with customer problems, from quality assurance for help with reliability problems, and purchasing for help with qualifying vendors. In addition to spending considerable time fixing problems on previously introduced products, engineers spent many hours in "information" and "update" meetings. In short, they spent too little time developing the right new products, experimenting with new technologies, or addressing new markets.

PreQuip's story is hardly unique. Most organizations we are familiar with spend their time putting out fires and pursuing projects aimed at catching up to their competitors. They have far too many projects going at once and all too often seriously over-commit their development resources. They spend too much time dealing with short-term pressures and not enough time on the strategic mission of product development.

Indeed, in most organizations, management directs all its attention to individual projects—it micromanages project development. But no single project defines a company's future or its market growth over time; the "set" of projects does. Companies need to devote more attention to managing the set and mix of projects. In particular, they should focus on how resources are allocated between projects. Management must plan how the project set evolves over time, which new projects get added when, and what role each project should play in the overall development effort.

The aggregate project plan addresses all of these issues. To create a plan, management categorizes projects based on the amount of resources they consume and on how they will contribute to the company's product line. Then, by mapping the project types, management can see where gaps exist in the development strategy and make more informed decisions about what types of projects to add and when to add them. Sequencing projects carefully, in turn, gives management greater control of resource allocation and utilization. The project map also reveals where development capabilities need to be strong. Over time, companies can focus on adding critical resources and on developing the skills of individual contributors, project leaders, and teams.

Finally, an aggregate plan will enable management to improve the way it manages the development function. Simply adding projects to the active list—a common practice at many companies—endangers the long-term health of the development process. Management needs to create a set of projects that is consistent with the company's development strategies rather than selecting individual projects from a long list of ad hoc proposals. And management must become involved in the development process before projects get started, even before they are fully defined. It is not appropriate to give one department—say, engineering or marketing—sole responsibility for initiating all projects because it is usually not in a position to determine every project's strategic worth.

Indeed, most companies—including PreQuip—should start the reformation process by eliminating or postponing the lion's share of their existing projects, eventually supplanting them with a new set of projects that fits the business strategy and the capacity constraints. The aggregate project plan provides a framework for addressing this difficult task.

How to Map Projects

The first step in creating an aggregate project plan is to define and map the different types of development projects; defining projects by type provides useful information about how resources should be allocated. The two dimensions we have found most useful for classifying are the degree of change in the product and the degree of change in the manufacturing process. The greater the changes along either dimension, the more resources are needed.

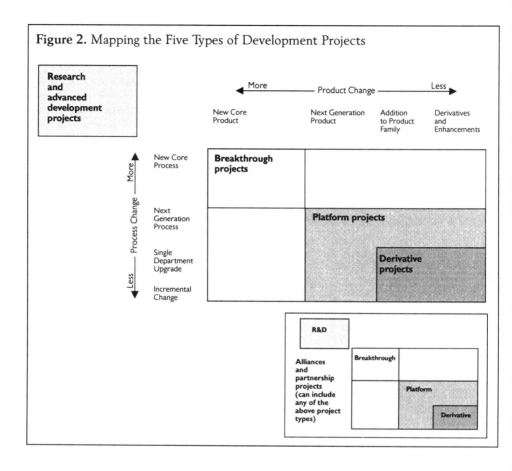

Figure 2. Mapping the Five Types of Development Projects

Using this construct, we have divided projects into five types. The first three—derivative, breakthrough, and platform—are commercial development projects. The remaining two categories are research and development, which is the precursor to commercial development, and alliances and partnerships, which can be either commercial or basic research. (See the chart "Mapping the Five Types of Development Projects.")

Each of the five project types requires a unique combination of development resources and management styles. Understanding how the categories differ helps managers predict the distribution of resources accurately and allows for better planning and sequencing of projects over time. Here is a brief description of each category.

Derivative projects range from cost-reduced versions of existing products to add-ons or enhancements for an existing production process. For example, Kodak's wide-angle, single-use 35mm camera, the Stretch, was derived from the no-frills Fun Saver introduced in 1990. Designing the Stretch was primarily a matter of changing the lens.

Development work on derivative projects typically falls into three categories: incremental product changes, say, new packaging or a new feature, with little or no manufacturing process change; incremental process changes, like a lower cost manufacturing process, improved reliability, or a minor change in materials used, with little or no product change; and incremental changes on both dimensions. Because design changes are usually minor, incremental projects typically are more clearly bounded and require substantially fewer development resources than the other categories. And because derivative projects are completed in a few months, ongoing management involvement is minimal.

Breakthrough projects are at the other end of the development spectrum because they involve significant changes to existing products and processes. Successful breakthrough projects establish core products and processes that differ fundamentally from previous generations. Like compact disks and fiber-optics cable, they create a whole new product category that can define a new market.

Because breakthrough products often incorporate revolutionary new technologies or materials, they usually require revolutionary manufacturing processes. Management should give development teams considerable latitude in designing new processes, rather than force them to work with existing plant and equipment, operating techniques, or supplier networks.

Platform projects are in the middle of the development spectrum and are thus harder to define. They entail more product and/or process changes than derivatives do, but they don't introduce the untried new technologies or materials that breakthrough products do. Honda's 1990 Accord line is an example of a new platform in the auto industry: Honda introduced a number of manufacturing process and product changes but no fundamentally new technologies. In the computer market, IBMs PS/2 is a personal computer platform; in consumer products, Procter & Gamble's Liquid Tide is the platform for a whole line of Tide brand products.

Well-planned and well-executed platform products typically offer fundamental improvements in cost, quality, and performance over preceding generations. They introduce improvements across a range of performance dimensions—speed, functionality, size, weight. (Derivative, on the other hand, usually introduce changes along only one or two dimensions.) Platforms also represent a significantly better system solution for the customer because of the extent of changes involved, successful platforms require considerable up-front planning and the involvement of not only engineering but also marketing, manufacturing, and senior management.

Companies target new platforms to meet the needs of a core group of customers but design them for easy modification into derivatives through the addition, substitution, or removal of features. Well-designed platforms also provide a smooth migration path between generations so neither the customer nor the distribution channel is disrupted.

Consider Intel's 80486 microprocessor, the fourth in a series. The 486 introduced a number of performance improvements; it targeted a core customer group—the high-end PC/workstation user—but variations addressed the needs of other users; and with software compatibility between the 386 and the 486, the 486 provided an easy migration path for existing customers. Over the life of the 486 platform, Intel will introduce a host of derivative products, each offering some variation in speed, cost, and performance and each able to leverage the process and product innovations of the original platform.

Platforms offer considerable leverage and the potential to increase market penetration, yet many companies systematically under-invest in them. The reasons vary, but the most common is that management lacks an awareness of the strategic value of platforms and fails to create well-thought-out platform projects. To address the problem, companies should recognize explicitly the need for platforms and develop guidelines for making them a central part of the aggregate project plan.

Research and development is the creation of the know-how and know-why of new materials and technologies that eventually translate into commercial development. Even though R&D lies outside the boundaries of commercial development, we include it here for two reason: it is the precursor to product and process development; and, in terms of future resource allocation, employees move between basic research and commercial development. Thus R&D projects compete with commercial development projects for resources. Because R&D is a creative, high-risk process, companies have different expectations about results and different strategies for funding and managing it than they do for commercial development. These differences can indeed be great, but a close relationship between R&D and commercial development is essential to ensure an appropriate balance and a smooth conversion of ideas into products.

Alliances and partnerships, which also lie outside the boundaries of the development map, can be formed to pursue any type of project—R&D, breakthrough, platform, or derivative. As such, the amount and type of development resources and management attention can vary widely.

Even though partnerships are an integral part of the project development process, many companies fail to include them in their project planning. They often separate the management of partnerships from the rest of the development organization and fail to provide them with enough development resources. Even when the partner company takes full responsibility for a project, the acquiring company must devote in-house resources to monitor the project, capture the new knowledge being created, and prepare for the manufacturing and sales of the new product.

All five development categories are vital for creating a development organization that is responsive to the market. Each type of project plays a different role; each requires different levels and mixes of resources; and each generates very different results. Relying on only one or two categories for the bulk of the development work invariably leads to suboptimal use of resources, an unbalanced product offering, and eventually, a less than competitive market position.

PreQuip's Project Map

Using these five project types, PreQuip set about changing its product mix as the first step toward reforming the product development process. It started by matching its existing project list to the five categories. PreQuip's product line consisted of four kinds of analytic instruments—mass spectrometers, gas and liquid chromatographs, and data handling and processing equipment—that identified and isolated chemical compounds, gases, and liquids. Its customers included scientific laboratories, chemical companies, and oil refineries—users that needed to measure and test accurately the purity of raw materials, intermediate by-products, and finished products.

PreQuip's management asked some very basic questions in its attempt to delineate the categories. What exactly was a breakthrough product? Would a three-dimensional graphics display constitute a breakthrough? How was a platform defined? Was a full-featured mass spectrometer considered a platform? How about a derivative? Was a mass spectrometer with additional software a derivative?

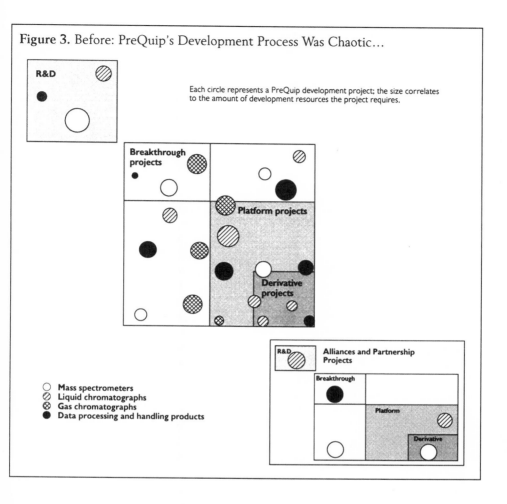

Figure 3. Before: PreQuip's Development Process Was Chaotic...

Each circle represents a PreQuip development project; the size correlates to the amount of development resources the project requires.

R&D

Breakthrough projects

Platform projects

Derivative projects

Alliances and Partnership Projects

R&D

Breakthrough

Platform

Derivative

○ Mass spectrometers
⊘ Liquid chromatographs
⊗ Gas chromatographs
● Data processing and handling products

None of these questions were easy to answer but after much analysis and debate, the management team agreed on the major characteristics for each project type and assigned most of PreQuip's 30 projects to one of the five categories. The map revealed just how uneven the distribution of projects had become—for instance, less than 20% of the company's projects were classified as platforms. (See the chart "Before: PreQuip's Development Process Was Chaotic....")

Management then turned its attention to those development projects that did not fit into any category. Some projects required substantial resources but did not represent breakthroughs. Others were more complicated than derivative projects but did not fall into PreQuip's definition of platforms. While frustrating, these dilemmas opened managers' eyes to the fact that some projects made little strategic sense. Why spend huge amounts of money developing products that at best would produce only incremental sales? The realization triggered a re-examination of PreQuip's customer needs in all product categories.

Consider mass spectrometers, instruments that identify the chemical composition of a compound. PreQuip was a top-of-the-line producer of mass spectrometers, offering a whole series of high-performance equipment with all the latest features but at a significant price premium. While this strategy had worked in the past, it no longer made sense in a maturing market; the evolution of mass spectrometer technology was predictable and well defined, and many competitors were able to offer the same capabilities, often at lower prices.

Increasingly, customers were putting greater emphasis on price in the purchasing decision. Some customers also wanted mass spectrometers that were easier to use and modular so they could be integrated into their own systems. Others demanded units with casings that could withstand harsh industrial environments. Still others required faster operating speeds, additional data storage, or self-diagnostic capabilities.

Taking all these customer requirements into account, PreQuip used the project map to rethink its mass spectrometer line. It envisaged a single platform complemented with a series of derivative products, each with a different set of options and each serving a different customer niche. By combining some new product design ideas—modularity and simplicity—with some new features that were currently under development, PreQuip created the concept of the C-101 platform, a low-priced, general-purpose mass spectrometer. In part because of its modularity, the product was designed to be simpler and cheaper to manufacture, which also helped to improve its overall quality and reliability. By adding software and a few new features, PreQuip could easily create derivatives, all of which could be assembled and tested on a single production line. In one case, a variant of the C-101 was planned for the high-end laboratory market. By strengthening the casing and eliminating some features, PreQuip also created a product for the industrial market.

Mapping out the new mass spectrometer line and the three other product lines was not painless. It took a number of months and involved a reconceptulization of the product lines, close management, and considerable customer involvement. To provide additional focus, PreQuip separated the engineering resources into three categories: basic R&D projects; existing products and customers, now a part of the manufacturing organization; and commercial product development.

To determine the number of breakthrough, platform, derivative, and partnered projects that could be sustained at any time, the company first estimated the average number of engineering months for each type of project based on past experience. It then allocated available engineering resources according to its desired mix of projects; about 50% to platform projects, 20% to derivative projects, and 10% each to breakthrough projects and partnerships. PreQuip then selected specific projects, confident that it would not overallocate its resources.

In the end, PreQuip canceled more than two-thirds of its development projects, including some high-profile pet projects of senior managers. When the dust had settled in mid-1990, PreQuip had just eleven projects: three platforms, one breakthrough, three derivatives, one partnership, and three projects in basic R&D. (see the chart "…After: PreQuip's Development Process Was Manageable.")

The changes led to some impressive gains: between 1989 and 1991, PreQuip's commercial development productivity improved by a factor of three. Fewer projects meant more actual work got done, and more work meant more products. To avoid over-committing resources and to improve productivity further, the company built a "capacity cushion" into its plan. It assigned only 75 full-time-equivalent engineers out

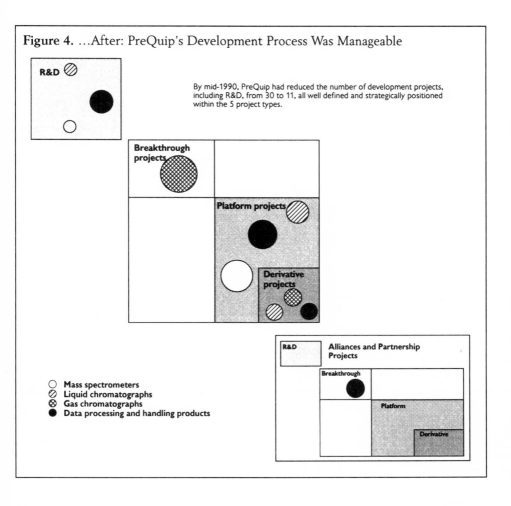

Figure 4. ...After: PreQuip's Development Process Was Manageable

By mid-1990, PreQuip had reduced the number of development projects, including R&D, from 30 to 11, all well defined and strategically positioned within the 5 project types.

R&D

Breakthrough projects

Platform projects

Derivative projects

R&D

Alliances and Partnership Projects

Breakthrough

Platform

Derivative

○ Mass spectrometers
⊘ Liquid chromatographs
⊗ Gas chromatographs
● Data processing and handling products

of a possible 80 to the 8 commercial development projects. By leaving a small percent of development capacity uncommitted, PreQuip was better prepared to take advantage of unexpected opportunities and to deal with crises when they arose.

Focus on the Platform

PreQuip's development map served for reallocating resources and for rethinking the mix of projects. Just as important, however, PreQuip no longer thought about projects in isolation; breakthrough projects shaped the new platforms, which defined the derivatives. In all four product lines, platforms played a particularly important role in the development strategy. This was not surprising considering the maturity of PreQuip's industry. For many companies, the more mature the industry, the more important it is to focus on platform projects.

Consider the typical industry life cycle. In the early stages of growth, innovative, dynamic companies gain market position with products that have dramatically superior performance along one or two dimensions. Whether they know it or not, these companies employ a breakthrough-platform strategy. But as the industry develops and the opportunity for breakthrough products decreases—often because the technology is shared more broadly—competitors try to satisfy increasingly sophisticated customers by rapidly making incremental improvements to existing products. Consciously or not, they adopt a strategy based on derivative projects. As happened with PreQuip, this approach ultimately leads to a proliferation of product lines and over-commitment of development resources. The solution lies in developing a few well-designed platform products, on each of which a generation of products can be built.

In the hospital bed industry, for example, companies that design, manufacture, sell, and service electric beds have faced a mature market for years. They are constantly under pressure to help their customers constrain capital expenditures and operating costs. Technologies are stable and many design changes are minor. Each generation of product typically lasts 8 to 12 years, and companies spend most of their time and energy developing derivative products. As a result, companies find themselves with large and unwieldy product lines.

In the 1980s, Hill-Rom, a leading electric-bed manufacturer, sought a new product strategy to help contain costs and maintain market share. Like other bed makers, its product development process was reactive and mired in too many low-payoff derivative projects. The company would design whatever the customer—a single hospital or nursing home—wanted, even if it meant significant commitments of development resources.

The new strategy involved a dramatic shift toward leveraging development and manufacturing resources. Hill-Rom decided to focus on hospitals and largely withdraw from the nursing home segment, as well as limit the product line by developing two new platform products—the Centra and the Century. The Centra was a high-priced product with built-in electronic controls, including communications capabilities. The Century was a simpler, less-complex design with fewer features. The products built off each platform shared common parts and manufacturing processes and provided the customer with a number of add-on options. By focusing development efforts on two platforms, Hill-Rom was able to introduce new technologies and new product features into the market faster and more systematically, directly affecting patient recovery and hospital staff productivity. This strategy led to a less chaotic development cycle as well as lower unit cost, higher product quality and more satisfied customers.

For companies that must react to constant changes in fashion and consumer tastes, a different relationship between platform and derivative projects makes sense. For example, Sony has pioneered its "hyper-variety" strategy in developing the Walkman: it directs the bulk of its Walkman development efforts at creating derivatives, enhancements, hybrids, and line extensions that offer something tailored to every niche, distribution channel, and competitor's product. As a result, in 1990, Sony dominated the personal audio system market with over 200 models based on just three platforms.

Platforms are critical to any product development effort, but there is no one ideal mix of projects that fits all companies. Every company must pursue the projects that match its opportunities, business strategy, and available resources. Of course, the mix evolves over time as projects move out of development into production, as business strategies change, as new markets emerge, and as resources are enhanced. Management needs to revisit the project mix on a regular basis—in some cases every six months, in others, every year or so.

Figure 5. PreQuip's Project Sequence

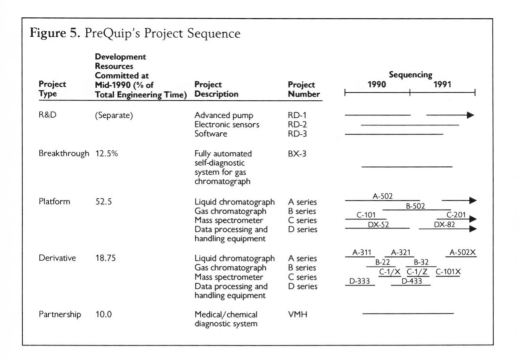

Project Type	Development Resources Committed at Mid-1990 (% of Total Engineering Time)	Project Description	Project Number	Sequencing 1990 1991
R&D	(Separate)	Advanced pump	RD-1	
		Electronic sensors	RD-2	
		Software	RD-3	
Breakthrough	12.5%	Fully automated self-diagnostic system for gas chromatograph	BX-3	
Platform	52.5	Liquid chromatograph	A series	A-502
		Gas chromatograph	B series	B-502
		Mass spectrometer	C series	C-101 C-201
		Data processing and handling equipment	D series	DX-52 DX-82
Derivative	18.75	Liquid chromatograph	A series	A-311 A-321 A-502X
		Gas chromatograph	B series	B-22 B-32
		Mass spectrometer	C series	C-1/X C-1/Z C-101X
		Data processing and handling equipment	D series	D-333 D-433
Partnership	10.0	Medical/chemical diagnostic system	VMH	

Steady Stream Sequencing: PreQuip Plans Future Development

Periodically evaluating the product mix keeps development activities on the right track. Companies must decide how to sequence projects over time, how the set of projects should evolve with the business strategy, and how to build development capabilities though such projects. The decisions about changing the mix are neither easy nor straightforward. Without an aggregate project plan, most companies cannot even begin to formulate a strategy for making those decisions.

PreQuip was no different. Before adopting an aggregate project plan, the company had no concept of project mix and no understanding of sequencing. Whenever someone with authority had an idea worth pursuing, the development department added the project to its active list. With the evolution of a project plan, PreQuip developed an initial mix and elevated the sequencing decision to a strategic responsibility of senior management. Management scheduled projects at evenly spaced intervals to ensure a "steady stream" of development projects. (See the chart "PreQuip's Project Sequence.")

A representative example of PreQuip's new strategy for sequencing projects is its new mass spectrometer, or C series. Introduced into the development cycle in late 1989, the C-101 was the first platform conceived as a system built around the new modular design. Aimed at the middle to upper end of the market, it was a versatile, modular unit for the laboratory that incorporated many of the existing electromechanical features into the new software. The C-101 was scheduled to enter manufacturing prototyping in the third quarter of 1990.

PreQuip positioned the C-1/X, the first derivative of the C-101, for the industrial market. It had a rugged casing designed for extreme environments and fewer software features than the C-101. It entered the development process about the time the C-101 moved into manufacturing prototyping and was staffed initially with two designers whose activities on the C-101 were drawing to a close.

Very similar to the C-1/X was the C-1/Z, a unit designed for the European market; the C-1/X team was expanded to work on both the C-1/X and the C-1/Z. The C-1/Z had some unique software and a different display and packaging but the same modular design. PreQuip's marketing department scheduled the C-101 to be introduced about 6 months before the C-1/X and the C-1/Z, thus permitting the company to reach a number of markets quickly with new products.

To leverage accumulated knowledge and experience, senior management assigned the team that worked on the C-1/X and the C-1/Z to the C-201 project, the next-generation spectrometer scheduled to replace the C-101. It too was of a modular design but with more computer power and greater software functionality. The C-201 also incorporated a number of manufacturing process improvements gleaned from manufacturing the C-101.

To provide a smooth market transition from the C-101 to the C-201, management assigned the remainder of the C-101 team to develop the C-101X, a follow-on derivative project. The C-101X was positioned as an improvement over the C-101 to attract customers who were in the market for a low-end mass spectrometer but were unwilling to settle for the aging technology of the C-101. Just as important, the project was an ideal way to gather market data that could be used to develop the C-201.

PreQuip applied this same strategy across the other three product categories. Every other year it planned a new platform, followed by two or three derivatives spaced at appropriate intervals. Typically, when a team finished work on a platform, management assigned part of the team to derivative projects and part to the other projects. A year or so later, a new team would form to work on the next platform, with some members having worked on the preceding generation and others not. This steady stream sequencing strategy worked to improve the company's overall market position while encouraging knowledge transfer and more rapid, systematic resource development.

An Alternative: Secondary Wave Planning

While the steady stream approach served PreQuip well, companies in different industries might consider alternative strategies. For instance, a "secondary wave" strategy may be more appropriate for companies that, like Hill-Rom, have multiple product lines, each with their own base platforms but with more time between succeeding generations of a particular platform.

The strategy works like this. A development team begins on a next-generation platform. Once the company completes that project, the key people from the team start work on another platform for a different product family. Management leaves the recently introduced platform on the market for a couple of years with a few derivatives introduced. As that platform begins to age and competitors' newer platforms challenge it, the company refocuses development resources on a set of derivatives in order to strengthen and extend the viability of the product line's existing platform. The wave of derivative projects extends the platform life and upgrades product offerings, but it also provides experience and feedback to the people working on the product line and prepares them for the next-generation platform development. They receive feedback from the market on the previous platform, information on competitors' platform offerings, and information on emerging market needs. Key people then bring that information together to define the next platform and the cycle begins again, built around a team, many of whose members have just completed the wave of derivative products.

A variation on the secondary wave strategy, one used with considerable success by Kodak, involves compressing the time between market introduction of major platforms. Rather than going off to work on another product family's platform following one platform's introduction, the majority of the development team goes to work immediately on a set of derivative products. This requires a more compressed and careful assessment of the market's response to the just-introduced platform and much shorter feedback loops regarding competitors' products. If done right, however, companies can build momentum and capture significant incremental market share. Once the flurry of derivative products has passed, the team goes to work on the next-generation platform project for the same product family.

Before 1987, Kodak conducted a series of advanced development projects to explore alternative single-use 35mm cameras—a roll of film packaged in an inexpensive camera. Once used, the film is processed and the camera discarded or recycled. During 1987, a group of Kodak development engineers worked on the first platform project which resulted in the market introduction and volume production of the Fling 35mm camera in January 1988. (The product was later renamed the Fun Saver.) As the platform neared completion, management reassigned the front-end development staff to two derivative projects; the Stretch, a panoramic, double-wide image version of the Fling, and the Weekend, a waterproof version.

By the end of 1988, Kodak had introduced both derivative cameras and was shipping them in volume. True to the definition of a derivative, both the Stretch and the Weekend took far fewer development resources and far less time than the Fling. They also required less new tooling and process engineering since they leveraged the existing automation and manufacturing process. The development team then went to work on the next-generation platform product—a Fun Saver with a built-in flash.

No matter which strategy a company uses to plan its platform-derivative mix—steady stream or secondary wave—it must have well-defined platforms. Indeed, in a number of industries we've studied, the companies that introduced new platforms at the fastest rate were usually able to capture the greatest market share over time.

In the auto industry, for example, different companies follow quite different sequencing schedules, with markedly different results. According to data collected in the late 1980s, European car companies changed the platform for a given product, on average, every 12 years, U.S. companies every 8 years, and Japanese companies every 4 years. A number of factors explain the differences in platform development cycles—historical and cultural differences, longer development lead times, and differences in development productivity.

In both Europe and the United States, the engineering hours and tooling costs of new products were much higher than in Japan. This translated into lower development costs for Japanese car makers, which allowed faster payback and shorter economic lives for all models. As a consequence, the Japanese could profitably conduct more projects and make more frequent and more extensive changes than both their

---

Figure 8. Eight Steps of an Aggregate Project Plan

1 Define project types as either breakthrough, platform, derivative, R&D, or partnered projects.

2 Identify existing projects and classify by project type.

3 Estimate the average time and resources needed for each project type based on past experience.

4 Identify existing resource capacity.

5 Determine the desired mix of projects.

6 Estimate the number of projects that existing resources can support.

7 Decide which specific projects to pursue.

8 Work to improve development capabilities.

European and U.S. competitors and thus were better positioned to satisfy customers' needs and capture market share.

The Long-Term Goal: Building Critical Capabilities

Possibly the greatest value of an aggregate project plan over the long-term is its ability to shape and build development capabilities, both individual and organizational. It provides a vehicle for training development engineers, marketers, and manufacturing people in the different skill sets needed by the company. For instance, some less experienced engineers initially may be better suited to work on derivative projects, while others might have technical skills more suited for breakthrough projects. The aggregate project plan lets companies play to employees' strengths and broaden their careers and abilities over time.

Thinking about skill development in terms of the aggregate project plan is most important for developing competent team leaders. Take, for instance, an engineer with five years of experience moving to become a project leader. Management might assign her to lead a derivative project first. It is an ideal training ground because derivative projects are the best defined, the least complex, and usually the shortest in duration of all project types. After the project is completed successfully, she might get promoted to lead a larger derivative project and then a platform project. And if she distinguished herself there and has the other required skills, she might be given the opportunity to work on a breakthrough project.

In addition to creating a formal career path within the sphere of development activities, companies should also focus on moving key engineers and other development participants between advanced research and commercial development. This is necessary to keep the transfer of technology fresh and creative and to reward engineers who keep their R&D efforts focused on commercial developments.

Honda is one company that delineates clearly between advanced research and product development—the two kinds of projects are managed and organized differently and are approached with very different expectations. Development engineers tend to have broader skills, while researchers' are usually more specialized. However, Honda encourages its engineers to move from one type of project to another if they demonstrate an idea that management believes may result in a commercially viable innovation. For example, Honda's new lean-burning engine, introduced in the 1992 Civic, began as an advanced research project headed by Hideyo Miyano. As the project moved from research to commercial development, Miyano moved too, playing the role of project champion throughout the entire development process.

Besides improving people's skills, the aggregate project plan can be used to identify weaknesses in capabilities, improve development processes, and incorporate new tools and techniques into the development environment. The project plan helps identify where companies need to make changes and how those changes are connected to product and process development.

As PreQuip developed an aggregate project plan, for example, it identified a number of gaps in its capabilities. In the case of the mass spectrometer, the demand for more software functionality meant PreQuip had to develop an expertise in software development. And with an emphasis on cost, modularity and reliability, PreQuip also had to focus on improving its industrial design skills.

As part of its strategy to improve design skills, the company introduced a new computer-aided design system into its engineering department, using the aggregate project plan as its guide. Management knew that one of the platform project teams was particularly adept with computer applications, so it chose that project as the pilot for the new CAD system. Over the life of the product, the teams' proficiency with the new system grew. When the project ended, management dispersed team members to other projects so they could train other engineers in using the new CAD system.

As PreQuip discovered, developing an aggregate project plan involves a relatively simple and straightforward procedure. But carrying it out—moving from a poorly managed collection of ad hoc projects to a robust set that matches and reinforces the business strategy—requires hard choices and discipline.

At all the companies we have studied, the difficulty of those choices makes imperative strong leadership and early involvement from senior management. Without management's active participation and direction, organizations find it next to impossible to kill or postpone projects and to resist the short-term pressures that drive them to spend most of their time and resources fighting fires.

Getting to an aggregate project plan is not easy but working through the process is a critical part of creating a sustainable development strategy. Indeed, while the specific plan is extremely important, the planning process itself is even more so. The plan will change as events unfold and managers make adjustments. But choosing the mix, determining the number of projects the resources can support, defining the sequence, and picking the right projects raise crucial questions about how product and process development ought to be linked to the company's competitive opportunities. Creating an aggregate project plan gives direction and clarity to the overall development effort and helps lay the foundation for outstanding performance.

Appendix

Bibliography
Readings on Project Portfolio Management

Aaker, D.A. and T.T. Tyebjee. 1978. A model for the selection of interdependent R&D projects. *IEEE Transactions on Engineering Management* 25(2): 30-36.

Adelson, R.M. 1965. Criteria for capital investment: an approach through decision theory. *Operational Research Quarterly* 16(1): 19-50.

Agarwal, R., L Roberge and M. Tanniru. 1994. MIS planning: a methodology for systems prioritization. *Information Management* 27(5): 261-74.

Agarwal, R., M.R. Tanniru and M. Dacruz. 1992. Knowledge-based support for combining qualitative and quantitative judgment in resource allocation decisions. *Journal of Management Information Systems* 9(1):165-84.

Albala, A. 1975. Stage approach for the evaluation and selection of R&D projects. *IEEE Transactions on Engineering Management* 22(4).

Aldrich, D. and T.E. Morton. 1975. Optimal funding paths for a class of risky R&D projects. *Management Science* 21: 491-500.

Alidi, A.S. 1996. Use of the analytic hierarchy process to measure the initial viability of industrial projects. *International Journal of Project Management* 14(4): 205-8.

Allen, D.H. and T.F.N. Johnson. 1971. Realism in LP modelling for project selection. *R&D Management* 1(1): 10-15.

Alston, F.M. 1986. Recovering IR&D/B&P costs. *NCMA Journal* (Summer): 55-59.

Anderson, D.R., D.J. Sweeney and T.A. Williams. 1994. *An Introduction to Management Science: Quantitative Approaches to Decision Making.* New York: West Publishing Co.

Archer, N.P. and F. Ghasemzadeh. 1996. Project portfolio selection techniques: a review and a suggested integrated approach. Management of Innovation and New Technology Working Paper 46, School of Business, McMaster University.

Archer, N.P. and F. Ghasemzadeh. 1999. An integrated framework for project portfolio selection. *International Journal of Project Management* 17(4): 207-16.

Archer, N.P. and F. Gasemzadeh. 1998. A decision support system for project portfolio selection. *International Journal of Technology Management* 16(1/3): 105-14

Archibald, R.D. 1976. *Managing High Technology Programs and Projects.* New York: Wiley.

Armstrong, J.S. and R. J. Brodie. 1994. Effects of portfolio planning methods on decision making: experimental results. *International Journal of Research in Marketing* 11: 73-84.

Ash, R. and D. E. Smith-Daniels. 1999. The effects of learning, forgetting, and relearning on decision rule performance in multiproject scheduling. *Decision Sciences* 30(1): 47-82.

Asher, D.I. 1962. A linear programming model for the allocation of R&D efforts. *IRE Transactions on Engineering Management* 9 (December): 154-57.

Atkinson, A.C. and A.H. Bobis. 1969. A mathematical basis for the selection of research projects. *IEEE Transactions on Engineering Management* 16(1): 2-8.

Augood, D.R. 1973. A review of R&D evaluation methods. *IEEE Transactions on Engineering Management* 20(4): 114-20.

Augood, D.R. 1975. A new approach to R&D evaluation. *IEEE Transactions on Engineering Management* 22(1): 2-11.

Averch, H. 1993. Criteria for evaluating research projects and portfolios. In *Assessing R&D Impacts: Methods and Practice*, B. Bozeman and J. Melkers, eds. Norwell, MA: Kluwer, pp. 264-77.

Bacon, C.J. 1992. The use of decision criteria in selecting information systems/technology investments. *MIS Quarterly* 16: 335-53.

Baker, L.T. 1969. Planning an independent research and development program. *Proceedings of the IEEE Aerospace Electronics Conference*, pp. 507-12.

Baker, N.R. 1974. R&D project selection models: an assessment. *IEEE Transactions on Engineering Management* 21(4): 165-71.

Baker, N.R. and J. Freeland. 1975. Recent advances in R&D benefit measurement and project selection models. *Management Science* 21(10): 1164-75.

Baker, N.R. and W.H. Pound. 1964. R&D project selection: where we stand. *IEEE Transactions on Engineering Management* 11(4): 124-34.

Balachandra, R. 1984. Critical signals for making the go/no go decisions in new product development. *Journal of Product Innovation Management* 2: 92-100.

Balachandra, R. and J.A. Raelin. 1980. How to abandon an R&D project. *Research Management* 18: 24-29.

Balthasar, H.U., R.A. Boschi and M.M. Menke. 1978. Calling the shots in R&D. *Harvard Business Review* 56(10).

Bard, J.F. 1990. Using multicriteria methods in the early stages of new product development. *Journal of the Operational Research Society* 41(8): 755-66.

Bard, J.F., R. Balachandra and P.E. Kaufmann. 1988. An interactive approach to R&D project selection and termination. *IEEE Transactions on Engineering Management* 35(3): 139-46.

Beale, P. and M. Freeman. 1991. Successful project execution: a model. *Project Management Journal* 22(4).

Becker, R.H. 1980. Project selection checklists for research, product development, and process development. *Research Management* 23(5): 34-36.

Bedell, R.J. 1983. Terminating R&D projects prematurely. *Research Management* 26(4): 32-35.

Beged-Dov, A.G. 1965. Optimal assignment of research and development projects in a large company using an integer programming model. *IEEE Transactions on Engineering Management* 12: 138-43.

Bell, D.C. and A.W. Read. 1970. The application of a research project selection method. *R&D Management* 1(1): 35-42.

Bell, D.C., J.E. Chilcott, A.W. Read and R. Salway. 1967. Application of a research project selection method in the North Eastern Region Scientific Services Department. Central Electricity Generating Board Report RH/H/RS, United Kingdom.

Bellman, R.E. and L.A. Zadeh. 1970. Decision-making in a fuzzy environment. *Management Science* 17(4): 141-75.

Bender, D.A., E.B. Pyle III, W.J. Westlake and D. Bryce. 1976. Simulation of R&D investment strategies. *Omega* 4(1): 67-77.

Benjamin, C.O. 1985. A linear goal programming model for public-sector project selection. *Journal of the Operational Research Society* 36: 13-23.

Bergman, S.W. and J.L. Gittins. 1985. R&D project-selection methods. In *Statistical Methods for Pharmaceutical Research Planning*. New York: Marcel Dekker.

Bernardo, J.J. 1977. An assignment approach to choosing R&D experiments. *Decision Sciences* 8: 489-501.

Black, K.M. 1988. IR&D: an essential element of national defense. *National Defense: Journal of the American Defense Preparedness Association* 72(437): 33-37.

Bobis, A.H., T.F. Cooke and J.H. Paden. 1971. A funds allocation method to improve the odds for research successes. *Research Management* 14: 34-49.

Bohanec, M., V. Rajkovic, B. Semolic and A. Pogacnik. 1995. Knowledge-based portfolio analysis for project evaluation. *Information & Management* 28(5): 293-302.

Booker, J.M. and M.C. Bryson. 1984. Annotated bibliography on decision analysis with applications to project management. Los Alamos National Laboratory, Los Alamos, NM, Technical Report LA-10027-MS.

Booker, J.M. and M.C. Bryson. 1985. Decision analysis in project management: an overview. *IEEE Transactions on Engineering Management* 32(1): 3-9.

Bordley, R.F. 1998. R&D project selection versus R&D project generation. *IEEE Transactions on Engineering Management* 45(4): 407-13.

Boschi, R.A., H.U. Balthasar and M.M. Menke. 1979. Quantifying and forecasting exploratory research success. *Research Management* 22(5): 14-21.

Boznak, R.G. 1996. Management of projects: A giant step beyond project management. *PM Network* 10(1): 27-30.

Brenner, M.S. 1994. Practical R&D project prioritization. *Research Technology Management* 37(5): 38-42.

Brewer, P.C., A.W. Gatian and J.A. Reeve. 1993. Managing uncertainty. *Management Accounting* (October): 39-45.

Brunsson, N. 1980. The functions of project evaluation. *R&D Management* 10(2): 61-65.

Buchanan, J.L. and H.G. Daellenbach. 1987. A comparative evaluation of interactive solution methods for multiple objective decision models. *European Journal of Operational Research* 29: 353-59.

Buckley, S.R. and D. Yen. 1990. Group decision support systems: concerns for success. *The Information Society* 7: 109-23.

Buss, M.D.J. 1983. How to rank computer projects. *Harvard Business Review* (January-February): 118-24.

Calantone, R.J., C.A. Di Benedetto and J.B. Schmidt. 1999. Using the analytic hierarchy process in new product screening. The *Journal of Product Innovation Management* 16(1): 65.

Canada, J.R. and J.A. White. 1980. *Capital Investment Decision Analysis for Management and Engineering.* Englewood Cliffs, NJ: Prentice-Hall.

Cardus, D.M., J. Fuhrer, A.W. Martin and R.M. Thrall. 1982. Use of benefit-cost analysis in the peer review of proposed research. *Management Science* 28(4): 439-45.

Cetron, M.J., J. Martino and L. Roepcke. 1967. The selection of R&D program content—survey of quantitative methods. *IEEE Transactions on Engineering Management* 14(1): 4-13.

Chapman, M.R. 1998. Benefits management—going beyond program management. *Proceedings of the Annual Project Management Institute Seminars & Symposium,* pp. 399-405.

Charnes, A. and A.C. Stedry. 1966. A chance-constrained model for real-time control in research and development management. *Management Science* 12(8): 353-62.

Chen, K. and N. Gorla. 1998. Information system project selection using fuzzy logic. *IEEE Transactions on Systems, Man and Cybernetics* 28(6): 849-55.

Chun, Y.H. 1994. Sequential decisions under uncertainty in the R&D project selection problem. *IEEE Transactions on Engineering Management* 40: 404-413.

Chung, C.A. and A.Md.A. Huda. 1998. Practical tools for project selection. In *Field Guide to Project Management,* D.I. Cleland, ed. New York: Wiley, pp. 37-47.

Churchman, C.W. and R.L. Ackoff. 1954. An approximate measure of value. *Operations Research* 2.

Churchman, C.W., R.L. Ackoff, and E.L. Arnoff. 1957. *Introduction to Operations Research.* New York: Wiley.

Clark, P. 1977. A profitability project selection method. *Research Management* 20(6).

Clarke, T.E. 1974. Decision-making in technologically based organizations: a literature survey of present practice. *IEEE Transactions on Engineering Management* 21(1): 9-23.

Clayton, R. 1971. A convergent approach to R&D planning and project selection. *Research Management* 14(5).

Cleland, D.I. 1999. The strategic context of projects. In *Project Management: Strategic Design and Implementation, Third Edition.* New York: McGraw-Hill, pp. 91-117.

Clemen, R. 1996. *Making Hard Decisions: An Introduction to Decision Analysis,* 2nd ed. Duxbury Press.

Clifton, Jr., D.S. and D.E. Fyffe. 1977. *Project Feasibility Analysis: A Guide to Profitable Ventures.* New York: Wiley.

Cochran, M.A., E.B. Pyle, III, L.C. Greene, H.A. Clymer, and A.D. Bender. 1971. Investment model for R&D project evaluation and selection. *IEEE Transactions on Engineering Management* 18(8).

Cochrane, J.L. and M. Zeleny, eds. 1973. *Multiple Criteria Decision Making.* Columbia, SC: University of South Carolina Press.

Coffin, M.A. and B.W. Taylor, III. 1996. Multiple criteria R&D project selection and scheduling using fuzzy logic. *Computers & Operations Research* 23(3): 207-20.

Collis, D.J. and E. Johnson. 1995. Portfolio planning at CIBA-GEIGY and the Newport investment proposal. Harvard Business School Publishing Case Study.

Comaford, C. 1997. Getting net projects into the pearly gates of ROI. *PC Week* (March 10).

Combe, M.W. 1998. Project prioritization in a large functional organization. *Proceedings of the Annual Project Management Institute Seminars & Symposium,* pp. 511-15.

Comstock, G.L. and D.E. Sjolseth. 1999. Aligning and prioritizing corporate R&D. *Research Technology Management* 42(3): 19-25.

Cook, W.D. and L.M. Seifford. 1982. R&D project selection in a multidimensional environment: a practical approach. *Journal of the Operational Research Society* 33: 397-405.

Cook, W.D. and Y. Roll. 1988. R&D project selection: productivity considerations. *R&D Management* 18(3): 251-56.

Cooley, S.J., J. Hehmeyer and P.J. Sweeney. 1986. Modeling R&D resource allocation. *Research Management* 29(1): 40-45.

Cooper, M.J. 1978. An evaluation system for project selection. *Research Management* 24: 29-33.

Cooper, R.G. 1979. The dimensions of industrial new product success and failure. *Journal of Marketing* 43 (Summer).

Cooper, R.G. 1981. An empirically derived new product project selection model. *IEEE Transactions on Engineering Management* 28(3).

Cooper, R.G. 1993. *Winning At New Products,* 2nd ed. Reading, MA: Addison-Wesley.

Cooper, R.G. and E.J. Kleinschmidt. 1987. What makes a new product winner: success factors at the project level. *R&D Management* 17(3).

Cooper, R.G. and E.J. Kleinschmidt. 1990. New product success factors: a comparison of 'kills' versus successes and failures. *R&D Management* 20(1).

Cooper, R.G. and E.J. Kleinschmidt. 1996. Winning business in product development: critical success factors. *Research Technology Management* 39(4): 18-29.

Cooper, R.G., S.J. Edgett and E.J. Kleinschmidt. 1997. Portfolio management in new product development: lessons from the leaders-I. *Research Technology Management* 40(5): 16-28.

Cooper, R.G., S.J. Edgett and E.J. Kleinschmidt. 1997. Portfolio management in new product development: lessons from the leaders-II. *Research Technology Management* 40(6): 43-58.

Cooper, R.G., S.J. Edgett and E.J. Kleinschmidt. 1998. Best practices for managing R&D portfolios. *Research Technology Management* 41(4): 20-33.

Cooper, R.G., S.J. Edgett and E.J. Kleinschmidt. 1998. *Portfolio Management for New Products.* Reading, MA: Addison-Wesley.

Cord, J. 1964. A method for allocating funds to investment projects when returns are subject to uncertainty. *Management Science* 19(5): 335-41.

Costello, D. 1983. A practical approach to R&D selection. *Technological Forecasting and Social Change* 23: 353-68.

Coulter, C., III. 1990. Multiproject management and control. *Cost Engineering* 32(10).

Cramer, R.M. and B.E. Smith. 1964. Decision models for the selection of research projects. *The Engineering Economist* 9(2): 1-20.

Crowder, H. E., J. Johnson and M. Padberg. 1983. Solving large-scale zero-one linear programming problems. *Operations Research* 31(5): 803-34.

Czajkowski, A.F. and S. Jones. 1986. Selecting interrelated R&D projects in space planning technology. *IEEE Transactions on Engineering Management* 33: 17-24.

Dalkey, N.C. 1969. *The Delphi Method: An Experimental Study of Group Opinion* (RM-5888-PR). Santa Monica, CA: The Rand Corporation.

Danila, N. 1989. Strategic evaluation and selection of R&D projects. *R&D Management* 19(1): 47-62.

David, H.A. 1963. *The Method of Paired Comparisons.* New York: Hafner Publishing.

Davis, E.W. and G.E. Heidorn. 1971. Optimal project scheduling under multiple resource constraints. *Management Science* 17(12): 803-816.

Dean, B.V. 1968. *Evaluating, Selecting, and Controlling R&D Projects.* New York: American Management Association.

Dean, B.V. 1972. A research laboratory performance model. In *Quantitative Decision Aiding Techniques for Research and Development,* M.J. Cetron, H. Davidson, and A.H. Rubenstein, eds. New York: Gordon and Breach.

Dean, B.V. and L.A. Roepcke. 1969. Cost effectiveness in R&D organizational resource allocation. *IEEE Transactions on Engineering Management* 16: 222-42.

Dean, B.V. and M.J. Nishry. 1965. Scoring and profitability models for evaluating and selecting engineering projects. *Operations Research* 13(4): 550-69.

Dean, B.V. and S.J. Mantel, Jr. 1968. A model for evaluating costs of implementing community projects. In *Analysis for Planning Programming Budgeting,* M. Alfandary-Alexander, ed. Potomac, MD: Washington Operations Research Council.

Dean, B.V. and S.S. Sengupta. 1962. Research budgeting and project selection. *IRE Transactions on Engineering Management* 19: 158-69.

Dean, B.V., D.R. Denzler and J.J. Watkins. 1992. Multiproject staff scheduling with variable resource constraints. *IEEE Transactions on Engineering Management* 29(1).

Dekluyver, C.A. and H. Moskowitz. 1984. Assessing scenario probabilities via inter-active goal programming. *Management Science* 30(3): 273-78.

Delbecq, A.L., A.H. Van de Ven and D.H. Gustafson. 1975. *Group Techniques for Program Planning*. Glenview, IL: Scott, Foresman.

DeMaio, A., R. Verganti and M. Corso. 1994. A multi-project management framework for new product development. *European Journal of Operational Research* 78(2): 178-91.

Dias, Jr., O.P. 1988. the R&D project selection problem with fuzzy coefficients. *Fuzzy Sets and Systems* 26(3): 299-316.

Dinsmore, P.C. 1996. Toward corporate project management: beefing up the bottom line with MOBP. *PM Network* 10(6): 10-13.

Dolk, D.R. and J.E. Kottemann. 1993. Model integration and a theory of models. *Decision Support Systems* 9: 51-63.

Dos Santos, B.L. 1989. Selecting information system projects: problems, solutions and challenges. *Proceedings of the Hawaii Conference on System Sciences*, pp. 1131-40.

Dyer, J.S. 1990. Remarks on the analytic hierarchy process. *Management Science* 36(3): 249-58.

Dyer, J.S. and Rakesh K. Sarin. 1979. Measurable multiattribute value functions. *Operations Research* 27(4): 810-22.

Eldukair, Z.A. 1990. Project correlation in portfolio theory. *Civil Engineering Systems* 7(3): 170.

Ellis, L.W. 1984. *The Financial Side of Industrial Research Management*. New York: Wiley.

Englund, R. and R.J. Graham. 1999. From experience: linking projects to strategy. *Journal of Product Innovation Management* 16(1): 52-64.

Enrick, N.L. 1980. Value analysis for priority setting and resource allocation. *Industrial Management* (September-October).

Eom, B.H. and S.M. Lee. 1990. A survey of decision support system applications. *Interfaces* 20: 65-79.

European Industrial Research Management Association. 1978. Top-down and bottom-up approaches to project selection. *Research Management* 21(2).

Evans, G.W. and R. Fairbairn. 1989. Selection and scheduling of advanced missions for NASA using 0-1 integer linear programming. *Journal of the Operational Research Society* 40(11): 971-81.

Ewusi-Mensah, K. and Z.H. Przasnyski. 1991. On information systems project abandonment: an exploratory study of organizational practice. *MIS Quarterly* (March): 67-85.

Fahrni, P. and M. Spatig. 1990. An application-oriented guide to R&D project selection and evaluation methods. *R&D Management* 20(2): 155-71.

Faust, R.E. 1971. Project selection in the pharmaceutical industry. *Research Management* 14(5).

Fisk, J.A. 1979. Goal programming model for output planning. *Decision Sciences* 10: 593-603.

Flinn, R.A. and E. Turban. 1970. Decision tree analysis for industrial research. *Research Management* 15(1): 27-34.

Forman, E.H., T.L. Saaty, M.A. Selly and R. Waldron. 1983. *Expert Choice.* McLean, VA: Decision Support Software.

Fox, G.E. and N.R. Baker. 1985. Project-selection decision making linked to a dynamic environment. *Management Science* 31(10): 1272-85.

Fox, G.E., N.R. Baker and J.L. Bryant. 1984. Economic models for R and D project selection in the presence of project interactions. *Management Science* 30(7): 890-902.

Frame, J.D. 1994. *The New Project Management.* San Francisco: Jossey-Bass.

Freeman, R.J. 1960. A stochastic model for determining the selection and allocation of the research budget. *IRE Transactions on Engineering Management* 17: 2-7.

Freestone, D.S. 1994. Reflections on pharmaceutical company project portfolio management. *Drug Information Journal* 28(3): 641.

French, S. 1984. Interactive multi-objective programming: its aims, applications and demands. *Journal of the Operational Research Society* 35: 827-34.

Garcia, A., and W. Cowdrey. 1978. Information systems: a long way from wall-carvings to CRTs. *Industrial Engineering* (April).

Garguilo, G.R., et al. 1981. Developing systematic procedures for directing research programs. *IRE Transactions on Engineering Management* 8: 24-29.

Gaynor, H. 1990. Selecting projects. *Research Technology Management* 33(4): 43-45.

Gear, A.E. 1974. A review of some recent developments in portfolio modeling in applied research and development. *IEEE Transactions on Engineering Management* 21(4): 119-25.

Gear, A.E. and A.G. Lockett. 1973. A dynamic model of some multistage aspects of research and development portfolios. *IEEE Transactions on Engineering Management* 20(1): 22-29.

Gear, A.E., A.G. Lockett and A.W. Pearson. 1971. Analysis of some portfolio models for R&D. *IEEE Transactions on Engineering Management* 18(2): 66-75.

Gee, R.E. 1971. A survey of current project selection practices. *Research Management* 14(5): 38-45.

Geoffrion, A.M., J.S. Dyer and A. Feinberg. 1972. An interactive approach for multicriterion optimization with an application to the operation of an academic department. *Management Science* 19(4): 357-68.

Gerstenfeld, A. 1976. A study of successful projects, unsuccessful projects, and projects in process in West Germany. *IEEE Transactions on Engineering Management* 23(3).

Ghasemzadeh, F. and N.P. Archer. 1998. Project portfolio selection through decision support. Management of Innovation and New Technology Working Paper 76. Michael G. DeGroote School of Business, McMaster University.

Ghasemzadeh, F., N.P. Archer, and P. Iyogun. 1996. A zero-one ILP model for project portfolio selection. Management of Innovation and New Technology Working Paper 59. School of Business, McMaster University.

Ghotb, F. and L. Warren. 1995. A case study comparison of the analytic hierarchy process and fuzzy decision methodology. *The Engineering Economist* 40(3): 233-47.

Gill, B., B. Nelson and S. Spring. 1996. Seven steps to strategic new product development. In *The PDMA Handbook of New Product Development*, Milton D. Rosenau, Jr., ed. New York: Wiley, pp. 19-33.

Ginzberg, M.J. 1979. Improving MIS project selection. *Omega* 7(6): 527-37.

Githens, G.D. 1998. Programs, portfolios, and pipelines: how to anticipate executives' strategic questions. *Proceedings of the Annual Project Management Institute Seminars & Symposium*, pp. 728-31.

Gluck, F.W. and R.N. Foster. 1975. Managing technological change: a box of cigars for Brad. *Harvard Business Review* (September-October): 139-49.

Gokhale, H. and M.L. Bhatia. 1997. A project planning and monitoring system for research projects. *International Journal of Project Management* 15(3): 159-63.

Golabi, K. 1987. Selecting a group of dissimilar projects for funding. *IEEE Transactions on Engineering Management* 34: 138-45.

Golabi, K., G.W. Kirkwood and A. Sicherman. 1981. Selecting a portfolio of solar energy projects using multi-attribute preference theory. *Management Science* 27(2): 174-89

Golden, B.L., E.A. Wasil and D.E. Levy. 1989. Applications of the analytic hierarchy process: a categorized, annotated bibliography. In *Analytic Hierarchy Process: Applications and Studies*, B.L. Golden, E.A. Wasil and P.T. Harker, eds. New York: Springer-Verlag.

Goldstein, P.M. and H.M. Singer. 1986. A note on economic models for R&D project selection in the presence of project interactions. *Management Science* 32(10): 1356-60.

Gordon, L.A. and G.E. Pinches. 1984. *Improving Capital Budgeting: A Decision Support System Approach*. Reading, MA: Addison-Wesley.

Graves, S.B. and J.L. Rinquest. 1992. Choosing the best solution in an R&D project selection problem with multiple objectives. *Journal of High Technology Management Research* 3(2).

Griffin, A. and A. Page. 1993. An interim report on measuring product development success and failure. *Journal of Product Innovation Management* 9(1): 291-308.

Guimaraes, T. and W. E. Paxton. 1984. Impact of financial methods project selection. *Journal of Systems Management* 35(2): 18-22.

Gupta, S.K. and T. Mandakovic. 1992. Contemporary approaches to R&D project selection: a literature search. In *Management of R&D and Engineering*, D.F. Kocaoglu, ed. Amsterdam: North-Holland.

Gupta, S.K., J. Kyparisis and C. Ip. 1992. Project selection and sequencing to maximize net present value of the total return. *Management Science* 38: 751-52.

Gustafson, D.H. G.K. Pai and G.C. Kramer. 1971. A weighted aggregate approach to R&D project selection. *AIIE Transactions* 3(1): 22-30.

Hajek, V.G. 1984. *Management of Engineering Projects*, 3rd ed. New York: McGraw-Hill.

Hall, D.L. and A. Nauda. 1988. A strategic methodology for IR&D project selection. In *Proceedings of the 1988 IEEE Engineering Management Conference*, pp. 59-66.

Hall, D.L. and A. Naudia. 1990. An interactive approach for selecting IR&D projects. *IEEE Transactions on Engineering Management* 37(2): 126-33.

Hannan, E.L. 1985. An assessment of some criticism of goal programming. *Computers and Operations Research* 12(6): 525-41.

Hansen, P. 1979. Methods of 0-1 programming. *Annals of Discrete Mathematics* 5: 53-70.

Harker, P.T. 1987. Alternative modes of questioning in the analytic hierarchy process. *Mathematical Modelling* 9: 353-60.

Harker, P.T. 1987. Incomplete pairwise comparisons in the analytic hierarchy process. *Mathematical Modelling* 9: 837-48.

Harker, P.T. 1989. The art and science of decision making: the analytic hierarchy process. In *The Analytic Hierarchy Process: Applications and Studies*, B.L. Golden, E.A. Wasil, and P.T. Harker, eds. New York: Springer-Verlag.

Harker, P.T. and L.G. Vargas. 1987. Theory of ratio scale estimation: Saaty's analytic hierarchy process. *Management Science* 33: 1383-1403.

Haspelagh, P. 1982. Portfolio planning: uses and limits. *Harvard Business Review* 60(1): 58-73.

Hayes, R. and W.J. Abernathy. 1980. Managing our way to economic decline. *Harvard Business Review* (July-Aug).

Hedley, B. 1997. Strategy for the business portfolio. *Long Range Planning* 10(1): 9-15.

Heidenberger, K. 1996. Dynamic project selection and funding under risk: a decision tree based MILP approach. *European Journal of Operational Research* 95(2): 284-298.

Helin, A.F. and W.E. Souder. 1974. Experimental test of a q-sort procedure for prioritizing R&D projects. *IEEE Transactions on Engineering Management* 21(4).

Hendriks, M.H.A., B. Voeten, and L. Kroep. 1999. Human resource allocation in a multi-project R&D environment. Resource capacity allocation and project portfolio planning in practice. *International Journal of Project Management* 17(3): 181-88.

Henriksen, A.D. and A.J. Traynor. 1999. A practical R&D project-selection scoring tool. *IEEE Transactions on Engineering Management* 46(2): 158-70.

Hertz, D.B. 1964. Risk analysis in capital investment. *Harvard Business Review* 42: 95-106.

Hertz, D.B. and H. Thomas. 1983. *Risk Analysis and Its Applications*. New York: Wiley.

Hespos, R.F. and P.A. Strassman. 1965. Stochastic decision trees for the analysis of investment decisions. *Management Science* 11(10): 244-59.

Hess, S.W. 1962. A dynamic programming approach to R&D budgeting and project selection. *IRE Transactions on Engineering Management* 9 (December): 170-79.

Hess, S.W. 1993. Swinging on the branch of a tree: project selection applications. *Interfaces* 23(6): 5-12.

Higgins, J.C. and K.M. Watts. 1986. Some perspectives on the use of management science techniques in R&D management. *R&D Management* 16(4): 291-96.

Hodder, J.E. and H.E. Riggs. 1985. Pitfalls in evaluating risky projects. *Harvard Business Review* 63(1).

Hopp, W.J. 1987. A sequential model of R&D investment over an unbounded time horizon. *Management Science* 33: 500-8.

Horesh, R. and B. Raz. 1982. Technological aspects of project-selection. *R&D Management* 12(3): 133-40.

Howard, R.A. 1988. Decision analysis: practice and promise. *Management Science* 34(6): 679-95.

Huber, G.P. 1981. The nature of organizational decision making and the design of decision support systems. *MIS Quarterly* (June).

Ignizio, J.P. 1976. *Goal Programming and Extensions*, Lexington, MA: Lexington Books.

Ignizio, J.P. 1978. A review of goal programming: a tool for multiobjective analysis. *Journal of the Operational Research Society* 29(11): 1114-22.

Ignizio, J.P. 1982. *Linear Programming in Single and Multiple Objective Systems*. Englewood Cliffs, NJ: Prentice-Hall.

Ignizio, J.P. and J.H. Perlis. 1979. Sequential linear goal programming: implementation via MPSX. *Computers and Operations Research* 6(3): 141-45.

Ijiri, Y. 1965. *Management Goals and Accounting for Control*. Chicago, IL: Rand McNalley.

Irving, R.H. and D.W. Conrath, 1988. The social context of multiperson, multiatribute decision-making. *IEEE Transactions on Systems, Man, and Cybernetics* (May-June).

Iyigun, M.G. 1993. A decision support system for R&D project selection and resource allocation under uncertainty. *Project Management Journal* 24(4): 5-13.

Jackson, B. 1983. Decision methods for selecting a portfolio of R&D projects. *Research Management* 26(5): 21-26.

Jain, H.K., M.R. Tanniru and B. Fazlollahi. 1991. MCDM approach for generating and evaluating alternatives in requirements analysis. *Information Systems Research* 2: 223-39.

Jenni, K., N. Merkhofer and C. Williams. 1995. The rise and fall of a risk-based priority system: lessons from DOE's environmental restoration priority system. *Risk Analysis* 15(3): 1-30.

Jiang, J.J. and G. Klein. 1999. Information system project-selection criteria variations within strategic classes. *IEEE Transactions on Engineering Management* 46(2): 171-76.

Jin, X.Y., A.L. Porter, F.A. Rossini and E.D. Anderson. 1987. R&D project selection and evaluation: a microcomputer-based approach. *R&D Management* 17(4): 277-88.

Johnson, C.R. 1980. Constructive critique of a hierarchical prioritization scheme employing paired comparisons. *Proceedings of the International Conference of Cybernetics and Society*, New York: IEEE.

Johnston, R.D. 1972. Project selection and evaluating. *Long Range Planning* (September).

Jones, K. and J. Weiskittel. 1997. Program management: a key for integrated healthcare delivery systems. *Proceedings of the Annual Project Management Institute Seminars & Symposium*, pp. 23-28.

Kamenetzky, R.D. 1982. The relationship between the analytic hierarchy process and the additive value function. *Decision Sciences* 13: 702-12.

Keefer, D.L. 1978. Allocation planning for R&D with uncertainty and multiple objectives. *IEEE Transactions on Engineering Management* 25(1): 8-14.

Keefer, D.L. and C.W. Kirkwood. 1978. A multiobjective decision analysis: budget planning for product engineering. *Journal of the Operational Research Society* 29(5): 435-42.

Keeney, R.L. 1992. *Value-Focused Thinking: A Path to Creative Decision-Making.* Cambridge, MA: Harvard University Press.

Keeney, R.L. and H. Raiffa. 1976. *Decisions With Multiple Objectives: Preference and Value Tradeoffs.* New York: Wiley.

Keown, A.J., B.W. Taylor, III and C.P. Duncan. 1979. Allocation of research and development funds: a zero-one goal programming approach. *Omega* 7: 345-51.

Khan, A.M. and D.P. Fiorino. 1992. The capital asset pricing model in project selection: a case study. *The Engineering Economist* 37(2):145-59.

Khorramshahgol, R. and H.M. Steiner. 1984. Quantifying organizational goals in project planning. In *Proceedings of the ASCE Symposium on Management Planning for Survival and Growth.*

Khorramshahgol, R. and J.P. Ignizio. 1984. Single and multiple decision making in a multiple objective environment. *Advances in Management Studies* 3(3/4): 181-92.

Khorramshahgol, R. and Y. Gousty. 1986. Delphic goal programming (DGP): a multiobjective cost/benefit approach to R&D portfolio analysis. *IEEE Transactions on Engineering Management* 33(3): 172-75.

Khorramshahgol, R., H. Azani and Y. Gousty. 1988. An integrated approach to project evaluation and selection. *IEEE Transactions on Engineering Management* 35(4): 265-69.

Khorramshahgol, R., Y. Gousty and H. Azani. 1986. An outline of a new methodology for resource analysis and planning of R&D projects and programs. In *Proceedings of the AFCET First International Congress on Industrial Engineering and Management.*

Khurana, A. and S.R. Rosenthal. 1997. Integrating the fuzzy front end of new product development. *Sloan Management Review* 38(2): 103-19.

King, J.L. and E.L. Schrem. 1978. Cost-benefit analysis in information systems. *Computer Surveys* 10(1): 20-34.

Kira, D.S., M.I. Dusy, D.H. Murray and B.J. Goranson. 1990. A specific decision support system (SDSS) to develop an optimal project portfolio mix under uncertainty. *IEEE Transactions on Engineering Management* 37(3): 213-21.

Klein, G. and P.O. Beck. 1987. A decision aid for selecting among information system alternatives. *MIS Quarterly* 11 (June): 177-85.

Klein, G., H. Moskowitz and A. Ravindran. 1986. Comparative evaluation of prior versus progressive articulation of preference in bicriterion optimization. *Naval Research Logistics Quarterly* 33: 309-23.

Knutson, J. 1999. A portfolio management system. *PM Network* 13(6): 21-23.

Kocaoglu, D.F. and M.G. Iyigun. 1994. Strategic R&D project selection and resource allocation with a decision support system application. In *Proceedings of the 1994 IEEE International Engineering Management Conference*, pp. 225-32.

Kocaoglu, D.G. 1983. A participative approach to program evaluation. *IEEE Transactions on Engineering Management* 30(3): 112-18.

Koh, W. 1994. Making decisions in committees: a human fallibility approach. *Journal of Economic Behavior in Organizations* 23(2): 195-214.

Kostoff, R.N. 1983. A cost/benefit analysis of commercial fusion-fission reactor development. *Journal of Fusion Energy* 3(2): 81-93.

Kostoff, R.N. 1988. Evaluation of proposed and existing accelerated research programs by the office of naval research. *IEEE Transactions on Engineering Management* 35: 271-79.

Krawiec, F. 1984. Evaluating and selecting research projects by scoring. *Research Management* 27(2): 21-25.

Krumm, F. and C.F. Rolle. 1992. Management and application of decision and risk analysis in Du Pont. *Interfaces* 22(6): 84-93.

Kruytbosch, C.E. 1989. The role and effectiveness of peer review. In *The Evaluation of Scientific Research*, D. Evered and S. Harnett, eds. Chichester, UK: Wiley, pp. 69-85.

Kurtulus, I.S. and E.W. Davis. 1982. Multi-project scheduling: categorization of heuristic rules performance. *Management Science* 28: 161-72.

Kurtulus, I.S. and S.C. Narula. 1985. Multiproject scheduling: analysis of project performance. *IIE Transactions* 17(1): 58-66.

Kuwahara, Y. and T. Yasutsugu. 1988. An empirical view of a managerial evaluation of overall R&D cost-effectiveness. In *Proceedings of the 1988 IEEE Engineering Management Conference*, pp. 67-71.

Kwak, N.K. and M.J. Schniederjans. 1985. A goal programming model as an aid in facility location analysis. *Computers & Operations Research* 12(2): 151-61.

Kyparisis, G.J., S.K. Gupta and C.-M. Ip. 1996. Project selection with discounted returns and multiple constraints. *European Journal of Operational Research* 94(1): 87-96.

Kyparisis, J. and R. Santhanam. 1995. A multiple criteria decision model for information system project selection. *Computers & Operations Research* 22(8).

Lautenschalger, G.J. 1989. A comparison of alternatives to conducting Monte Carlo analysis for determining parallel analysis criteria. *Multivariate Behavioral Research* 24(3): 365-95.

Law, A.M. and W. Kelton. 1990. *Simulation Modeling and Analysis,* 2nd ed. New York: McGraw-Hill.

Lee, J., S. Lee and Z.T. Bae. 1986. R&D project selection: behavior and practice in a newly industrializing country. *IEEE Transactions on Engineering Management* 33(3): 141-47.

Lee, M. and K. Om. 1997. The concept of effectiveness in R&D project selection. *International Journal of Technology Management* 13(5/6): 511-24.

Lee, S.M. 1972. *Goal Programming for Decision Analysis.* Philadelphia: Auerbach Publishers.

Levine, H.A. 1999. Project portfolio management: a song without words? *PM Network* 13(7): 25-27.

Liberatore, M.J. 1987. An extension of the analytic hierarchy process for industrial R&D project selection and resource allocation. *IEEE Transactions on Engineering Management* 34(1): 12-18

Liberatore, M.J. 1988. A decision support system linking research and development project selection with business strategy. *Project Management Journal* 19(5): 14-21.

Liberatore, M.J. 1988. An expert system for R&D project selection. *Mathematics and Computer Modeling* 11: 260-65.

Liberatore, M.L. and G.J. Titus. 1983. The practice of management science in R&D project selection. *Management Science* 29(8): 962-74.

Lim Kai, H. and S.R. Swenseth. 1993. An iterative procedure for reducing problem size in large scale AHP problems. *European Journal of Operational Research* 67: 64-67.

Lin, W.T. 1980. A survey of goal programming applications. *Omega* 8(1): 115-17.

Lockett, G. and M. Stratford. 1987. Ranking of research projects: experiments with two methods. *Omega* 15(5): 395-400.

Lockett, G., B. Hetherington, P. Yallup, M. Stratford and B. Cos. 1986. Modeling a research portfolio using AHP: a group decision process. *R&D Management* 16(2): 151-60.

Lovelace, R.F. 1987. R&D planning techniques. *R&D Management* 17(4): 241-51.

Lucas, H.C. and J.R. Moore. 1976. A multiple criterion scoring approach to information system project selection. *Infor* 14(1): 1-12.

Luehrman, T.A. 1998. Strategy as a portfolio of real options. *Harvard Business Review* (September-October): 89-99.

Madey, G.R. and Dean, B.V. 1985. Strategic planning for investment in R&D using decision analysis and mathematical programming. *IEEE Transactions on Engineering Management* 32(2).

Magee, J.F. 1964. How to use decision trees in capital investment. *Harvard Business Review* 42(5): 79-96.

Maher, P.M. and A.H. Rubenstein. 1974. Factors affecting adoption of a quantitative method for R&D project selection. *Management Science* 21(2): 119-29.

Malach, J.D. 1998. Phase gate management—best practices and methods. *Proceedings of the Annual Project Management Institute Seminars & Symposium*, pp. 893-98.

Mandakovic, T.F. and W.E. Souder. 1985. A flexible hierarchical model for project-selection. *R&D Management* 15(1): 23-29.

Mandakovic, T.F. and W.E. Souder. 1985. An interactive decomposable heuristic for project selection. *Management Science* 31(10): 1257-71.

Mandakovic, T.F. and W.E. Souder. 1990. Experiments with microcomputers to facilitate the use of project selection models. *Journal of Engineering Technology Management* 7(1): 1-16.

Mann, G.A. 1979. VERT: a risk analysis tool for program management. *Defense Management* (May-June).

Mansfield, E. 1968. *Industrial Research and Technological Innovation.* New York: Norton.

Mansfield, E., J. Rapoport, J. Schnee, S. Wagner, and M. Hamburger. 1971. *Research and Innovation in the Modern Corporation.* New York: Norton.

Mantel Jr., S.J., J.R. Evans, and V.A. Tipnis. 1985. Decision analysis for new process technology. In *Project Management: Methods and Studies*, B.V. Dean, ed. Amsterdam: North-Holland.

Martino, J.P. 1993. *Technological Forecasting for Decision Making*, 3rd ed. New York: McGraw-Hill.

Martino, J.P. 1995. *Research and Development Project Selection.* New York: Wiley.

Mason, B.M., W.E. Souder and E.P. Winkofsky. 1980. R&D budgeting and project selection: a review of practices and models. *ISMS*.

Matheson, D., J. Matheson and M. Menke. 1993. *R&D Decision Quality Association Benchmarking Study.* Palo Alto, CA: Strategic Decisions Group.

Matheson, J.E. 1984. Overview of R&D decision analysis. In *Readings on the Principles and Applications of Decision Analysis*, R. Howard and J. Matheson, eds. Palo Alto, CA: Strategic Decisions Group.

Matheson, J.E. and M.M. Menke. 1994. Using decision quality principles to balance your R&D portfolio. *Research Technology Management* 37(3): 38-43.

Mathieu, R.G. and J.E. Gibson. 1993. A methodology for large scale R&D planning based on cluster analysis. *IEEE Transactions on Engineering Management* 30(3).

McFarlan, F.W. 1981. Portfolio approach to information systems. *Harvard Business Review* 38: 142-50.

McGuire, P.E. 1973. *Evaluating New-Product Proposals.* New York: New York Conference Board, Inc.

McKeen, J.D. and T. Guimaraes. 1985. Selecting MIS projects by steering committee. *Communications of the ACM* 28(12): 1344-52.

Mehrez A. and Z. Sinuary-Stern. 1983. Resource allocation to the interrelated risky projects using multiattribute utility function. *Management Science* 29(4): 430-30.

Mehrez, A. 1988. Selecting R&D projects: a case study of the expected utility approach. *Technovation* 8: 299-311.

Mehrez, A. and A.P. Sethi. 1989. Hierarchical planning of project-selection problems with information purchasing. *Journal of the Operational Research Society* 40(2): 267-79.

Mehrez, A., S. Mossery and Z. Sinuany-Stern. 1982. Project selection in a small university R&D laboratory. *R&D Management* 12(4): 169-74.

Melone, N.P. and T.J. Wharton. 1984. Strategies for MIS project selection. *Journal of Systems Management* 9: 26-33.

Meredith, J.R. and S.J. Mantel, Jr. 1995. *Project Management: A Managerial Approach.* New York: Wiley.

Merrifield, B.. 1978. Industrial project selection and management. *Industrial Marketing Management* 7(5): 324-30.

Merrifield, D.B. 1978. How to select successful R&D projects. *Management Review* (December).

Mian, S.A. and C.X. Dai. 1999. Decision-making over the project life cycle: an analytical hierarchy approach. *Project Management Journal* 30(1): 40-52.

Miller, B. 1997. Linking corporate strategy to the selection of IT projects. *Proceedings of the Annual Project Management Institute Seminars & Symposium*, pp. 55-59.

Mjelde, K. 1983. Resource allocation with tree constraints. *Operations Research* 31: 881-90.

Mohanty, R.P. 1992. Project selection by a multiple-criteria decision-making method: an example from a developing country. *International Journal of Project Management* 10(1).

Mohanty, R.P. and M.K. Siddiq. 1989. Multiple projects—multiple resources scheduling: a multi-objective analysis. *Engineering and Production Economics* (October).

Moolman, G.C. and W.J. Fabrycky. 1997. A capital budgeting model based on the project portfolio approach: avoiding cash flows per project. *The Engineering Economist* 42(2): 111-35.

Moore Jr., J.R. and N.R. Baker. 1969. An analytical approach to scoring model design—application to research and development project selection. *IEEE Transactions on Engineering Management* 16: 90-98.

Moore Jr., J.R. and N.R. Baker. 1969. Computational analysis of scoring models for R&D project selection. *Management Science* 16(4): 212-32.

Moore, J.H. 1979. A framework for MIS software development projects. *MIS Quarterly* 3(1): 29-38.

Morison, A. and R. Wensley. 1991. Boxing up or boxed in? A short history of the Boston Consulting Group share/growth matrix. *Journal of Marketing Management* 7: 105-29.

Morris, P.A., E.O. Teisberg and A.L. Kolbe. 1991. When choosing R&D projects, go with the long shots. *Research Technology Management* 34(1): 35-40.

Moselhi, O. and B. Deb. 1993. Project selection considering risk. *Construction Management Economics* 11(1): 45-52.

Motley, C.M. and R.D. Newton. 1959. The selection of projects for industrial research. *Operations Research* 7(6): 740-51.

Mukherjee, K.. 1994. Application of an interactive method for MOLIP in project selection decision: a case from Indian coal mining industry. *International Journal of Production Economics* 36: 203-11.

Muralidhar, K., R. Santhanam and R.L. Wilson. 1990. Using the analytic hierarchy process for information system project selection. *Information & Management* 18: 87-95.

Murphy, C.K.. 1993. Limits on the analytic hierarchy process from its consistency index. *European Journal of Operational Research* 65: 138-39.

Narasimhan, R. 1980. Goal programming in a fuzzy environment. *Decision Sciences* 11: 325-36.

Naumann, J.D. and S. Palvia. 1982. A selection model for system development tools. *MIS Quarterly* 6: 39-48.

Naylor, T.H. 1984. A matrix management approach to strategic planning. In *Optimization Models for Strategic Planning*, T.H. Naylor and C. Thomas, eds. Amsterdam: North-Holland.

Nelson, B., B. Gill and S. Spring. 1997. Building on the stage/gate: An enterprise-wide architecture for new product development. *Proceedings of the Annual Project Management Institute Seminars & Symposium*, pp. 67-72.

Neumann, S., N. Ahituv and M. Zviran. 1992. A measure for determining the strategic relevance of IS to the organization. *Information Management* 22(5): 281-99.

Newton, D.P. and A.W. Pearson. 1994. Application of option pricing theory to R&D. *R&D Management* 24(1): 83-89.

Nutt, A.B. 1965. An approach to research and development effectiveness. *IEEE Transactions on Engineering Management* (September).

Oral, M., O. Kettani and P. Lang. 1991. A methodology for collective evaluation and selection of industrial R&D projects. *Management Science* 37(7): 871-85.

Page, A.L. 1993. Assessing new product development practices and performance: establishing crucial norms. *Journal of Product Innovation Management* 10(4): 273-90.

Pan, S.D. and R.S. Chen. 1981. An integrative approach to R&D cost budgeting. *Southern Business Review* 7: 25-32.

Paolini Jr., A. and M.A. Glaser. 1977. Project selection methods that pick winners. *Research Management* 20(3): 26-29.

Pearson, A.W. 1983. Project-selection in an organizational context. *IEEE Transactions on Engineering Management* 21: 152-58.

Pessemier, E.A. and N.R. Baker. 1971. Project and program decisions in research and development. *R&D Management* 2(1).

Pinto, J.K. and D.P. Slevin. 1987. Critical factors in successful project implementation. *IEEE Transactions on Engineering Management* 34(1): 22-27.

Plebani, L.P. and H.K. Jain. 1981. Evaluating research proposals with group techniques. *Research Management* 24: 34-38.

Pound, W.H. 1964. Research project selection: testing a model in the field. *IEEE Transactions on Engineering Management* 11 (March).

Raelin, J.A. and R. Balachandra. 1986. R&D project termination in hi-tech industries. *IEEE Transactions on Engineering Management* 32(1): 16-23.

Ramsey, J.E. 1978. *Research and Development: Project Selection Criteria.* UMI Research Press.

Ramsey, J.E. 1981. Selecting R&D projects for development. *Long Range Planning* (February).

Rasmussen, L.M. 1986. Zero-one programming with multiple criteria. *European Journal of Operational Research* 26: 83-95.

Reisman, A. 1965. Capital budgeting for interrelated projects. *The Journal of Industrial Engineering* 15(1): 59-64.

Remer, D.S., S.B. Stokdyk and M. Van Driel. 1993. Survey of project evaluation techniques currently used in industry. *International Journal of Production Economics* 32: 103-15.

Reynard, E.L. 1979. A method for relating research spending to net profit. *Research Management* (December).

Ricciuti, M. 1991. Project management: easy ways to manage multiple IS projects. *Datamation* 37(22).

Riggs, J.L, S.B. Brown and R.P. Trueblood. 1994. Integration of technical, cost, and schedule risks in project management. *Computers & Operations Research* 21(5): 521-33.

Riggs, J.L., M. Goodman, R. Finley and T. Miller. 1992. A decision support system for predicting project success. *Project Management Journal* 23(3): 37-43.

Ringuest, J.L. and S.B. Graves. 1989. The linear multi-objective R&D project selection problem. *IEEE Transactions on Engineering Management* 36(1): 54-57.

Ringuest, J.L. and S.B. Graves. 1990. The linear R&D project selection problem: an alternative to net present value. *IEEE Transactions on Engineering Management* 37: 143-46.

Robinson, B., and C. Lakhani. 1975. Dynamic models for new product planning. *Management Science* (June).

Roman, D.D. 1986. *Managing Projects: A Systems Approach.* New York: Elsevier.

Romero, C. 1986. A survey of generalized goal programming. *European Journal of Operational Research* 25: 183-91.

Rosen, E.M. and W.E. Souder. 1965. A method for allocating R&D expenditures. *IEEE Transactions on Engineering Management* 12(3): 87-93.

Rosenau, Jr., M.D. 1991. *Successful Project Management*, 2nd ed. New York: Van Nostrand Reinhold.

Rosenthal, R.E. 1985. Concepts, theory and techniques—principles of multiobjective optimization. *Decision Sciences* 15: 133-52.

Roussel, P.A., K.N. Saad and T.J. Erickson. 1991. *Third Generation R&D: Managing the Link to Corporate Strategy.* Boston: Harvard Business School Press.

Rubenstein, A.H. and H.H. Schroder. 1977. Managerial differences in assessing probabilities of technical success for R&D projects. *Management Science* 24(2): 137-48.

Ruhl, J.M. and L.M. Parker. 1994. The effects of experience and the firm's environment on manager's project selection decisions. *Journal of Management Issues* 6(3): 331-49.

Rzasa, P.V., T.W. Faulkner and N.L. Sousa. 1990. Analyzing R&D portfolios at Eastman Kodak. *Research Technology Management* 33(1): 27-32.

Saaty, T.L. 1977. A scaling method for priorities in hierarchical structure. *Journal of Mathematical Psychology* 15(3): 234-81.

Saaty, T.L. 1982. *Decision Making for Leaders*. Belmont, CA: Lifetime Learning Publications.

Saaty, T.L. 1986. Axiomatic foundation of the analytic hierarchy process. *Management Science* 32(7): 841-55.

Saaty, T.L. 1990. An exposition of the AHP in reply to the paper "Remarks on the analytical hierarchy process." *Management Science* 36(3): 259-68.

Saaty, T.L. 1990. Decision making, scaling, and number crunching. *Decision Sciences* 20: 404-9.

Saaty, T.L. and L.G. Vargas. 1982. *The Logic of Priorities*. Boston: Kluwer-Nijhoff.

Saaty, T.L., P.C. Rogers and R.Pell. 1980. Portfolio selection through hierarchies. *The Journal of Portfolio Management* 6(3): 16-21.

Saaty,T.L.. 1980. *The Analytic Hierarchy Process*. New York: McGraw-Hill.

Sanchez, A.M. 1989. R&D selection strategy: an empirical study in Spain. *R&D Management* 19(1): 63-68.

Santhanam, R. and J. Kyparsis. 1995. A multiple criteria decision model for information system project selection. *Computers & Operations Research* 22(8): 807-18.

Santhanam, R., K. Muralidhar and M. Schniederjans. 1989. A zero-one goal programming approach for information system project selection. *Omega* 17(6): 583-93.

Schmidt, R.L. 1993. A model for R&D project selection with combined benefit, outcome and resource interactions. *IEEE Transactions on Engineering Management* 40(4): 403-10.

Schmidt, R.L. and J.R. Freeland. 1992. Recent progress in modelling R&D project selection processes. *IEEE Transactions on Engineering Management* 39(2): 189-200.

Schniederjans, M.J. and R. Santhanam. 1993. A multi-objective constrained resource information system project selection method. *European Journal of Operational Research* 70: 244-53.

Schniederjans, M.J. and R.L. Wilson. 1991. Using the analytic hierarchy process and goal programming for information system project selection. *Information Management* 20: 333-42.

Schroder, H.H. 1971. R&D project evaluation and selection models for development: a survey of the state of the art. *Socio-Economic Planning Science* 5(1): 25-39.

Schuyler, J.R. 1996. *Decision Analysis in Projects: Learn to Make Faster, More Confident Decisions*. Upper Darby, PA: Project Management Institute.

Schwartz, S.L. and I. Vertinsky. 1977. Multi-attribute investment decisions: a study of R&D project selection. *Management Science* 24(3): 285-301.

Scott, Gary J. 1996. Expanding the role of the project director as the CIO in the information technology industry. *Project Management Journal* 27(3): 5-15.

Seidmann, A. and A. Arbel. 1984. Microcomputer selection process for organizational information management. *Information & Management* 7: 317-29.

Sharpe, P. and T. Keelin. 1998. How SmithKline Beecham makes better resource-allocation decisions. *Harvard Business Review* (March-April): 4-10.

Sharpe, W.F. 1963. A simplified model for portfolio analysis. *Management Science* 9(1): 277-93.

Sharpe, W.F. 1964. Capital asset prices: a theory of market equilibrium under conditions of risk. *Journal of Finance*, pp. 425-42.

Shoval, P. and R. Giladi. 1996. Determination of an implementation order for IS projects. *Information Management* 31(2): 67-74.

Silvennoinen, P. 1994. R&D project selection for promoting the efficiency of energy use. *R&D Management* 24(4): 317-24.

Silverman, B.G. 1981. Project appraisal methodology: a multidimensional R&D benefit/cost assessment tool. *Management Science* 27(7): 802-24.

Skolnick, A. 1969. A structure and scoring method for judging alternatives. *IEEE Transactions on Engineering Management* 16(2): 72-83.

Smith, S. and J. Barker. 1999. Benefit-cost ratio: selection tool or trap? *PM Network* 13(5): 23-26.

Sommer, R.J. 1998. Portfolio management for projects—a new paradigm. *Proceedings of the Annual Project Management Institute Seminars & Symposium*, pp. 462-64.

Souder, W.E. 1967. Selecting and staffing R&D projects via operations research. *Chemical Engineering Progress* 63(11): 27-37.

Souder, W.E. 1972. A scoring methodology for assessing the suitability of management science models. *Management Science* 18(10): B526-43.

Souder, W.E. 1972. Comparative analysis of R&D investment models. *AIIE Transactions* 1(2): 57-64.

Souder, W.E. 1973. Analytical effectiveness of mathematical models for R&D project selection. *Management Science* 19(8): 907-23.

Souder, W.E. 1973. Utility and perceived acceptability of R&D project selection models. *Management Science* 19(12): 1384-94.

Souder, W.E. 1975. Achieving organizational consensus with respect to R&D project selection criteria. *Management Science* 21(6): 669-81.

Souder, W.E. 1975. Field studies with a q-sort/nominal-group process for selecting R&D projects. *Research Policy* 4: 172-88.

Souder, W.E. 1978. A system for using R&D project evaluation methods. *Research Management* 21(5): 29-37.

Souder, W.E. 1980. *Management Decision Methods for Managers of Engineering and Research*. New York: Van Nostrand Reinhold.

Souder, W.E. 1984. *Project Selection and Economic Appraisal*. New York: Van Nostrand Reinhold.

Souder, W.E. 1988. Project evaluation and selection. In *Project Management Handbook*, D.I. Cleland and W.R. King, eds. New York: Van Nostrand Reinhold.

Souder, W.E. and T. Mandakovic. 1986. R&D project selection models. *Research Management* 29(4): 36-42.

Souder, W.E., P.M. Maher and A.H. Rubenstein. 1972. Two successful experiments in project selection. *Research Management* 15(5): 44-54.

Soyibo, A. 1985. Goal programming methods and applications: a survey. *Journal of Information and Optimization Sciences* 6(3): 247-64.

Speranza, M.G. and C. Vercellis. 1993. Hierarchical models for multi-project planning and scheduling. *European Journal of Operational Research* 64: 312-25.

Spradlin, C.T. and D.M. Kutoloski. 1999. Action-oriented portfolio management. *Research Technology Management* 42(2): 26-32.

Sprague Jr., R.H. and E.D. Carlson. 1982. *Building Effective Decision Support Systems*. Englewood Cliffs, NJ: Prentice-Hall.

Srinivasan, V. and Y.H. Kim. 1987. Evaluating interrelated capital projects: an alternative framework. *The Engineering Economist* 33(1): 13-30.

Stadje, W. 1993. Optimal selection of R&D projects. *Applied Mathematical Optimization* 28(2): 149-60.

Stahl, M.J. and A.M. Harrel. 1983. Identifying operative goals by modeling project selection decisions in research and development. *IEEE Transactions on Engineering Management* 30(4).

Steele, L.W. 1988. What we've learned: selecting R&D programs and objectives. *Research Technology Management* 31(2): 17-36.

Steuer, R.E. 1986. *Multiple Criteria Optimization: Theory, Computation and Application*. New York: Wiley.

Stewart, T.J. 1981. A descriptive approach to multiple-criteria decision making. *Journal of the Operational Research Society* 32: 45-53.

Stewart, T.J. 1991. A multi-criteria decision support system for R&D project selection. *Journal of the Operational Research Society* 42(1): 17-26.

Stinson, J.P., E.W. Davis, and S.M. Khumawala. 1978. Multiple resource constrained scheduling using branch and bound. *AIIE Transactions* 10(3): 252-59.

Szakonyi, R. 1985. Keeping R&D projects on track. *Research Management* 28(1): 29-34.

Taggart, J.H. and T.J. Blaxter. 1992. Strategy in pharmaceutical R&D: a portfolio risk matrix. *R&D Management* 22(3): 241-54.

Talbot, F.B. and J.H. Patterson. 1978. An efficient integer programming algorithm with network cuts for solving resource constrained scheduling problems. *Management Science* 24(11): 1163-74.

Taylor, B.W. and A.J. Keown. 1978. A goal programming application of capital project selection in the production area. *AIIE Transactions* 10: 52-57.

Taylor, B.W., L.J. Moore and E.R. Clayton. 1982. R&D project selection and manpower allocation with integer nonlinear goal programming. *Management Science* 28(10): 1149-58.

Teghem Jr., J. and P.L. Kunsch. 1986. A survey of techniques for finding efficient solutions to multi-objective integer linear programming. *Asia Pacific Journal of Operations Research* 3: 95-108.

Themelis, N.J. 1976. Evaluation and selection of projects in industrial research. *Journal of Management* (January): 15-20.

Thierauf, R.J. 1982. *Decision Support Systems for Effective Planning and Control. A Case Study Approach.* Englewood Cliffs, NJ: Prentice-Hall.

Tiggemann, R.F., D.A. Dworaczyk and H. Sabel. 1998. Project portfolio management: a powerful strategic weapon in pharmaceutical drug development. *Drug Information Journal* 32(3): 813.

Todd, P. and I. Benbasat. 1993. An experimental investigation of the relationship between decision makers, decision aids, and decision making effort. *Infor* 31(2): 80-100.

Townsend, H.W.R., and G.E. Whitehouse. 1977. We used risk analysis to move our computer. *Industrial Engineering* (May).

Tsubakitani, S. and R.F. Deckro. 1990. A heuristic for multi-project scheduling with limited resources in the housing industry. *European Journal of Operational Research* 49: 80-91.

Tukana, S. and R. Weber. 1996. An empirical test of the strategic-grid model of information systems planning. *Decision Science* 27(4): 735-63.

Turban, E. 1995. *Decision Support and Expert Systems,* 4th ed. Englewood Cliffs, NJ: Prentice Hall.

Tymon, W.G. and R.F. Lovelace. 1986. A taxonomy of R&D control models and variables affecting their use. *R&D Management* 16(3): 233-41.

Uenohara, M. 1991. A management view of Japanese corporate R&D. *Research Technology Management* 34(6): 17-23.

Van de Ven, A. and A.L. Delbecq. 1971. Nominal versus interacting group processes for committee decision-making effectiveness. *Academy of Management Journal* (June): 203-12.

Vazsonyi, A. 1978. Decision support systems: the new technology of decision making? *Interfaces* (November).

Venkatraman, R. and S. Venkatraman. 1995. R&D project selection and scheduling for organizations facing product obsolescence. *R&D Management* 25(1): 57-70.

Wallin, C.C. and J.J. Gilman. 1986. Determining the optimum level for R&D spending. *Research Management* 29(5): 19-24.

Watters, L.D. 1967. Research and development project selection: interdependence and multiperiod probabilistic budget constraints. Ph.D. dissertation, Arizona State University, Tempe, AZ.

Weingartner, H.M. 1963. *Mathematical Programming and the Analysis of Capital Budgeting Problems*. Englewood Cliffs, NJ: Prentice-Hall.

Weingartner, H.M. 1966. Capital budgeting of interrelated projects: survey and synthesis. *Management Science* 12: 485-516.

Whalen, T. 1984. Decision making under uncertainty with various assumptions about available information. *IEEE Transactions on Systems, Man, and Cybernetics* 14: 888-990.

Whaley, W.M. and R.A. Williams. 1971. A profits-oriented approach to project selection. *Research Management* 14(5).

Wheelwright, S.C. and K.B. Clark. 1992. Creating project plans to focus product development. *Harvard Business Review* (March-April): 2-14.

Wiegand, F.M. 1990. Managing multiple capital projects in the electric utility industry. *Project Management Journal* 21(3): 13-17.

Wilder, C., B. Caldwell and M.J. Garvey. 1998. Trends: the big puzzle—multiproject management is redefining the way companies handle technology, people, and vendors to make all the pieces fit. *InformationWeek* (August 3): 36-41.

Williams, D.J. 1969. A study of a decision model for R&D project selection. *Operational Research Quarterly* 20(3): 361-73.

Wiloughby, T.C. 1975. Origins of systems projects. *Journal of Systems Management* (October).

Wind, Y. and T.L. Saaty. 1980. Marketing applications of the analytic hierarchy process. *Management Science* 26(7): 641-58.

Wind, Y. and V. Mahajan. 1981. Designing product and business portfolios. *Harvard Business Review* 59: 155-65.

Wind, Y., V. Mahajan and D.J. Swire. 1983. an empirical comparison of standardized portfolio models. *Journal of Marketing* 47: 89-99.

Wind, Y., V. Mahajan and R.N. Cardozo. 1981. *New Product Forecasting*. Lexington, MA: Lexington Books.

Winkofsky, E.P., N.R. Baker and D.J. Sweeny. 1981. A decision process model of R&D resource allocation in hierarchical organizations. *Management Science* 27(3): 268-83.

Winkofsky, E.P., R.M. Mason and W.E. Souder. 1980. R&D budgeting and project selection: a review of practices and models. In *Managing Research Innovation*, B.V. Dean and J.L. Goldhar, eds. Amsterdam: North-Holland.

Winsen, J.K. 1996. Project NPV as a portfolio of derivative securities. A discrete time analysis. *Resources Policy* 22(3): 161.

Yip, G.S. 1984. Market selection and direction: role of product portfolio planning. Harvard Business School Publishing Case Study.

Zaas, B.M. and M.M. Geaney. 1997. A new era of program management: steering systems integration solutions with next generation management. *Proceedings of the Annual Project Management Institute Seminars & Symposium*, pp. 3-11.

Zahedi, F. 1985. Database management system evaluation and selection decision. *Decision Sciences* 15(1): 91-116.

Zahedi, F. 1986. The analytic hierarchy process—a survey of the method and its applications. *Interfaces* 16(4).

Zaloom, V.A. 1973. Project selection methods. *Journal of Systems Management* (August): 14-17.

Zapalac, R., K. Kuemmler and T. Malagon. 1994. Establishing management information systems for multiproject programs. *Journal of Management in Engineering* 10(1).

Zeleney, M. 1982. *Multiple Criteria Decision Making*. New York: McGraw-Hill.

Zinkhan, F.C. and J.A. Boyd. 1995. Combining net present value and strategic attractiveness to evaluate drug development alternatives. *Journal of Pharmaceutical Marketing & Management* 9(4): 19.

Zionts, S. and J. Wallenius. 1976. An interactive programming method for solving the multiple criteria problem. *Management Science* 22(6): 652-63.

About the Authors

(Biography is as of date of original publication)

Norman P. Archer is professor of management science and information systems at the Michael G. DeGroote School of Business, McMaster University.

Joh Barker is chief financial officer with SMS Consulting Group with over 20 years experience in information technology and finance.

Merrill S. Brenner is a research associate in management information systems at Air Products and Chemicals, Inc., Allentown, Pennsylvania.

Dianne N. Bridges is a senior consultant with PM Solutions, Inc., who has dealt with portfolio management issues in government, insurance, and information technology.

Martin D.J. Buss is the director of planning for Philip Morris International and previously was a senior consultant with Arthur D. Little, Inc.

Kim B. Clark is a professor of business administration at the Harvard Business School, teaching technology and operations management.

David I. Cleland is Ernest D. Roth Professor and professor of engineering management at the University of Pittsburgh.

Margaret W. Combe is with the Northwestern Mutual Life Insurance Company.

Robert G. Cooper is professor of marketing at the Michael DeGroote School of Business, McMaster University.

Lowell D. Dye is account manager with PM Solutions, Inc., where he consults and develops and conducts courses in the area of project management.

Scott J. Edgett is associate professor of marketing at the Michael DeGroote School of Business and director of the Product Development Institute, McMaster University.

Wolter J. Fabrycky is the Lawrance Professor Emeritus of industrial and systems engineering and a senior research scientist at Virginia Polytechnic Institute and State University.

J. Davidson Frame is professor of management science at the School of Business and Public Management at the George Washington University.

Fereidoun Ghasemzadeh is a Ph.D. candidate in the program in management science/systems at the Michael DeGroote School of Business, McMaster University.

Bob Gill is with Product Development Partners, Inc.

Anne DePiante Henriksen is associate professor of manufacturing and engineering in the College of Integrated Science and Technology, James Madison University.

James J. Jiang is associate professor of computer information systems at the College of Administration and Business, Louisiana Tech University.

Tom Keelin is worldwide managing director of the Strategic Decisions Group.

Anil Khurana is assistant professor of operations management at the School of Management, Boston University.

Gary Klein is Couger Professor of Information Systems at the University of Colorado.

Elko J. Kleinschmidt is professor of marketing at the Michael DeGroote School of Business and director of the engineering and management program at McMaster University.

David M. Kutoloski is an associate senior scientist in the Decision Sciences Department at Eli Lilly and Company.

Harvey A. Levine is a principal of The Project Knowledge Group.

Timothy A. Luehrman is professor of finance at Thunderbird, the American Graduate School of International Management.

Samuel J. Mantel, Jr. is the Joseph S. Stern Professor of Management (emeritus) in the College of Business Administration, Cincinnati University.

James E. Matheson is director of the research and development consulting practice at Strategic Decisions Group.

Michael M. Menke is a founding principal of Strategic Decisions Group.

Jack R. Meredith is professor of management in the College of Business Administration, Cincinnati University.

G. Chris Moolman is a program manager with LIW, Denel, South Africa and adjunct faculty of the Graduate School of Engineering at the University of Pretoria.

Beebe Nelson is with Product Development Partners, Inc.

James S. Pennypacker is director of the Center for Business Practices, a division of PM Solutions, Inc.

Stephen R. Rosenthal is professor of operations management and director of the Manufacturing Roundtable at the School of Management, Boston University.

Paul Sharpe is vice president and director of project management in neuroscience at SmithKline Beecham in Harlow, England.

Stephen Smith is lecturer in information systems at the University of Melbourne.

Renee J. Sommer is with The Avanti Group, Inc.

C. Thomas Spradlin is a senior research scientist in the Decision Sciences Department at Eli Lilly and Company.

Steve Spring is with Duncan-Nevison.

Ann Jensen Traynor is a B.S. degree candidate in mechanical engineering at Brigham Young University.

Steven C. Wheelwright is professor of business administration at the Harvard Business School.

About the Center for Business Practices

The Center for Business Practices is a knowledge center created to capture, organize, and transfer business practice knowledge to project stakeholders in order to help them excel in their competitive environments in today's rapidly changing business world.

The CBP harnesses project management knowledge and expertise and integrates it into all products to deliver the maximum amount of fact-based information to customers. By adding information from external knowledge databases, original research, and other knowledge-based services to internally developed knowledge, the CBP provides comprehensive, accurate, and timely information on the most effective business practices.

CBP Knowledge Products

The Center for Business Practices is a premier deliverer of business practice knowledge in a variety of publications and on the web, which includes a publicly accessible section of the CBP KnowledgeBank (www.pmsolutions.com/center) that offers a comprehensive list of links to websites with business practice knowledge.

• CBP KnowledgeBank

Business practice knowledge is acquired from both internal and external sources and stored in repositories—physical and electronic. These repositories comprise the CBP KnowledgeBank, which is also designed to add value to the information and knowledge by packaging and presenting it for easy access.

• CBP Management Bookstore

The CBP reviews and sells the best literature on the market for understanding how to manage your organization and its projects effectively. Visit the CBP Management Bookstore at www.pmsolutions .com center.

• Project Management Best Practices Report

Discover best practices that lead to consistent results and improved project performance. Areas covered in this succinctly

---

CBP KnowledgeBoard

John R. Adams
Western Carolina University

David I. Cleland
University of Pittsburgh (emer.)

J. Kent Crawford
PM Solutions, Inc

Paul C. Dinsmore
Dinsmore Associates

John Kennel
NCR Corporation (ret.)

James R. Snyder
SmithKline Beecham (ret.)

Frank Toney
Executive Initiative Institute
University of Phoenix

J. Rodney Turner
Erasmus University

Ronald P.C. Waller
Johnson Controls, Inc. (ret.)

Neal Whitten
The Neal Whitten Group

written monthly newsletter include: Portfolio Management, Project Office Implementation, Enterprise PM, Professional Development, PM Maturity and Assessment, Team Building, PM Processes, Performance Metrics.

• *Project Management Practices Book Series*

The PM Practices Series features books that detail the best practices related to the implementation of project management. Current books under development include enterprise project management, competency standards for project managers, project management competency standards for organizations, managing multiple projects, and essentials of project management. Authors are encouraged to discuss publication of their work—contact the Center for Business Practices directly.

CBP Consortium

The CBP Consortium brings together a community of business leaders, academics, and researchers—the business practice thought leaders—to develop a greater understanding of how businesses can better use project management to create value. Knowledge is transferred through forums, surveys, and online discussions within this community of project management practice.

CBP Research

The CBP sponsors original research that will contribute to the success of organizations. Subject areas include: Value of Project Management, Portfolio Management, Project Office Implementation, Enterprise PM, PM Maturity and Assessment. Contact the CBP for information about sponsorship and/or publishing research.

For More Information

The Center for Business Practices is a division of PM Solutions, Inc. For more information contact James S. Pennypacker, Director, Center for Business Practices, 316 West Barnard St., West Chester, PA 19382; 610.701.9337; jpennypacker@pmsolutions.com.

Index